Grassroots

Grassroots

with Readings

THE WRITER'S WORKBOOK

SEVENTH EDITION

Susan Fawcett

Alvin Sandberg

HOUGHTON MIFFLIN COMPANY   Boston New York

Senior Sponsoring Editor: Mary Jo Southern
Development Editor: Marilyn Weissman
Associate Editor: Kellie Cardone
Editorial Associate: Danielle Richardson
Senior Project Editor: Rosemary Winfield
Senior Production/Design Coordinator: Sarah Ambrose
Senior Manufacturing Coordinator: Priscilla Bailey
Senior Marketing Manager: Annamarie Rice
Senior Designer: Henry Rachlin

Cover: Photograph copyright by Steve Satushek, Gettyone.com, 2001.
Chapter and unit openers and interior design elements: Steve Satushek/The Image Bank, copyright 2001.

Acknowledgments appear on page 478.

Printed in the U.S.A.

Library of Congress Catalog Card number: 2001-131491

Student Edition without Readings ISBN: 0-618-11558-7
Student Edition with Readings ISBN: 0-618-11579-X
Instructor's Annotated Edition with Readings ISBN: 0-618-11586-2

8 9 10 11 12 13 -PO- 07 06 05 04

As part of Houghton Mifflin's ongoing
commitment to the environment, this text
has been printed on recycled paper.

Contents

UNIT 2   *Writing Complete Sentences*   74

UNIT 3   *Using Verbs Effectively*   *104*

Preface

Grassroots with Readings combines in one book the exciting Seventh Edition of our widely used basic writing text *Grassroots* and twenty-two high-interest reading selections. *Grassroots* grew out of our classroom experience at Bronx Community College of the City University of New York; it is designed for students who have not yet mastered the basic writing skills so necessary for success in college and in many careers. Through clear, paced lessons and a variety of engaging practices and writing assignments, *Grassroots* has helped more than a million students write better.

In *Grassroots with Readings*, instructors who wish to incorporate reading in their basic writing classes may choose from a diverse group of readings chosen with an eye to thought-provoking subject matter, stylistic excellence, and ethnic and gender balance. Authors include Amy Tan, Malcolm X, Anna Quindlen, Julia Alvarez, Daniel Goleman, Maya Angelou, and Dave Barry. Each selection is accompanied by a headnote, vocabulary glosses, comprehension questions, and writing assignments.

In this new Seventh Edition, we have kept the carefully honed grammar and sentence-skills lessons that prompt so many instructors and students to tell us that *Grassroots* keeps fulfilling its promise: to help students become better writers. We have added Internet strategies for writing for today's college students; strengthened our coverage of the writing process; increased the number of reading selections; added material for ESL students; and, of course, updated and replaced practice material throughout the book.

Features of the Seventh Edition

- **Addition of Internet Strategies** Because so many students now have access to computers and spend considerable time online, techniques for using the Internet for help with writing have been added to all of the writing chapters. Chapters 1 through 5 each conclude with a section called Internet Strategies, which helps students use search engines effectively, find links that are relevant to their own writing, evaluate websites, find online writing centers for additional writing and grammar help, and more.

- **Enhanced Coverage of the Writing Process** Chapter 3 now contains Part H, "Looking at a Paragraph from Start to Finish." This section is meant to encourage students to understand (and tolerate) the recursiveness of the writing process—the messy and sometimes dead-end striving to arrive at a cogent topic sentence, better support, and clearer writing. All the prewriting techniques and strategies for developing an effective paragraph discussed in Chapters 2 and 3 are used as draft material for the final paragraph.

- **New High-Interest Practice Material** Twenty percent of the practice sets have been replaced with engaging new paragraphs, essays, and continuous discourses for proofreading and editing. These exercises sustain interest as students apply the concepts they have learned. Topics include Stephen King's online writing, how to build better relationships, Jane Goodall's lifelong efforts to understand and save chimpanzees, Tiger Woods' childhood, vanishing languages, credit card debt, J. K. Rowling's phenomenal Harry Potter success, cancer survivor and Tour de France winner Lance Armstrong, and many more inspiring people as well as issues relevant to students' lives.

- **More New Material**   We have also replaced many Unit Writing Assignments, a fifth of the individual items in sentence-level practices, and many quotations in the Quotation Bank. We have added a spell-check section, including a practice that students should find amusing, to Chapter 31, "Spelling."

- **Other Improvements**   For clarity and ease of use, we have numbered practices consecutively within each chapter. For students' motivation and convenience, we have provided in the directions the number of errors that students should find in each of the Unit proofreading practices. For instructors' convenience, we have added the labels "Answers will vary" and "Sample answers" in the Instructor's Annotated Edition.

- **New Appendix for ESL Students**   Appendix B, "Some Guidelines for Students of English as a Second Language" now joins Appendix A, "Parts of Speech Review." Topics in Appendix B include count and noncount nouns, verbs with gerunds and infinitives, and prepositions with gerunds. Short practices provide students with the opportunity to work with the material.

- **Nine New Reading Selections**   We have replaced five reading selections and added four more, for a total of nine new readings. These include Rosa Parks' own version of what happened on the day her refusal to give up her seat on a bus launched her into the civil rights movement, the myths behind the advantages of bottled water, the influence of the Barbie doll on women's self-image, and the history of the *tortilla* in the life of artist and author José Antonio Burciaga.

- **Extensive Ancillary Package**   Available on adoption of the text, the following ancillaries provide the instructor with rich materials to expand his or her teaching options:

  Instructor's Annotated Edition

  A Test Package that includes approximately seventy-five tests with 25 percent newly created activities

  Student Answer Key

  Grammar CD-ROM with more than 1,200 practice exercises written specifically for the *Grassroots* level. This dynamic CD contains exercises, tutorials, instructional reviews, and practice and assessment tests for the *Grassroots* audience. When packaged with *Grassroots*, the CD is available to students for a nominal charge.

  Computerized diagnostic and chapter tests that provide additional test materials for instructors' use.

  Houghton Mifflin website that includes resources for students and instructors. Students can access Online Writing and Grammar Centers along with a variety of reading and writing tests. Instructors' resources include a Web tutorial, discipline-focused articles, book-specific websites, and ordering information.

Organization of the Text

The range of materials and flexible format of *Grassroots* make this worktext adaptable to almost any teaching/learning situation: classroom, laboratory, or self-teaching. Each chapter is a self-contained lesson, so instructors may teach the chapters in any sequence that fits their course designs. *Grassroots with Readings* is versatile enough to support many different approaches to basic writing instruction.

Acknowledgments

The authors wish to thank those people whose thoughtful comments and suggestions helped them develop the Seventh Edition.

Larry Baden, Colorado Christian University

Barbara Bretcko, Raritan Valley Community College

Judy D. Covington, Trident Technical College

Jane P. Gamber, Hutchinson Community College

Sherry K. Gell, Brevard Community College

Jennifer Hurd, Harding University

Steve Kaufman, Minneapolis Community & Technical College

Patsy Krech, The University of Memphis

Rebecca Smith Mann, Guilford Technical Community College

Joy Marsh, Casper College

Mary Ann Merz, Oklahoma City Community College

Eugene H. McCarthy, Middlesex Community College

Sue B. Palmer, Brevard Community College

Dee Pruitt, Florence-Darlington Technical College

Martha Rose, Johnson and Wales University

Roseann Torsiello, Berkeley College

Willie Jean Smith, University of Arkansas at Pine Bluff

Linda Whisnant, Guilford Technical Community College

Note on the Readings

The reading selections have been grouped according to the topics listed here. Suggestions for using specific readings with unit Writers' Workshops appear, where appropriate, in one of the notes of each group.

Historical Events
Rosa Parks, "Montgomery, Alabama, 1955"
Leonard Pitts, Jr., "Just One More"

Language
Daniel Meier, "One Man's Kids"
Ana Veciana-Suarez, "For a Parent, There's No Language Dilemma"

Fathers
Leo Buscaglia, "Papa, the Teacher"
Li-Young Lee, "One Human Hand"

Immigrant Experience
Julia Alvarez, "Yolanda"
Ranbir Sidhu, "Esperanto"

Medical Science
Courtland Milloy, "The Gift"
Patsy Garlan, "A Link to the Living"

Books
Malcolm X, "A Homemade Education"
Maya Angelou, "Mrs. Flowers"

Cultural Expectations
Anna Quindlen, "Barbie at 35"
Dave Barry, "Sports Nuts"
Amy Tan, "Four Directions"

Marriage
Francine Klagsbrun, "Forever"
Shoba Narayan, "In This Arranged Marriage, Love Came Later"

Manufacture
José Antonio Burciaga, *"Tortillas"*
Barbara Garson, "Perfume"
Liza Gross, "The Hidden Life of Bottled Water"

Self-Help
Joseph T. Martorano/John P. Kildahl, "Say Yes to Yourself"
Daniel Goleman, "Emotional Intelligence"

Grassroots

UNIT 1

Writing Forceful Paragraphs

The goal of *Grassroots* is to make you a better writer, and Unit 1 is key to your success. In this unit, you will

- Learn the importance of subject, audience, and purpose
- Learn the parts of a good paragraph
- Practice the paragraph-writing process
- Learn how to revise and improve your paragraphs
- Apply these skills to exam questions and short essays

Spotlight on Writing

My mother used to take me with her into the woods, to ponds where she would do her washing. These were the days before such things as washing machines, and we had no running water in the house, no electricity in the house. So when she washed clothing—and she washed the clothing for everyone in the family—she used to take it all in a big bundle into the woods, where rainwater settled into ponds. The ponds were like part of the marsh, but it would be fresh water—water you could wash clothing in. There used to be a soap called Octagon that came in an eight-sided bar, and she used that to get to the dirt in the clothing. Some people who had a few bucks had a scrub board, but she didn't. She would just beat the clothing on the rock until the dirt would sort of dissolve and float out. This water wasn't hot, mind you; it was cold water. And then she would wring the water out of each item and spread the clothes out on low trees to dry in the sun. We would be gone most of the day on those days when she washed, and when the clothes were almost dry, she would bundle them up and we would go back home.

Sidney Poitier, *The Measure of a Man: A Spiritual Autobiography*

- Sidney Poitier's words bring to life a scene from his childhood in the Bahamas. Are any details especially vivid? Which ones?

- Words have power: they can make us remember, see, feel, or think in a certain way.

    Unit 1 will introduce you to the power of writing well.

Writing Ideas
- A memory of someone doing a chore that is now done by a machine or by technology

- Your favorite (or least favorite) childhood or adulthood chore

Good writing is the end result of a *writing process*, a series of steps the writer has taken. This chapter will give you an overview of that process—explored in more depth throughout Unit 1—as well as some tips on how to approach your writing assignments.

PART A   *The Writing Process*

Experienced writers go through a *process* consisting of steps like these:

1
Prewriting
- Thinking about possible subjects
- Freely jotting ideas on paper or computer
- Narrowing the subject and writing it as one sentence
- Deciding which ideas to include
- Arranging ideas in a plan or outline

2
Writing
- Writing a first draft

3
Rewriting
- Rethinking, rearranging, and revising as necessary
- Writing one or more new drafts
- Proofreading for grammar and spelling errors

Writing is a personal and sometimes messy process. Writers don't all perform these steps in the same order, and they may have to go through some steps more than once. However, most writers *prewrite, write, rewrite*—and *proofread*. The rest of this unit and much of the book will show you how.

Practice 1   Self-Assessment

Choose a paper that you wrote recently for an English class or for some other class, and think about the *process* you followed in writing it. With a group of three or four classmates, or in your notebook, answer these questions:

1. Did I do any planning or prewriting—or did I just start writing the paper?

2. How much time did I spend improving and revising my paper?

3. Was I able to spot and correct my own grammar and spelling errors?

4. In the past, have any instructors or others made useful comments about my writing?

5. What one change in my writing process would most improve my writing? (Taking more time for prewriting? Spending more time revising? Improving my grammar or spelling skills?)

PART B   *Subject, Audience, and Purpose*

As you begin a writing assignment, give some thought to your *subject, audience,* and *purpose.*

When your instructor assigns a broad subject, try to focus on one aspect that interests you. For example, suppose the broad subject is *music,* and you play the conga drums. You might focus on why you play them rather than some other instrument, or on what drumming means to you. If the broad subject is *a change you have made,* you might focus on how you recently improved your study habits.

Whenever possible, choose subjects you know and care about: observing your neighborhood come to life in the morning, riding a dirt bike, helping a child become more confident, learning more about your computer, achieving a dream. Ask yourself:

● What special experience or knowledge do I have?

● What angers, saddens, or inspires me?

● What do I love to do?

● What news story affected me recently?

● What community problem do I have ideas about solving?

Your answers to such questions will suggest promising writing ideas.

How you approach your subject will depend on your *audience,* your readers. Are you writing for classmates, a professor, people who know about your subject, or people who do not? For instance, if you are writing about weight training and your readers have never been inside a gym, you will approach your subject in a simple and basic way, perhaps stressing the benefits of weightlifting. An audience of bodybuilders, however, already knows these things; for them, you would write in more depth, perhaps focusing on how to develop one muscle group.

Finally, keeping your *purpose* in mind helps you know what to write. Do you want to explain something to your readers, convince them that a certain point of view is correct, entertain them, or just tell a good story? If your purpose is to persuade parents to support having school uniforms, you can explain that uniforms lower clothing costs and may reduce student crime. However, if your purpose is to convince students that uniforms are a good idea, you might approach the subject differently, emphasizing how stylish the uniforms look or why students from other schools feel that uniforms improve their school atmosphere.

Practice 2

List five subjects you might like to write about. For ideas, reread the questions on page 5.

1. _____

2. _____

3. _____

4. _____

5. _____

Practice 3

With a group of three or four classmates, or on your own, jot down ideas for the following two writing tasks. Notice how your points and details differ, depending on your audience and purpose. (If you are not employed, write about a job with which you are familiar.)

1. For a new coworker, you plan to write a description of a typical day on your job. Your purpose is to help train this person, who will perform the same duties you do. Your supervisor will need to approve what you write.

2. For one of your closest friends, you plan to write a description of a typical day on your job. Your purpose is to make your friend laugh because he or she has been feeling down recently.

PART C   *Guidelines for Submitting Written Work*

Learn your instructor's requirements for submitting written work, as these may vary from class to class. Here are some general guidelines. Write in any special instructions.

1. Choose sturdy white $8\frac{1}{2}$-by-11-inch paper, lined if you write by hand, plain if you use a computer or type.

2. Clearly write your name, the date, and any other required information, using the format requested by your instructor.

3. If you write by hand, do so neatly in black or dark blue ink.

4. Write on only one side of the paper.

5. Double-space if you write on computer or type. Some instructors also want handwriting double-spaced.

6. Leave margins of at least one inch on all sides.

7. Number each page of your assignment, starting with page 2. Place the numbers at the top of each page, either centered or in the top right corner.

Other guidelines: _____

_____

_____

 Chapter Highlights

Tips for Succeeding in This Course

● Remember that writing is a process: prewriting, writing, and rewriting.

● Before you write, always be clear about your subject, audience, and purpose.

● Follow your instructor's guidelines for submitting written work.

Internet Strategies

The Internet can be an excellent tool at all stages of the writing process. The strategies that end each chapter in Unit 1 will help you use the Internet effectively as you (1) prepare to write, (2) write, and (3) revise and edit.

Using a Search Engine

A search engine allows you to type in words and find related Web pages that may or may not be relevant to your seach. A number of search engines are available, including Google, Excite, Yahoo!, and Altavista to name only a few. You can experiment with different search engines until you find one that meets your needs. Here are some pointers to keep in mind as you use search engines:

- Be as specific as possible when you type in keywords. For example, if you would like to search for pages related to *education,* ask yourself, "Which aspects of education interest me most?" If you use *education* as a keyword, you will be overwhelmed by the huge number of general and specific pages that will be presented. However, if you decide that you are most interested in writing or learning about *charter schools, home schooling, elementary education,* or *higher education,* to name a few topics, you can focus your search more specifically. Your search will yield more pages that are closely related to your topic.

- When you find a helpful page that relates to your area of interest, *bookmark* it. Look at the toolbar at the top of your Web page and find the button that says *bookmark* or *favorite,* and hit *add.* This will save your page in a central location so that you can return to it without having to type in the address.

- If you are not getting the results that you want, try another search engine!

- Here are the addresses of several search engines you may find useful:

    Google: http://www.google.com
    Altavista: http://www.altavista.com
    Excite: http://www.excite.com
    HotBot: http://www.hotbot.com
    Yahoo: http://www.yahoo.com

Each chapter in this unit has an Internet Strategies section. The goal of the exercises is to help you gain the skills to write a short paper by using the Internet as your source for prewriting, writing, and rewriting.

Choosing a Topic and Finding Relevant Sites

1. Choose one subject from the list you wrote in Practice 2, page 6, or choose one of these subjects: *sports, education, money,* or *careers.* Now focus on just *one interesting aspect* of this subject and search the web. Find three to five websites that you believe might help you write a paper later. (Before you leave each site, answer questions 2 and 3). List the addresses here:

    _____

    _____

    _____

    _____

2. Bookmark the websites on your computer so that you can return to them as you continue your Internet project.

3. Answer the following questions about each site you bookmarked. You will need this information later.

    a. What is the subject of the site? _____

    b. For what audience is the site intended?_____

    c. What is the purpose of the site (to entertain, to inform, to sell something, and so on)? _____

    a. _____

    b. _____

    c. _____

    a. _____

    b. _____

    c. _____

    a. _____

    b. _____

    c. _____

CHAPTER 2

Prewriting to Generate Ideas

PART A *Freewriting*
PART B *Brainstorming*
PART C *Clustering*
PART D *Keeping a Journal*
Internet Strategies

One of the authors of this book used to teach ice skating. On the first day of class, the students practiced falling. Once they knew how to fall without fear, they were free to learn to skate.

Writing is much like ice skating: The more you practice, the better you get. If you are free to make mistakes, you'll want to practice, and you'll look forward to new writing challenges.

The problem is that many people avoid writing. Faced with an English composition or a report at work, they put it off and then scribble something at the last minute. Other people sit staring at the blank page—writing a sentence, crossing it out, unable to get started. In this chapter, you will learn four useful prewriting techniques that will help you jump-start your writing process and put ideas on paper: freewriting, brainstorming, clustering, and keeping a journal.

PART A	Freewriting

Freewriting is a method many writers use to warm up and get ideas on paper. Here are the guidelines: For five or ten full minutes, write without stopping about anything that comes into your head. Don't worry about grammar or about writing complete sentences; just set a timer and go. If you get stuck, repeat or rhyme the last word you wrote, but keep writing nonstop until the timer sounds.

Afterward, read what you have written, and underline any parts you like. Here is one student's first freewriting, with her underlinings:

> Freewrite free without stopping hopping hoping moping coping, <u>coping since Mark left.</u> Singing, ringing, sun glowing, water glittering. Hope he'll be a great artist someday, paint thick golden suns sparkling on crackly green waves. Peaceful calm coasting ships—my pen coasting along like a ship—getting lost coasting—this doesn't feel like writing—feels like flying, sailing, swooping, like something quick and quiet except for the sound of all these pens maybe 30 pens on paper scratch scratch hiss hiss and sleeves <u>right-handed sleeves, left-handed sleeves dragging in the ink</u> sink pink skies and fast blue sounds. <u>Fast ink is a blue sound, the sea is a blue sound.</u> Mark's brush paints silver songs hearts singing up and down the waves—singing an always song.

- This example has the vital energy of many freewritings.
- Why do you think the student underlined what she did?
- Would you have underlined any other words or phrases? Why?

_____

_____

Freewriting is a wonderful way to let ideas pour onto paper without getting stuck by worrying too soon about correctness or "good writing." Sometimes freewriting produces nonsense, but often it provides interesting ideas for further thinking and writing.

Practice 1

1. Set a timer for ten minutes, or have someone time you. Freewrite without stopping for the full ten minutes. Repeat or rhyme words if you get stuck, but keep writing! Don't let your pen or pencil leave the page.

2. When you finish, write down one or two words that describe how you feel

   while freewriting. _____

3. Now read your freewriting. Underline any words or lines you like—anything that strikes you as powerful, moving, funny, or important. If nothing strikes you, that's okay.

Practice 2

Try two more freewritings at home, each one ten minutes long. Do them at different times of the day when you have a few quiet moments. If possible, use a timer: set it for ten minutes, and then write fast until it rings. Later, read your freewritings, and underline any striking lines or ideas.

Focused Freewriting

In _focused freewriting,_ you try to focus your thoughts on one subject as you freewrite. The subject can be one assigned by your instructor, one you choose, or one you discover in unfocused freewriting.

Here is one student's focused freewriting on the topic *someone who strongly influenced me.*

> Thin, thinner, weak, weaker. You stopped cooking for yourself—forced yourself to choke down cans of nutrition. Your chest caved in; your bones stuck out. You never asked, Why me? With a weak laugh you asked, Why not me? I had a wonderful life, a great job, a good marriage while it lasted. Have beautiful kids. Your wife divorced you—couldn't stand to watch you die, couldn't stand to have her life fall apart the way your body was falling apart. I watched you stumble, trip over your own feet, sink, fall down. I held you up. Now I wonder which one of us was holding the other one up. I saw you shiver in your summer jacket because you didn't have the strength to put on your heavy coat. Bought you a feather-light winter jacket, saw your eyes fill with tears of pleasure and gratitude. You said they would find you at the bottom of the stairs. When they called to tell me we'd lost you, the news wasn't unexpected, but the pain came in huge waves. Heart gave out, they said. Your daughter found you crumpled at the foot of the stairs. How did you know? What else did you guess?
>
> Daniel Corteau, student

- This student later used his freewriting as the basis for an excellent paragraph.

- Underline any words or lines that you find especially striking or powerful. Be prepared to discuss your choices.

- How was the writer influenced by the man he describes?

Practice 3

Reread your earlier freewritings, and notice your underlinings. Do you find any words or ideas that you would like to write more about? List two or three of them here:

_____

_____

_____

_____

_____

Practice 4

Now choose one word or idea from your freewriting or from the following list. Focus your thoughts on it, and do a ten-minute focused freewriting. Try to stick to the topic, but don't worry too much about it. Just keep writing! When you finish, read and underline as usual.

1. finding
2. shoes
3. the biggest lie
4. a dream
5. someone who influenced you
6. your experiences with writing
7. the smell of _____
8. strength

PART B	*Brainstorming*

Brainstorming means freely jotting ideas about a topic. As in freewriting, the purpose of brainstorming is to get as many ideas as possible onto paper so that you will have something to work with later. Just write down everything that comes to mind about a topic—words and phrases, ideas, details, examples, little stories. Once you have brainstormed, read over your list, underlining any ideas you might want to develop further.

Here is one student's brainstorming list on *an interesting job:*

> midtown messenger
>
> frustrating but free
>
> I know the city backwards and forwards
>
> good bike needed
>
> fast, ever-changing, dangerous
>
> drivers hate messengers—we dart in and out of traffic
>
> old clothes don't get respect
>
> I wear the best Descent racing gear, a Giro helmet
>
> people respect you more
>
> I got tipped $100 for carrying a crystal vase from the showroom to Wall Street in 15 minutes
>
> other times I get stiffed
>
> lessons I've learned—controlling my temper
>
> having dignity
>
> staying calm no matter what—insane drivers, deadlines, rudeness
>
> weirdly, I like my job

As he brainstormed, this writer produced many interesting facts and details about his job as a bicycle messenger, all in just a few minutes. He might want to underline the ideas that most interest him—perhaps the time he was tipped $100—and then brainstorm again for more details.

Practice 5

Choose one of the following topics that interests you, and write it at the top of your paper. Then brainstorm! Write anything that comes into your head about the topic. Let your ideas flow.

1. a singer or a musician
2. the future
3. an intriguing job
4. a story in the news

5. the best/worst class I've had
6. making a difference
7. a place to which I never want to return
8. a community problem

After you fill a page with your list, read it over, underlining the most interesting ideas. Draw arrows to connect related ideas. Do you find one idea that might be the subject of a paper?

PART C   *Clustering*

Some writers find *clustering* or *mapping* an effective way to get ideas on paper. To begin clustering, write one idea or topic—usually one word—in the center of your paper. Then let your mind make associations, and write those ideas down, branching out from the center, like this:

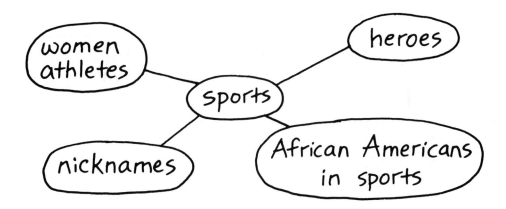

When one idea suggests other ideas, details, or examples, jot those around it in a cluster. When you finish, pick the cluster that most interests you, and write further. You might want to freewrite for more ideas.

track, tennis

getting more endorsements

Women athletes

drugs

Do heroes make mistakes?

Anthony Mason

What is a hero?

heroes

big $?
skill?
admirable values?

Sports

nicknames

African Americans in sports

baseball

Carl Malone, the Mailman— he always delivers

Glen Robinson—Big Dog he's got the bark he's got the bite

Lady Magic

Jackie Robinson, first in majors

Larry Doby, first in American League

way names relate to qualities, skills, body type

Neon Deion Sanders, blazing with gold jewelry

progress

audience love names, fun to shout

Sir Charles Barkley— he's king of the court

more managers and coaches needed

Jumbo Elliot 6'7", 297 pounds

Practice 6

Read over the clustering map on page 14. If you were giving advice to the writer, which cluster or branch do you think would make the most interesting paper? Why?

Practice 7

Choose one of these topics or another topic that interests you. Write it in the center of a piece of paper and then try clustering. Keep writing down associations until you have filled the page.

1. movies
2. a pet
3. a lesson
4. sports
5. my hometown
6. self-esteem
7. a relative
8. someone I don't understand

PART D   *Keeping a Journal*

Keeping a journal is an excellent way to practice your writing skills and to discover ideas for future writing. Most of all, your journal is a place to record your private thoughts and important experiences. Set aside a section of your notebook, or get yourself a special book with $8\frac{1}{2}$-by-11-inch lined paper. Every night, or several times a week, write for at least ten minutes in your journal.

What you write about will be limited only by your imagination. Here are some ideas:

- Write in detail about things that matter to you—family relationships, falling in (or out) of love, an experience at school or work, something important you just learned, something you did well.

- List your personal goals, and brainstorm possible steps toward achieving them.

- Write about problems you are having, and "think on paper" about ways to solve them.

- Comment on classroom instruction or assignments, and evaluate your learning progress. What needs work? What questions do you need to ask? Write out a study plan for yourself and refer to it regularly.

- Write down your responses to your reading—class assignments, newspaper items, magazine articles that impress or anger you.

- Read through the quotations at the end of this book until you find one that strikes you. Then copy it into your journal, think about it, and write. For example, Agnes Repplier says, "It is not easy to find happiness in ourselves, and it is not possible to find it elsewhere." Do you agree with her?

● Be alert to interesting writing topics all around you. If possible, carry a notebook during the day for "fast sketches." Jot down moving or funny moments, people, or things that catch your attention—an overworked waitress in a restaurant, a scene at the day-care center where you leave your child, a man trying to persuade an officer not to give him a parking ticket.

You will soon find that ideas for writing will occur to you all day long. Before they slip away, capture them in words.

Practice 8

Write in your journal for at least ten minutes three times a week.

At the end of each week, read what you have written. Underline striking passages, and put a check beside interesting topics and ideas that you would like to write more about.

As you complete the exercises in this book and work on the writing assignments, try all four techniques—freewriting, brainstorming, clustering, and keeping a journal—and see which ones work best for you.

Practice 9

From your journal, choose one or two passages that you might want to rewrite and allow others to read. Put a check beside each of those passages so that you can find them easily later. Underline the parts you like best. Can you already see ways you might rewrite and improve the writing?

Chapter Highlights

To get started and to discover your ideas, try these techniques.

● **Freewriting:** writing for five or ten minutes about anything that comes into your head

● **Focused freewriting:** freewriting for five or ten minutes about one topic

● **Brainstorming:** freely jotting many ideas about a topic

● **Clustering:** making word associations on paper

● **Keeping a journal:** writing regularly about things that interest and move you

Internet Strategies

Look at your information about the sites you bookmarked in Chapter 1. Revisit the sites. Do you still believe that they will be helpful as you write about the topic you chose? If not, narrow your search or revisit some of the other sites you found. Bookmark any additional useful sites.

Using Prewriting Techniques

Complete one of the following activities, using your bookmarked sites:
1. Do a focused freewriting for five or ten minutes on the content of the best site you found. If you have time, freewrite on all three sites. When you have finished, decide whether you still want to write about your original topic or whether you want to re-focus or narrow your topic even further.

2. Brainstorm on your topic and on the content of the best site you found. Jot down everything that comes to mind. When you have finished, read over your list, and underline any ideas you want to develop further.

3. Create a cluster or a map of ideas related to your topic. Use the content of your bookmarked sites to add further details, ideas, or examples. When you have finished, look over your cluster and decide which branch would make the most interesting essay.

Assessing Your Topic

Now that you have used one prewriting activity to further develop your topic, think about how well you could write a brief paper about it. Answer the following questions:

- Will you be able to develop your idea fully? _____

- Will you be able to use your bookmarked sites to support your

  main idea and overall topic? _____

- Will you need to do additional research on the Web to get informa-

  tion to support your main idea? _____

If you answered no to the first two questions or if you need to do additional research, you should rethink your topic or examine your focused freewriting, brainstorming, or clustering for another idea. If you believe that your topic can be developed and that your bookmarked sites will help you, you are ready to begin to think about writing your Internet-based paper.

CHAPTER 3

Developing Effective Paragraphs

The *paragraph* is the basic unit of writing. This chapter will guide you through the process of writing paragraphs.

PART A *Defining the Paragraph and the Topic Sentence*

A *paragraph* is a group of related sentences that develop one main idea. Although a paragraph has no definite length, it is often four to twelve sentences long. A paragraph usually appears with other paragraphs in a longer piece of writing—an essay, a letter, or an article, for example.

A paragraph looks like this on the page:

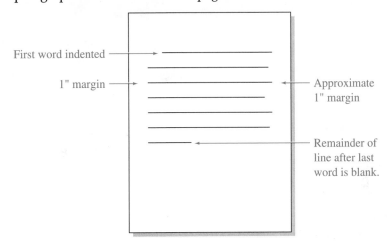

First word indented

1" margin

Approximate 1" margin

Remainder of line after last word is blank.

- Clearly *indent* the first word of every paragraph about one-half inch or five spaces on the keyboard. On a computer, you can usually tab over (once) for a paragraph indent.

- Extend every line of a paragraph as far as it will go to the right-hand margin. If you are working on a computer, the line wraps automatically.

- However, if the last word of the paragraph comes before the end of the line, leave the rest of the line blank.

Topic Sentence and Body

Most paragraphs contain one main idea to which all the sentences relate. The *topic sentence* states this main idea. The *body* of the paragraph supports this main idea with specific details, facts, and examples.

> When I was growing up, my older brother Joe was the greatest person in my world. If anyone teased me about my braces or buckteeth, he fiercely defended me. When one boy insisted on calling me "Fang," Joe threatened to knock his teeth out. It worked—no more teasing. My brother always chose me to play on his baseball teams though I was a terrible hitter. Even after he got his driver's license, he didn't abandon me. Instead, every Sunday, the two of us went for a drive. We might stop for cheeseburgers, go to a computer showroom, drive past some girl's house, or just laugh and talk. It was one of childhood's mysteries that such a wonderful brother loved me.
>
> Jeremiah Woolrich, student

- The first sentence of this paragraph is the *topic sentence.* It states in a general way the main idea of the paragraph: that *Joe was the greatest person in my world.*

Although the topic sentence can appear anywhere in the paragraph, it is often the first sentence.

- The rest of the paragraph, the *body*, fully explains this statement with details about braces and buckteeth, baseball teams, Sunday drives, cheeseburgers, and so forth.

- Note that the final sentence provides a brief conclusion so that the paragraph *feels* finished.

Practice 1

Each group of sentences below can be arranged and written as a paragraph. Circle the letter of the sentence that would be the best topic sentence. REMEMBER: The topic sentence states the main idea of the entire paragraph and includes all the other ideas.

EXAMPLE:
a. Speed-walking three times a week is part of my routine.

b. Staying healthy and fit is important to me.

c. Every night, I get at least seven hours of sleep.

d. I eat as many fresh fruits and vegetables as possible.

(Sentence b is more general than the other sentences; it would be the best topic sentence.)

1. a. My father looks handsome in his old-fashioned top hat and tails.
   b. My mother is seated before him wearing a lacy gown.
   c. I will always treasure a faded wedding picture of my parents.
   d. In the background is the old arched gate of my grandparents' garden.

2. a. In 1988, three students at a Philadelphia high school for the arts were singing in the men's room.
   b. Singing dates in Philadelphia clubs led to their first recording contract.
   c. A fourth student came by, added a bass note, and was asked to join the group, then called Unique Attraction.
   d. The group Boyz II Men rose quickly from lunch-hour vocalizing to international fame.
   e. Their first album, *Coolie High Harmony*, earned platinum.
   f. Today the Boyz' silky mix of doo-wop and gospel is loved all over the world.

3. a. Physical courage allows soldiers or athletes to endure bodily pain or danger.
   b. Those with social courage dare to expose their deep feelings in order to build close relationships.
   c. Those rare people who stand up for their beliefs despite public pressure possess moral courage.
   d. Inventors and artists show creative courage when they break out of old ways of seeing and doing things.
   e. Psychologist Rollo May claimed that there are four different types of courage.

4. a. Many old toys and household objects are now collectors' items.
   b. A Barbie or Madame Alexander doll from the 1950s can bring more than $1,000.
   c. Old baseball cards are worth money to collectors.
   d. Fiesta china, made in the 1930s, has become popular again.

5. a. You should read the ingredients on every package of food you buy.
   b. Children should not eat mandelona, which is made from peanuts soaked in almond flavoring.
   c. Avoid buying food from bins that do not list ingredients.
   d. If your child is allergic to peanuts, you need to be constantly on the alert.
   e. In a restaurant, tongs may have been used to pick up items containing peanuts.

PART B   *Narrowing the Topic and Writing the Topic Sentence*

This chapter will guide you through the process of writing paragraphs of your own. Here are the steps we will discuss:

1. Narrowing the topic and writing the topic sentence

2. Generating ideas for the body

3. Selecting and dropping ideas

4. Grouping ideas in a plan

5. Writing and revising the paragraph

6. Writing the final draft

Narrowing the Topic

Often your first step as a writer will be *narrowing* a broad topic—one assigned by your instructor, one you have thought of yourself, or one suggested by a particular writing task, like a letter. That is, you must cut the topic down to size and choose one aspect that interests you.

Assume, for example, that you are asked to write a paragraph describing a person you know. The trick is to choose someone you would *like* to write about, someone who interests you and would probably also interest your audience of readers.

At this point, many writers find it helpful to think on paper by *brainstorming, freewriting,* or *clustering.** As you jot down or freely write ideas, ask yourself questions. Whom do I love, hate, or admire? Who is the funniest or most unusual person I know? Is there a family member or friend about whom others might like to read?

Suppose you choose to write about your friend Beverly. *Beverly* is too broad a topic for one paragraph. Therefore, you should limit your topic further, choosing just one of her qualities or acts. What is unusual about her? What might interest others? Perhaps what stands out in your mind is that Beverly is a determined person who doesn't let difficulties defeat her. You have now *narrowed* your broad topic to just *Beverly's determination.*

---

*Brainstorming is discussed further in Part C. Also see Chapter 2 for more information about prewriting.

Writing the Topic Sentence

The *topic sentence* states your narrowed topic clearly in sentence form. It makes one point that the rest of your paragraph will support and explain. A topic sentence can be very simple *(Beverly is a determined person)*, or, better yet, it can state your attitude or point of view about the topic *(Beverly inspires admiration because she is so determined)*. A good topic sentence should be limited and complete.

Your topic sentence should be *limited*. It should make a point that is neither too broad nor too narrow to be supported in a paragraph. As a rule, the more specific and well-defined the topic sentence, the better the paragraph. Which of these topic sentences do you think will produce the best paragraphs?

> (1) My recent trip to Colorado was really bad.
> (2) My recent trip to Colorado was disappointing because the weather ruined my camping plans.

- Topic sentence (1) is so broad that the paragraph could include almost anything.

- Topic sentence (2), on the other hand, is *limited* enough to provide the main idea for a good paragraph: how terrible weather ruined the writer's camping plans.

> (3) The Each-One-Reach-One tutoring program encourages academic excellence at Chester Elementary School.
> (4) Tutoring programs can be found all over the country.

- Topic sentence (3) is limited enough to provide the main idea for a good paragraph. Reading this topic sentence, what do you expect the paragraph to include?

_____

_____

- Topic sentence (4) lacks a limited point. Reading this sentence, someone cannot guess what the paragraph will be about.

In addition, the topic sentence must be a *complete sentence*; it must contain a subject and a verb and express a complete thought.* Do not confuse a topic with a topic sentence. For example, *the heroism of Christopher Reeve* cannot be a topic sentence because it is not a complete sentence. Here is one possible topic sentence: *Christopher Reeve's work with other spinal-cord injury patients makes him a true hero.*

For now, it is best to place your topic sentence at the beginning of the paragraph. After you have mastered this pattern, you can try variations. Placed first, the topic sentence clearly establishes the focus of your paragraph and helps grab the reader's attention. Wherever the topic sentence appears, all other sentences must relate to it and support it with specific details, facts, examples, arguments, and explanations. If necessary, you can revise the topic sentence later to make it more accurately match the paragraph you have written.

---

*For more work on writing complete sentences, see Chapters 6 and 7.

Do not begin a topic sentence with *This paragraph will be about . . .* or *I am going to write about . . .* These extra words contribute nothing. Instead, make your point directly. Make every word in the topic sentence count.

Practice 2

Put a check beside each topic sentence that is limited enough to be the topic sentence of a good paragraph. If you think a topic sentence is too broad, limit the topic according to your own interests; then write a new, specific topic sentence.

EXAMPLES: ✔   E-mail has changed my life in three ways.

Rewrite: _____

I am going to write about cell phones.

Rewrite: *Talking on a cell phone can distract drivers to the point of causing accidents.*

1.   Working in the complaint department taught me tolerance.

Rewrite: _____

_____

2.   A subject I want to write about is money.

Rewrite: _____

_____

3.   This paragraph will discuss food.

Rewrite: _____

_____

4.   Some things about college have been great.

Rewrite: _____

_____

5.   Single parents often have a hard time.

Rewrite: _____

_____

6.   Living in a one-room apartment forces a person to be organized.

Rewrite: _____

_____

PART C — Generating Ideas for the Body of the Paragraph

Rich, supporting detail is one key to effective writing. A good way to generate ideas for the body of a paragraph is by *brainstorming,* freely jotting down ideas. This important step may take just a few minutes, but it gets your ideas on paper and may pull ideas out of you that you didn't even know you had.

Freely jot down anything that might relate to your topic—details, examples, little stories. Don't worry at this point if some ideas don't seem to belong. For now, just keep jotting.

Here is a possible brainstorming list for the topic sentence *Beverly inspires admiration because she is so determined.*

1. saved enough money for college

2. worked days, went to school nights

3. has beautiful brown eyes

4. nervous about learning to drive but didn't give up

5. failed road test twice—passed eventually

6. her favorite color—wine red

7. received degree in accounting

8. she is really admirable

9. with lots of will power, quit smoking

10. used to be a heavy smoker

11. married to Virgil

12. I like Virgil too

13. now a good driver

14. never got a ticket

15. hasn't touched another cigarette

As you saw in Part B, some writers also brainstorm or use other prewriting techniques *before* they write the topic sentence. Do what works best for you.

Practice 3

Here are three topic sentences. For each one, brainstorm, freewrite, or cluster for several specific details that you might use to develop an interesting paragraph.

1. The room was decorated with items from every stage of my (his, her) life.

_____

_____

_____

2. _____ gave a wonderful party for _____.

_____

_____

_____

3. The best course I ever took was _____.

_____

_____

_____

Practice 4

Now choose one of the topic sentences that you rewrote for Practice 2. Write that topic sentence here.

Topic sentence: _____

_____

Next, brainstorm. On a sheet of notebook paper, write anything that comes to you about your topic sentence. Just let your ideas pour onto paper! Try to fill the page.

Practice 5

Many writers adjust the topic sentence after they have finished drafting the paragraph. In a group of three or four classmates, study the body of each of the following paragraphs. Then, working together, write the most exact and interesting topic sentence you can.

1. Topic sentence: _____

_____

    The chairs in Celia's living room are printed with pony heads and stand on legs that resemble hooves. The bases of her four table lamps are statues of cowboys or cowgirls, each topped with a matching shade. On three walls, floor-to-ceiling shelves sag under the weight of Roy Rogers and Hopalong Cassidy lunch boxes from the 1940s and hundreds of salt-and-pepper shakers in the form of cowboy boots or cacti. The most amazing object in Celia's collection is a huge motorized bucking bronco that guests in her house can ride.

2. Topic sentence: _____

_____

    Frigid air would hit us in the eyes when we stepped out the door to catch the school bus. Even though our faces were wrapped in scarves and our heads covered with wool caps, the cold snatched our breath away. A thin layer of snow crunched loudly under our boots as we ran gasping out to the road. I knew that the famous Minnesota wind chill was pulling temperatures well below zero, but I tried not to think about that. Instead, I liked to see how everything in the yard was frozen motionless, even the blades of grass that shone like little glass knives.

Ari Henson, student

PART D *Selecting and Dropping Ideas*

This may be the easiest step in paragraph writing because all you have to do is to select those ideas that best support your topic sentence and drop those that do not. Also drop ideas that just repeat the topic sentence but add nothing new to the paragraph.

Here is the brainstorming list for the topic sentence *Beverly inspires admiration because she is so determined.* Which ideas would you drop? Why?

1. saved enough money for college
2. worked days, went to school nights
3. has beautiful brown eyes
4. nervous about learning to drive but didn't give up
5. failed road test twice—passed eventually
6. her favorite color—wine red
7. received degree in accounting
8. she is really admirable
9. with lots of will power, quit smoking
10. used to be a heavy smoker
11. married to Virgil
12. I like Virgil too
13. now a good driver
14. never got a ticket
15. hasn't touched another cigarette

You probably dropped ideas 3, 6, 11, and 12 because they do not relate to the topic. You also should have dropped idea 8 because it merely repeats the topic sentence.

Practice 6

Now read through your own brainstorming list in Practice 4. Select the ideas that best support your topic sentence, and cross out those that do not. In addition, drop ideas that merely repeat the topic sentence. You should be able to give good reasons for keeping or dropping each idea in the list.

PART E *Arranging Ideas in a Plan or an Outline*

Now choose an *order* in which to arrange your ideas. First, group together ideas that have something in common, that are related or alike in some way. Then decide which ideas should come first, which second, and so on. Many writers do this by numbering the ideas on their list.

Here are the ideas for a paragraph about Beverly arranged in one possible way.

worked days, went to school nights
saved enough money for college
received degree in accounting

nervous about learning to drive but didn't give up
failed road test twice—passed eventually
now a good driver
never got a ticket

used to be a heavy smoker
with lots of will power, quit smoking
hasn't touched another cigarette

- How are the ideas in each group related? _____

_____

- Does it make sense to discuss college first, driving second, and smoking last?

Why? _____

_____

Keep in mind that there is more than one way to arrange ideas. As you group your own brainstorming list, think of what you want to say; then arrange ideas accordingly.*

Practice 7

On a separate sheet of paper, group the ideas from your brainstorming list into a plan. First, group together related ideas. Then decide which ideas will come first, which second, and so on.

PART F   *Writing and Revising the Paragraph*

Writing the First Draft

By now, you should have a clear plan or outline from which to write the first draft of your paragraph. The *first draft* should contain all the ideas you have decided to use, in the order in which you have chosen to present them. Writing on every other line will leave room for later changes.

———

*For more work on choosing an order, see Chapter 4, Part B.

Explain your ideas fully, including details that will interest or amuse the reader. If you are unsure about something, put a check in the margin and come back to it later, but avoid getting stuck on any one word, sentence, or idea. If possible, set the paper aside for several hours or several days; this will help you read it later with a fresh eye.

Practice 8

On a separate sheet of paper, write a first draft of the paragraph you have been working on.

Revising

Whether you are a beginning writer or a professional, you must *revise*—that is, rewrite what you have written in order to improve it. You might cross out and rewrite words or entire sentences. You might add, drop, or rearrange details.

As you revise, keep the reader in mind. Ask yourself these questions:

- Is my topic sentence clear?

- Can the reader easily follow my ideas?

- Is the order of ideas logical?

- Will this paragraph keep the reader interested?

In addition, revise your paragraph for *support* and for *unity*.

Revising for Support

Make sure your paragraph contains excellent *support*—that is, specific details, facts, and examples that fully explain your topic sentence.

Avoid simply repeating the same idea in different words, especially the idea in the topic sentence. Repeated ideas are just padding, a sign that you need to brainstorm or freewrite again for new ideas. Which of the following two paragraphs contains the best and most interesting support?

> A.   Every Saturday morning, Fourteenth Street is alive with activity. From one end of the street to the other, people are out doing everything imaginable. Vendors sell many different items on the street, and storekeepers will do just about anything to get customers into their stores. They will use signs, and they will use music. There is a tremendous amount of activity on Fourteenth Street, and just watching it is enjoyable.
>
> B.   Every Saturday morning, Fourteenth Street is alive with activity. Vendors line the sidewalks, selling everything from cassette tapes to wigs. Trying to lure customers inside, the shops blast pop music into the street or hang brightly colored banners announcing "Grand Opening Sale" or "Everything Must Go." Shoppers jam the sidewalks, both serious bargain hunters and families just out for a stroll, munching chilidogs as they survey the merchandise. Here and there, a panhandler hustles for handouts, taking advantage of the Saturday crowd.

- The body of *paragraph A* contains vague and general statements, so the reader gets no clear picture of the activity on Fourteenth Street.

- The body of *paragraph B*, however, includes many specific *details* that clearly explain the topic sentence: *vendors selling everything from cassette tapes to wigs, shops blasting pop music, brightly colored banners.*

- What other details in paragraph B help you see just how Fourteenth Street is alive with activity?

_____

_____

_____

Practice 9

Check the following paragraphs for strong, specific support. Mark places that need more details or explanation, and cross out any weak or repeated words. Then revise and rewrite each paragraph *as if you had written it,* inventing and adding support when you need to.

Paragraph A: Aunt Alethia was one of the most important people in my life. She had a strong influence on me. No matter how busy she was, she always had time for me. She paid attention to small things about me that no one else seemed to notice. When I was successful, she praised me. When I was feeling down, she gave me pep talks. She was truly wise and shared her wisdom with me. My aunt was a great person who had a major influence on my life.

Paragraph B: Just getting to school safely can be a challenge for many young people. Young as he is, my son has been robbed once and bullied on several occasions. The robbery was very frightening, for it involved a weapon. What was taken was a small thing, but it meant a lot to my son. It angers me that just getting to school is so dangerous. Something needs to be done.

Revising for Unity

While writing, you may sometimes drift away from your topic and include information that does not belong in the paragraph. It is important, therefore, to revise your paragraph for *unity;* that is, to drop any ideas or sentences that do not relate to the topic sentence.

This paragraph lacks unity:

(1) Franklin Mars, a Minnesota candy maker, created many popular candy snacks. (2) Milky Way, his first bar, was an instant hit. (3) Snickers, which he introduced in 1930, also sold very well. (4) Milton Hershey developed the very first candy bar in 1894. (5) M&Ms were a later Mars creation, supposedly designed so that soldiers could enjoy a sugar boost without getting sticky trigger fingers.

- What is the topic sentence in this paragraph? _____

- Which sentence does *not* relate to the topic sentence? _____

- Sentence (4) has nothing to do with the main idea, that *Franklin Mars created many popular candy snacks.* Therefore, sentence (4) should be dropped.

Practice 10

Check the following paragraphs for unity. If a paragraph is unified, write U in the blank. If it is not, write the number of the sentence that does not belong in the paragraph.

1. _____ (1) Personalized license plates have become very popular since they were introduced in the 1970s. (2) These "vanity plates" allow car owners to express their sense of humor, marital status, pet peeves, or ethnic pride. (3) Of course, every car must display a plate on the rear bumper or in the back window. (4) California was one of the first states to allow vanity plates, and its drivers created such messages as NUTS 2U and 55IZ2LO. (5) Now in some states, as many as one in seven autos has a personalized plate. (6) A recent *Car and Driver* poll picked the nation's best vanity plates, including NT GUILTY (on an Arkansas sports car) and NOBODY (on a Rolls Royce in California).

2. _____ (1) Families who nourish their children with words as well as food at dinner time produce better future readers. (2) Researchers at Harvard University studied the dinner conversations of sixty-eight families. (3) What they found was that parents who use a few new words in conversation with their three- and four-year-olds each night quickly build the children's vocabularies and their later reading skills. (4) The researchers point out that children can learn from eight to twenty-eight new words a day, so they need to be "fed" new words. (5) Excellent "big words" for preschoolers include *parachute, emerald, instrument,* and *education,* the researchers say.

3. _____ (1) Swimming is excellent exercise. (2) Swimming vigorously for just twelve minutes provides aerobic benefits to the heart. (3) Unlike jogging and many other aerobic sports, however, swimming does not jolt the bones and muscles with sudden pressure. (4) Furthermore, the motions of swimming, such as reaching out in the crawl, stretch the muscles in a healthy, natural way. (5) Some swimmers wear goggles to keep chlorine or salt out of their eyes while others do not.

Peer Feedback for Revising

You may wish to show your first draft or read it aloud to a respected friend or classmate. Ask this person to give an honest reader response, not to rewrite your work. To elicit useful responses, ask specific questions of your own, or use the Peer Feedback Sheet on the following page. You may want to photocopy the sheet rather than write on it so that you can revise it.

Practice 11

Now read the first draft of your paragraph with a critical eye. Revise and rewrite it, checking especially for a clear topic sentence, strong support, and unity.

Practice 12

Exchange *revised* paragraphs with a classmate. Ask specific questions or use the Peer Feedback Sheet.

When you *give* feedback, try to be as honest and specific as possible; saying a paper is "good," "nice," or "bad" doesn't really help the writer. When you *receive* feedback, think over your classmate's responses; do they ring true?

Now revise a second time, with the aim of writing a fine paragraph.

PEER FEEDBACK SHEET

To: _____ From: _____ Date: _____

1. What I like about this piece of writing is _____
_____
_____
_____
_____

2. Your main point seems to be _____
_____
_____
_____
_____
_____

3. These particular words or lines struck me as powerful.

   Words or lines: I like them because

   _____   _____
   _____   _____
   _____   _____
   _____   _____
   _____   _____

4. Some things aren't clear to me. These lines or parts could be improved
   (meaning not clear; supporting points missing; order seems mixed up;
   writing not lively).

   Lines or parts: Need improving because

   _____   _____
   _____   _____
   _____   _____
   _____   _____

5. The one change you could make that would most improve this piece of
   writing is
_____
_____
_____
_____
_____

PART G   *Writing the Final Draft*

When you are satisfied with your revisions, recopy your paper. Be sure to include all your corrections, and write neatly and legibly—a carelessly scribbled paper seems to say that you don't care about your work.

The first draft of the paragraph about Beverly, with the writer's changes, and the revised final draft follow. Compare them.

First Draft with Revisions

(1) Beverly inspires admiration because she is so determined. (2) Although
doing what? add details
she could not afford to attend college right after high school, she worked to save
How long?! Better support needed—show her hard work!
money. (3) It took a long time, but she got her degree. (4) She is now a good dri-

ver. (5) At first, she was very nervous about getting behind the wheel and even
The third time,
failed the road test twice, but she didn't quit. (6) She passed eventually.
Drop Virgil—he doesn't belong
(7) Her husband, Virgil, loves to drive; he races cars on the weekend. (8) Anyway,

Beverly has never gotten a ticket. (9) A year ago, Beverly quit smoking. (10) For
how long??   *too general—add details here*
a while, she had a rough time, but she hasn't touched a cigarette. (11) Now she
better conclusion needed
says that the urge to smoke has faded away. (12) She doesn't let difficulties

defet her.   *(Guide the reader better from point to point! Choppy—)*

Final Draft

(1) Beverly inspires admiration because she is so determined. (2) Although she could not afford to attend college right after high school, she worked as a cashier to save money for tuition. (3) It took her five years working days and going to school nights, but she recently received a B.S. in accounting. (4) Thanks to this same determination, Beverly is now a good driver. (5) At first, she was very nervous about getting behind the wheel and even failed the road test twice, but she didn't give up. (6) The third time, she passed, and she has never gotten a ticket. (7) A year ago, Beverly quit smoking. (8) For a month or more, she chewed her nails and endless packs of gum, but she hasn't touched a cigarette. (9) Now she says that the urge to smoke has faded away. (10) When Beverly sets a goal for herself, she doesn't let difficulties defeat her.

- This paragraph provides good support for the topic sentence. The writer has made sentences (2) and (3) more specific by adding *as a cashier; for tuition; five years working days and going to school nights;* and *recently received a B.S. in accounting.*

- What other revisions did the writer make? How do these revisions improve the paragraph? _____

_____

_____

_____

_____

- *Transitional expressions* are words and phrases that guide the reader smoothly from point to point. In sentence (5) of the final draft, *at first* is a transitional expression showing time. What other transitional expressions of time are used? _____

_____

- What phrase provides a transition from sentence (3) to (4)?

_____

- Note that the last sentence now provides a brief *conclusion* so that the paragraph *feels* finished.

Proofreading

Finally, carefully *proofread* your paper for grammatical and spelling errors, consulting your dictionary and this book as necessary. Errors in your writing will lower your grades in almost all college courses. Writing errors may also affect your job opportunities. Units 2 through 8 of this textbook will help you improve your grammar, punctuation, and spelling skills.

Some students find it useful to point to each word and say it softly. This also helps them catch errors, as well as any words they may have left out as they wrote, especially little words like *and, at, of,* and *on*.

In which of these sentences have words been omitted?

> (1) Despite its faulty landing gear, the 747 managed land safely.
> (2) Plans for the new gym were on display the library.
> (3) Mr. Sampson winked at his reflection in the bathroom mirror.

- Words are missing in sentences (1) and (2).
- Sentence (1) requires *to* before *land*.
- What word is omitted in sentence (2)? _____
- Where should this word be placed? _____

Practice 13

Proofread these sentences for omitted words. Add the necessary words above the lines. Some sentences may already be correct.

EXAMPLE: People were not always able~~to~~ tell time accurately.

1. People used to guess the time day by watching the sun move across the sky.

2. Sunrise and sunset were easy recognize.

3. Recognizing noon easy, too.

4. However, telling time by the position of sun was very difficult at other times.

5. People noticed that shadows lengthened during the day.

6. They found it easier to tell time by looking at the shadows than by looking the sun.

7. People stuck poles into the ground to time by the length of the shadows.

8. Those the first shadow clocks, or sundials.

9. In 300 B.C., Chaldean astronomer invented a more accurate, bowl-shaped sundial.

10. Today, most sundials decorative, but they can still be used to tell time.

Practice 14

Proofread the final draft of your paragraph, checking for grammar or spelling errors and omitted words.

PART H   *Looking at a Paragraph from Start to Finish*

As you may already know, writing is not an orderly process that goes neatly from step to step. When we write, we often return to prewriting strategies, like freewriting or brainstorming or clustering, to get more ideas. We may rewrite a topic sentence several times to focus our thinking and to make our main point clearer. We may rewrite drafts to organize and present our material as effectively as possible. As we write, we may come to new conclusions or make important decisions.

Here is the writing progress of one student, Melanie Wells. She began by doing a focused freewriting about her year-old kittens to come up with a specific topic to explore further. Her writing process ended in discovery.

Here is her focused freewriting:

> Cat fell into the toilet last night. Try for a sip, try for a drink, closer, closer, splash, in! How embarrassing. Gives new meaning to the words "toilet water." These kittens are so funny, they're big, almost a year old now, not really kittens any more. MUST give them names. Maybe call one Pushpin because he's obsessed by pushpins. Came home one night—cards, clippings, notices all over the floor. He had pulled off every pushpin on the bulletin board. Other one jumps for light switches, never reaches them, just kind of falls back down—but so funny to watch. These kittens remind me so much of Patches and Shadow. Dead for years now—took me so long to decide to get new ones—still miss the older ones sometimes. The two new ones are so different from each other—but so much like the older ones. Wonder why I can't name them—nothing seems to fit.

Melanie Wells considered several of the ideas that appeared in her freewriting. She thought about writing a humorous piece about her kittens but she wasn't sure what point she wanted to make. She considered writing about her former cats, Shadow and Patches, but she decided that she would rather look forward than backward. Eventually, she decided to write about her difficulty in naming her kittens. She would be exploring new territory because she didn't understand why she was having such a hard time with their names.

Her first try at a topic sentence was "Naming my new kittens is a real problem for me." Here is the first draft of her paragraph:

> Naming my new kittens is a real problem for me. The animal shelter where I got them from had called them Froggy and Frumpy. Can you imagine those names for such adorable kittens? Who would ever name them that? Everyone tried to help me. My roommate suggested that I call them Reader and Writer. My best friend suggested Zippity and Doodah. My youngest sister suggested Cuddles and Bubbles. My brother suggested Joe and Max. Somehow none of the names seem right. Nothing I call them seems to fit them. What would you do in my situation?

When Wells read her first draft, she felt dissatisfied. She had described the problem, but she hadn't come to any conclusions. She hadn't learned anything.

She looked back at her freewriting, and this time she decided to pay attention to the ways in which the new kittens were similar to her old cats, Patches and Shadow. She decided to do some brainstorming. Here are her brainstormed lists:

How Kitten 1 Is Like Patches	**How Kitten 2 Is Like Shadow**
Looks like Patches	Looks like Shadow
Face	Face
Body	Body
Love them both	Love them both
Miss the first Patches	Miss the first Shadow
Acts like Patches	Acts like Shadow
Does similar things	Does similar things
Has the personality of Patches	Has the personality of Shadow

Her second try at a topic sentence was "My new kittens have amazing resemblances to the cats I used to have." She soon realized, however, that some points on her list were irrelevant (loving all the cats; missing Patches and Shadow). She also realized that most of the points on her list were not specific enough. Here is the second draft of her paragraph:

> My new kittens have amazing resemblances to the cats I used to have. The new kittens don't resemble each other at all. My older cats, Patches and Shadow, also didn't resemble each other at all. But each new kitten really is very much like one of the older cats. One of them looks just like Patches. He also acts like Patches and has the same temperament. The other one looks very much like Shadow, though not as much as the other one looks like Patches. The temperaments of the new and old cats are the same too. They are both nervous and intense. They are both laid back and cuddly. The resemblances are really astonishing.

When Wells read her second draft, she felt even more dissatisfied than before. Her descriptions were vague and general instead of clear and specific. She had repeated herself several times. She also realized that a reader was bound to get confused about which cat or cats she was describing.

Wells did not give up. She decided to try another prewriting strategy, clustering. She produced two separate clusters, one that compared Kitten 1 with Patches and another that compared Kitten 2 with Shadow. Here are her clusters::

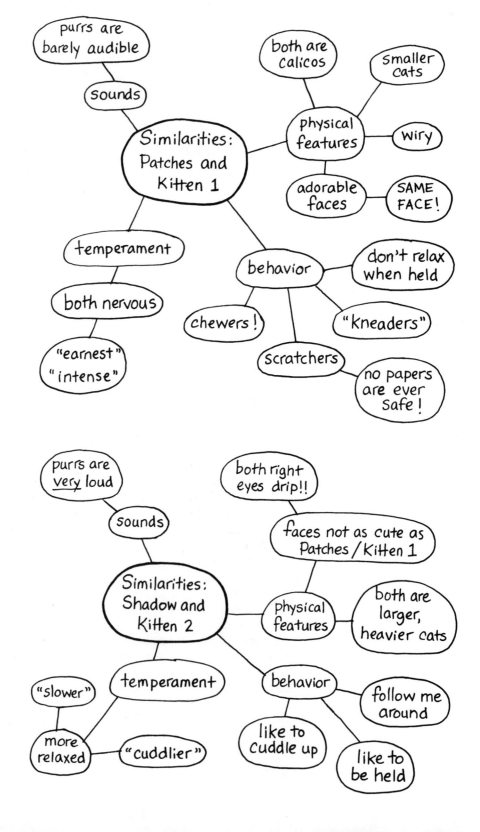

Wells was pleased with the number of specific details that her clustering had produced. Looking over her freewriting, her brainstormed lists, her two clusters, and her first two drafts, she suddenly was reminded of her trip to the animal clinic the day before. With that memory, she discovered a new direction for her paragraph—and the answer to the problem of naming her cats. The third version of her topic sentence was as follows: "Although I have been unable to name my new kittens for almost a year now, their names have been under my nose the whole time."

Here is the third draft of her paragraph.

> Although I have been unable to name my new kittens for almost a year now, their names have been under my nose the whole time. The animal shelter called them Froggy and Frumpy. I knew I had to rename them, but nothing seemed to fit. My roommate suggested that I call them Reader and Writer. My best friend suggested Zippity and Doodah. My sister suggested Cuddles and Bubbles. My brother suggested Joe and Max. Somehow none of the names seemed right, and the kittens have been unnamed for almost a year. Throughout the year, though, the kittens have reminded me of old cats, Patches and Shadow. Kitten 1 looks like Patches: he is small, wiry calico with the same adorable face. Like Patches, he is intense, nervous, and fearful. Like Patches, he never relaxes when I hold him. Kitten 2 looks like Shadow: he is bigger, heavier, and gray-brown. Like Shadow, he has a drippy right eye. Like Shadow, he follows me everywhere; he purrs like a Mack truck. Yesterday, when I took the kittens to the animal clinic for shots, I was asked there names. Immediately I replied, "Patches and Shadow." Of course, of course. My kittens names are Patches and Shadow.

Although Wells could see that her paragraph had some problems, she felt that she was finally on the right track. This time she was satisfied with her ideas; she needed only to improve her writing.

First, she looked at her topic sentence. She realized that "their names have been under my nose" included an overused expression ("under my nose"). She also decided that the picture "names under my nose" didn't make sense. So she decided, once again, to rewrite her topic sentence. Her fourth and final topic sentence became "Yesterday's visit to the Barnstable Animal Clinic solved a problem that has been bothering me for a year." (Wells later noticed that this topic sentence was similar to the topic sentence in her first draft, "Naming my new kittens is a real problem for me." However, the writing process, which had helped her to explore and make discoveries, had given her a solution to the problem.)

She then decided to combine all the sentences about the names that other people had suggested. Those sentences were taking up too much of the paragraph. She liked the comparisons she had written about the cats, so she kept those sentences very much as they were. She decided, however, to drop "he purrs like a Mack truck." Like "names under my nose," the description used a trite expression and was not accurate anyway. When she read the last sentence, the paragraph didn't feel finished to her. She decided to add one more sentence to make it feel more complete.

Here is Melanie Wells' final draft. She knew that she would have to proofread it for omitted words, spelling errors, and other mistakes, but she was satisfied with both her ideas and the way she had expressed them.

Yesterday's visit to the Barnstable Animal Clinic solved a problem that has been bothering me for a year. My adorable kittens, somehow named froggy and frumpy by a busy animal shelter, needed new names. Well-meaning friends and relatives had offered many suggestions—Reader and Writer, Zippity and Doodah, Cuddles and Bubbles, Joe and Max—but none seemed to fit. Throughout the year, though, the kittens have reminded me of old cats, Patches and Shadow. Kitten 1 looks like Patches: he is small, wiry calico with the same adorable face. Like Patches, he is intense, nervous, and fearful. Like Patches, he never relaxes when I hold him. Kitten 2 looks like Shadow: he is bigger, heavier, and gray-brown. Like Shadow, he has a drippy right eye. Like Shadow, he follows me everywhere. Yesterday, when I took the kittens to the animal clinic for shots, I was asked there names. Immediately I replied, "Patches and Shadow." Of course. How could I not have not known. My kittens names are Patches and Shadow. They were never meant to be called anything else.

When Wells proofread her paragraph, she found only a few errors. Here is her corrected version.

Yesterday's visit to the Barnstable Animal Clinic solved a problem that has been bothering me for a year. My adorable kittens, somehow named froggy and frumpy by a busy animal shelter, needed new names. Well-meaning friends and relatives had offered many suggestions—Reader and Writer, Zippity and Doodah, Cuddles and Bubbles, Joe and Max—but none seemed to fit. Throughout the year, though, the kittens have reminded me of old cats, Patches and Shadow. Kitten 1 looks like Patches: he is small, wiry calico with the same adorable face. Like Patches, he is intense, nervous, and fearful. Like Patches, he never relaxes when I hold him. Kitten 2 looks like Shadow: he is bigger, heavier, and gray-brown. Like Shadow, he has a drippy right eye. Like Shadow, he follows me everywhere. Yesterday, when I took the kittens to the animal clinic for shots, I was asked there names. Immediately I replied, "Patches and Shadow." Of course. How could I not have not known. My kittens names are Patches and Shadow. They were never meant to be called anything else.

Working on a computer, Wells was able to make her corrections in only a few minutes. Then she used a spell checker to check her spelling. Proofreading her paragraph for the last time, she felt satisfied.

Practice 15   Writing and Revising Paragraphs

The assignments that follow will give you practice in writing and revising basic paragraphs. In each assignment, aim for (1) a clear topic sentence and (2) sentences that fully support and explain the topic sentence. As you write, refer to the checklist in the Chapter Highlights on page 39.

Paragraph 1: Describe a public place. Reread paragraph B on page 28. Then choose a place in your neighborhood that is "alive with activity"—a park, street, restaurant, or club. In your topic sentence, name the place and say when it is most active; for example, "Every Saturday night, the Planet Hollywood Café is alive with activity." Begin by freewriting or by jotting down as many details about the scene as possible. Then describe the scene. Arrange your observations in a logical order. Revise for support, making sure that your details are so lively and interesting that your readers will see the place as clearly as you do.

Paragraph 2: Choose your time of day. Many people have a favorite time of day—the freshness of early morning, 5 p.m. when work ends, late at night when the children are asleep. In your topic sentence, name your favorite time of day. Then develop the paragraph by explaining why you look forward to this time and exactly how you spend it. Remember to conclude the paragraph; don't just stop.

Paragraph 3: Describe a person. Choose someone you strongly admire (or do not admire). In your topic sentence, focus on just *one* of the person's qualities. For example, "I admire Jamal's courage (athletic ability, unusual sense of humor, and so on)." Then discuss two or three incidents or actions that clearly show this quality. Freewrite, brainstorm, or cluster for details and examples. Revise for unity; make sure that every sentence supports your topic sentence. Check your final draft for omitted words.

Paragraph 4: Create a holiday. Holidays honor important people, events, or ideas. If you could create a new holiday for your town or state, or for the country, what would that holiday be? In your topic sentence, name the holiday and tell exactly whom or what it honors. Then explain why this holiday is important, and discuss how it should be celebrated. Take a humorous approach if you wish. For instance, you might invent a national holiday in honor of the first time you got an A in English composition. As you revise, make sure you have arranged your ideas in a logical order. Proofread carefully.

✔ Chapter Highlights

Checklist for Writing an Effective Paragraph

1. Narrow the topic: Cut the topic down to one aspect that interests you and will probably interest your readers.

2. Write the topic sentence. (You may wish to brainstorm or freewrite first.)

3. Brainstorm, freewrite, or cluster ideas for the body: Write down anything and everything that might relate to your topic.

4. Select and drop ideas: Select those ideas that relate to your topic and drop those that do not.

5. Group together ideas that have something in common; then arrange the ideas in a plan.

6. Write your first draft.

7. Read what you have written, making any necessary corrections and additions. Revise for support and unity.

8. Write the final draft of your paragraph neatly and legibly, making sure to indent the first word.

9. Proofread for grammar, punctuation, spelling, and omitted words. Make neat corrections in ink.

Internet Strategies

The Topic Sentence

By now you have narrowed your Internet search subject, explored three sites with information about that subject, and done some prewriting. Perhaps you have enough material for a paragraph or for an even longer paper. As you know, most paragraphs contain a topic sentence to which all the sentences relate. The topic sentence states the main idea of the paragraph.

Exploring Topic Sentences

1. Read over your prewriting and website information from the end of the last chapter. Do you have enough material and ideas to write a good paragraph? On the lines below, write a topic sentence for your paragraph.

   Topic sentence: _____

   _____

   _____

2. Now read over your topic sentence as if someone else had written it. Is the topic limited enough? Is it a complete sentence? If not, write a better topic sentence here:

   Revised topic sentence: _____

   _____

   _____

Generating Ideas for the Body

Take time to look at the different pages that each bookmarked site presents. Websites usually have pages that go into more detail, either on the main topic of the site or on different aspects of the topic. Visit the different pages of each site. Doing this may help you narrow your topic further, if necessary, or give you new insights into your topic.

Developing Your Paragraph

Now think about your topic sentence, prewriting, and website information. Revisit your bookmarked sites. Then brainstorm, freewrite, or cluster on specific details that will help you further develop an interesting paragraph. As you can see, following these steps can provide enough good material for even a multiparagraph paper.

Links

Sites often present links to other relevant sites. For instance, a site that focuses on writer Toni Morrison may contain a biography and a bibliography of Morrison's work. This site may have links to other sites. You may, for example, be able to visit Morrison's home by looking at pictures on the Web or go to sites that have the texts of Morrison's works.

Exploring Links

1. Look at your bookmarked sites. Are links to other sites presented? If so, visit a few, and see if they will help you further develop your paper or give you ideas that you might want to write more about in the future. You can bookmark any sites that you find helpful.

2. Write the addresses of the links that you found helpful, and write a sentence about how they might help you develop your writing.

_____

_____

_____

_____

_____

_____

_____

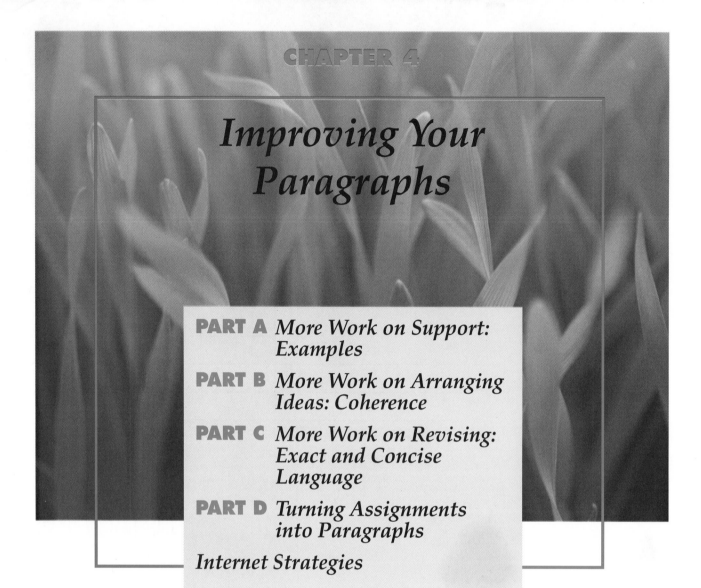

In Chapter 3, you practiced the steps of the paragraph-writing process. This chapter builds on that work. It explains several skills that can greatly improve your writing: using examples; achieving coherence; choosing exact, concise language; and turning assignments into paragraphs.

PART A　　　　*More Work on Support: Examples*

One effective way to make your writing specific is by using *examples*. Someone might write, "Divers in Monterey Bay can observe many beautiful fish. For instance, tiger-striped treefish are common." The first sentence makes a general statement about the beautiful fish in Monterey Bay. The second sentence gives a specific example of such fish: *tiger-striped treefish*.

Use one, two, or three well-chosen examples to develop a paragraph.

> Many of the computer industry's best innovators were young when they first achieved success. For example, David Filo and Jerry Yang were graduate students at Stanford when they realized that their hobby of listing the best pages on the World Wide Web might become a business. They created Yahoo!, a Web index now used by more than 500,000 people every day. Another youthful example is Marc Andreesen, who helped start the software company Netscape and designed one of the most popular computer programs ever, the Navigator. At age twenty-four, Andreesen suddenly had $58 million in the bank. A third young computer genius is Masayoshi Son. As a Berkeley undergraduate, he started importing the Space Invaders video game from his native Japan and made a small fortune. After graduation, at twenty-four, Son returned to Japan, started the Softbank company, and built a worldwide computer empire.

● The writer begins this paragraph with a topic sentence about the youth of many computer innovators.

● What three examples does the writer provide as support?

Example 1: _____

Example 2: _____

Example 3: _____

● Note that the topic sentence and the examples make a rough plan for the paragraph.

The simplest way to tell a reader that an example will follow is to say so, using a transitional expression: *For example, David Filo . . .*

Transitional Expressions to Introduce Examples

for example	for instance
to illustrate	another example

Practice 1

Each example in a paragraph must clearly relate to and explain the topic sentence. Each of the following topic sentences is followed by several examples. Circle the letter of any example that does not clearly illustrate the topic sentence. Be prepared to explain your choices.

EXAMPLE: Some animals and insects camouflage themselves in interesting ways.

a. Snowshoe rabbits turn from brown to white in winter, thus blending into the snow.

b. The cheetah's spotted coat makes it hard to see in the dry African bush.

c. The bull alligator smashes its tail against the water and roars during mating season.

d. The walking stick is brown and irregular, much like the twigs among which this insect hides.

1. Mrs. Makarem is well loved in this community for her generous heart.
   a. Her door is always open to neighborhood children, who stop by for lemonade or advice.
   b. When the Padilla family had a fire, Mrs. Makarem collected clothes and blankets for them.
   c. "Hello, dear," she says with a smile to everyone she passes on the street.
   d. Born in Caracas, Venezuela, she has lived on Bay Road for thirty-two years.

2. A number of unusual, specialized scholarships are offered by colleges across the United States.
   a. North Carolina State University offers up to $7,000 to undergraduates with the last name Gatlin or Gatling.
   b. The University of Vienna in Austria has funds for "noncommunist creative writers ages 22 to 35."
   c. Left-handed, financially needy students can get special scholarships at Juniata College in Pennsylvania.
   d. Wisconsin's Ripon College offers $1,500 to students with a 3.0 average who once were Badger Girls or Badger Boys.

3. English borrows words from many other languages.
   a. The Spanish *la reata* gives us *lariat*, "a rope."
   b. The expression *gung ho* comes from the Chinese *keng ho*, which literally means "more fire."
   c. *Diss* is a term meaning "disrespect."
   d. *Kimono* is the Japanese word for "thing for wearing."

4. On March 16, 2000, the U.S. stock market had a record-breaking day.
   a. The Dow Jones industrial average is based on the stock prices of thirty solid companies (Wal-Mart, American Express, Microsoft, and so on).
   b. Reflecting price trends for stocks and bonds, the Dow Jones had its largest one-day point gain, up nearly 500 points.
   c. Huge numbers of investors who had been pouring money into high-tech stocks suddenly returned to buying stocks of solid, quality companies.
   d. Closing the day at 10,630.60 points, the Dow went 118.66 points beyond its past record for gaining points, set on September 8, 1998.

5. In recent years, scientists have learned that human genes play a role in causing many diseases.
   a. Once thought to be an illness of the past, T.B.—tuberculosis—is common again.
   b. New research shows that women with a certain pair of genes have an increased chance of getting breast cancer.
   c. The discovery that cystic fibrosis has a genetic cause is suggesting new treatments.
   d. Sickle cell anemia has long been known to have a genetic cause.

Practice 2

The secret of good illustration lies in well-chosen and well-written examples. Think of one example that illustrates each of the following general statements. Write out the example in sentence form—one to three sentences—as clearly and exactly as possible.

1. Many films today have amazing special effects.

   Example: _____

   _____

2. Television programs have reached new lows in the past few years.

   Example: _____

   _____

3. Dan is always buying strange gadgets.

   Example: _____

   _____

4. Even when she is very busy, Grace finds ways to exercise.

   Example: _____

   _____

5. Children often say surprising things.

   Example: _____

   _____

Practice 3   Writing Assignment

Write a paragraph developed by examples. Make sure your topic sentence can be supported by examples. Prewrite and pick the best one to three examples to explain your topic sentence. Here are some ideas:

disastrous wedding stories   ads that appeal to _____

great places to study on campus   offensive talk-show topics

PART B — *More Work on Arranging Ideas: Coherence*

Every paragraph should have *coherence*. A paragraph *coheres*—holds together—when its ideas are arranged in a clear and logical order.

Sometimes the order of ideas will flow logically from your topic. However, three basic ways to organize ideas are *time order*, *space order*, and *order of importance*.

Time Order

Time order means arranging ideas chronologically, from present to past or from past to present. Careful use of time order helps to avoid such confusing writing as *Oops, I forgot to mention before that . . .*

Most instructions, histories, processes, and stories follow the logical order of time.

Susan Krabacher is an example of a person who completely redirected her life. After suffering an unhappy childhood, she became a model for *Playboy* magazine. She modeled for sixteen years, but by her early thirties, she felt depressed and unfocused. Then an unexpected trip to Haiti gave her a new direction. Krabacher expected to see poverty (especially compared with her own life of luxury), but she was totally unprepared for the state-run hospital in Haiti's capital city. Overwhelmed by the sight of starving, abandoned, and dying children, she was soon raising money, building medical facilities and housing, and occasionally living in Haiti under extreme conditions. Krabacher has since established the Foundation for Worldwide Mercy and Sharing, which funds orphanages, clinics, schools, and hospital wards. Her dream, she says, is for the children to grow up to take over her job in their country.

- The paragraph moves in time from Susan Krabacher's childhood to her new life's work of providing for starving, abandoned, and dying children in Haiti.

- Note how some transitional expressions—*after, for sixteen years, by her early thirties, then, soon, since*—show time and connect the events in the paragraph.

Transitional Expressions to Show Time

first, second, third

then, next, finally

before, during, after

soon, the following month, the next year

Practice 4

Arrange each set of sentences in time order, numbering them 1, 2, 3, and so on. Be prepared to explain your choices.

1. In eighty years, the T-shirt rose from simple underwear to fashion statement.

    _____ During World War II, women factory workers started wearing T-shirts on the job.

    _____ Hippies in the 1960s tie-dyed their T-shirts and wore them printed with messages.

    _____ Now, five billion T-shirts are sold worldwide each year.

    _____ The first American T-shirts were cotton underwear, worn home by soldiers returning from France after World War I.

2. Scientists who study the body's daily rhythms can suggest the ideal time of day for different activities.

    _____ Taking vitamins with breakfast will help the body absorb them.

    _____ Allergy medication should be taken just before bedtime to combat early-morning hay fever—usually the worst of the day.

    _____ The best time to work out is 3 p.m. to 5 p.m., when strength, flexibility, and body temperature are greatest.

    _____ Ideal naptime is 1 p.m. to 3 p.m., when body temperature falls, making sleep easier.

3. The short life of Sadako Sasaki has inspired millions to value peace.

_____ Sadako was just two years old in 1945 when the atom bomb destroyed her city, Hiroshima.

_____ From her sickbed, Sadako set out to make 1,000 paper cranes, birds that, in Japan, symbolize long life and hope.

_____ Although she died before making 1,000, classmates finished her project and published a book of her letters.

_____ At age eleven, already a talented runner, she was crushed to learn that she had leukemia, caused by radiation from the bomb.

_____ Now, every year, the Folded Crane Club places 1,000 cranes at the foot of a statue of Sadako, honoring her wish that all children might enjoy peace and a long life.

Practice 5   Writing Assignment

Have you ever been through something that lasted only a few moments but was unforgettable—for example, a sports victory, an accident, or a kiss? Write a paragraph telling about such an event. As you prewrite, pick the highlights of the experience and arrange them in time order. As you write, try to capture the drama of what happened. Use transitional expressions of time to make the story flow smoothly.

Space Order

Space order means describing a person, a place, or a thing from top to bottom, from left to right, from foreground to background, and so on.

Space order is most often used in descriptions because it moves from detail to detail, like a camera's eye.

> When the city presses in on me, I return in my mind to my hometown in St. Mary, Jamaica. I am alone, high in the mango tree on our property on the hilltop. The wind is blowing hard as usual, making a scared noise as it passes through the lush vegetation. I look down at the coconut growth with its green flooring of banana plants. Beyond that is a wide valley and then the round hills. Farther out lies the sea, and I count the ships as they pass to and from the harbor while I relax on my special branch and eat mangoes.
>
> Daniel Dawes, student

● The writer describes this scene from his vantage point high in a tree. His description follows space order, moving from the plants below him, farther out to the valley and the hills, and then even farther, to the sea.

● Notice how *transitional expressions* indicating space—*beyond that, then,* and *farther out*—help the reader to follow and "see" the details.

Transitional Expressions to Show Space Order

to the left, in the center, to the right

behind, beside, in front of

next, beyond that, farther out

Practice 6

Arrange each set of details according to space order, numbering them 1, 2, 3, and so on. Be prepared to explain your choices.

1. After the party, the living room was a complete mess.

   _____ greasy pizza boxes on the coffee table

   _____ empty soda cans on the floor

   _____ deflated balloons on the ceiling light

   _____ pictures hanging at odd angles on the wall

2. We took in the sights of Rue Sherbrook West in Montreal.

   _____ grand towers of the Ritz Carlton hotel

   _____ lunch-hour crowds on the sidewalks

   _____ pigeons sitting on top of the streetlights

   _____ an airplane passing in the blue sky

3. The taxicab crawled through rush-hour traffic in the rain-drenched city.

   _____ fare meter on dashboard ticking relentlessly

   _____ headlights barely piercing the stormy gray dusk

   _____ windshield wipers losing their battle with the latest cloudburst

   _____ back-seat passengers frantically checking their watches

   _____ driver wishing hopelessly that he could be home watching Rosie O'Donnell

Practice 7   Writing Assignment

Select an object that interests you. It can be something natural—like a plant or a wasp's nest, or something made by human hands—like a police shield or a cellular phone. Study the object closely; then describe it in a detailed paragraph. Arrange the details in space order, from top to bottom, left to right, and so forth. As you revise, make sure your sentences flow clearly and smoothly.

Order of Importance

Order of importance means starting your paragraph with the most important idea.

> State legislators should provide more money to community colleges. Most important, more teachers are needed. Faculty size has not kept pace with the great increase in community college students. Therefore, classes keep getting larger, and students get less personal attention. In addition, colleges need better learning facilities. Many community colleges occupy old buildings. Classrooms are often small and in poor condition. These schools often lack the well-equipped science labs and computer centers needed to prepare students in the twenty-first century. Finally, community colleges also need more parking lots. Currently, students spend so much time looking for parking spaces that they are frequently late to class.

- The three reasons in this paragraph are discussed from the most important reason to the least important.

- Note that the words *most important, in addition,* and *also* help the reader move from one reason to another.

Sometimes you may wish to begin with the least important idea and build toward a climax at the end of the paragraph. Paragraphs arranged from the least important idea to the most important idea can have dramatic power.

> Although my fourteen-year-old daughter learned a great deal from living with a Pennsylvania Amish family last summer, adjusting to their strict lifestyle was difficult for her. Kay admitted that the fresh food served on the farm was great, but she missed her diet colas. More difficult was the fact that she had to wear long dresses—no more jeans and baby tees. Still worse in her view were the hours. A suburban girl and self-confessed night person, my daughter had to get up at 5 a.m. to milk cows! By far the most difficult adjustment concerned boys. If an Amish woman is not married, she cannot spend time with males, and this rule now applied to Kay. Yes, she suffered and complained, but by summer's end, she was a different girl—more open-minded and proud of the fact that all these deprivations put her more in touch with herself.
>
> Lucy Auletta, student

- The adjustment difficulties this writer's daughter had are arranged from least

  to most important. How many difficulties are discussed? _____

- Note how the words *more difficult, still worse,* and *by far the most difficult adjustment* help the reader move from one idea to the next.

Transitional Expressions to Show Importance

first, next, finally

more, most

less, least

Practice 8

Arrange the ideas that develop each topic sentence in order of importance, numbering them 1, 2, and 3. Begin with the most important idea, or reverse the order if you think that a paragraph would be more effective if it began with the least important idea. Be prepared to explain your choices. Then, on a separate sheet of paper, write the ideas in a paragraph.

1. For three reasons, joining a serious study group is an excellent idea.

    _____ A study group will expose you to new points of view and effective study habits.

    _____ Joining a study group is a good way to make new friends.

    _____ Statistics show that students who regularly attend a study group get better grades and are less likely to drop out of college.

2. Steven Spielberg's *E.T.* is one of the world's most successful movies.

   _____ It will be re-released on its twentieth anniversary.

   _____ The re-release will delight audiences with new computer-generated enhancements and never-before-seen footage.

   _____ The 1982 heartwarmer has already grossed more than $700 million in ticket sales.

3. At 2 a.m., arriving on the scene of a rollover with injuries, the fire rescue team had to act quickly.

   _____ One team member lit flares and placed them on the road to warn other drivers to slow down.

   _____ On the ambulance radio, a team member called for "sanders" to drop sand on local roads, which were becoming slippery in the falling snow.

   _____ A lone woman, conscious with head injuries, was carefully moved from the driver's seat into the ambulance.

   _____ Someone held the woman's dog, who was shivering but seemed unhurt.

Practice 9   Writing Assignment

Your college is offering free classes in photography, money management, or fitness for senior citizens in the area. Choose just one of these classes, and write a paragraph encouraging local seniors to sign up. Discuss the three most important reasons why this class would benefit them, and arrange these reasons in order of importance—least to most important or most to least important, whichever you think would make a better paragraph. Don't forget to use transitional expressions. If you wish, use humor to win over your audience.

PART C   *More Work on Revising: Exact and Concise Language*

Good writers do not settle for the first words that spill onto their paper or computer screen. Instead, they *revise* what they have written, replacing vague words with exact language and repetitious words with concise language.

Exact Language

As a rule, the more specific, detailed, and exact the language is, the better the writing. Which sentence in each of the following pairs contains the more vivid and exact language?

> (1) The office was noisy.
>
> (2) In the office, phones jangled, faxes whined, and copy machines hummed.
>
> (3) What my tutor said made me feel good.
>
> (4) When my tutor whispered, "Fine job," I felt like singing.

● Sentence (2) is more exact than sentence (1) because *phones jangled, faxes whined, and copy machines hummed* provides more vivid information than the general word *noisy.*

● What exact words does sentence (4) use to replace the general words *said* and

    made me feel good? _____

    You do not need a large vocabulary to write exactly and well, but you do need to work at finding the right words to fit each sentence.

Practice 10

These sentences contain vague language. Revise each one, using vivid and exact language wherever possible.

EXAMPLE: A man went through the crowd.

        Revise: A man in a blue leather jacket pushed through the crowd.

1. An automobile went down the street.

    Revise: _____

    _____

2. This apartment has problems.

    Revise: _____

    _____

3. When Allison comes home, her pet greets her.

    Revise: _____

    _____

4. This magazine is interesting.

    Revise: _____

    _____

5. The expression on his face made me feel comfortable.

    Revise: _____

    _____

6. My job is fun.

    Revise: _____

    _____

7. There was a big storm here last week.

    Revise: _____

    _____

8. Hobbies can be nice.

Revise:_____

_____

9. The emergency room has a lot of people in it.

Revise:_____

_____

10. Your paper is okay.

Revise:_____

_____

Concise Language

Concise writing never uses five or six words when two or three will do. It avoids repetitious and unnecessary words that add nothing to the meaning of a sentence. As you revise your writing, cross out unnecessary words and phrases.

Which sentence in each of the following pairs is more concise?

> (1) Because of the fact that Larissa owns an antiques shop, she is always poking around in dusty attics.
>
> (2) Because Larissa owns an antiques shop, she is always poking around in dusty attics.
>
> (3) Mr. Tibbs entered a large, dark blue room at the end of the hallway.
>
> (4) Mr. Tibbs entered a room that was large in size and dark blue in color at the end of the hallway.

- Sentences (2) and (3) are concise; sentences (1) and (4) are wordy.

- In sentence (1), *because of the fact that* is a wordy way of saying *because*.

- In sentence (4), *in size* and *in color* just repeat which ideas?

_____

Of course, conciseness does not mean writing short, choppy sentences. It does mean dropping unnecessary words and phrases.

Practice 11

The following sentences are wordy. In a group with two or three others, make each sentence more concise by deleting unnecessary words. Write your revised sentences on the lines provided.

EXAMPLE: Venice, an Italian city in Italy, is trying to reduce the huge number of visitors who go to see it.

Revise: _Venice, a city in Italy, is trying to reduce its huge number of visitors._

1. For a great many hundreds of years, this beautiful city of great loveliness has been a major tourist attraction.

   Revise: _____

   _____

2. The reasons why people go to Venice are because they want to see its priceless art and architecture, its famous bridges, and the canals that serve as streets.

   Revise: _____

   _____

3. At this time now, however, Venice is being destroyed by floods, polluted air and water that foul the atmosphere, and tourists who visit it.

   Revise: _____

   _____

4. Experts believe in their opinion that day trippers are the greatest problem of Venice's tourist problems.

   Revise: _____

   _____

5. The day trippers, who come only for a day trip, do not spend much money, thus contributing very little to the city's economy of money.

   Revise: _____

   _____

6. They contribute hugely and in large amounts, however, to the city of Venice's congestion, transportation, and sanitation nightmares.

   Revise: _____

   _____

7. Recently, the city decided to scare off day trippers by scaring them with a negative publicity campaign that gave bad publicity about the city.

   Revise: _____

   _____

8. Posters posted all over the place showed tourists being devoured and eaten by Venice's well-known and famous pigeons.

   Revise: _____

   _____

9. An immense giant toilet plunger became the symbol of a city that some say is the city that is the most romantic city in the world.

   Revise: _____

   _____

10. A very interesting fact is that, unfortunately, the campaign has not stopped tourists from pouring into Venice at the rate of more than ten million tourists a year.

Revise: _____

_____

Practice 12   Review

Following are statements from real accident reports collected by an insurance company. As you will see, these writers need help with more than their fenders!

In a group with four or five classmates, read each statement and try to understand what each writer *meant* to say. Then revise each statement so that it says, exactly and concisely, what the writer intended.

1. "The guy was all over the place. I had to swerve a number of times before I hit him."

2. "The telephone pole was approaching fast. I was attempting to swerve out of its path when it struck my front end."

3. "Coming home, I drove into the wrong house and collided with a tree I don't have."

4. "I was on my way to the doctor's with rear-end trouble when my universal joint gave way, causing me to have an accident."

5. "I was driving my car out of the driveway in the usual manner when it was struck by the other car in the same place it had been struck several times before."

Practice 13   Review

Choose a paragraph or paper you wrote recently. Read it with a fresh eye, checking for exact and concise language. Then rewrite it, eliminating all vague or wordy language.

PART D   *Turning Assignments into Paragraphs*

In Chapter 3, Part B, you learned how to narrow down a broad topic and write a specific topic sentence. Sometimes, however, your assignment may take the form of a specific question, and your job may be to answer the question in one paragraph.

For example, this question asks you to take a stand on—for or against—a particular issue.

Are professional athletes overpaid?

You can often turn this kind of question into a topic sentence:

(1) Professional athletes are overpaid.

(2) Professional athletes are not overpaid.

(3) Professional athletes are sometimes overpaid.

- These three topic sentences take different points of view.
- The words *are, are not,* and *sometimes* make each writer's opinion clear.

Sometimes you will be asked to agree or disagree with a statement:

(4) Salary is the most important factor in job satisfaction. Agree or disagree.

- This is really a question in disguise: *Is salary the most important factor in job satisfaction?*

In the topic sentence, make your opinion clear, and repeat key words.

(5) Salary is the most important factor in job satisfaction.

(6) Salary is not the most important factor in job satisfaction.

(7) Salary is only one among several important factors in job satisfaction.

- The words *is, is not,* and *is only one among several* make each writer's opinion clear.
- Note how the topic sentences repeat the key words from the statement—*salary, important factor, job satisfaction.*

Once you have written the topic sentence, follow the steps described in Chapter 2—freewriting, brainstorming, or clustering; selecting; grouping—and then write your paragraph. Be sure that all ideas in the paragraph support the opinion you have stated in the topic sentence.

Practice 14

Here are four exam questions. Write one topic sentence to answer each of them. REMEMBER: Make your opinion clear in the topic sentence, and repeat key words from the question.

1. Should computer education be required in every public high school?

   Topic sentence: _____

   _____

2. Would you advise your best friend to buy a new car or a used car?

   Topic sentence: _____

   _____

3. Is there too much bad news on television news programs?

Topic sentence: _____

_____

4. How have your interests changed in the past five years?

Topic sentence: _____

_____

Practice 15

Imagine that your instructor has just written the exam questions from Practice 14 on the board. Choose the question that most interests you, and write a paragraph answering that question. Prewrite, select, and arrange ideas before you compose your paragraph. Then read your work, making neat corrections in ink.

Practice 16

Here are four statements. Agree or disagree, and write a topic sentence for each.

1. All higher education should be free. Agree or disagree.

Topic sentence: _____

_____

2. Expecting one's spouse to be perfect is the most important reason for the high divorce rate in the United States. Agree or disagree.

Topic sentence: _____

_____

3. Parents should give children money when they need it, rather than give children an allowance. Agree or disagree.

Topic sentence: _____

_____

4. Silence is golden. Agree or disagree.

Topic sentence: _____

_____

Practice 17

Choose the statement in Practice 16 that most interests you. Then write a paragraph in which you agree or disagree.

Chapter Highlights

To improve your writing, try these techniques:

- Use well-chosen examples to develop a paragraph.

- Organize your ideas by time order.

- Organize your ideas by space order.

- Organize your ideas by order of importance, either from the most important to the least or from the least important to the most.

- Use language that is exact and concise.

- Turn assignment questions into topic sentences.

Internet Strategies

Writing from a Web Source

You can use your bookmarked sites to gather information for a paper or to support your main idea. However, always assess the sites you have chosen to make sure that they provide valid, factual information. For example, a site on the subject of homelessness produced by a homeless advocacy group may present accurate statistics on aspects of homelessness, but the site may not give you the entire picture. Look for sites that present a balanced view of the subject. If you have one site that is sponsored by a homeless advocacy group, look for a site sponsored by a person or group that discusses the problems the homeless bring to society in general.

Notice the three-letter extension on the end of every Internet address. The extensions read as follows:

.com for company
.edu for educational institution
.gov for governmental agency
.org for nonprofit organization

The extension on each website will help you assess the information contained in that site. For example, information found on university sites (*.edu*) is often more reliable than information found on company sites (*.com*) because company sites are often promoting products that they sell.

Evaluating Websites

Ask yourself the following questions about each of your chosen sites and write your answers below.

1. Who is the author or owner of the site? What is its three-letter extension?

     a. _____

     b. _____

     c. _____

     d. _____

     e. _____

2. Do you think the person or organization that produced the site might have any bias toward the subject? Why? How might you detect bias?

a. _____

_____

b. _____

_____

c. _____

_____

d. _____

_____

e. _____

_____

3. Will the information, examples, or statistics presented on the site be weighted one way or another? Why or why not?

a. _____

b. _____

c. _____

d. _____

e. _____

Using Examples

Your sites might provide you with examples that you can use in the body of your paper. Write a topic sentence below for three different paragraphs. Look at your sites to see if you can support each topic sentence with examples. Choose the best examples, and write them after the topic sentence.

Topic sentence: _____

_____

Example(s): _____

_____

Topic sentence: _____

_____

Example(s): _____

_____

Topic sentence: _____

_____

Example(s): _____

_____

CHAPTER 5

Moving from Paragraph to Essay

PART A *Defining the Essay and the Thesis Statement*

PART B *The Process of Writing an Essay*

Internet Strategies

So far, you have written single paragraphs, but to succeed in college and at work, you will need to handle longer writing assignments as well. This chapter will help you apply your paragraph-writing skills to planning and writing short essays.

PART A — Defining the Essay and the Thesis Statement

An *essay* is a group of paragraphs about one subject. In many ways, an essay is like a paragraph in longer, fuller form. Both have an introduction, a body, and a conclusion. Both explain one main idea with details, facts, and examples.

However, an essay is not just a padded paragraph. An essay is longer because it contains more ideas.

The paragraphs in an essay are part of a larger whole, so each one has a special purpose.

● The *introductory paragraph* opens the essay and tries to catch the reader's interest. It usually contains a *thesis statement,* one sentence that states the main idea of the entire essay.

● The *body* of an essay contains one, two, three, or more paragraphs, each one making a different point about the main idea.

● The *conclusion* brings the essay to a close. It might be a sentence or a paragraph long.

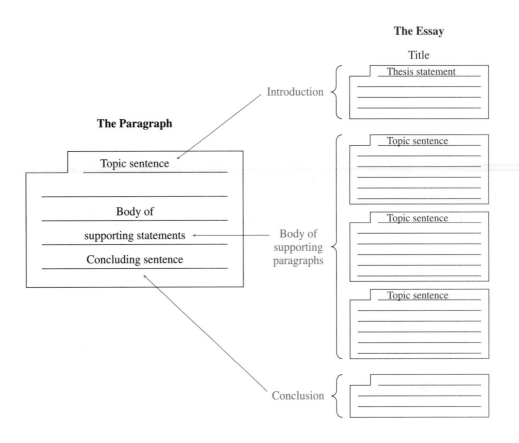

Here is a student essay:

Tae Kwon Do
Wineth Williams

(1) Tae kwon do is a Korean martial art. It is a way of fighting and self-defense based on an understanding of both body and mind. As a college student, I discovered tae kwon do. Even though I was physically fit and planned to become a police officer, I thought that women needed special skills to protect themselves. Tae kwon do teaches these skills and much more. The person who practices tae kwon do gains discipline, maturity, and a changed self-concept.

(2) First, the discipline of tae kwon do helps the student to outfight and outsmart her opponent. For a while, I didn't appreciate the discipline. We had to move in certain ways, and we had to yell. Yelling made me laugh. Our teacher told us to shout with great force, "Keeah!" Yelling keeps the mind from focusing on being tired and helps the fighter call out the life force, or "chi," from inside her. Once we started sparring, I also had to get past not wanting to hurt anyone. Later I understood that if I punched or kicked my opponent, it meant that he or she should have been blocking and was not using good skills.

(3) Second, with practice, tae kwon do increases maturity. I have a hot temper. Before tae kwon do, I would walk dark streets and take chances, almost daring trouble. I reacted to every look or challenge. Practicing this martial art, I started to see the world more realistically. I developed more respect for the true danger in the streets. I spoke and behaved in ways to avoid trouble. My reactions became less emotional and more rational.

(4) Finally, after a year or so, tae kwon do can change the student's self-concept. This happened to me. On one hand, I became confident that I had the skills to take care of business if necessary. On the other hand, the better I got, the

more I acted like a pussycat instead of a lion. That may sound strange, but inside myself, I knew that I had nothing to prove to anybody.

(5) As I discovered firsthand, the practice of tae kwon do can bring personal benefits that go far beyond self-defense.

- The last sentence in the introduction (underlined) is the *thesis statement*. The thesis statement must be general enough to include the topic sentence of every paragraph in the body of the essay.

- Underline the topic sentences of paragraphs (2), (3), and (4). Note that the thesis statement and the topic sentences make a rough plan of the entire essay.

- *Transitional expressions* are words and phrases that guide the reader from point to point and from paragraph to paragraph. What transition does this student use between paragraphs (1) and (2)? Between (2) and (3)? Between (3) and (4)?

_____

- The last paragraph provides a brief *conclusion*.*

Practice 1

To help you understand the structure of an essay, complete this plan for "Tae Kwon Do." Under each topic sentence, jot down the writer's two or three main supporting points, as if you were making a plan for the essay. (In fact, the writer probably made such a plan before she wrote her first draft.)

Paragraph 1. INTRODUCTION

        Thesis statement: The person who practices tae kwon do gains discipline, maturity, and a changed self-concept.

Paragraph 2. Topic sentence: First, the discipline of tae kwon do helps the student to outfight and outsmart her opponent.

Point 1: _____

Point 2: _____

Point 3: _____

Paragraph 3. Topic sentence: Second, with practice, tae kwon do increases maturity.

Point 1: _____

Point 2: _____

Paragraph 4. Topic sentence: Finally, after a year or so, tae kwon do can change the student's self-concept.

Point 1: _____

Point 2: _____

Point 3: _____

Paragraph 5. CONCLUSION

_____

*To read essays by other students, see the Writers' Workshops in Units 3, 6, 7, and 8.

Practice 2

Discuss with several classmates or write your answers to these questions.

1. Did Wineth Williams' introduction (paragraph 1) catch and hold your interest? Would this essay be just as good or better if it had no introduction but started right in with the thesis statement? Why or why not?

2. In paragraph (4), the writer says she now can "take care of business." Is this language appropriate for a college essay? Will readers know what this means?

3. Is the conclusion effective, or is it too short?

4. Williams' audience was her English class. Her purpose (though not directly stated in the essay) was to let people know some of the benefits that come from practicing tae kwon do. Did she achieve her purpose?

5. What did you like best about the essay? What, if anything, would you change?

PART B   *The Process of Writing an Essay*

Whether you are writing a paragraph or an essay, the writing process is the same. Of course, writing an essay will probably take longer. In this section, you will practice these steps of the essay-writing process:

- Narrowing the subject and writing the thesis statement
- Generating ideas for the body of the essay
- Selecting and arranging ideas in a plan
- Writing and revising your essay

Narrowing the Subject and Writing the Thesis Statement

While an essay subject should be broader than a paragraph topic, a good essay subject also must be narrow enough to write about in detail. For example, the topic *jobs* is broad enough to fill a book. But the far narrower topic *driving a bulldozer at the town dump* could make a good essay. Remember to select or narrow your subject in light of your intended audience and purpose. Who are your readers, and what do you want your essay to achieve?

Writing the *thesis statement* forces you to narrow the topic further: *Driving a bulldozer for the Department of Highways was the best job I ever had*. That could be an intriguing thesis statement, but the writer could focus it even more: *For three reasons, driving a bulldozer for the Department of Highways was the best job I ever had*. The writer might discuss one reason in each of three paragraphs.

Here are two more examples of the narrowing process:

(1) Subject:	music
Narrowed subject:	Babyface Edmunds, songwriter to the stars
Thesis statement:	Hit maker Babyface Edmunds studies a singer's personality and style before he writes a song.
(2) Subject:	pets
Narrowed subject:	Pains and pleasures of owning a parrot
Thesis statement:	Owning a parrot will enrich your life with noise, occasional chaos, and lots of laughs.

● On the basis of each thesis statement, what do you expect the essays to

discuss? _____

_____

    Although the thesis statement must include all the ideas in the body of the essay, it should also be clear and specific. Which of these thesis statements is specific enough for a good essay?

> (1) Three foolproof techniques will help you avoid disastrous first dates.
> (2) NBA basketball is the most exciting sport in the world.
> (3) Dr. Villarosa is a competent and caring physician.

● Thesis statements (1) and (3) are both specific. From (1), a reader might expect to learn about the "three foolproof techniques," each one perhaps explained in a paragraph.

● On the basis of thesis statement (3), what supporting points might the essay

discuss? _____

_____

● Thesis statement (2), however, is too broad for an essay—or even a book. It gives the reader (and writer) no direction.

Practice 3

Choose one of these topics for your own essay. Then narrow the topic, and write a clear and specific thesis statement.

> The benefits of a sport or practice
>
> The most fascinating/boring/important job I ever had
>
> Qualities of an excellent husband/wife/partner

Narrowed subject: _____

_____

Thesis statement: _____

_____

Generating Ideas for the Body of the Essay

Writers generate support for an essay just as they do for a paragraph—by prewriting to get as many interesting ideas as possible. Once you know your main point and have written a thesis statement, use your favorite prewriting method—freewriting, for example. If you feel stuck, change to brainstorming or clustering. Just keep writing.

Practice 4

Now generate as many good ideas as possible to support your thesis statement. Fill at least one or two pages with ideas. As you work, try to imagine how many paragraphs your essay will contain and what each will include.

Selecting and Arranging Ideas in a Plan

Next, underline or mark the most interesting ideas that support your thesis statement. Cross out the rest.

Make a rough plan or outline that includes an introductory paragraph, two or three paragraphs for the body of the essay, and a brief conclusion. Choose a logical order in which to present your ideas. Which idea will come first, second, third?

For example, the bulldozer operator might explain why that job was "the best" with three reasons, arranged in this order: 1. *On the job, I learned to operate heavy equipment.* 2. *Working alone at the controls gave me time to think.* 3. *One bonus was occasionally finding interesting items beside the road.* This arrangement moves logically from physical skills to mental benefits to a surprising bonus.

Practice 5

Read over your prewriting pages, selecting your best ideas and a logical order in which to present them. Make an outline or a plan that includes an introduction and a thesis statement; two or three supporting paragraphs, each with a clear topic sentence; and a brief conclusion.

Writing and Revising Your Essay

Drafting

Now write your first draft. Try to express your ideas clearly and fully. If a section seems weak or badly written, put a check in the margin and go on; you can come back to that section later, prewriting again if necessary for fresh ideas. Set aside your draft for an hour or a day.

Revising and Proofreading

Revising may be the most important step in the writing process. Reread your essay as if you were reading someone else's work, marking it up as you answer questions like these:

- Are my main idea and my thesis statement clear?
- Have I supported my thesis in a rich and convincing way?
- Does each paragraph in the body clearly explain the main idea?
- Does my essay have a logical order and good transitions?
- Are there any parts that don't belong or don't make sense?
- What one change would most improve my essay?*

You also might wish to ask a respected friend to read or listen to your essay, giving peer feedback before you revise.**

Practice 6

Now read your first draft to see how you can improve it. Trust your instincts about what is alive and interesting and what is dull. Take your time. As you revise, try to make this the best paper you have ever written.

---

* See Chapter 3, Part F, for more revising ideas.
** See Chapter 3, page 31, for a sample Peer Feedback Sheet.

Finally, write a new draft of your essay, using the format preferred by your instructor. Proofread carefully, correcting any grammar or spelling errors.

Practice 7

Exchange essays with a classmate. Write a one-paragraph evaluation of each other's work, saying as specifically as possible what you like about the essay and what might be improved. If you wish, use the Peer Feedback Sheet (page 31).

Possible Topics for Essays

1. The Best/Worst Class I Ever Had

2. Three Things That _____ Taught Me

3. Two Surefire Ways to Relax

4. The Bill I Most Hated to Pay

5. How to Solve a Community Problem

6. A Major Decision

7. Tips for the New Driver (College Student, NBA Draft Pick, Dieter, and so forth)

8. A Valuable/Worthless Television Show

9. Why _____ Is a Great Entertainer

10. A Good Friend

11. Can Anger Be Used Constructively?

12. What Success Meant in My High School (Family, Country)

13. How I Fell in Love with Books (German Shepherds, Rock Climbing, Video Games, and so forth)

14. Why Teenagers Have Babies

15. What Childhood Taught Me About Boys/Girls in Society

✔ Chapter Highlights

Checklist for Writing an Effective Essay

- Narrow the topic in light of your audience and purpose. Be sure you can discuss the topic fully in a short essay.

- Write a clear thesis statement. If you have trouble, freewrite or brainstorm first; then narrow the topic and write the thesis statement.

- Freewrite, brainstorm, or cluster to generate facts, details, and examples to support your thesis statement.

- Plan or outline your essay, choosing from two to three main ideas to support the thesis statement.

- Write a topic sentence that expresses each main idea.

- Decide on a logical order in which to present the paragraphs.

- Plan the body of each paragraph, using all you have learned about support and paragraph development.

- Write the first draft of your essay.

- Revise as necessary, checking your essay for support, unity, and coherence.

- Proofread carefully for grammar, punctuation, and spelling.

Internet Strategies

Using Online Writing Centers

If you are in need of writing and grammar assistance, online writing centers (commonly called OWLS) are one of the best things to come out of using the Internet. Many sites offer excellent help with grammar problems. Some offer twenty-four-hour-a-day help by having tutors available to answer questions. A few sites will read your paper and give you some feedback, but you will have to do some searching to find sites that provide such services.

Here is a list of sites to visit. Some provide lists of OWLS, and others are addresses for specific writing labs or centers. Visit some different sites, and decide which ones might be helpful to you. Bookmark those sites for later use.

National Writing Centers Association: Writing Centers Online
www.departments.colgate.edu/NWCAOWLS.html
> This site provides a comprehensive listing in alphabetical order of writing centers in the United States.

LEO: Literacy Education Online (St. Cloud State University)
http://leo.stcloudstate.edu
> This site provides links to writing aids, based on self-diagnosed problems.

Online Writing Lab (Purdue University)
http://owl.english.purdue.edu
> This site is one of the most famous OWLS on the Web. It provides writing help, links to other writing labs, and Internet links for various subjects.

The Elements of Style Online
http://www.bartleby.com/141
> This is an online version of the original classic reference book on effective writing by William Strunk, Jr.

Guide to Grammar and Writing
http://webster.commnet.edu/grammar/index.htm
> *or*
> http://ccc.commnet.edu/grammar/
> These sites offer coverage of basic grammar and usage rules, with examples for each point; sample letters, résumés, and memos; guidance on the writing process; quizzes; and related websites. The site also has an online form for submitting your grammar questions.

On-Line English Grammar
http://www.edunet.com/english/grammar/
> This site is an easy-to-use source for basic points of English grammar.

Choosing a Topic Sentence

Each group of sentences could be unscrambled and written as a paragraph. Circle the letter of the sentence that would be the best topic sentence.

1. a. Rooftops and towers made eye-catching shapes against the winter sky.

    b. Far below, the faint sounds of slush and traffic were soothing.

    c. From the apartment-house roof, the urban scene was oddly relaxing.

    d. Stoplights changing color up and down the avenues created a rhythmic pattern invisible from the street.

2. a. Julio Iglesias, the Spanish singer, has settled in Miami.

    b. Famous Mexican actress and singer Lucía Méndez has moved there, as has Venezuelan soap star José Luis Rodríguez.

    c. The largest Spanish-language TV networks now have headquarters in Miami.

    d. In recent years, Miami has become the Hollywood of Latin America.

Selecting Ideas

Here is a topic sentence and a brainstormed list of possible ideas for a paragraph. Check "Keep" for ideas that best support the topic sentence and "Drop" for ideas that do not.

Topic sentence: Oprah Winfrey is a force for tremendous good in the United States.

Keep   **Drop**

_____   _____   1. on her TV show, often features a psychologist who helps people improve their relationships

_____   _____   2. through her book club, inspired millions to start reading and each month introduces a vast audience to new and old authors

_____   _____   3. proves that women don't need to be thin to be beautiful, popular, famous, and greatly loved.

_____   _____   4. was born in 1954 on a farm in Mississippi

_____   _____   5. at age six was sent to Milwaukee; kept cockroaches in a jar as substitute for farm animals

_____   _____   6. is a well-known example of someone who overcame many obstacles, including childhood abuse and racial prejudice.

_____   _____   7. another example of someone who has overcome abuse and prejudice is Tina Turner

_____   _____   8. now in her sixties, Turner still has the magic—certainly defies the stereotype of "senior citizen"

_____ _____ 9. not only charitable herself — Winfrey awards money on her show to people who help others; supports everyone's generosity

_____ _____ 10. has a segment, "Remembering Your Spirit," at the end of each show to encourage viewers to think about their own spirituality

Examining a Paragraph

Read this paragraph and answer the questions.

(1) Students at some American colleges are learning a lot from trash by studying "garbology." (2) Wearing rubber gloves, they might sift through the local dump, counting and collecting treasures that they examine back at the laboratory. (3) First, they learn to look closely and to interpret what they see, thus reading the stories that trash tells. (4) More important, they learn the truth about what Americans buy, what they eat, and how they live. (5) Students at the University of Arizona, for instance, were surprised to find that low-income families in certain areas buy more educational toys for their children than nearby middle-income families. (6) Most important, students say that garbology courses can motivate them to be better citizens of planet Earth. (7) One young woman, for example, after seeing from hard evidence in her town's landfill how many people really recycled their glass, cans, and newspapers and how many cheated, organized an annual recycling awareness day.

1. Write the number of the topic sentence in the paragraph. _____

2. What kind of order does this writer use? _____

3. Students learn three things in garbology courses. (a) Write the numbers of the sentences stating these. (b) Which two ideas are supported by examples?

   (a) _____   (b) _____

UNIT 1 *Writers' Workshop*

Describe an Interesting Person

Good writers are masters of careful observation and exact language. Read this student's description of her classmate, aloud if possible. Underline any words or details that strike you as well written or powerful.

> In this paragraph, I will describe my classmate Benny. His most riveting feature is the contrast between his close-cropped black hair and his light skin. Two slight scars on his left cheek add to instead of detract from his appearance. His eyelashes are not prominent, but dark brown eyes gaze at you from under a canopy of thick black eyebrows. His nose is short and straight, befitting his oval face. The cheekbones high but not prominent, and the well-kept mustache gives a promise of luxuriant growth if given free rein. Benny's mouth small and full, and though the braces are off-putting, that shy smile will someday break a lot of hearts. All these factors put together with a mischievous gleam in his eyes draw the picture an intelligent, personable young man.
>
> *Carmen Crawford, student*

1. How effective is Carmen Crawford's description of Benny?

   _____ Good topic sentence?   _____ Rich supporting details?

   _____ Logical organization?   _____ Effective conclusion?

2. Underline the words, details, and sentences you like best. Put a check beside anything that needs improvement.

3. Now discuss your underlinings with your group or class. Try to explain why a particular word or sentence is effective. For instance, in the second sentence, the interesting word *riveting* introduces a contrast between Benny's "close-cropped black hair" (we can almost see it) and his light skin.

4. The best descriptions feel as if they were observed from real life, not memory. Do you think Carmen Crawford was *with* Benny when she wrote about him. Why?

5. Is the topic sentence as good as the rest of the paragraph? If not, how might you change it?

6. Last, proofread for grammar, spelling, and omitted words. Do you see any error patterns (the same type of error made two or more times) that this student should watch out for?

Writing and Revising Ideas

1. Describe a classmate.

2. Describe an interesting person from your neighborhood or job.

For help with writing your paragraph, see Chapter 3 and Chapter 4, Parts B and C. As you revise your first draft, pay special attention to writing a clear, catchy topic sentence supported by well-observed (even riveting) details.

UNIT 1 *Writing Assignments*

As you complete each writing assignment, remember to perform these steps:

● Write a clear, complete topic (or thesis) sentence.

● Use freewriting, brainstorming, or clustering to generate ideas for the body of your paragraph or essay.

● Arrange your best ideas in a plan.

● Revise for support, unity, coherence, and exact language.

● Proofread for grammar, punctuation, and spelling errors.

Writing Assignment 1: *Discuss one requirement for a happy family life.* Complete this topic sentence: "A basic requirement for a happy family life is _____." What do you believe a family should have? Is it something material, like a house or a certain amount of money? Is it related to the number or types of people in the family? Does it have to do with nonmaterial things, like communication or support? Begin by jotting down all the reasons why you would require this particular thing. Then choose the three most important reasons, and arrange them in order of importance—either from the least to the most important or the reverse. Explain each reason, making clear to the reader why you feel as strongly as you do.

Writing Assignment 2: *Interview a classmate about an achievement.* Write about a time when your classmate achieved something important, like winning a sales prize at work, losing thirty pounds, or helping a friend through a bad time. To gather interesting facts and details, ask your classmate questions like these, and take notes: *Is there one accomplishment of which you are very proud? Why was this achievement so important? Did it change the way you feel about yourself?* Keep asking questions until you feel you can give your reader a vivid sense of your classmate's triumph.

In your first sentence, state the person's achievement—for instance, *Getting her first A in English was a turning point in Jessica's life.* Then explain specifically why the achievement was so meaningful.

Writing Assignment 3: *Describe an annoying trait.* Choose someone you like or love, and describe his or her most annoying habit or trait. In your topic sentence, name the trait. For instance, you might say, "My husband's most annoying trait is carelessness." Then give one to three examples explaining the topic sentence. Make your examples as specific as possible; be sure they support the topic sentence.

Writing Assignment 4: *Develop a paragraph with examples.* Below are topic sentences for possible paragraphs. Pick the topic sentence that most interests you, and write a paragraph using one to three examples to explain the topic sentence. If you prefer, choose a quotation from the Quotation Bank at the end of this book, and explain it with one or more examples.

a. A sense of humor can make difficult times easier to bear.

b. Mistakes can be great teachers.

c. Television commercials often insult my intelligence.

UNIT 2

Writing Complete Sentences

The sentence is the basic unit of all writing, so good writers must know how to write clear and correct sentences. In this unit, you will

- Learn to spot subjects and verbs
- Practice writing complete sentences
- Learn to avoid or correct any sentence fragments

Spotlight on Writing

My grandfather has misplaced his words again. He is trying to find my name in the kaleidoscope of images that his mind has become. His face brightens like a child's who has just remembered his lesson. He points to me and says my mother's name. I smile back and kiss him on the cheek. It doesn't matter what names he remembers anymore. Every day he is more confused, his memory slipping back a little further in time. Today he has no grandchildren yet. Tomorrow he will be a young man courting my grandmother again, quoting bits of poetry to her. In months to come, he will begin calling her Mama.

Judith Ortiz Cofer, "The Witch's Husband"

- How does the writer feel about her grandfather? Which sentences tell you this?

- Why do you think the writer arranges the last three sentences in the order that she does?

 **Writing Ideas**
- A visit with a loved (or feared) relative
- Your relationship with someone who has a disability

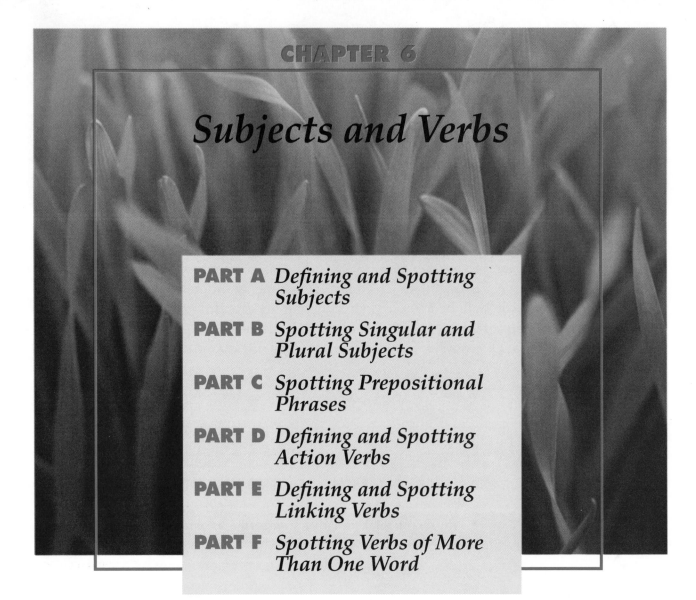

CHAPTER 6

Subjects and Verbs

PART A · Defining and Spotting Subjects

The sentence is the basic unit of all writing. To write well, you need to know how to write correct and effective sentences. A *sentence* is a group of words that expresses a complete thought about something or someone. It contains a subject and a verb.

> (1) _____ jumped over the black Buick, scaled the building, and finally reached the roof.
> (2) _____ needs a new coat of paint.

These sentences might be interesting, but they are incomplete.

● In sentence (1), *who* jumped, scaled, and reached? Bruce Willis, Mariah Carey, the English teacher?

- Depending on *who* performed the action—jumping, scaling, or reaching—the sentence can be exciting, surprising, or strange.

- What is missing is the *who* word—the *subject*.

- In sentence (2), *what* needs a new coat of paint? The house, the car, the old rocking chair?

- What is missing is the *what* word—the *subject*.

For a sentence to be complete, it must contain a *who* or *what* word—a *subject*. The subject tells you *who* or *what* does something or exists in a certain way.

The subject is often a *noun*, a word that names a person, place, or thing (such as *Mariah Carey, English teacher,* or *house*). However, a *pronoun (I, you, he, she, it, we,* or *they*) also can be the subject.*

Practice 1

In each of these sentences, the subject (the *who* or *what* word) is missing. Fill in your own subject to make the sentence complete.

EXAMPLE: A(n) _____ fox _____ dashed across the road.

1. The _____ skidded across the ice.

2. The _____ was eager to begin the semester.

3. Because of the crowd, the _____ slipped out unnoticed.

4. For years, _____ piled up in the back of the closet.

5. The cheerful yellow _____ brightened Sheila's mood.

6. _____ and _____ were scattered all over the doctor's desk.

7. The _____ believed that his _____ would return someday.

8. The _____ was in bad shape. The _____ was falling in, and the _____ were all broken.

As you may have noticed, the subject can be a noun only, but it can also include *words that describe the noun* (such as *the, cheerful,* or *yellow*).

The noun or pronoun alone is called the *simple subject;* the noun or pronoun plus the words that describe it are called the *complete subject.*

> (3) Three yellow roses grew near the path.
> (4) A large box was delivered this morning.

- The simple subject of sentence (3) is the noun *roses*.

- The complete subject is *three yellow roses*.

- What is the simple subject of (4)? _____

- What is the complete subject of (4)? _____

———

*For more work on pronoun subjects, see Chapter 21, Part F.

Practice 2

Circle the *simple* subject in each sentence. (A person's complete name—though more than one word—is considered a simple subject.)

EXAMPLE: A famous (writer) breaks new ground—for others.

(1) Stephen King has been a best-selling author for a long time. (2) In 2000, however, he became the first best-selling author to publish in an online format only. (3) King's online story drew a huge audience immediately. (4) Half a million readers downloaded "Riding the Bullet." (5) They could read the horror story online but were not permitted to print it. (6) According to reports, however, their terror was as chilling as ever. (7) Only one mystery remained in the end. (8) The author found himself unable to download his own story. (9) It was available only in PC-readable formats. (10) Macintosh users, including King, were left chilling out in cyberspace!

Practice 3

In these sentences, the complete subject has been omitted. You must decide where it belongs and fill in a complete subject (a *who* or *what* word along with any words that describe it). Write in any complete subject that makes sense.

EXAMPLE: Raced down the street.

My worried friend raced down the street.

1. Trained day and night for the big event.

_____

2. Has a dynamic singing voice.

_____

3. Landed in the cornfield.

_____

4. After the show, applauded and screamed for fifteen minutes.

_____

5. Got out of the large gray van.

_____

PART B   *Spotting Singular and Plural Subjects*

Besides being able to spot subjects in sentences, you need to know whether a subject is singular or plural.

> (1) The man jogged around the park.

- The subject of this sentence is *the man.*
- Because *the man* is one person, the subject is *singular.*

Singular means only one of something.

> (2) The man and his friend jogged around the park.

- The subject of sentence (2) is *the man and his friend.*
- Because *the man and his friend* refers to more than one person, the subject is *plural.*

Plural means more than one of something.

Practice 4

Here is a list of possible subjects of sentences. If the subject is singular, put a check in the Singular column; if the subject is plural, put a check in the Plural column.

Possible Subjects	Singular (one)	Plural (more than one)
EXAMPLES: an elephant	✔	___
children	___	✔
1. our cousins	___	___
2. a song and a dance	___	___
3. Kansas	___	___
4. their trophy	___	___
5. women	___	___
6. a rock star and her band	___	___
7. his three pickup trucks	___	___
8. salad dressing	___	___

Practice 5

Circle the complete subjects in these sentences. Then, in the space at the right, write *S* if the subject is singular or *P* if the subject is plural.

EXAMPLE: (Spike Lee) inspired a new generation of African-American filmmakers.   *S*

1. Lee's first hit was *She's Gotta Have It* in 1986.   ___

2. Many African-American moviemakers have had success since then.   ___

3. These young artists write, direct, and even act in their own movies.   ___

4. Often their goal is to combine exciting entertainment with a social message.   ___

5. John Singleton wrote and directed the acclaimed *Boyz N the Hood* at age twenty-three.   ___

6. *Poetic Justice* and *Higher Learning* followed soon after.   ___

7. Reading turned another young man into a filmmaker.   ___

8. At nineteen, Matty Rich made *Straight Out of Brooklyn,* after studying more than 250 film books!   ___

9. The talented Hudlin brothers produced *House Party, Boomerang,* and *Bebe's Kids*.   ___

10. Reginald Hudlin later directed *The Great White Hype,* a popular satire on the world of boxing.   ___

PART C   *Spotting Prepositional Phrases*

One group of words that may confuse you as you look for subjects is the prepositional phrase. A *prepositional phrase* contains a *preposition* (a word like *at, from, in,* or *of*) and its *object* (a *noun* or *pronoun*). Here are some prepositional phrases:*

Prepositional Phrase	= Preposition	+ Object
at work	at	work
behind her	behind	her
of the students	of	the students
on the blue table	on	the blue table

---

*For more work on prepositions, see Chapter 23.

The object of a preposition *cannot* be the subject of a sentence. Therefore, crossing out prepositional phrases can help you find the real subject.

> (1) On summer evenings, girls in white dresses stroll under the trees.
>
> (2) ~~On summer evenings,~~ girls ~~in white dresses~~ stroll ~~under the trees.~~
>
> (3) From dawn to dusk, we hiked.
>
> (4) The president of the college will speak tonight.

● In sentence (1), you may have trouble spotting the subject. However, once the prepositional phrases are crossed out in (2), the subject, *girls*, is easy to see.

● Cross out the prepositional phrase in sentence (3). What is the subject of the sentence? _____

● Cross out the prepositional phrase in sentence (4). What is the subject of the sentence? _____

Here are some common prepositions you should know:

Common Prepositions

about	beside	off
above	between	on
across	by	over
after	during	through(out)
against	except	to
along	for	toward
among	from	under
around	in	until
at	into	up
before	like	with
behind	of	without

Practice 6

Cross out the prepositional phrase or phrases in each sentence. Then circle the *simple* subject of the sentence.

EXAMPLE: (Millions) ~~of people~~ walk ~~on the Appalachian Trail~~ each year.

1. That famous trail stretches from Springer Mountain in Georgia to Mount Katahdin in Maine.

2. One quarter of the trail goes through Virginia.

3. The majority of walkers hike ~~for one day.~~

4. Of the four million trail users, two hundred people complete the entire trail every year.

5. For most hikers, the trip through fourteen states takes four or five months.

6. In the spring, many hardy souls begin their 2,158 mile-long journey.

7. These lovers of the wilderness must reach Mount Katahdin before winter.

8. On the trail, men and women battle heat, humidity, bugs, blisters, muscle sprains, and food and water shortages.

9. After beautiful green scenery, the path becomes rocky and mountainous.

10. Hikers in the White Mountains of New Hampshire struggle against high winds.

11. A pebble from Georgia is sometimes added to the pile of stones at the top of Mount Katahdin.

12. At the bottom of the mountain, the conquerors of the Appalachian Trail add their names to the list of successful hikers.

PART D   *Defining and Spotting Action Verbs*

(1) The pears _____ on the trees.

(2) Robert _____ his customer's hand and _____ her dog on the head.

These sentences tell you what or who the subject is—*the pears* and *Robert*—but not what each subject does.

● In sentence (1), what do the pears do? Do they *grow, ripen, rot, stink,* or *glow?*

● All these *action verbs* fit into the blank space in sentence (1), but the meaning of the sentence changes depending on which action verb you use.

● In sentence (2), what actions did Robert perform? He might have *shaken, ignored, kissed, patted,* or *scratched.*

● Depending on which verb you use, the meaning of the sentence changes.

● Some sentences, like sentence (2), contain two or more action verbs.

For a sentence to be complete, it must have a *verb.* **An** *action verb* **tells what action the subject is performing.**

Practice 7

Fill in each blank with an action verb.

1. Shaquille O'Neal _____ through the air for a slam dunk.

2. An artist _____ the scene at the waterfront.

3. When the rooster _____, the dogs _____ .

4. A fierce wind _____ and _____.

5. The audience _____ while the conductor _____ .

6. This new kitchen gadget _____ and _____ any vegetable you can imagine.

7. When the dentist _____ his drill, Charlene _____.

8. Will Smith _____ and _____ across the stage.

Practice 8

Circle the action verbs in these sentences. Some sentences contain more than one action verb.

(1) Sometimes the combination of talent and persistence explodes into well-deserved fame and fortune. (2) For almost a year, J. K. Rowling survived on public assistance in Edinburgh, Scotland. (3) Almost every day that year, she brought her baby to a coffee shop near their damp, unheated apartment. (4) In the warmth of the café, the divorced, unemployed mother sat and wrote. (5) Almost at the end of her endurance, she finally finished her first book. (6) Today, Rowling's Harry Potter books sell millions of copies. (7) The fourth Harry Potter book made publishing history, with a record-breaking 3.8 million copies in its first printing. (8) Each book tells about Harry's adventures, both in the everyday world (the Muggles' world) and at a new grade level at Hogwarts School of Witchcraft and Wizardry. (9) The imaginative (and very funny) series about the courageous young wizard-in-training attracts and enthralls adults as well as children. (10) In fact, the *New York Times* began a children's bestseller list for the first time—after months of Harry Potter books in slots 1, 2, and 3 on the adult bestseller list!

PART E   *Defining and Spotting Linking Verbs*

The verbs you have been examining so far show action, but a second kind of verb simply links the subject to words that describe or rename it.

> (1) Aunt Claudia sometimes seems a little strange.

- The subject in this sentence is *Aunt Claudia,* but there is no action verb.
- Instead, *seems* links the subject, *Aunt Claudia,* with the descriptive words *a little strange.*

Aunt Claudia	seems	a little strange.
↓	↓	↓
subject	linking verb	descriptive words

(2) They are reporters for the newspaper.

- The subject is *they*. The word *reporters* renames the subject.
- What verb links the subject, *they*, with the word *reporters*? _____

For a sentence to be complete, it must contain a *verb*. A *linking verb* links the subject with words that describe or rename that subject.

Here are some linking verbs you should know:

Common Linking Verbs	
be (am, is, are, was, were)	look
act	seem
appear	smell
become	sound
feel	taste
get	

- The most common linking verbs are the forms of *to be*, but verbs of the senses, such as *feel, look,* and *smell,* also may be used as linking verbs.

Practice 9

The subjects and descriptive words in these sentences are boxed. Circle the linking verbs.

1. Jerry sounds sleepy today.
2. Ronda always was the best debater on the team.
3. His brother often appeared relaxed and happy.
4. By evening, Harvey felt confident about the exam.
5. Mara and Maude became talent scouts.

Practice 10

Circle the linking verbs in these sentences. Then underline the subject and the descriptive word or words in each sentence.

1. The sweet potato pie tastes delicious.
2. You usually seem energetic.
3. During the summer, she looks calm.
4. Under heavy snow, the new dome roof appeared sturdy.
5. Raphael is a gifted animal trainer.
6. Lately, I feel very competent at work.
7. Luz became a medical technician.
8. Yvonne acted surprised at her baby shower.

PART F *Spotting Verbs of More Than One Word*

All the verbs you have dealt with so far have been single words—*look, walked, saw, are, were,* and so on. However, many verbs consist of more than one word.

> (1) Sarah is walking to work.

- The subject is *Sarah*. What is *Sarah* doing?
- Sarah is walking.
- *Walking* is the *main verb. Is* is the *helping verb*; without *is, walking* is not a complete verb.

> (2) Should I have written sooner?

- The subject is *I*.
- *Should have written* is the *complete verb*.
- *Written* is the *main verb. Should* and *have* are the *helping verbs*; without *should have, written* is not a complete verb.

> (3) Do you eat fish?

- What is the subject? _____
- What is the main verb? _____
- What is the helping verb? _____

The *complete verb* **in a sentence consists of all the helping verbs and the main verb.**

Practice 11

The blanks following each sentence tell you how many words make up the complete verb. Fill in the blanks with the complete verb; then circle the main verb.

EXAMPLE: Ordinary people have been fighting crime in many creative ways.

   ____have____   ____been____   (fighting)

1. They are turning their fear of crime into preventive action.

   _____   _____

2. Do you know about community policing programs?

   _____   _____

3. These programs have increased all over the country, from Florida to Oregon.

   _____   _____

4. Many volunteers have been walking the streets in civilian crime patrols.

   _____   _____   _____

5. Suspicious activities are reported to the police.

   _____   _____

6. Walkie-talkies, car patrols, and volunteer security guides can be very helpful in civilian crime prevention programs.

   _____   _____

7. Neighborhood groups in Brooklyn, New York, have found those measures particularly effective in their campaign against burglaries.

   _____   _____

8. Residents of some communities have been photographing drug dealers and exchanges. _____   _____   _____

9. On the basis of these photographs, police have made drug raids.

   _____   _____

10. Private citizens are arranging recreation, tutoring, and leadership programs for restless teenagers. _____   _____

11. They have also created antiviolence training for students in public schools.

    _____   _____

12. In Los Angeles, California, people have been campaigning against violence through billboards and television ads.

    _____   _____   _____

13. Are these measures working?

    _____   _____

14. Because of community action, crime has decreased in both large cities and small towns. _____   _____

15. Perhaps someday all neighborhoods will be safer.

    _____   _____

Practice 12

Box the simple subject, circle the main verb, and underline any helping verbs in each of the following sentences.

EXAMPLE: Most people have wondered about the beginning of the universe.

1. Scientists have developed one theory.

2. According to this theory, the universe began with a huge explosion.

3. The explosion has been named the Big Bang.

4. First, all matter must have been packed into a tiny speck under enormous pressure.

5. Then, about 15 billion years ago, that speck burst with amazing force.

6. Everything in the universe has come from the original explosion.

7. In fact, the universe still is expanding from the Big Bang.

8. All of the planets and stars are moving away from each other at an even speed.

9. Will it expand forever?

10. Experts may be debating that question for a long time.

Practice 13   Writing Assignment

Whether you have just graduated from high school or have worked for several years, the first year of college can be difficult. Imagine that you are writing to an incoming student who needs advice and encouragement. Pick one serious problem you had as a first-year student, and explain how you coped with it. State the problem clearly. Use examples from your own experience or the experience of others to make your advice more vivid.

✔ Chapter Highlights

- **A sentence contains a subject and a verb, and expresses a complete thought:**

  S   V
  Jennifer swims every day.

  S   V
  The two students have tutored in the writing lab.

- **An action verb tells what the subject is doing:**

  Toni Morrison *writes* novels.

- **A linking verb links the subject with words that describe or rename it:**

  Her novels *are* bestsellers.

- **Don't mistake the object of a prepositional phrase for a subject:**

  S   PP
  The red car [in the showroom] is a Corvette.

  PP   S
  [In my dream,] *a sailor and his parrot* were singing.

Circle the simple subjects, crossing out any confusing prepositional phrases. Then underline the complete verbs. If you have difficulty with this review, consider rereading the lesson.

Nobel Peace Prize Winners

(1) In 1901, a committee presented the first yearly Nobel Peace Prize. (2) That important prize honors individuals for outstanding work toward world peace. (3) Mother Teresa and Nelson Mandela are among the well-known winners of the award. (4) Those champions of peace devoted their lives to the welfare of others. (5) However, less famous figures also have been honored for their work toward a more peaceful world.

(6) Dr. Joseph Rotblat received the prize in 1995 for his opposition to nuclear weapons. (7) During World War II, he worked for the secret U.S. Manhattan Project. (8) In 1944, however, the talented physicist resigned from that atomic bomb project and has campaigned against atomic weapons ever since.

(9) In 1996, two peace workers shared the prize. (10) Bishop Carlos Belo and José Ramos-Horta had struggled for years against the military occupation of East Timor. (11) The award brought the tragedy of their land to the attention of the world. (12) The efforts of these two brave men eventually contributed to the independence of East Timor.

(13) In 1999, an organization won the award. (14) The Nobel Peace Prize went to Doctors Without Borders, a group of physicians dedicated to providing aid to victims of natural and human-made disasters, regardless of country or political "side." (15) Volunteer doctors from all over the world have courageously helped victims from Kosovo to East Timor, from Sierra Leone to Afghanistan.

(16) The president of South Korea was the award winner in 2000. (17) Kim Dae Jung has been reaching out for peace with North Korea—a miracle in the mind of many.

CHAPTER 7

Avoiding Sentence Fragments

PART A Writing Sentences with Subjects and Verbs

PART B Writing Sentences with Complete Verbs

PART C Completing the Thought

PART A — Writing Sentences with Subjects and Verbs

Which of these groups of words is a sentence? Be prepared to explain your answers.

(1) People will bet on almost anything.

(2) For example, every winter the Nenana River in Alaska.

(3) Often make bets on the date of the breakup of the ice.

(4) Must guess the exact day and time of day.

(5) Recently, the lucky guess won $300,000.

- In (2), you probably wanted to know what the Nenana River *does*. The idea is not complete because there is no *verb*.

- In (3) and (4), you probably wanted to know *who* often makes bets on the date of the breakup of the ice and *who* must guess the exact day and time of day.

The ideas are not complete. What is missing? _____

● But in sentences (1) and (5), you knew *who did what.* These ideas are complete.

Why? _____

_____

Below is the same group of words written as complete sentences:

(1) People will bet on almost anything.

(2) For example, every winter the Nenana River in Alaska freezes.

(3) The townspeople often make bets on the date of the breakup of the ice.

(4) Someone must guess the exact day and time of day.

(5) Recently, the lucky guess won $300,000.

Every *sentence* must have both a subject and a verb—and must express a complete thought.

A *fragment* lacks either a subject or a complete verb—or does not express a complete thought.

Practice 1

All of the following are *fragments;* they lack a subject, a verb, or both. Add a subject, a verb, or both in order to make the fragments into sentences.

EXAMPLE: Raising onions in the backyard.

Rewrite: *Charles is raising onions in the backyard.* _____

1. Laughed loudly at the comedian's jokes.

   Rewrite: _____

2. Melts easily.

   Rewrite: _____

3. That couple on the street corner.

   Rewrite: _____

4. One of the fans.

   Rewrite: _____

5. Manages a Software City store.

   Rewrite: _____

6. The tip of her nose.

   Rewrite: _____

7. A DVD player.

   Rewrite: _____

8. Makes me nervous.

   Rewrite: _____

9. Tuition and fees.

    Rewrite: _____

10. A person who likes to take risks.

    Rewrite: _____

PART B
Writing Sentences with Complete Verbs

Do not be fooled by incomplete verbs.

> (1) She leaving for the city.
>
> (2) The students gone to the cafeteria for dessert.

- *Leaving* seems to be the verb in (1).
- *Gone* seems to be the verb in (2).

But . . .

- An *-ing* word like *leaving* is not by itself a verb.
- A word like *gone* is not by itself a verb.

> (1) She $\left.\begin{matrix} is \\ was \end{matrix}\right\}$ leaving for the city.
>
> (2) The students $\left.\begin{matrix} have \\ had \end{matrix}\right\}$ gone to the cafeteria for dessert.

- To be a verb, an *-ing* word (called a *present participle*) must be combined with some form of the verb *to be*.*

Helping Verb	Main Verb
am	
is	
are	
was	
were	jogging
has been	
have been	
had been	

*For a detailed explanation of present participles, see Chapter 11.

- To be a *verb*, a word like *gone* (called a *past participle*) must be combined with some form of *to have* or *to be.**

Helping Verb	Main Verb
am	
is	
are	
was	
were	
has	forgotten
have	
had	
has been	
have been	
had been	

Practice 2

All of the following are fragments; they have only a partial or an incomplete verb. Complete each verb in order to make these fragments into sentences.

EXAMPLE: Both children grown tall this year.

Rewrite: *Both children have grown tall this year.*

1. The Australian winning the tennis match.

   Rewrite: _____

2. Her parents gone to the movies.

   Rewrite: _____

3. Steve's letter published in the *Miami Herald*.

   Rewrite: _____

4. My physics professor always forgetting the assignment.

   Rewrite: _____

5. This sari made of scarlet silk.

   Rewrite: _____

6. For the past two years, Joan working at a computer company.

   Rewrite: _____

7. You ever been to Alaska?

   Rewrite: _____

_____

*For a detailed explanation of past participles, see Chapter 10.

8. Yesterday, Ed's wet gloves taken from the radiator.

Rewrite: _____

Practice 3

All of the following are fragments; they lack a subject, and they contain only a partial verb. Make these fragments into sentences by adding a subject and by completing the verb.

EXAMPLE: Written by Ray Bradbury.

Rewrite: _This science fiction thriller was written by Ray Bradbury._____

1. Forgotten the password.

   Rewrite: _____

2. Now running the copy center.

   Rewrite: _____

3. Making sculpture from old car parts.

   Rewrite: _____

4. Been working at the state capitol building.

   Rewrite: _____

5. Creeping along the windowsill.

   Rewrite: _____

6. Driven that tractor for years.

   Rewrite: _____

7. Slept through the TV program.

   Rewrite: _____

8. Been to a wrestling match.

   Rewrite: _____

Practice 4

Fragments are most likely to occur in paragraphs or longer pieces of writing. Proofread the paragraph below for fragments; check for missing subjects, missing verbs, or incomplete verbs. Circle the number of every fragment; then write your corrections above the lines.

(1) On a routine day in 1946, a scientist at the Raytheon Company his hand into his pants pocket for a candy bar. (2) The chocolate, however, a messy, sticky mass of gunk. (3) Dr. Percy Spencer had been testing a magnetron tube. (4) Could the chocolate have melted from radiation leaking from the tube? (5) Spencer sent out for a bag of popcorn kernels. (6) Put the kernels near the tube. (7) Within

minutes, corn popping wildly onto the lab floor. (8) Within a short time, Raytheon working on the development of the microwave oven. (9) Microwave cooking the first new method of preparing food since the discovery of fire more than a million years ago. (10) ~~Was~~ the first cooking technique that did not directly or indirectly apply fire to food.

PART C   *Completing the Thought*

Can these ideas stand by themselves?

> (1) Because oranges are rich in vitamin C.
>
> (2) Although Sam is sleepy.

- These ideas have a subject and a verb (find them), but they cannot stand alone because you expect something else to follow.

- Because oranges are rich in vitamin C, then *what?* Should you *eat them, sell them,* or *make marmalade?*

- Although Sam is sleepy, *what will he do?* Will he *wash the dishes, walk the dog,* or *go to the gym?*

> (1) Because oranges are rich in vitamin C, *I eat one every day.*
>
> (2) Although Sam is sleepy, *he will work late tonight.*

- These sentences are now complete.

- Words like *because* and *although* make an idea incomplete unless another idea is added to complete the thought.*

Practice 5

Make these fragments into sentences by adding some idea that completes the thought.

EXAMPLE: Because I miss my family, ___I am going home for the weekend._____

1. As May stepped off the elevator, _____

2. If you are driving to Main Street, _____

3. While Kimi studied chemistry, _____

4. Because you believe in yourself, _____

5. Although spiders scare most people, _____

6. Unless the surgery is absolutely necessary, _____

_____

*For more work on this type of sentence, see Chapter 14.

7. Whenever I hear Macy Gray sing, _____

8. Although these air conditioners are expensive to run, _____

_____

Can these ideas stand by themselves?

(3) Graciela, who has a one-year-old daughter.

(4) A course that I will always remember.

● In each of these examples, you expect something else to follow. Graciela, who has a one-year-old daughter, *is doing what?* Does she *attend town meetings, knit sweaters,* or *fly planes?*

● A course that I will always remember *is what?* The thought must be completed.

(3) Graciela, who has a one-year-old daughter, *attends Gordon College.*

(4) A course that I will always remember *is documentary filmmaking.*

● These sentences are now complete.*

Practice 6

Make these fragments into sentences by completing the thought.

EXAMPLE: Kent, who is a good friend of mine, <u>rarely writes to me.</u>_____

1. The horoscopes that appear in the daily papers _____

2. Couples who never argue _____

3. Robert, who is a superb pole-vaulter, _____

4. Radio programs that ask listeners to call in are _____

5. A person who has coped with a great loss _____

6. My dog, which is the smartest animal alive, _____

_____

7. Libraries that are up-to-date _____

8. The video that we watched last night _____

9. A person who becomes upset easily _____

10. A country that I have always wanted to visit _____

_____

*For more work on this type of sentence, see Chapter 18, Part A.

Practice 7

To each fragment, add a subject, a verb, or whatever is required to complete the thought.

1. Visiting the White House.

   Rewrite: _____

2. That digital clock blinking for hours.

   Rewrite: _____

3. People who can't say no to their children.

   Rewrite: _____

4. Make tables from driftwood they find on the beach.

   Rewrite: _____

5. Over the roof and into the garden.

   Rewrite: _____

6. Raúl completed a culinary arts program, and now he a well-known chef.

   Rewrite: _____

7. Chess, which is a difficult game to play.

   Rewrite: _____

8. Whenever Dolly starts to yodel.

   Rewrite: _____

Practice 8

Proofread the paragraph for fragments. Circle the number of every fragment, and then write your corrections above the lines.

(1) The Special Olympics is an international program. (2) That is held for mentally retarded children and adults. (3) Special Olympics athletes train and compete in regular sports. (4) Which include floor hockey, skiing, soccer, swimming, speed skating, and tennis. (5) The Special Olympics winter and summer international games are held every other year. (6) Although 150 countries participate in the world games. (7) Special Olympics are also held yearly at local and state levels. (8) Altogether, more than a million athletes participate. (9) Whereas Special Olympics competitors may not swim as fast or jump as high as Olympics stars. (10) They are very eager to do their best. (11) Their courage and accomplishments inspire everyone. (12) And change these athletes' lives forever.

Practice 9   Writing Assignment

Working in a small group, choose one of the sentences below that could begin a short story.

1. As soon as Sean replaced the receiver, he knew he had to take action.
2. Suddenly, the bright blue sky turned dark.
3. No matter where she looked, Elena could not find her diary.

Next, each person in the group should write his or her own short story, starting with that sentence. First decide what type of story yours will be—science fiction, romance, action, comedy, murder mystery, and so on; perhaps each person will choose a different type. It may help you to imagine the story later becoming a TV show. As you write, be careful to avoid fragments, making sure each thought has a subject and a complete verb—and expresses a complete thought.

Then exchange papers, checking each other's work for fragments. If time permits, read the papers aloud to the group. Are you surprised by the different ways in which that first sentence was developed?

✔ Chapter Highlights

A sentence fragment is an error because it lacks

- **a subject:**

  Was buying a gold ring. *(incorrect)*
  Diamond Jim was buying a gold ring. *(correct)*

- **a verb:**

  The basketball game Friday at noon. *(incorrect)*
  The basketball game *was played* Friday at noon. *(correct)*

- **a complete thought:**

  While Teresa was swimming. *(incorrect)*
  While Teresa was swimming, she lost a contact lens. *(correct)*

  The woman who bought your car. *(incorrect)*
  The woman who bought your car is walking down the highway. *(correct)*

Chapter Review

Circle the number of each fragment. Correct it in any way that makes sense, changing it into a separate idea or adding it to another sentence.

A. (1) Steel drums wonderful and unusual musical instruments. (2) Steel bands use them to perform calypso, jazz, and popular music. (3) And even classical symphonies. (4) Steel drums were invented in Trinidad. (5) Where they were made from the ends of discarded oil drums. (6) That had been left by the British navy. (7) Although the first steel drums produced only rhythm. (8) Now they can be tuned to play up to five octaves. (9) Steel orchestras produce music. (10) That surrounds and delights listeners without the use of amplifiers. (11) The worldwide popularity of steel drums has been increasing steadily. (12) The Trinidad All Steel Percussion Orchestra was a smash hit. (13) When it first performed in England a number of years ago. (14) Recently, the Northern Illinois University Steel Band has been thrilling audiences from the United States to Taiwan.

B. (1) In 1986, people in the Ganges Delta of India began wearing masks to protect themselves from Bengal tigers. (2) These deadly tigers protected in the region. (3) Killing up to sixty people a year. (4) Someone noticed. (5) That the big cat attacked only from behind. (6) Workers put face masks on the back of their heads. (7) The inexpensive rubber masks showed a pale-faced human with a thin mustache. (8) The results excellent. (9) The confused animals thought the masks were real faces and did not attack.

C. (1) Braille, which is a system of reading and writing now used by blind people all over the world. (2) Was invented by a fifteen-year-old French boy. (3) In 1824, when Louis Braille entered a school for the blind in Paris. (4) He found that the library had only fourteen books for the blind. (5) These books used a system that he and the other blind students found hard to use. (6) Most of them just gave up. (7) Louis Braille devoted himself to finding a better way. (8) Working with the French army method called night-writing. (9) He came up with a new system in 1829. (10) Although his classmates liked and used Braille. (11) It not widely accepted in England and the United States for another hundred years.

D. (1) Not all employers have a problem with employees who sleep on the job. (2) In fact, when workers get that after-lunch draggy feeling. (3) Some employers encourage them to nap. (4) Sleep researchers believe that people have a natural tendency to fall asleep. (5) During the afternoon. (6) Short naps energize workers. (7) And improve both safety and performance. (8) Of course, nappers always have found ways to catch a few winks. (9) They snooze at (or under) desks and in cars, closets, cafeterias, meeting rooms, and bathroom stalls. (10) Now, however, more and more companies providing "relaxation rooms" and "nap nooks." (11) Camille and Bill Anthony, authors of *The Art of Napping at Work,* are even promoting a new holiday, National Workplace Napping Day. (12) Because it falls on the Monday after the end of daylight-saving time. (13) Employees can make up the lost hour of sleep by napping at work. (14) To learn more, read the Anthonys' book. (15) Which includes chapters on napping places, napping policies, and the future of workplace napping!

Proofreading and Revising

Proofread the following essay to eliminate all sentence fragments. Circle the number of every fragment. (You should find fourteen.) Then correct the fragments in any way you choose—by connecting them to a sentence before or after, by completing any incomplete verbs, and so on. Make your corrections above the lines.

Unfreezing the Photograph

(1) On June 8, 1972, a nine-year-old child became the symbol of every innocent victim of the Vietnam War. (2) Naked and screaming in pain. (3) Phan Thi Kim Phuc was photographed fleeing down a South Vietnamese country road. (4) The South Vietnamese air force, directed by the United States, had just carried out a napalm bombing. (5) Which had mistakenly hit South Vietnamese families in the village of Trang Bang.

(6) That photograph is frozen in time and memory. (7) It won a Pulitzer Prize. (8) For Vietnamese photographer Nick Ut. (9) The photograph also is credited with stepping up the effort to stop the Vietnam War. (10) Some people want to know more about Kim Phuc, however. (11) What happened to her, and where she now?

(12) After shooting the photograph. (13) Nick Ut rushed Kim Phuc to the nearest hospital. (14) Huge sections of her skin had been destroyed by the napalm. (15) Not expected to live. (16) She did survive, though, and was transferred to a hospital in Saigon. (17) Her chin had been fused to her chest by scar tissue, and what remained of her left arm was stuck to her rib cage. (18) Nick Ut visited her frequently and set up a bank account for donations for her medical treatment. (19) After undergoing seventeen skin grafts in fourteen months. (20) Kim Phuc was released. (21) The war still raging, and her home in Trang Bang had been destroyed.

(22) The heroic survivor became a political symbol for North Vietnam. (23) Which took over South Vietnam in 1975. (24) Kim Phuc was interviewed constantly by Western journalists, and her story was used to arouse anti-American and antiwar feelings. (25) She enrolled in medical school in 1982, but the Vietnamese government ended her studies. (26) To use her full-time for

political purposes. (27) Four years later, the government allowed her to move to Cuba to study pharmacology.

(28) In Havana, she met and married another Vietnamese student, Bui Huy Toan. (29) Returning in 1992 from their honeymoon in Moscow. (30) She and her husband risked everything for political freedom. (31) They got off the plane at a refueling stop in Canada. (32) With no luggage, no money, and no friends, Kim Phuc phoned Nick Ut, who had helped her so many times. (33) Eventually, Kim Phuc and her husband settled in Ontario. (34) In 1998, were awarded Canadian citizenship.

(35) Kim Phuc cofounded the Chicago-based Kim Foundation. (36) Which funds surgery for children who are victims of war. (37) Today, she devotes her time to the foundation. (38) And to visiting world capitals as a goodwill ambassador for UNESCO. (39) She says that people can learn the tragedy of war from her. (40) At the Vietnam Memorial in Washington, D.C., Kim Phuc even extended love and forgiveness to those responsible for her lifelong physical and emotional pain.

Discuss an Event That Influenced You

Readers of a final draft can easily forget that they are reading the *end result* of someone else's writing process. The following paragraph is one student's response to the assignment *Write about an event in history that influenced you.*

In your class or group, read it aloud if possible. As you read, underline any words or lines that strike you as especially powerful.

Though the Vietnam War ended almost before I was born, it changed my life. My earliest memory is of my father. A grizzled Vietnam warrior who came back spat upon, with one less brother. He wore a big smile playing ball with my brother and me, but even then I felt the grin was a coverup. When the postwar reports were on, his face became despondent. What haunted his heart and mind, I could not know, but I tried in my childish way to reason with him. A simple "It'll be all right, Dad" would bring a bleak smirk to his face. When he was happy, I was happy. When he was down, I was down. Soon the fatherly horseplay stopped, and once-full bottles of liquor were empty. He was there in body. Yet not there. Finally, he was physically gone. Either working a sixty-hour week or out in the streets after a furious fight with my mother. Once they divorced, she moved us to another state. I never came to grips with the turmoil inside my father. I see him as an intricate puzzle, missing one piece. That piece is his humanity, tangled up in history and blown up by a C-19.

Brian Pereira, student

1. How effective is Brian Pereira's paragraph?

   _____ Good topic sentence?   _____ Rich supporting details?

   _____ Logical organization?   _____ Effective conclusion?

2. Discuss your underlinings with the group or class. Did others underline the same parts? Explain why you feel particular words or details are effective. For instance, the strong words *bleak smirk* say so much about the father's hopeless mood and the distance between him and his young son.

3. The topic sentence says that the writer's life changed, yet the body of the paragraph speaks mostly about his troubled father. Does the body of the paragraph explain the topic sentence?

4. What order, if any, does this writer follow?

5. If you do not know what a "C-19" is in the last sentence, does that make the conclusion less effective for you?

6. Would you suggest any changes or revisions?

7. Proofread for grammar and spelling. Do you notice any error patterns (two or more errors of the same type) that this student should watch out for?

> Brian Pereira's fine paragraph was the end result of a difficult writing process. Pereira describes his process this way:
>
> > The floor in my room looked like a writer's battleground of crumpled papers. Before this topic was assigned, I had not the slightest idea that this influence even existed, much less knew what it was. I thought hard, started a sentence or two, and threw a smashed paper down in disgust, over and over again. After hours, I realized it—the event in history that influenced me was Vietnam, even though I was too young to remember it! That became my topic sentence.

Writing and Revising Ideas

1. Discuss an event that influenced you.

2. Choose your best recent paper and describe your own writing process—what you did well and not so well.

For help with writing your paragraph, see Chapter 3 and Chapter 4, Part B (see "Time Order"). Give yourself plenty of time to revise. Stick with it, trying to write the best possible paper. Pay special attention to fully supporting your topic with interesting facts and details.

UNIT 2 *Writing Assignments*

As you complete each writing assignment, remember to perform these steps:

- Write a clear, complete topic sentence.
- Use freewriting, brainstorming, or clustering to generate ideas for your paragraph, essay, or memo.
- Arrange your best ideas in a plan.
- Revise for support, unity, coherence, and exact language.
- Proofread for grammar, punctuation, and spelling errors.

Writing Assignment 1: *Write about someone who changed jobs.* Did you, someone you know, or someone you know about change jobs because of a new interest or love for something else? Describe the person's first job and feelings of job satisfaction (or lack of them). What happened to make the person want to make a job switch? How long did the switch take? Was it difficult or easy to accomplish? Describe the person's new job and feelings of job satisfaction (or lack of them). Proofread for fragments.

Writing Assignment 2: *Describe your place in the family.* Your psychology professor has asked you to write a brief description of your place in the family—as an only child, the youngest child, the middle child, or the oldest child. Did your place provide you with special privileges or lay special responsibilities on you? For instance, youngest children may be babied; oldest children may be expected to act like parents. Did your place in the family have an effect on you as an adult? In your topic sentence, state what role your place in the family played

in your development: *Being the _____ child in my family has made me*

_____. Proofread for fragments.

Writing Assignment 3: *Explain your feelings about a prized possession.* If your home caught fire and you could save just one thing you owned, what would it be? (Assume no one was harmed.) A reporter saw you run out of your house with your prized possession. She asks you why it means so much to you. If your explanation is interesting enough, it will be quoted in her newspaper story. Proofread for any fragments.

Writing Assignment 4: *Ask for a raise.* Compose a memo to a boss, real or imagined, persuading him or her to decide to raise your pay. In your first sentence, state that you are asking for an increase. Be specific: Note how the quality of your work, your extra hours, or any special projects you have been involved in have made the business run more smoothly or become more profitable. Do not sound vain, but do praise yourself honestly. Use the memo style shown here. Proofread for fragments.

MEMORANDUM

TO: Chris Clark, Front Office Manager

FROM: Mary Ellen Taylor

DATE: September 25, 2000

SUBJECT: Salary Increase

I am writing this memo to request . . .

UNIT 3

Using Verbs Effectively

Every sentence contains at least one verb. Because verbs often are action words, they add interest and punch to any piece of writing. In this unit, you will

- Learn to use present, past, and other verb tenses correctly

- Learn when to add -*s* or -*ed*

- Recognize and use past participle forms

- Recognize -*ing* verbs, infinitives, and other special forms

Spotlight on Writing

Notice how vividly this writer describes the scene before her. Her verbs are underlined.

A huge glittering tower <u>sparkles</u> across the Florida marshlands. Floodlights <u>reach</u> into the heavens all around it, rolling out carpets of light. Helicopters and jets <u>blink</u> around the launch pad like insects drawn to flame. Oz never <u>filled</u> the sky with such diamond-studded improbability. Inside the cascading lights, a giant trellis <u>holds</u> a slender rocket to its heart, on each side a tall thermos bottle filled with solid fuel the color and feel of a hard eraser, and on its back a sharp-nosed space shuttle, clinging like the young of some exotic mammal. A full moon <u>bulges</u> low in the sky, its face turned toward the launch pad, its mouth open.

Diane Ackerman, "Watching a Night Launch of the Space Shuttle"

- Well-chosen verbs help bring this description to life. Which verbs most effectively help you see and experience the scene?

- In the last sentence, the author describes the moon as if it were watching the launch—with "its mouth open." Why do you think she does this?

Writing Ideas
- The takeoff of a rocket, plane, speedboat, or other vehicle
- A historical event that you believe was important

CHAPTER 8

Present Tense (Agreement)

PART A Defining Agreement

A subject and a present tense verb *agree* if you use the correct form of the verb with each subject. The chart on the following page shows which form of the verb to use for each kind of pronoun subject (we discuss other kinds of subjects later).

Verbs in the Present Tense

(example verb: to write)

Singular		**Plural**	
If the subject is	the verb is	If the subject is	the verb is
↓	↓	↓	↓
1st person: I	write	1st person: we	write
2nd person: you	write	2nd person: you	write
3rd person: he she it }	writes	3rd person: they	write

Practice 1

Fill in the correct present tense form of the verb.

1. You *ask* questions.   1. He _____ questions.

2. They *decide*.   2. She _____.

3. I *remember*.   3. He _____.

4. They *wear* glasses.   4. She _____ glasses.

5. We *hope* so.   5. He _____ so.

6. I *laugh* often.   6. She _____ often.

7. We *study* daily.   7. He _____ daily.

8. He *amazes* me.   8. It _____ me.

Add *-s* or *-es* to a verb in the present tense only when the subject is *third person singular (he, she, it)*.

Third Person Singular

If the subject is	the verb in the present tense must take an *-s* or *-es*.
he she it	wins promises wishes

Practice 2

Write the correct form of the verb in the space to the right of the pronoun subject.

EXAMPLE: **to see**

I _____*see*_____

they _____*see*_____

she _____*sees*_____

to find	to ask	to go
he _____	I _____	it _____
they _____	she _____	you _____
you _____	he _____	we _____

to rest	to hold	to select
I _____	it _____	she _____
they _____	we _____	he _____
she _____	you _____	I _____

Practice 3

First, underline the subject (always a pronoun) in each sentence below. Then circle the correct verb form. REMEMBER: If the subject of the sentence is *he, she,* or *it* (third person singular), the verb must end in *-s* or *-es* to agree with the subject.

1. According to Deborah Tannen, author of the book *You Just Don't Understand*, we sometimes (fail, fails) to understand how men and women communicate.

2. They often (differ, differs) in predictable ways.

3. In the book, she (describe, describes) the following argument between a husband and wife.

4. For the third time in twenty minutes, they (drive, drives) through the same neighborhood.

5. She (press, presses) him to stop and ask for directions.

6. He (insist, insists) on finding the way himself.

7. In the twilight, they (struggle, struggles) to read street signs.

8. To the woman, it (make, makes) no sense not to get help.

9. She (remind, reminds) him about their tardiness.

10. He (keep, keeps) driving.

11. According to Tannen, they (represent, represents) common male-female differences.

12. Like many other men, he (feel, feels) strong when finding his own way but weak when asking for help.

13. Like many women in this situation, she (misunderstand, misunderstands) his need for independence.

14. She just (get, gets) angry or (criticize, criticizes) him.

15. Stereotypes or truth? You (decide, decides) for yourself about the accuracy of Tannen's analysis.

PART B   *Troublesome Verb in the Present Tense: TO BE*

A few present tense verbs are formed in special ways. The most common of these verbs is *to be*.

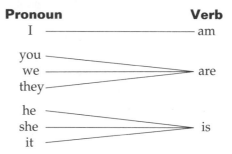

The chart also can be read like this:

Pronoun		Verb
I	———————————	am
you		
we		are
they		
he		
she		is
it		

Practice 4

Use the charts to fill in the present tense form of *to be* that agrees with the subject.

1. She _____is_____ a member of the Olympic softball team.

2. We _____ both carpenters, but he _____ more skilled than I.

3. We _____ sorry about your accident; you _____ certainly unlucky with rollerblades.

4. They _____ salmon fishermen.

5. He _____ a drummer in the firefighters' band.

6. I _____ a secret jazz singer.

7. Because she _____ a native of Morocco, she _____ able to speak both Arabic and French.

8. I _____ too nervous to sleep because we _____ having an accounting exam tomorrow.

9. So you _____ the one we have heard so much about!

10. It _____ freezing outside, but she _____ opening all the windows.

11. Of course we _____ excited about the rodeo.

12. Try this seafood soup; it _____ delicious.

13. They _____ interpreters at the United Nations.

14. I _____ sure that she _____ a marine biologist.

15. If it _____ sunny tomorrow, we _____ going hot air ballooning.

PART C *Troublesome Verb in the Present Tense: TO HAVE*

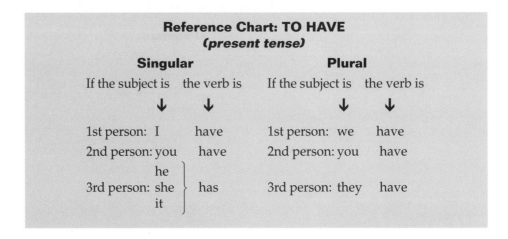

The chart also can be read like this:

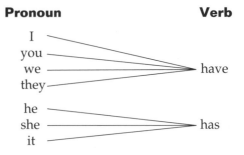

Practice 5

Fill in the present tense form of *to have* that agrees with the subject. Use the charts.

1. He _____ a cabin on Lake Superior.

2. You _____ a wonderful sense of style.

3. We _____ to taste these pickled mushrooms.

4. It _____ to be spring because the cherry trees _____ pink blossoms.

5. She _____ the questions, and he _____ the answers.

6. You _____ a suspicious look on your face, and I _____ to know why.

7. They _____ plans to build a fence, but we _____ plans to relax.

8. You _____ one ruby earring, and she _____ the other.

9. It _____ to be repaired, and I _____ just the person to do it for you.

10. If you _____ $50, they _____ an offer you can't refuse.

PART D   *Troublesome Verb in the Present Tense: TO DO (+ NOT)*

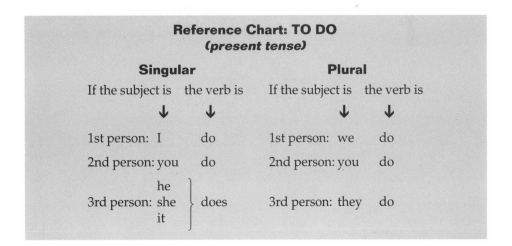

Reference Chart: TO DO
(present tense)

	Singular			**Plural**	
	If the subject is	the verb is		If the subject is	the verb is
	↓	↓		↓	↓
1st person:	I	do	1st person:	we	do
2nd person:	you	do	2nd person:	you	do
3rd person:	he she it	does	3rd person:	they	do

The chart also can be read like this:

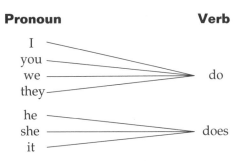

Pronoun	**Verb**
I you we they	do
he she it	does

Practice 6

Use the charts to fill in the correct present tense form of *to do*.

1. She always _____ well in math courses.

2. I always _____ badly under pressure.

3. It _____ matter if you forget to vote.

4. They most certainly _____ sell muscle shirts.

5. You _____ the nicest things for people!

6. If you _____ the dishes, I'll _____ the laundry.

7. He _____ seem sorry about forgetting your dog's birthday.

8. You sometimes _____ surprise me.

9. _____ they dance the tarantella?

10. _____ she want to be a welder?

To Do + Not

Once you know how to use *do* and *does*, you are ready for *don't* and *doesn't*.

do + not = don't
does + not = doesn't

Practice 7

In the Positive columns, fill in the correct form of *to do* (*do* or *does*) to agree with the pronoun. In the Negative columns, fill in the correct form of *to do* with the negative *not* (*don't* or *doesn't*).

Pronoun	Positive	Negative
1. he	_____	_____
2. we	_____	_____
3. I	_____	_____
4. they	_____	_____
5. she	_____	_____
6. they	_____	_____
7. it	_____	_____
8. you	_____	_____

Practice 8

Fill in either *doesn't* or *don't* in each blank.

1. If they _____ turn down that music, I'm going to scream.

2. It just _____ make sense.

3. You _____ have to reply in writing.

4. He _____ always lock his door at night.

5. We _____ mind the rain.

6. If she _____ stop calling collect, I _____ want to talk to her.

7. He _____ know the whole truth, and they _____ want to know.

8. They _____ want to miss *Larry King Live* tonight.

9. Although you _____ like biking five miles a day to work, it _____ do your health any harm.

10. When I _____ try, I _____ succeed.

Practice 9   Review

As you read this paragraph, fill in the correct present tense form of *be, have,* or *do* in each sentence. Make sure all your verbs agree with their subjects.

(1) He _____ the expertise of a James Bond or an Indiana Jones, but he _____ the real thing, not a movie hero performing fantasy stunts. (2) Right now, he _____ calm, even though he _____ ready to leap from the open door of a Navy aircraft. (3) On his back he _____ an oversized parachute capable of supporting both him and the extra hundred pounds of special equipment packed in his combat vest. (4) When he _____ hit the water, he _____ ready to face the real challenge: finding and defusing a bomb sixty feet under rough, murky seas. (5) He _____ a mission and a very tight time frame, and he _____ not want to let the enemy know he _____ there. (6) Swimming underwater in special scuba gear, he _____ not release any air bubbles to mark the water's surface. (7) Working in semidarkness, performing dangerous technical tasks, he quickly _____ the job. (8) However, unlike media heroes, he _____n't work alone. (9) He _____ a member of a highly trained team of Navy SEALs. (10) Among the most respected special forces in the world, they _____ commando divers ready for hazardous duty on sea, air, and land.

PART E — *Changing Subjects to Pronouns*

So far, you have worked on pronouns as subjects (*I, you, he, she, it, we, they*) and on how to make verbs agree with them. Often, however, the subject of a sentence is not a pronoun but a noun—like *dog, banjo, Ms. Callas, José and Robert, swimming* (as in *Swimming keeps me fit*).

To be sure that your verb agrees with your subject, *mentally* change the subject into a pronoun, and then select the correct form of the verb.

If the subject is	it can be changed to the pronoun
1. the speaker himself or herself	I
2. masculine and singular (*Bill, one man*)	he
3. feminine and singular (*Sondra, a woman*)	she
4. neither masculine nor feminine and singular (a thing or an action) (*this pen, love, running*)	it
5. a group that includes the speaker (I) (*the family and I*)	we
6. a group of persons or things not including the speaker (*Jake and Wanda, several pens*)	they
7. the person or persons spoken to	you

Practice 10

Change the subjects into pronouns. REMEMBER: If you add *I* to a group of people, the correct pronoun for the whole group is *we*; if you add *you* to a group, the correct pronoun for the whole group is *you*.

Possible Subject	Pronoun
EXAMPLE: Frank	*he*
1. a huge moose	_____
2. a calculator and a checkbook	_____
3. Sheila	_____
4. my buddies and I	_____
5. you and the other actors	_____
6. the silk scarf	_____
7. Frank and Ted	_____
8. her son	_____

9. their power drill   _____

10. scuba diving   _____

Practice 11   Review

Change each subject into a pronoun. Then circle the present tense verb that agrees with that subject. (Use the reference chart if you need to.)

EXAMPLES: Harry = _____*he*_____   Harry (whistle,(whistles).)

Sam and I = _____*we*_____   Sam and I (walk,)walks).

1. Camilla = _____   1. Camilla (own, owns) a horse farm.

2. Their concert = _____   2. Their concert (is, are) sold out.

3. You and Ron = _____   3. You and Ron (seem, seems) exhausted.

4. The men and I = _____   4. The men and I (repair, repairs) potholes.

5. This blender = _____   5. This blender (grate, grates) cheese.

6. This beach = _____   6. This beach (is, are) deserted.

7. Our printer = _____   7. Our printer (jam, jams) too often.

8. Folk dancing = _____   8. Folk dancing (is, are) our current passion.

9. The museum and garden = _____ 9. The museum and garden (is, are) open.

10. Aunt Lil and I = _____   10. Aunt Lil and I (like, likes) Swedish massages.

PART F   *Practice in Agreement*

Practice 12   Review

Circle the correct verb in each sentence, making sure it agrees with its subject.

Not Exactly Rocky Road

(1) Ben Cohen and Jerry Greenfield (is, are) famous. (2) Yet most people (do, does) not even know their last names. (3) Their friendly, unkempt faces (stares,

stare) at us every time we (tear, tears) the top from a pint of their sherbet or frozen yogurt. (4) Their ice cream business (run, runs) in a rather unusual way. (5) Of course, the company (has, have) to make a profit. (6) However, Ben and Jerry also (believe, believes) in having fun and in giving back to the community.

(7) One important goal (is, are) to make the factory in Vermont an enjoyable place to work. (8) Ben (call, calls) himself the firm's Minister of Joy. (9) He (lead, leads) a Joy Gang consisting of six employees. (10) Ben and this unusual group (roam, roams) the factory, acting goofy and making the daily grind more fun. (11) Urged on by the Joy Gang, employees (celebrate, celebrates) such little-known holidays as National Clash-Dressing Day. (12) On Clash Day, the company (award, awards) prizes like glow-in-the-dark rubber lobsters to the worker wearing the ugliest outfit. (13) The Joy Gang also (sponsor, sponsors) monthly events like delicious Italian dinners served to workers on the night shift.

(14) On a more serious note, the company (give, gives) each worker fifty hours off a year to volunteer in community programs. (15) For this time, the worker (receive, receives) full pay. (16) A loan fund (offer, offers) money to help employees start socially responsible businesses. (17) Other benefits (include, includes) profit sharing, maternity and paternity leave, free massages, and three pints of ice cream a day.

(18) Ben and Jerry (admit, admits) that they are not great managers. (19) A new, more traditional manager now (handle, handles) the business. (20) In fact, Unilever, a consumer-products giant, now (own, owns) the company. (21) As the original founders, however, Ben and Jerry still (love, loves) their jobs. (22) Every day, they (roar, roars) to work on their Harley-Davidsons.

Practice 13   Review

In each blank, write the *present tense* form of one of the verbs from this list. Your sentences can be funny; just make sure that each verb agrees with each subject.

talk	punch	tickle	drink
kiss	arrive	sing	dance

(1) Many famous people _____ at the party. (2) Tiger Woods _____ a baby. (3) Madonna and I _____ near the punchbowl, not far from the Vice President, who _____ with a small poodle. (4) Several rock stars _____ in one corner

of the room. (5) Then Eddie Murphy _____ , and everybody

goes home.

Practice 14   Review

The sentences that follow have singular subjects and verbs. To gain skill in verb agreement, rewrite each sentence, changing the subject from *singular* to *plural*. Then make sure the verb agrees with the new subject. Keep all verbs in the present tense.

EXAMPLE: The train stops at Cold Spring.

Rewrite: _____The trains stop at Cold Spring._____

1. The movie ticket costs too much.

   Rewrite: _____

2. The pipeline carries oil from Alaska.

   Rewrite: _____

3. A white horse grazes by the fence.

   Rewrite: _____

4. My brother knows American Sign Language.

   Rewrite: _____

5. The family needs good health insurance.

   Rewrite: _____

6. The backup singer wears green contact lenses.

   Rewrite: _____

7. My niece wants an iguana.

   Rewrite: _____

8. A wave laps softly against the dock.

   Rewrite: _____

Practice 15   Review

The sentences that follow have plural subjects and verbs. Rewrite each sentence, changing the subject from *plural* to *singular*. Then make sure the verb agrees with the new subject. Keep all verbs in the present tense.

1. My cousins raise sheep.

   Rewrite: _____

2. The engines roar loudly.

   Rewrite: _____

3. The students manage money wisely.

   Rewrite: _____

4. The inmates watch *America's Most Wanted*.

   Rewrite: _____

5. Overhead, seagulls ride on the wind.

   Rewrite: _____

6. Good card players know when to bluff.

   Rewrite: _____

7. On Saturday, the pharmacists stay late.

   Rewrite: _____

8. The jewels from Bangkok are on display.

   Rewrite: _____

Practice 16   Review

Rewrite this paragraph in the present tense by changing the verbs.

(1) Every day, a father whacked golf balls into a net in the family garage. (2) Every day, a six-month-old in a highchair watched his father intently. (3) When the baby started to walk, his parents gave him a short putter, which he dragged around. (4) When he was nine months old, he carefully picked up the putter. (5) He did an exact imitation of his father's little waggle, swung, and sent a ball perfectly into the net. (6) Thunderstruck, the father and mother realized that they had a genius. (7) From the age of eighteen months, the toddler practiced his pitch and putt strokes on a golf course. (8) At age three, Tiger Woods exclaimed on a TV show that he wanted to beat Jack Nicklaus some day. (9) He did that at age twenty-one, winning the Masters with the lowest score in tournament history. (10) At age twenty-four, he shattered U.S. Open records by a twelve under par and a fifteen-stroke victory, and he tied Nicklaus' record of the lowest score ever in a U.S. Open.

_____

_____

_____

_____

_____

_____

_____

_____

_____

_____

_____

PART G *Special Problems in Agreement*

So far, you have learned that if the subject of a sentence is third person singular (*he, she, it*) or a word that can be changed into *he, she,* or *it,* the verb takes *-s* or *-es* in the present tense.

In special cases, however, you will need to know more before you can make your verb agree with your subject.

Focusing on the Subject

> (1) A box of chocolates sits on the table.

- *What* sits on the table?
- Don't be confused by the prepositional phrase before the verb—*of chocolates.*
- Just one *box* sits on the table.
- *A box* is the subject. *A box* takes the third person singular verb—*sits.*

A box (of chocolates) sits on the table.
↓   ↓
subject   verb
(singular)   *(singular)*

> (2) The children in the park play for hours.

- *Who* play for hours?
- Don't be confused by the prepositional phrase before the verb—*in the park.*
- *The children* play for hours.
- *The children* is the subject. *The children* takes the third person plural verb—*play.*

The children (in the park) play for hours.
↓   ↓
subject   verb
(plural)   *(plural)*

> (3) The purpose of the exercises is to improve your spelling.

- *What* is to improve your spelling?
- Don't be confused by the prepositional phrase before the verb—*of the exercises.*
- *The purpose* is to improve your spelling.
- *The purpose* is the subject. *The purpose* takes the third person singular verb—*is.*

The purpose (of the exercises) is to improve your spelling.
↓   ↓
subject   verb
(singular)   *(singular)*

As you can see from these examples, sometimes what seems to be the subject is really not the subject. Prepositional phrases (groups of words beginning with *of, in, at,* and so on) *cannot* contain the subject of a sentence. One way to find the subject of a sentence that contains a prepositional phrase is to ask yourself *what makes sense as the subject*.

My friends from the old neighborhood often { visits / visit } me.

- Which makes sense as the subject of the sentence: *my friends* or *the old neighborhood?*

(a) My friends . . . visit me.

(b) The old neighborhood . . . visits me.

- Obviously, sentence (a) makes sense; it clearly expresses the intention of the writer.

Practice 17

Now try these sentences. Cross out any confusing prepositional phrases, and circle the correct verb.

1. The blue jays in my yard (squawk, squawks) loudly.

2. The traffic lights along Clark Street (blink, blinks) to a salsa beat.

3. The price of the repairs (seem, seems) high.

4. His popularity with teenagers (amaze, amazes) me.

5. The coffee stains on his résumé (show, shows) his carelessness.

6. The secret to success (is, are) often persistence.

7. The cause of many illnesses (is, are) poor diet.

8. The polar bear in the zoo (miss, misses) the Arctic.

9. My cousins from Kenya (run, runs) in marathons.

10. The laboratories on the fifth floor (has, have) new equipment.

Spotting Special Singular Subjects

Either of the students
Neither of the students
Each of the students   } seems happy.
One of the students
Every one of the students

- *Either, neither, each, one,* and *every one* are the real subjects of these sentences.

- *Either, neither, each, one,* and *every one* are special singular subjects. They always take a singular verb.

- REMEMBER: The subject is never part of a prepositional phrase, so *the students* cannot be the subject.

Practice 18

Circle the correct verb.

1. One of the forks (is, are) missing.

2. Each of my brothers (wear, wears) cinnamon after-shave lotion.

3. Each of us (carry, carries) a snakebite kit.

4. Neither of those excuses (sound, sounds) believable.

5. One of the taxi drivers (see, sees) us.

6. Either of the watches (cost, costs) about $30.

7. Neither of those cities (is, are) the capital of Brazil.

8. One of the butlers (commit, commits) the crime, but which one?

9. One of the desserts in front of you (do, does) not contain sugar.

10. Each of the cars (have, has) a CD player.

Practice 19

On separate paper, write five sentences using the special singular subjects. Make sure your sentences are in the present tense.

Using THERE to Begin a Sentence

> (1) *There* is a squirrel in the yard.
> (2) *There* are two squirrels in the yard.

- Although sentences sometimes begin with *there*, *there* cannot be the subject of a sentence.

- Usually, the subject *follows* the verb in sentences that begin with *there*.

To find the real subject (so you will know how to make the verb agree), mentally drop the *there* and rearrange the sentence to put the subject at the beginning.

(1) There is a squirrel in the yard.
becomes

A squirrel   *is* in the yard.
↓   ↓
subject   verb
(singular)   *(singular)*

(2) There are two squirrels in the yard.
becomes

Two squirrels   *are* in the yard.
↓   ↓
subject   verb
(plural)   *(plural)*

BE CAREFUL: Good writers avoid using *there* to begin a sentence. Whenever possible, they write more directly: *Two squirrels are in the yard.*

Practice 20

In each sentence, mentally drop the *there* and rearrange the sentence to put the subject at the beginning. Then circle the verb that agrees with the subject of the sentence.

1. There (is, are) a daycare center on campus.

2. There (is, are) a scarecrow near the barn.

3. There (is, are) two scarecrows near the barn.

4. There (is, are) one good reason to quit this job—my supervisor.

5. There (is, are) six customers ahead of you.

6. There (is, are) a water fountain in the lounge.

7. There (is, are) a house and a barn in the wheat field.

8. There (is, are) only two shopping days left before my birthday.

9. There (is, are) thousands of plant species in the rain forest.

10. There (is, are) a single blue egg in the nest over the kitchen door.

Practice 21

On a separate sheet of paper, rewrite each sentence in Practice 1 so that it does not begin with *there is* or *there are*. (You may add or change a word or two if you like.) Sentences (1) and (2) are done for you.

EXAMPLES: 1. A daycare center is on campus.

2. A scarecrow hangs near the barn.

Choosing the Correct Verb in Questions

(1) Where is Bob?
(2) Where are Bob and Lee?
(3) Why are they singing?
(4) Have you painted the hall yet?

● In questions, the subject usually *follows* the verb.

● In sentence (1), the subject is *Bob*. *Bob* takes the third person singular verb *is*.

● In sentence (2), the subject is *Bob and Lee*. *Bob and Lee* takes the third person plural verb *are*.

● What is the subject in sentence (3)? _____ What verb does it take? _____

● What is the subject in sentence (4)? _____ What verb does it take? _____

If you can't find the subject, mentally turn the question around:

> (1) Bob is . . .
> (2) Bob and Lee are . . .

Practice 22

Circle the correct verb.

1. Where (is, are) my leather bomber jacket?

2. (Have, Has) our waiter gone to lunch?

3. How (is, are) your children enjoying summer camp?

4. Who (is, are) those people on the fire escape?

5. Which (is, are) your day off?

6. Why (do, does) she want to buy another tractor?

7. (Have, Has) you considered taking a cruise next year?

8. Where (is, are) Don's income tax forms?

9. (Have, Has) the groundhog raided the zucchini patch today?

10. Well, what (do, does) you know about that?

Practice 23

On separate paper, write five questions of your own. Make sure that your questions are in the present tense and that the verbs agree with the subjects.

Using WHO, WHICH, and THAT as Relative Pronouns

When you use a relative pronoun—*who, which,* or *that*—to introduce a dependent idea, make sure you choose the correct verb.*

> (1) I know a woman *who* plays expert chess.

- Sentence (1) uses the singular verb *plays* because *who* relates or refers to *a woman* (singular).

> (2) Suede coats, *which* stain easily, should not be worn in the rain.

- Sentence (2) uses the plural verb *stain* because *which* relates to the subject *suede coats* (plural).

> (3) Computers *that* talk make me nervous.

- Sentence (3) uses the plural verb *talk* because *that* relates to what word?

_____

*For work on relative pronouns, see Chapter 18.

Practice 24

Write the word that the *who, which,* or *that* relates or refers to in the blank at the right; then circle the correct form of the verb.

EXAMPLE: I like people who (is, (are)) creative.   _people_

1. My office has a robot that (fetch, fetches)

   the mail.   _____

2. Never buy food in cans that (have, has)

   dented containers.   _____

3. My husband, who (take, takes) marvelous

   photographs, won the Nikon Prize.   _____

4. He likes women who (is, are) very ambitious.   _____

5. The old house, which (sit, sits) on a cliff

   above the sea, is called Balston Heights.   _____

6. Students who (love, loves) to read usually

   write well.   _____

7. I like a person who (think, thinks) for

   himself or herself.   _____

8. The only airline that (fly, flies) to

   Charlottesville is booked solid.   _____

9. People who (live, lives) in glass houses

   should invest in blinds.   _____

10. Most students want jobs that (challenge,

    challenges) them.   _____

Practice 25   Review

Proofread the following paragraph for a variety of verb agreement errors. First underline all present tense verbs. Then correct any errors above the lines.

(1) Many people who love exciting theater and talented actors admires Anna Deveare Smith. (2) She is well known for her thought-provoking one-woman shows. (3) Many of these dramas explores social conflicts in America and use just one actor. (4) Often, Smith herself brilliantly plays the roles of many different characters. (5) For example, one play, *Twilight: Los Angeles, 1992,* examine the Los Angeles riots and the beatings of Rodney King and Reginald Denny. (6)

Amazingly, Smith, who is African-American, bring to life all the people involved: white people, black people, Korean shopkeepers, angry rioters, and frightened citizens. (7) Through Smith, theatergoers understand a moment in history from many points of view. (8) How do she achieve this? (9) Once a shy and withdrawn child, Anna Deveare Smith now works to open her mind and heart to the experiences of others. (10) She believes that both successful acting and successful democracy requires us to grow in tolerance. (11) Besides writing plays, this talented woman appears occasionally in Hollywood films and teaches drama at Stanford University in Palo Alto, California.

Practice 26   Writing Assignment

In a group of three or four classmates, choose an area of the building or campus that contains some interesting action—the hallway, the cafeteria, or a playing field. Go there now and observe what you see, recording details and using verbs in the present tense. Choose as many good action verbs as you can. Keep observing and writing for ten minutes. Then head back to the classroom and write a first draft of a paragraph.

Next, exchange papers within your group. The reader should underline every verb, checking for verb agreement, and tell the writer what he or she liked about the writing and what could be improved.

✔ Chapter Highlights

- **A subject and a present tense verb must agree:**

    The light flickers. *(singular subject, singular verb)*

    The lights flicker. *(plural subject, plural verb)*

- **Only third person singular subjects** *(he, she, it)* **take verbs ending in** *-s* **or** *-es.*

- **Three troublesome present tense verbs are** *to be, to have,* **and** *to do.*

- **When a prepositional phrase comes between a subject and a verb, the verb must agree with the subject.**

    The *chairs* on the porch *are* painted white.

- **The subjects** *either, neither, each, one,* **and** *every one* **are always singular.**

    Neither of the mechanics *repairs* transmissions.

- **In a sentence beginning with** *there is* **or** *there are,* **the subject follows the verb.**

    There are three *oysters* on your plate.

- **In questions, the subject usually follows the verb.**

    Where are *Kimi and Fred?*

- **Relative pronouns** *(who, which,* **and** *that)* **refer to the word with which the verb must agree.**

    A *woman who* has children must manage time skillfully.

Chapter Review

Proofread this essay carefully for verb agreement. First, underline all present tense verbs. Then correct each verb agreement error.

Making Relationships Work

(1) Our partners sometimes cause us pain. (2) They criticize us, make unfair demands, and rejects us. (3) If one of these behaviors happen occasionally, we generally ignore it. (4) When it occurs often, we seek explanations for it.

(5) We usually blame our partner for these problems. (6) He is selfish, unfair, or inconsiderate. (7) She is immature, insecure, or depressed. (8) The hurtful behavior are a result of their poor communication skills or fear of expressing love.

(9) When we finishes our analyses, we want to share our conclusions with our partners. (10) We expect them to change after they finds out about all the things that is wrong with them. (11) To our surprise, our partners defend themselves. (12) Even worse, they tell us what is wrong with *us.* (13) Then each of us say things that are even more painful to the other. (14) Neither of us feel better. (15) Why does things go from bad to worse like that?

(16) The points in this essay comes from the book *Reconcilable Differences* by Andrew Christensen and Neil Jacobson. (17) These authors explore conflicts in relationships. (18) They stress that no person is like anyone else. (19) There is always differences. (20) However, differences are not defects. (21) Differences needs to be understood. (22) Once they are understood, they are much easier to accept. (23) Amazingly enough, change often happen by itself when people feel understood and accepted.

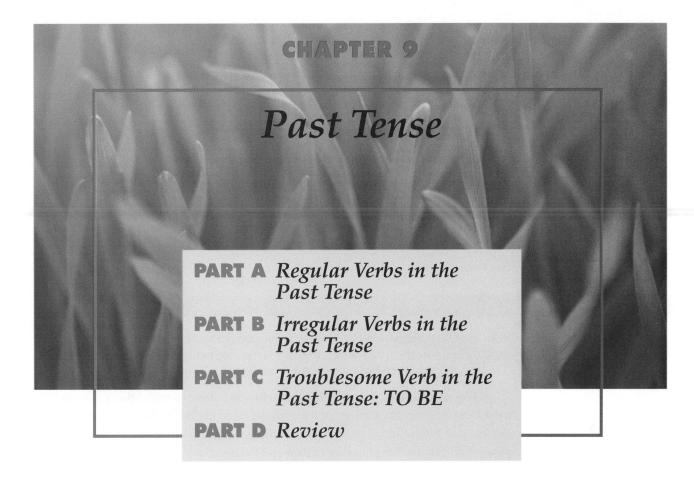

CHAPTER 9

Past Tense

PART A *Regular Verbs in the Past Tense*

PART B *Irregular Verbs in the Past Tense*

PART C *Troublesome Verb in the Past Tense: TO BE*

PART D *Review*

PART A   Regular Verbs in the Past Tense

Verbs in the past tense express actions that occurred in the past. The italicized words in the following sentences are verbs in the past tense.

> (1) They *noticed* a dent in the fender.
>
> (2) She *played* the guitar very well.
>
> (3) For years I *studied* yoga.

- What ending do all these verbs take? _____

- In general, what ending do you add to put a verb in the past tense?

  _____

- Verbs that add *-d* or *-ed* to form the past tense are called *regular verbs*.

Practice 1

Some of the verbs in these sentences are in the present tense; others are in the past tense. Circle the verb in each sentence. Write *present* in the column at the right if the verb is in the present tense; write *past* if the verb is in the past tense.

1. Ricardo stroked his beard. _____

2. Light travels 186,000 miles in a second. _____

3. They donate blood every six months.   _____

4. Magellan sailed around the world.   _____

5. The lake looks calm as glass.   _____

6. Yesterday, Rover buried many bones.   _____

7. Mount St. Helens erupted in 1980.   _____

8. That chemical plant pollutes our water.   _____

9. A robin nested in the mailbox.   _____

10. He owns two exercise bikes.   _____

Practice 2

Read the following paragraph, written in the present tense. The verbs are shown in italics. Then, on the blank lines, rewrite the entire paragraph in the past tense, changing every verb to the correct past tense form.*

(1) Again this year, Carnival *transforms* Rio de Janiero, Brazil, into one of the most fantastic four-day parties on the planet. (2) On the Friday before Ash Wednesday, thousands of visitors *pour* into the city. (3) They *watch* all-night parades and *admire* the glittering costumes. (4) They *cheer, sweat,* and *dance* the samba. (5) Of course, preparation *starts* long before. (6) For months, members of the samba schools (neighborhood dance clubs) *plan* their floats, *practice* samba steps, and *stay* up nights making their costumes. (7) Using bright fabrics, sequins, feathers, and chains, both men and women *create* spectacular outfits. (8) Each samba school *constructs* a float that *features* a smoke-breathing dragon or a spouting waterfall. (9) During Carnival, judges *rate* the schools on costumes, dancing, and floats, and then they *award* prizes. (10) Together, Brazilians and their visitors *share* great music, drink, food, fun, and the chance to go a little bit crazy.

_____

_____

_____

_____

_____

_____

_____

_____

_____

_____

_____

_____

_____
*If you have questions about spelling, see Chapter 31.

As you can see from this exercise, many verbs form the past tense by adding either *-d* or *-ed*.

Furthermore, in the past tense, agreement is not a problem, except for the verb *to be*. This is because verbs in the past tense have only one form, no matter what the subject is.

Practice 3

The verbs have been omitted from this paragraph. Choose verbs from the list below, and write a past tense form in each blank space. Do not use any of the verbs twice.

approach	wink	shriek	stay
rustle	cry	leap	cook
move	burn	chase	help
camp	arrive	climb	laugh

(1) Last December, Tom and I _____ overnight in Everglades National Park. (2) We _____ at sunset and _____ eggs and beans over a campfire. (3) Suddenly, the dry grass near us _____ , and a very large alligator _____ . (4) We _____ and _____ into the van, where we _____ all night.

Practice 4

Fill in the past tense of each verb.

1. In 1923, Luis Angel Firpo _____ (challenge) Jack Dempsey.

2. Firpo _____ (want) to be the new heavyweight champion of the world.

3. The two boxers _____ (battle) in the fiercest title bout ever.

4. Excitement _____ (fill) the air as 85,000 fans _____ (crowd) into New York City's Polo Grounds.

5. Scalpers _____ (charge) as much as $150 for a ticket.

6. From the opening bell, the fighters _____ (slug) it out.

7. Dempsey _____ (knock) Firpo down seven times and _____ (close) in to end the fight.

8. To everyone's surprise, Firpo _____ (unload) a powerful right-hand punch to Dempsey's jaw.

9. The champion _____ (sail) through the ropes and out of the ring.

10. Only his legs _____ (remain) in view as they _____ (twist) in the air.

11. The dazed Dempsey _____ (stagger) back into the ring and

    barely _____ (manage) to finish the round.

12. Dempsey _____ (open) the second round by quickly
    flooring Firpo twice.

13. Then the champ _____ (flatten) Firpo with a left to the jaw.

14. Bleeding, Firpo _____ (try) hard to get up, but

    he _____ (stiffen) and _____ (pass) out.

15. The whole match _____ (last) just three minutes and fifty-
    seven seconds.

PART B   *Irregular Verbs in the Past Tense*

Instead of adding -d or -ed, some verbs form the past tense in other ways.

> (1) He *threw* a knuckle ball.
> (2) She *gave* him a dollar.
> (3) He *rode* from his farm into the town.

- The italicized words in these sentences are also verbs in the past tense.

- Do these verbs form the past tense by adding -d or -ed? _____

- *Threw, gave,* and *rode* are the past tense of verbs that do not add -d or -ed to form
  the past tense.

- Verbs that do not add -d or -ed to form the past tense are called *irregular verbs*.

A chart listing common irregular verbs follows.

Reference Chart: Irregular Verbs

Simple Form	Past	Simple Form	Past
be	was, were	fall	fell
become	became	feed	fed
begin	began	feel	felt
blow	blew	fight	fought
break	broke	find	found
bring	brought	fly	flew
build	built	forget	forgot
burst	burst	forgive	forgave
buy	bought	freeze	froze
catch	caught	get	got
choose	chose	give	gave
come	came	go	went
cut	cut	grow	grew
dive	dove (dived)	have	had
do	did	hear	heard
draw	drew	hide	hid
drink	drank	hold	held
drive	drove	hurt	hurt
eat	ate	keep	kept

Reference Chart: Irregular Verbs (*continued*)

Simple Form	Past	Simple Form	Past
know	knew	shine	shone (shined)
lay	laid	shrink	shrank (shrunk)
lead	led	sing	sang
leave	left	sit	sat
let	let	sleep	slept
lie	lay	speak	spoke
lose	lost	spend	spent
make	made	spring	sprang
mean	meant	stand	stood
meet	met	steal	stole
pay	paid	strike	struck
put	put	swim	swam
quit	quit	swing	swung
read	read	take	took
ride	rode	teach	taught
ring	rang	tear	tore
rise	rose	tell	told
run	ran	think	thought
say	said	throw	threw
see	saw	understand	understood
seek	sought	wake	woke
sell	sold	wear	wore
send	sent	win	won
set	set	wind	wound
shake	shook	write	wrote

Learn the unfamiliar past tense forms by grouping together verbs that change from present tense to past tense in the same way. For example, some irregular verbs change *ow* in the present to *ew* in the past:

bl<u>ow</u>	bl<u>ew</u>	kn<u>ow</u>	kn<u>ew</u>
gr<u>ow</u>	gr<u>ew</u>	thr<u>ow</u>	thr<u>ew</u>

Another group changes from *i* in the present to *a* in the past:

beg<u>i</u>n	beg<u>a</u>n	s<u>i</u>ng	s<u>a</u>ng
dr<u>i</u>nk	dr<u>a</u>nk	spr<u>i</u>ng	spr<u>a</u>ng
r<u>i</u>ng	r<u>a</u>ng	sw<u>i</u>m	sw<u>a</u>m

As you write, refer to the chart. If you are unsure of the past tense form of a verb that is not in the chart, check a dictionary. For example, if you look up the verb *go* in the dictionary, you will find an entry like this:

go \ went \ gone \ going

The first word listed is used to form the *present* tense of the verb (I *go*, he *goes*, and so on). The second word is the *past* tense (I *went*, he *went*, and so on). The third word is the *past participle* (*gone*), and the last word is the *present participle* (*going*).

Some dictionaries list different forms only for irregular verbs. If no past tense is listed, you know that the verb is regular and that its past tense ends in *-d* or *-ed*.

Practice 5

Use the chart to fill in the correct form of the verb in the past tense.

1. Beryl Markham _____ (grow) up in Kenya, East Africa.

2. As a child, this adventurer _____ (go) hunting with African tribesmen.

3. Once, while a lion attacked her, she _____ (lie) still, thus saving her own life.

4. At age seventeen, she _____ (seek) a license to train horses, becoming the first woman trainer in Kenya.

5. Her friend Tom Black _____ (teach) her how to fly a small plane, the *D. H. Gipsy Moth.*

6. By her late twenties, she _____ (be) a licensed pilot.

7. As Africa's first female bush pilot, Markham regularly

    _____ (fly) across East Africa, carrying supplies, mail, and passengers.

8. In 1936, she _____ (make) a solo flight across the Atlantic Ocean.

9. Despite poor flying conditions, fatigue, and low fuel, she

    _____ (keep) her plane in the air for more than twenty hours.

10. Markham _____ (set) a record as the first woman to fly alone nonstop from England to Nova Scotia.

11. In 1942, she _____ (write) *West with the Night,* a book about her thrilling life.

12. Reprinted in 1983, this book _____ (become) a great success.

Practice 6

Use the chart to fill in the correct past tense form of each verb.

(1) Joe _____ (begin) his job search in an organized way.

(2) He _____ (think) carefully about his interests and abilities.

(3) He _____ (spend) time in the library and

_____ (read) books like *What Color Is Your Parachute?* and

Job-Hunting on the Internet. (4) He _____ (speak) to people

with jobs that _____ (have) special appeal for him. (5) After he

_____ (understand) his own skills and goals, he

_____ (draw) up a straightforward, one-page résumé. (6) His

clear objectives statement _____ (lay) a strong foundation that

_____ (tell) prospective employers about his job preferences.
(7) After listing his educational experience, he _____ (give) his
past employment, with his most recent job experience first. (8) Rather than
writing a boring description of each job, he _____ (take) the
opportunity to briefly explain his own contribution to the company. (9) For
references, he _____ (choose) four people who
_____ (know) him well. (10) He _____
(send) his résumé to his references and _____ (speak) to each
of them about his hopes and dreams. (11) Finally, Joe _____
(feel) ready to answer newspaper ads, search for jobs online, and explore every
lead he _____ (get). (12) That night at a family barbecue, however, his Uncle George _____ (come) up to him with the perfect job offer. (13) Hamlet's words _____ (ring) in Joe's head:
"The readiness is all." (14) Since the offer _____ (be) a result of
his hard work and not dumb luck, Joe _____ (forgive) his
uncle with shouts of joy.

Practice 7

Look over the list of irregular verbs on pages 130 and 131. Pick out the ten verbs that
give you the most trouble, and list them here.

Simple	Past	Simple	Past
_____	_____	_____	_____
_____	_____	_____	_____
_____	_____	_____	_____
_____	_____	_____	_____
_____	_____	_____	_____

Now, on a separate sheet of paper, write one paragraph using *all ten* verbs. Your
paragraph may be humorous; just make sure your verbs are correct.

PART C Troublesome Verb in the Past Tense: TO BE

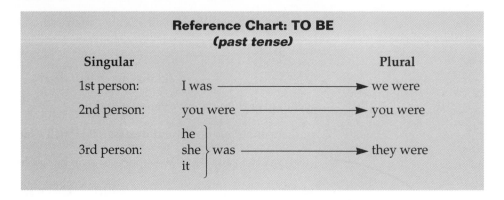

Reference Chart: TO BE
(past tense)

	Singular		Plural
1st person:	I was	→	we were
2nd person:	you were	→	you were
3rd person:	he she it } was	→	they were

● Note that the first and third person singular forms are the same—*was*.

Practice 8

In each sentence, circle the correct past tense of the verb *to be*—either *was* or *were*.

1. Our instructor (was, were) a pilot and skydiver.
2. You always (was, were) a good friend.
3. Georgia O'Keeffe (was, were) a great twentieth-century American painter.
4. Why (was, were) they an hour early for the party?
5. Carlos Santana (was, were) a big Grammy Award winner in 2000.
6. She (was, were) hungry, but they (was, were) famished.
7. The president and the first lady (was, were) both here.
8. I (was, were) seven when my sister (was, were) born.
9. Carmen (was, were) a Republican, but her cousins (was, were) Democrats.
10. Some people say that Greg Louganis (was, were) the world's greatest diver.
11. The bride and groom (was, were) present, but where (was, were) the ring?
12. (Was, Were) you seasick on your new houseboat?
13. Either they (was, were) late, or she (was, were) early.
14. Who (was, were) the woman we saw you with last night?
15. At this time last year, Sarni and I (was, were) in Egypt.

To Be + Not

Be careful of verb agreement if you use the past tense of *to be* with *not* as a contraction.

was + not = wasn't

were + not = weren't

Practice 9

In each sentence, fill in the blank with either *wasn't* or *weren't*.

1. The printer cartridges _____ on sale.

2. That papaya _____ cheap.

3. He _____ happy about the opening of the nuclear power plant.

4. _____ you once an actress?

5. She _____ bored, was she?

6. This fireplace _____ built properly.

7. When I saw I saw Bonnie, she and Charles _____ dating.

8. The parents _____ willing to tolerate drug dealers near the school.

9. That _____ the point!

10. My pet lobster _____ in the aquarium.

11. Three of the paintings _____ on exhibit.

12. That history quiz _____ so bad.

13. He and I liked each other, but we _____ able to agree about anything.

14. I _____ sure that he knew how to swim.

15. Many young couples _____ able to afford homes.

PART D   *Review*

Practice 10   Review

Read the following paragraph for meaning. Then write a different past tense verb in every blank.

(1) In 1861, a French naturalist _____ through a dense jungle of Cambodia in Southeast Asia. (2) He _____ to a clearing and _____ across the treetops. (3) He _____ in amazement. (4) Five enormous towers _____ above him. (5) With a pounding heart, he _____ to the most gorgeous temple imaginable. (6) He _____ 250 feet to the top of the highest tower. (7) A huge abandoned city _____ for miles all

around him. (8) Carvings of gods and goddesses _____ the

palaces and monuments. (9) Unlike the ruins of Greece and Rome, every stone in

these buildings _____ in place. (10) Local people

_____ this marvelous lost city Angkor. (11) Five hundred

years before, it had been the largest city in Asia. (12) Then for unknown reasons,

its entire population _____ .

Practice 11   Review

Rewrite this paragraph, changing the verbs to the past tense.*

(1) Above the office where I work is a karate studio. (2) Every day as I go through my files, make out invoices, and write letters, I hear loud shrieks and crashes from the studio above me. (3) All day long, the walls tremble, the ceiling shakes, and little pieces of plaster fall like snow onto my desk. (4) Sometimes, the noise does not bother me; at other times, I wear earplugs. (5) If I am in a very bad mood, I stand on my desk and pound out reggae rhythms on the ceiling with my shoe. (6) However, I do appreciate one thing. (7) The job teaches me to concentrate, no matter what.

_____

_____

_____

_____

_____

_____

_____

Practice 12   Writing Assignment

With three or four classmates, invent a group fairy tale. Take five minutes to decide on a subject for your story. On a clean sheet of paper, the first student should write the first sentence—in the past tense, of course. Use vivid action verbs. Each student should write a sentence in turn until the fairy tale is finished.

Have a group member read your story aloud. As you listen, make sure the verbs are correct. Should any verbs be replaced with livelier ones?

---

*See also Chapter 24, "Consistent Tense," for more practice.

✔ Chapter Highlights

- **Regular verbs add *-d* or *-ed* in the past tense:**

  We *decided*.

  The frog *jumped*.

  He *outfoxed* the fox.

- **Irregular verbs in the past tense change in irregular ways:**

  We *took* a marketing course.

  Owen *ran* fast.

  Jan *brought* pineapples.

- ***To be* is the only verb that takes more than one form in the past tense:**

I was	we were
you were	you were
he she it } was	they were

Chapter Review

Fill in the past tense form of each verb in parentheses. Some verbs are regular; others are irregular.

Scientist and Hero

(1) Marie Curie _____ (lead) a heroic life. (2) Honored as one of the most brilliant scientists of the twentieth century, she also _____ (triumph) over great hardship and loss.

(3) Born in Poland in 1867, Marie Curie _____ (begin) life as the daughter of a poor chemistry professor. (4) While a young woman, she _____ (postpone) her own studies and _____ (finance) her older sister's medical education with the money she _____ (earn) as a governess. (5) Then Curie's turn _____ (come). (6) She _____ (move) to Paris in 1891 and _____ (become) the first woman to enroll in the Sorbonne, the greatest university in France. (7) For three years, she _____ (study) hard and _____ (live) in poverty. (8) Her work _____ (pay) off. (9) The young scholar _____ (graduate) first in her class with a degree in physical

science. (10) One year later, she _____ (complete) another degree, in mathematics.

(11) The eleven years from 1895 to 1906 _____ (be) the happiest of her life. (12) She _____ (marry) Pierre Curie, a well-known scientist. (13) The devoted couple _____ (raise) two daughters and _____ (work) together every day on their research in radiation. (14) In 1898, Madame Curie _____ (find) two new radioactive elements. (15) One _____ (be) radium. (16) The other she _____ (call) polonium, after her native land. (17) In 1903, the Curies _____ (share) the Nobel Prize in physics. (18) When the French Legion of Honor _____ (offer) Pierre Curie membership, he _____ (refuse) it because his wife _____ (be) left out.

(19) A truck _____ (strike) and _____ (kill) Pierre Curie in 1906. (20) This bitter blow _____ (drive) Madame Curie further into her work. (21) She _____ (step) into Pierre Curie's professorship to become the first woman teacher at the Sorbonne. (22) Then, in 1911, she _____ (achieve) a second Nobel Prize, this one in chemistry.

(23) During World War I, the world-famous doctor _____ (risk) her life driving an ambulance and treating soldiers at the battlefront. (24) Later, she _____ (establish) research centers in Paris and Warsaw, _____ (lecture) in many countries, and _____ (continue) her studies. (25) Madame Curie _____ (die) in 1934 of cancer, caused by years of exposure to radioactivity.

© 2001 Houghton Mifflin Company

CHAPTER 10

The Past Participle in Action

PART A *Defining the Past Participle*

Every verb has one form that can be combined with helping verbs like *has* and *have* to make verbs of more than one word. This form is called the *past participle*.

(1) She has solved the problem.
(2) I have solved the problem.
(3) He had solved the problem already.

- Each of these sentences contains a two-part verb. Circle the first part, or *helping verb,* in each sentence, and write each helping verb in the blanks that follow:

  (1) _____

  (2) _____

  (3) _____

- Underline the second part, or *main verb,* in each sentence. This word, a form of

  the verb *to solve,* is the same in all three. Write it here: _____

- *Solved* is the past participle of *to solve.*

The past participle never changes, no matter what the subject is, no matter what the helping verb is.

PART B — *Past Participles of Regular Verbs*

Fill in the past participle in each series below:

Present Tense	Past Tense	Helping Verb + Past Participle
(1) Beth dances.	(1) Beth danced.	(1) Beth has _____.
(2) They decide.	(2) They decided.	(2) They have _____.
(3) He jumps.	(3) He jumped.	(3) He has _____.

- Are the verbs *to dance, to decide,* and *to jump* regular or irregular?

  _____ How do you know? _____

- What ending does each verb take in the past tense? _____

- Remember that any verb that forms its past tense by adding *-d* or *-ed* is a *regular* verb. What past participle ending does each verb take?

  _____

The past participle forms of regular verbs look exactly like the past tense forms. Both end in *-d* or *-ed*.

Practice 1

The first sentence in each of these pairs contains a one-word verb in the past tense. Fill in the past participle of the same verb in the blank in the second sentence.

EXAMPLE: She designed jewelry all her life.

She has _____designed_____ jewelry all her life.

1. Several students worked in the maternity ward.

   Several students have _____ in the maternity ward.

2. The pot of soup boiled over.

   The pot of soup has _____ over.

3. The chick hatched.

   The chick has _____.

4. We congratulated Jorgé.

   We have _____ Jorgé.

5. Nelson always studied in the bathtub.

   Nelson has always _____ in the bathtub.

6. Many climbers scaled this mountain.

   Many climbers have _____ this mountain.

7. The landlord asked for a rent increase.

   The landlord has _____ for a rent increase.

8. Sylvia located her long-lost cousin in New Jersey.

   Sylvia has _____ her long-lost cousin in New Jersey.

9. The satellite circled Jupiter.

   The satellite has _____ Jupiter.

10. They signed petitions to save the seals.

    They have _____ petitions to save the seals.

Practice 2

Write the missing two-part verb in each of the following sentences. Use the helping verb *has* or *have* and the past participle of the verb written in parentheses.

EXAMPLE: ____Have____ you ever _____wished_____ (to wish) for a new name?

1. Some of us _____ _____ (to want) new names at one time or another.

2. Many famous people _____ _____ (to fulfill) that desire.

3. Some _____ _____ (to use) only their first names.

4. Madonna Louise Ciccone _____ _____ (to drop) everything but Madonna.

5. Cherilyn LaPiere _____ _____ (to shorten) her name to Cher.

6. Roseann O'Donnell _____ _____ (to preserve) her last name but is best known as Rosie, the TV talk-show host.

7. Other celebrities _____ _____ (to retain) their first names and taken new last names.

8. Winona Horowitz _____ _____ (to convert) her last name to Ryder.

9. Steveland Judkinds _____ _____ (to turn) into Stevie Wonder.

10. Still others _____ _____ (to replace) their names altogether.

11. For many years, Caryn Johnson _____ _____ (to call) herself Whoopi Goldberg.

12. Carlos Irwin Estevez _____ _____ (to transform) himself into Charlie Sheen.

13. Annie Mae Bullock _____ _____ (to rename) herself Tina Turner.

14. Gordon Matthew Sumner _____ _____ (to change) into Sting.

15. What new name would you _____ _____ (to pick) for yourself?

PART C   *Past Participles of Irregular Verbs*

Present Tense	Past Tense	Helping Verb + Past Participle
(1) He sees.	(1) He saw.	(1) He has seen.
(2) I take vitamins.	(2) I took vitamins.	(2) I have taken vitamins.
(3) We sing.	(3) We sang.	(3) We have sung.

- Are the verbs *to see*, *to take*, and *to sing* regular or irregular? _____

- Like all irregular verbs, *to see*, *to take*, and *to sing* do not add *-d* or *-ed* to show past tense.

- Most irregular verbs in the past tense are also irregular in the past participle— like *seen*, *taken*, and *sung*.

- Remember that past participles must be used with helping verbs.*

Because irregular verbs change their spelling in irregular ways, there are no easy rules to explain these changes. Here is a list of some common irregular verbs.

---

*For work on incomplete verbs, see Chapter 7, Part B.

Reference Chart: Irregular Verbs

Simple Form	Past	Past Participle
be	was, were	been
become	became	become
begin	began	begun
blow	blew	blown
break	broke	broken
bring	brought	brought
build	built	built
burst	burst	burst
buy	bought	bought
catch	caught	caught
choose	chose	chosen
come	came	come
cut	cut	cut
dive	dove (dived)	dived
do	did	done
draw	drew	drawn
drink	drank	drunk
drive	drove	driven
eat	ate	eaten
fall	fell	fallen
feed	fed	fed
feel	felt	felt
fight	fought	fought
find	found	found
fly	flew	flown
forget	forgot	forgotten
forgive	forgave	forgiven
freeze	froze	frozen
get	got	gotten (got)
give	gave	given
go	went	gone
grow	grew	grown
have	had	had
hear	heard	heard
hide	hid	hidden
hold	held	held

Reference Chart: Irregular Verbs *(continued)*

Simple Form	Past	Past Participle
hurt	hurt	hurt
keep	kept	kept
know	knew	known
lay	laid	laid
lead	led	led
leave	left	left
let	let	let
lie	lay	lain
lose	lost	lost
make	made	made
mean	meant	meant
meet	met	met
pay	paid	paid
put	put	put
quit	quit	quit
read	read	read
ride	rode	ridden
ring	rang	rung
rise	rose	risen
run	ran	run
say	said	said
see	saw	seen
seek	sought	sought
sell	sold	sold
send	sent	sent
set	set	set
shake	shook	shaken
shine	shone (shined)	shone (shined)
shrink	shrank (shrunk)	shrunk
sing	sang	sung
sit	sat	sat
sleep	slept	slept
speak	spoke	spoken
spend	spent	spent
spring	sprang	sprung

Reference Chart: Irregular Verbs (*continued*)

Simple Form	Past	Past Participle
stand	stood	stood
steal	stole	stolen
strike	struck	struck
swim	swam	swum
swing	swung	swung
take	took	taken
teach	taught	taught
tear	tore	torn
tell	told	told
think	thought	thought
throw	threw	thrown
understand	understood	understood
wake	woke (waked)	woken (waked)
wear	wore	worn
win	won	won
wind	wound	wound
write	wrote	written

You already know many of these past participle forms. One way to learn the unfamiliar ones is to group together verbs that change from the present tense to the past tense to the past participle in the same way. For example, some irregular verbs change from *ow* in the present to *ew* in the past to *own* in the past participle.

bl_ow_	bl_ew_	bl_own_
gr_ow_	gr_ew_	gr_own_
kn_ow_	kn_ew_	kn_own_
thr_ow_	thr_ew_	thr_own_

Another group changes from *i* in the present to *a* in the past to *u* in the past participle:

beg_i_n	beg_a_n	beg_u_n
dr_i_nk	dr_a_nk	dr_u_nk
r_i_ng	r_a_ng	r_u_ng
s_i_ng	s_a_ng	s_u_ng
spr_i_ng	spr_a_ng	spr_u_ng
sw_i_m	sw_a_m	sw_u_m

As you write, refer to the chart. If you are unsure of the past participle form of a verb that is not on the chart, check a dictionary. For example, if you look up the verb *see* in the dictionary, you will find an entry like this:

see \ saw \ seen \ seeing

The first word listed is the present tense form of the verb (*I see, she sees,* and so on). The second word listed is the past tense form (*I saw, she saw,* and so on). The third word is the past participle form (*I have seen, she has seen,* and so on), and the last word is the present participle form.

Some dictionaries list different forms only for irregular verbs. If no past tense or past participle form is listed, you know that the verb is regular and that its past participle ends in *-d* or *-ed*.

Practice 3

The first sentence in each pair contains an irregular verb in the past tense. Fill in *has* or *have* plus the past participle of the same verb to complete the second sentence.

EXAMPLE: I ate too much.

I ___have___ _____eaten_____ too much.

1. The river rose over its banks.

   The river _____ _____ over its banks.

2. She sold her 1956 Buick.

   She _____ _____ her 1956 Buick.

3. For years, we sang in a barbershop quartet.

   For years, we _____ _____ in a barbershop quartet.

4. Crime rates fell recently.

   Crime rates _____ _____ recently.

5. Ralph gave me a red satin bowling jacket.

   Ralph _____ _____ me a red satin bowling jacket.

6. They thought carefully about the problem.

   They _____ _____ carefully about the problem.

7. I kept all your love letters.

   I _____ _____ all your love letters.

8. The Joneses forgot to confirm the reservation.

   The Joneses _____ _____ to confirm the reservation.

9. The pond froze solid.

   The pond _____ _____ solid.

10. The children knew about those caves.

    The children _____ _____ about those caves.

Practice 4

Now you will be given only the first sentence with its one-word verb in the past tense. Rewrite the entire sentence, changing the verb to a two-word verb: *has* or *have* plus the past participle of the main verb.

EXAMPLE: He took his credit cards with him.

He has taken his credit cards with him.

1. They brought their Great Dane to the party.

   _____

2. T. J. drove a city bus for two years.

   _____

3. She chose a van Gogh poster for the hallway.

   _____

4. I saw a white fox near the barn.

   _____

5. A tornado tore through the shopping center.

   _____

6. Margo became more self-confident.

   _____

7. Councilman Gomez ran a fair campaign.

   _____

8. The old barn stood there for years.

   _____

9. Sam read about the islands of Fiji.

   _____

10. Our conversations were very helpful.

   _____

Practice 5   Review

For each verb in the chart that follows, fill in the present tense (third person singular form), the past tense, and the past participle. BE CAREFUL: Some of the verbs are regular, and some are irregular.

Simple	Present Tense (he, she, it)	Past Tense	Past Participle
know	knows	knew	known
catch			

Simple	Present Tense (he, she, it)	Past Tense	Past Participle
stop			
break			
reach			
bring			
fly			
fall			
feel			
take			
go			
see			
do			
buy			
make			
answer			
hold			
say			

Practice 6   Review

Complete each sentence by filling in the helping verb *has* or *have* and the past participle of the verb in parentheses. Some verbs are regular, and some are irregular.

EXAMPLES: Millions _____have_____ _____heard_____ (hear) her sing.

She _____has_____ _____used_____ (use) words and music to connect with others.

Gloria Estefan

(1) Singer Gloria Estefan _____ _____ (inspire) millions of fans. (2) Since she joined the Miami Sound Machine in 1975, her albums _____ _____ (sell) millions of copies, and rousing songs like "Rhythm of the Night" _____ _____ (take) their place in the memory banks of a generation. (3) For more than twenty years, Estefan and her husband, Emilio, _____ _____ (be) marriage partners as well as business partners.

(4) Yet Estefan _____ _____ (endure) many hardships. (5) Born in Cuba in 1957, she _____ _____ (see) her father imprisoned for political activities, and she _____ _____ (know) poverty. (6) After fleeing with her family to Miami, she often stayed home to care for her sister and her dying father while her mother worked. (7) Ever since those early years, however, Estefan _____ _____ (find) strength in music—in singing and playing her guitar.

(8) Her talent _____ _____ (turn) misfortune into real fortune. (9) She and her husband _____ _____ (become) rich in friends as well as in material things. (10) But this is not a fairy tale: A 1990 bus tour accident broke Estefan's back, and she _____ _____ (suffer) through pain, four hundred stitches, and two metal rods near her spine. (11) Her song "Coming Out of the Dark" captures the spiritual power she _____ _____ (rely) on all her life.

(12) Gloria Estefan _____ _____ (raise) money for hurricane victims and _____ _____ (volunteer) her time to publicize the dangers of jet skis (after a young man died racing a jet ski into her boat). (13) She _____ _____ (win) two Grammies, one for best Tropical Latin album, and she _____ _____ (write) a song for the Olympics, "Reach."

Practice 7   Review

Now check your work in the preceding exercises, or have it checked. Do you see any patterns in your errors? Do you tend to miss regular or irregular verbs? To help yourself learn, copy all four forms of each verb that you missed into your notebook in a chart like the one on the next page. Use the chart to study.

Personal Review Chart

Simple	Present Tense (he, she, it)	Past Tense	Past Participle
go	goes	went	gone

PART D *Using the Present Perfect Tense*

The *present perfect tense* is composed of the present tense of *to have (has* or *have)* plus the past participle.

Present Perfect Tense

Singular

I *have* spoken

you *have* spoken

he
she } *has* spoken
it

Plural

we *have* spoken

you *have* spoken

they *have* spoken

Let us see how this tense is used.

---

(1) They *sang* together last Saturday.

(2) They *have sung* together for three years now.

- In sentence (1), the past tense verb *sang* tells us that they sang together on one occasion, Saturday, but are no longer singing together. The action began and ended in the past.

- In sentence (2), the present perfect verb *have sung* tells us something entirely different: that they have sung together in the past and *are still singing together now*.

(3) Janet *sat* on the beach for three hours.

(4) Valerie *has* just *sat* on the beach for three hours.

- Which woman is probably still sunburned? _____

- In sentence (3), Janet's action began and ended at some time in the past. Perhaps it was ten years ago that she sat on the beach.

- In (4), the present perfect verb *has sat* implies that, although the action occurred in the past, it *has just happened,* and Valerie had better put some lotion on her sunburn *now.*

- Notice how the word *just* emphasizes that the action occurred very recently.

Use the *present perfect tense* **to show either (1) that an action began in the past and has continued until now or (2) that an action has just happened.**

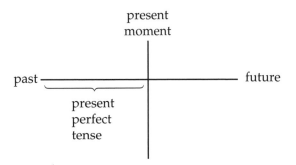

In writing about an action that began in the past and is still continuing, you will often use time words like *for* and *since.*

(5) We have watched the fireworks *for* three hours.

(6) John has sung in the choir *since* 1980.

In writing about an action that has just happened, you will often use words like *just, recently, already,* and *yet.*

(7) I have *just* finished the novel.

(8) They have *already* gone to the party.

Practice 8

Paying close attention to meaning, circle the verb that best completes each sentence.

EXAMPLES: In recent years, many unusual museums (appeared, have appeared). For example, the International Museum of Cartoon Art first (opened, has opened) in 1974 in Greenwich, Connecticut.

1. The idea for the museum (came, has come) from cartoonist Mort Walker, the creator of "Beetle Bailey."

2. In the beginning, his museum (had, has had) only a small collection of original cartoons.

3. However, since 1974, the collection (grew, has grown) to include valuable first drawings of Mickey Mouse, Batman, Flash Gordon, Road Runner, Dumbo, Popeye, Garfield, and many others.

4. In 1995, the museum (moved, has moved) to a beautiful new building in Boca Raton, Florida.

5. For the past several years, visitors (laughed, have laughed) at classic comic books, cartoon movies, and the interactive Laugh Center.

6. Another interesting museum, the Bata Shoe Museum in Toronto, Canada, (gained, has gained) worldwide attention in 1995.

7. For years now, the Bata (held, has held) the world's largest collection of shoes.

8. In 1995, the museum (moved, has moved) its huge shoe collection into a new building shaped like a shoebox!

9. On a recent day, Elvis Presley's blue and white loafers, John Lennon's Beatle boot, and Queen Victoria's ivory satin flats (seemed, have seemed) to be the favorite items on view.

10. However, several history students never (got, have gotten) past the Bata's world-famous exhibit of Native American footwear.

Practice 9

Fill in either the *past* tense or the *present perfect* tense form of each verb in parentheses.

(1) For the past few years, Camille Norris _____ (to spend) too much money on clothes, restaurant meals, and gifts for others. (2) Six months ago, she _____ (to decide) that enough was enough. (3) She _____ (to make) a list of her credit-card debts and _____ (to find) the debt with the highest interest rate. (4) Every month since then, she _____ (to focus) on paying off that charge card. (5) She _____ (to pay) only the minimum amount due on the rest of her bills. (6) When she _____ (to review) her finances last week, however she _____ (to be) still unsatisfied. (7) She _____ (to want) faster results. (8) Unsure of the next step, she _____ (to telephone) Consumer Credit Counseling Services and _____ (to e-mail) Money Management by Mail for free help with her debt problems. (9) Since then, she _____ (to feel) much better. (10) She even _____ (to have) no compulsion to buy more "stuff"!

PART E	*Using the Past Perfect Tense*

The *past perfect tense* is composed of the past tense of *to have (had)* plus the past participle.

Past Perfect Tense	
Singular	**Plural**
I *had* spoken	we *had* spoken
you *had* spoken	you *had* spoken
he she } *had* spoken it	they *had* spoken

Let us see how this tense is used.

> (1) Because Bob *had broken* his leg, he *wore* a cast for six months.

● The actions in both parts of this sentence occurred entirely in the past, but one occurred before the other.

● At some time in the past, Bob *wore* (past tense) a cast on the leg that he *had broken* (past perfect tense) at some time before that.

When you are writing in the past tense, use the past perfect tense to show that something happened at an even earlier time.

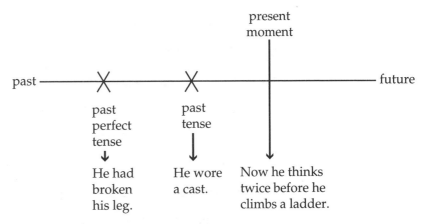

As a general rule, the present perfect tense is used in relation to the present tense, and the past perfect tense is used in relation to the past tense. Read the following pairs of sentences, and note the time relation.

> (2) Sid *says* (present) he *has found* (present perfect) a good job.
> (3) Sid *said* (past) he *had found* (past perfect) a good job.
> (4) Grace *tells* (present) us she *has won* (present perfect) first prize.
> (5) Grace *told* (past) us she *had won* (past perfect) first prize.

Practice 10

Choose either the present perfect or the past perfect tense of the verb in parentheses to complete each sentence. Match present perfect tense with present tense and past perfect tense with past tense.

1. The newspaper reports that the dictator _____ _____ (to leave) the country.

2. The newspaper reported that the dictator _____ _____ (to leave) the country.

3. I plan to buy a red convertible; I _____ _____ (to want) a convertible for three years now.

4. Last year, I bought a red convertible; I _____ _____ (to want) a convertible for three years before that.

5. Mel _____ _____ (to choose) the steepest trail up the mountain; he was thoroughly worn out.

6. Mel _____ _____ (to choose) the steepest trail up the mountain; he is thoroughly worn out.

7. I am worried about my cat; she _____ _____ (to drink) bubble bath.

8. I was worried about my cat; she _____ _____ (to drink) bubble bath.

9. Sam told us that he _____ _____ (to decide) to major in restaurant management.

10. Sam tells us that he _____ _____ (to decide) to major in restaurant management.

PART F   *Using the Passive Voice*

So far in this chapter, you have combined the past participle with forms of *to have*. But the past participle also can be used with forms of *to be (am, is, are, was, were)*.

> (1) That jam was made by Aunt Clara.

- The subject of the sentence is *that jam*. The verb has two parts: the helping verb *was* and the past participle *made*.

- Note that the subject, *that jam*, does not act but is acted on by the verb. *By Aunt Clara* tells us who performed the action.

That jam *was made* by Aunt Clara.

When the subject is acted on or receives the action, it is passive, and the verb *(to be + past participle)* **is in the** *passive voice.*

Now compare the passive voice with the active voice in these pairs of sentences:

> (2) **Passive voice:** Free gifts are given by the bank.
>
> (3) **Active voice:** The bank gives free gifts.
>
> (4) **Passive voice:** We were photographed by a tourist.
>
> (5) **Active voice:** _____

- In sentence (2), the subject, *free gifts,* is passive; it receives the action. In sentence (3), *the bank* is active; it performs the action.

- Note the difference between the passive verb *are given* and the active verb *gives*.

- However, the tense of both sentences is the same. The passive verb *are given* is in the present tense, and so is the active verb *gives*.

- Rewrite sentence (4) in the active voice. Be sure to keep the same verb tense in the new sentence.

Write in the passive voice only when you want to emphasize the receiver of the action rather than the doer. Usually, however, write in the active voice because sentences in the active voice are livelier and more direct.

Practice 11

Underline the verb in each sentence. In the blank at the right, write *A* if the verb is written in the active voice and *P* if the verb is in the passive voice.

EXAMPLE: Nelson Mandela is <u>respected</u> worldwide as a leader.   _P_

1. Nelson Mandela was born in South Africa on July 18, 1918, a member of the Xhosa tribe.   _____

2. Under the apartheid government, only whites enjoyed basic rights, not the black majority.   _____

3. As a young lawyer, Mandela defended many black clients.   _____

4. They were charged with such crimes as "not owning land" or "living in the wrong area."   _____

5. Several times, Mandela was arrested for working with the African National Congress, a civil rights group.   _____

6. In 1961, he sadly gave up his lifelong belief in nonviolence.   _____

7. Training guerrilla fighters, he was imprisoned again, this time with a life sentence.   _____

8. Thirty years in jail did not break Mandela.   _____

9. Offered freedom to give up his beliefs, he said no.   _____

10. Finally released in 1990, this man became a symbol of hope for a new South Africa.   _____

11. In 1994, black and white South Africans lined up to vote in the first free elections.   _____

12. Gray-haired, iron-willed Nelson Mandela was elected president of his beloved country.   _____

Practice 12

In each sentence, underline both parts of the passive verb, and circle the complete subject. Then draw an arrow from the verb to the word or words it acts on.

EXAMPLE: (I) was approached by Professor Martin.

1. The skaters were applauded vigorously by the crowd.

2. The corn is picked fresh every morning.

3. These flowered bowls were imported from Mexico.

4. Milos, my cat, was ignored by the mouse.

5. Hasty promises are often broken.

6. An antique train set was sold at the auction.

7. The speech was memorized by both actors.

8. Customers are lured into the store by loud music and bright signs.

9. Dutch is spoken on Curaçao.

10. Our quarrel was quickly forgotten.

Practice 13

Rewrite each sentence, changing the verb from the passive to the active voice. Make all necessary verb and subject changes. Be sure to keep each sentence in the original tense.

EXAMPLE: Newspaper headlines are made by harmful or fatal medical errors. Harmful or

fatal medical errors make newspaper headlines.

1. His patient's healthy leg was amputated by a surgeon in Florida.

_____

_____

2. Instead of an anesthetic, a seven-year-old was given Adrenalin by a doctor.

_____

_____

3. A journalist in Boston was killed by an overdose of a chemotherapy drug.

_____

_____

4. In fact, from 44,000 to 98,000 Americans are fatally injured every year by medical errors.

   _____

5. Because of unreported mistakes, even higher numbers are estimated by experts.

   _____

6. Partly as a result of publicity, their procedures were improved by many hospitals.

   _____

   _____

7. Also as a result of publicity, more precautions are taken by patients.

   _____

   _____

8. Questions are asked by them.

   _____

   _____

9. Lists of medications with doses and dosage times are carried by them.

   _____

10. The National Patient Safety Foundation's website (www.npsf.org) is visited by computer users for information. _____

    _____

PART G   *Using Past Participles as Adjectives*

Sometimes the past participle is not a verb at all, but an *adjective*, a word that describes a noun or pronoun.*

(1) Jay is *married*.
(2) The *broken* window looks terrible.
(3) Two *tired* students slept in the hall.

- In sentence (1), *married* is the past participle of the verb *to marry*, but here it is not a verb. Instead, it describes the subject, *Jay*.
- *Is* links the subject, *Jay,* with the descriptive word, *married*.

---

*For more work on adjectives, see Chapter 22.

- In sentence (2), *broken* is the past participle form of *to break,* but it is used as an adjective to describe the noun *window.*

- In sentence (3), what past participle is an adjective? _____

- Which word does it describe? _____

Past participles like *married, broken,* and *tired* are often used as adjectives.

Some form of the verb *to be* usually links descriptive past participles with the subjects they describe, but here are a few other common linking verbs that you learned in Chapter 6, Part E.

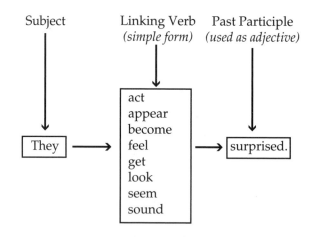

Subject	Linking Verb *(simple form)*	Past Participle *(used as adjective)*
They	act appear become feel get look seem sound	surprised.

Practice 14

Underline the linking verb in each sentence. Then circle the descriptive past participle or participles that complete the sentences.

EXAMPLES: The window was (polish, (polished)).

Harry seems very (worry, (worried)) these days.

1. This product is (guarantee, guaranteed) not to explode.

2. Nellie seems (qualify, qualified) for the job.

3. Your aunt appears (delight, delighted) to see you again.

4. After we read the chapter, we were still (confuse, confused).

5. The science laboratory is (air-condition, air-conditioned).

6. David feels (appreciate, appreciated) in his new job.

7. Did you know that one out of two American couples gets (divorce, divorced)?

8. We were (thrill, thrilled) to meet Venus and Serena Williams.

9. During the holidays, Paul feels (depress, depressed).

10. She is (interest, interested) in theater production.

11. You look so (dignify, dignified) in that tuxedo.

12. The garnet ring she wore was (borrow, borrowed).

13. I can't help you; my hands are (tie, tied).

14. Are the potatoes (fry, fried), (bake, baked), or (boil, boiled)?

15. After the trip, we felt (rest, rested), (pamper, pampered), and (relax, relaxed).

Practice 15

Below is a list of verbs. Use the past participles of the verbs as adjectives, to describe each noun in the exercise. Then use your adjective-noun combination in a sentence. Use a different past participle for each noun.

bore	freeze	park	train
delight	hide	pollute	wear
dry	lose	tire	worry
embarrass	daze	toast	wrinkle

EXAMPLE: the _____ dried _____ fruit

We served the dried fruit for dessert.

1. a(n) _____ sheet

   _____

2. the _____ river

   _____

3. a(n) _____ man

   _____

4. a(n) _____ child

   _____

5. the _____ emeralds

   _____

6. these _____ muffins

   _____

7. that _____ bear

   _____

8. a(n) _____ nurse

   _____

9. several _____ cars

   _____

10. two _____ passengers

    _____

Practice 16

Proofread the following ad copy for past participle errors. First, underline all the past participles. Then make any corrections above the line.

(1) We are please to introduce three automobiles this year, each one created

by our experience team of engineers. (2) Our racy new sport model, the

Hormone, is guaranteed to provide adventure on the road. (3) It comes equip with a powerful fuel-injected engine, steel-belt tires, and orange flames painted across the hood. (4) Growing families will prefer the Sesame ST. (5) Blue and modest on the outside, the Sesame ST's interior is make for parents and children. (6) Its plastic upholstery is printed with yellow Big Bird designs. (7) Pop-out soda and hamburger holders come preinstall, and the sound system is program for soft rock only, so your kids can't tune in to grunge, hard rock, or rap stations. (8) For the budget-minded car shopper, we offer the Chintz. (9) It comes equip with a two-cylinder engine, steering wheel, and seats. (10) Recently, on *The Tonight Show with Jay Leno,* the Chintz was name "the car that gives you less for less."

Practice 17

Combine each pair of short sentences. First, find and underline the past participle. Then rewrite the two short sentences as one smooth sentence, using the past participle as an adjective.

EXAMPLE: The book is lost. It is worth $1,000.

The lost book is worth $1,000.

1. The pie was purchased. It tasted homemade.

2. This rug has been dry-cleaned. It looks new.

3. His grades have fallen. He can bring them up.

4. The envelope was sealed. Harriet opened it.

5. The player was injured. The coach took her out of the game.

6. Your report is typed. It looks very neat.

7. This bowl is broken. Can you fix it?

8. The weather forecast was revised. It calls for sunshine.

9. These gold chains are overpriced. Do not buy them.

_____

10. The box was locked. Divers brought it to the surface.

_____

Practice 18

The sentences in the left column are in the present tense; those in the right column are in the past tense. If the sentence is shown in the present tense on the left, write the sentence in the past tense on the right, and vice versa. REMEMBER: Only the _linking verb,_ never the past participle, changes to show tense.

Present Tense

Past Tense

EXAMPLES: Smoking is forbidden.

Smoking was forbidden.
_____

Lunches are served.
_____

Lunches were served.

1. Your car is repaired.

1. _____

2. _____

2. The store looked closed.

3. _____

3. My feelings were hurt.

4. The seats are filled.

4. _____

5. She is relaxed.

5. _____

6. _____

6. You seemed qualified for the job.

7. He is supposed to meet us.*

7. _____

8. They are used to hard work.*

8. _____

9. _____

9. It was written in longhand.

10. You are expected at noon.

10. _____

Practice 19   Writing Assignment

In a group of four or five classmates, write a wacky restaurant menu, using all the past participles as adjectives that you can think of: _steamed_ fern roots, _fried_ cherries, _caramel-coated_ hamburgers, and so forth. Brainstorm. Get creative. Then arrange your menu in an order that makes sense (if that is the correct term for such a menu!).

✔ Chapter Highlights

● **Past participles of regular verbs add -_d_ or -_ed_, just like their past tense forms:**

Present	Past	Past Participle
decide	decided	decided
jump	jumped	jumped

_____

*For more work on _supposed_ and _used,_ see Chapter 32, "Look-Alikes/Sound-Alikes."

- Past participles of irregular verbs change in irregular ways:

Present	Past	Past Participle
bring	brought	brought
see	saw	seen
take	took	taken

- Past participles can combine with *to have:*

  He *has edited* many articles for us. *(present perfect tense)*

  He *had edited* many articles for us. *(past perfect tense)*

- Past participles can combine with *to be:*

  The report *was edited* by Mary. *(passive voice)*

- Past participles can be used as adjectives:

  The *edited* report arrived today. *(adjective)*

Chapter Review

Proofread this student's essay for past participle errors. Correct each error above the line.

Three Ways to Be a Smarter Learner

(1) Once in a great while, a person is born with a photographic memory, allowing him or her to memorize a lot of information with almost no effort. (2) However, most of us have struggle on our own to find the best ways to learn. (3) We have stayed up all night studying. (4) We have mark up our textbooks, highlighting and underlining like skill tattoo artists. (5) Maybe, in frustration, we have even questioned our own intelligence. (6) Although everyone has his or her own learning style, three techniques have make me and others better learners.

(7) The first technique is simple—sit at the front of the class! (8) A student who has choose to sit up front is more likely to stay alert and involve than students at the back and sides. (9) By sitting away from windows or talkative friends, many students discover that they take a greater interest in the classroom subject and take better notes. (10) An extra benefit of sitting up front is that teachers are often impress by students with whom they make eye contact, students whose behavior says, "I care about this class."

(11) Second, make a smart friend. (12) During the first week of class, exchange phone numbers with another front-row student. (13) You are looking

for an intelligent, responsible classmate who seems committed to learning—not for a pizza buddy or a date. (14) Students who have agree in advance to help each other can call if they miss a class. (15) What was discuss that day? (16) Was homework assign or a test announced? (17) Two students who "click" might want to become study partners, meeting regularly to review material and prepare for tests.

(18) Third, ask questions. (19) The student who has sit up front, made a study friend, and pay close attention in class should not be worried about asking the professor questions. (20) Learning a subject is like building a tower. (21) Each new level of understanding must be build solidly on the level below. (22) If an important point or term is unclear, ask for help, in or after class.

(23) Students who use these techniques will be rewarded with increase understanding and better grades—even before they have pull out their pastel highlighters.

Maurice Jabbar, student

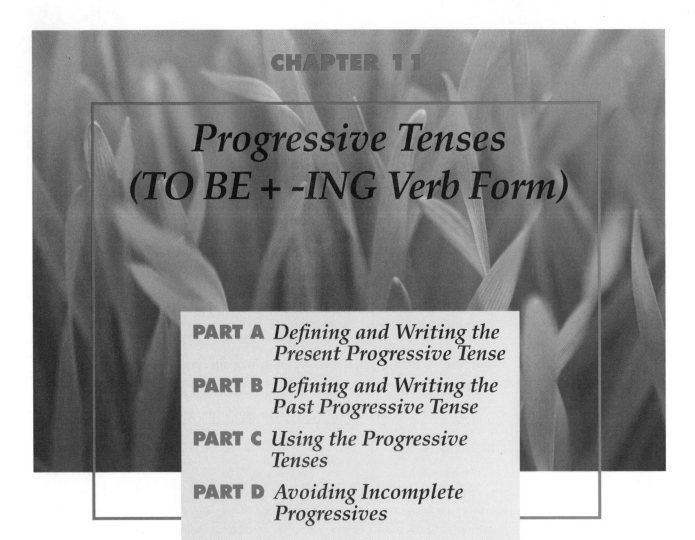

CHAPTER 11

Progressive Tenses (TO BE + -ING Verb Form)

PART A Defining and Writing the Present Progressive Tense

PART B Defining and Writing the Past Progressive Tense

PART C Using the Progressive Tenses

PART D Avoiding Incomplete Progressives

PART A Defining and Writing the Present Progressive Tense

Verbs in the *present progressive tense* have two parts: the present tense form of *to be* (*am, is, are*) plus the *-ing* (or present participle) form of the main verb.

Present Progressive Tense	
(example verb: to play)	
Singular	**Plural**
I am playing	we are playing
you are playing	you are playing
he	
she } is playing	they are playing
it	

Compare the present tense with the present progressive tense below.

> (1) Larry works at the bookstore.
>
> (2) Larry is working at the bookstore.

● Sentence (1) is in the present tense. Which word tells you this?

_____

● Sentence (2) is also in the present tense. Which word tells you this?

_____

● Note that the main verb in sentence (2), *working*, has no tense. Only the helping verb *is* shows tense.

Practice 1

Change each one-word present tense verb in the left-hand column to a two-part present progressive verb in the right-hand column. Do this by filling in the missing helping verb (*am, is,* or *are*).

Present Tense	Present Progressive Tense
EXAMPLES: I fly.	I ____*am*____ flying.
He wears my sweater.	He ____*is*____ wearing my sweater.

1. Elsa and I set goals together.
2. They eat quickly.
3. He plans the wedding.
4. Our work begins to pay off.
5. We pose for the photographer.
6. Maryann smiles.
7. Sal does his Elvis impression.
8. I speak Portuguese to Manuel.
9. My grandson gets silly.
10. You probably wonder why.

1. Elsa and I _____ setting goals together.
2. They _____ eating quickly.
3. He _____ planning the wedding.
4. Our work _____ beginning to pay off.
5. We _____ posing for the photographer.
6. Maryann _____ smiling.
7. Sal _____ doing his Elvis impression.
8. I _____ speaking Portuguese to Manuel.
9. My grandson _____ getting silly.
10. You _____ probably wondering why.

REMEMBER: Every verb in the present progressive tense must have two parts: a helping verb (*am, is,* or *are*) and a main verb ending in -*ing*. The helping verb must agree with the subject.

Practice 2

Below are sentences in the regular present tense. Rewrite each one in the present progressive tense by changing the verb to *am, is,* or *are* plus the *-ing* form of the main verb.

EXAMPLE: We play cards.

We are playing cards.

1. The telephone rings.

   _____

2. Dexter wrestles with his math homework.

   _____

3. James and Judy work in the emergency room.

   _____

4. I keep a journal of thoughts and observations.

   _____

5. We polish all our old tools.

   _____

PART B — *Defining and Writing the Past Progressive Tense*

Verbs in the *past progressive tense* have two parts: the past tense form of *to be* (*was* or *were*) plus the *-ing* form of the main verb.

Past Progressive Tense
(example verb: to play)

Singular	Plural
I was playing	we were playing
you were playing	you were playing
he she it was playing	they were playing

Compare the past tense with the past progressive tense below.

(1) Larry worked at the bookstore.

(2) Larry was working at the bookstore.

● Sentence (1) is in the past tense. Which word tells you this?

_____

● Sentence (2) is also in the past tense. Which word tells you this?

_____

● Notice that the main verb in sentence (2), *working,* has no tense. Only the helping verb *was* shows tense.

Practice 3

Change each one-word past tense verb in the left-hand column to a two-part past progressive verb in the right-hand column. Do this by filling in the missing helping verb (*was* or *were*).

Past Tense	Past Progressive Tense
EXAMPLES: I flew.	I ____was____ flying.
He wore my sweater.	He ___was___ wearing my sweater.

1. Elsa and I set goals together.
2. They ate quickly.
3. He planned the wedding.
4. Our work began to pay off.
5. We posed for the photographer.
6. Maryann smiled.
7. Sal did his Elvis impression.
8. I spoke Portuguese to Manuel.
9. My grandson got silly.
10. You probably wondered why.

1. Elsa and I _____ setting goals together.
2. They _____ eating quickly.
3. He _____ planning the wedding.
4. Our work _____ beginning to pay off.
5. We _____ posing for the photographer.
6. Maryann _____ smiling.
7. Sal _____ doing his Elvis impression.
8. I _____ speaking Portuguese to Manuel.
9. My grandson _____ getting silly.
10. You _____ probably wondering why.

Practice 4

Below are sentences in the past tense. Rewrite each sentence in the past progressive tense by changing the verb to *was* or *were* plus the *-ing* form of the main verb.

EXAMPLE: You cooked dinner.

You were cooking dinner.
_____

1. The two linebackers growled at each other.

_____

2. Leroy examined his bank receipt.

_____

3. We watched the news.

_____

4. Marsha read the *Wall Street Journal*.

_____

5. He painted like a professional artist.

_____

PART C   *Using the Progressive Tenses*

As you read these sentences, do you hear the differences in meaning?

> (1) Lenore *plays* the piano.
> (2) Dave *is playing* the piano.

- Which person is definitely at the keyboard right now?

- If you said Dave, you are right. He is *now in the process of playing* the piano. Lenore, on the other hand, *does* play the piano; she may also paint, write novels, and play center field, but we do not know from the sentence what she *is doing right now.*

- The present progressive verb *is playing* tells us that the action is *in progress.*

   Here is another use of the present progressive tense:

> (3) Tony *is coming* here later.

- The present progressive verb *is coming* shows *future* time: Tony is going to come here.

> (4) Linda *washed* her hair last night.
> (5) Linda *was washing* her hair when we arrived for the party.

- In sentence (4), *washed* implies a completed action.

- The past progressive verb in sentence (5) has a special meaning: that Linda was *in the process* of washing her hair when something else happened (we arrived).

- To say, "Linda *washed* her hair *when* we arrived for the party" means that first we arrived, and then Linda started washing her hair.

   Writers in English use the progressive tenses *much less often* than the present tense and past tense. Use the progressive tense only when you want to emphasize that something is or was in the process of happening.

Use the *present progressive tense (am, is, are + -ing)* **to show that an action is in progress now or that it is going to occur in the future.**

Use the *past progressive tense (was, were + -ing)* **to show that an action was in progress at a certain time in the past.**

Practice 5

Read each sentence carefully. Then circle the verb or verbs that best express the meaning of the sentence.

EXAMPLE: Right now, we (write, (are writing)) letters.

1. Thomas Edison (held, was holding) 1,093 patents.

2. Darrell (loves, is loving) to solve problems.

3. Where is Ellen? She (drives, is driving) to Omaha.

4. Most mornings we (get, are getting) up at seven.

5. Believe it or not, I (thought, was thinking) about you when you phoned.

6. My dog Gourmand (eats, is eating) anything at all.

7. At this very moment, Gourmand (eats, is eating) the sports page.

8. Max (fried, was frying) onions when the smoke alarm (went, was going) off.

9. Please don't bother me now; I (study, am studying).

10. Newton (sat, was sitting) under a tree when he (discovered, was discovering) gravity.

11. When Soo-Ling lived in Nevada, she (drove, was driving) through the desert every day.

12. The *Andrea Doria,* a huge pleasure ship, (sank, was sinking) on July 25, 1956.

13. Right now, she (plans, is planning) her future.

14. Through a scheduling error, runner Eddie Hart (missed, was missing) his race at the 1972 Olympics.

15. The last time I (saw, was seeing) Sandy, he (headed, was heading) toward the Lone Star Café.

PART D   *Avoiding Incomplete Progressives*

Now that you can write both present and past progressive verbs, avoid mistakes like this one:

We having fun. *(incomplete)*

● Can you see what is missing?

● All by itself, the *-ing* form *having* is not a verb. It has to have a helping verb.

● Because the helping verb is missing, *we having fun* has no time. It could mean *we are having fun* or *we were having fun.*

● *We having fun* is not a sentence. It is a fragment of a sentence.*

———

*For more on this type of fragment, see Chapter 7, Part B.

Practice 6

Each group of words below is incomplete. Put an X over the exact spot where a word is missing. Then, in the Present Progressive column, write the word that would complete the sentence in the *present progressive tense.* In the Past Progressive column, write the word that would complete the sentence in the *past progressive tense.*

	Present Progressive	Past Progressive
EXAMPLE: He X having fun.	<u>is</u> (He is having fun.)	<u>was</u> (He was having fun.)
1. Mario balancing his checkbook.	_____	_____
2. Fran and I watching the sunrise.	_____	_____
3. You taking a computer course.	_____	_____
4. A big log floating down the river.	_____	_____
5. That woman always playing poker.	_____	_____
6. The professors laughing loudly.	_____	_____
7. I trying to give up caffeine.	_____	_____
8. Fights about money getting me down.	_____	_____
9. Jean and Marie opening a café.	_____	_____
10. Thick fog blanketing the city.	_____	_____
11. He fixing up old cars.	_____	_____
12. That child reading already.	_____	_____
13. Your pizza getting cold.	_____	_____
14. Her study skills improving.	_____	_____
15. They discussing the terms of the new contract.	_____	_____

Practice 7   Writing Assignment

Write a brief account that begins, "We are watching an amazing scene on TV. A man is ripping open an enormous brown box." Write four or five more sentences describing the unfolding action in the present progressive tense—as if the action is taking place now. Then read over what you have written, checking the verbs.

Now rewrite the whole account in the past progressive tense. The new version will begin, "We were watching an amazing scene on TV. A man was ripping open an enormous brown box."

✔ Chapter Highlights

● **The progressive tenses combine *to be* with the *-ing* verb form:**

> present progressive tense: I *am reading.* He *is reading.*
> past progressive tense: I *was reading.* He *was reading.*

● **The *-ing* verb form must have a helping verb to be complete:**

> She playing the tuba. *(incorrect)*
> She *is playing* the tuba. *(correct)*

● **The present progressive tense shows that an action is in progress now:**

> Aunt Belle *is waxing* her van.

● **The present progressive tense can also show that an action will take place in the future:**

> Later today, Aunt Belle *is driving* us to the movies.

● **The past progressive tense shows that an action was in progress at a certain time in the past:**

> Aunt Belle *was waxing* her van when she heard thunder.

Chapter Review

Proofread this paragraph for incomplete progressive verbs. Write the missing verbs above the lines.

(1) One of the most important scientific projects in history is going on right now. (2) Scientists studying the role of human genes in everything from hair color to intelligence to a tendency toward obesity. (3) This huge effort is called the Human Genome Project. (4) Its goal is to map every gene in the human body— three billion elements in all. (5) Scientists finding the genes that cause or contribute to many diseases. (6) This valuable information leading to new cures and to other discoveries—like bacteria that eat up oil spills and then die. (7) On the other hand, ethical problems arising. (8) Some insurance companies are refusing to insure healthy people who carry certain genes. (9) In the future, will employers be allowed to use genetic tests the way some now use lie detectors or drug tests? (10) Will parents try to plan the physical traits or intelligence of their babies? (11) Because of questions like these, some critics finding genetic research more like a Pandora's box than a magic bullet.

CHAPTER 12

Fixed-Form Helping Verbs and Verb Problems

PART A — *Defining and Spotting the Fixed-Form Helping Verbs*

You already know the common—and changeable—helping verbs: *to have, to do,* and *to be.* Here are some helping verbs that do not change:

Fixed-Form Helping Verbs

can	could
will	would
may	might
shall	should
must	

The fixed-form helping verbs do not change, no matter what the subject is. They always keep the same form.

Practice 1

Fill in each blank with a fixed-form helping verb.

1. You _____ do it!

2. This _____ be the most exciting presidential debate ever held.

3. I _____ row while you watch for crocodiles.

4. Rico _____ go to medical school.

5. In South America, the elephant beetle _____ grow to twelve inches in length.

6. If the committee _____ meet today, we _____ have a new budget on time.

7. We _____ rotate the crops this season.

8. Violent films _____ cause children to act out violently.

9. You _____ have no difficulty finding a sales position.

10. Janice _____ teach users to do research on the Internet.

PART B   *Using the Fixed-Form Helping Verbs*

> (1) Al will stay with us this summer.
> (2) Susan can shoot a rifle well.

- *Will* is the fixed-form helping verb in sentence (1). What main verb does it

  help? _____

- *Can* is the fixed-form helping verb in sentence (2). What main verb does it

  help? _____

- Notice that *stay* and *shoot* are the simple forms of the verbs. They do not show tense by themselves.

When a verb has two parts—a fixed-form helping verb and a main verb—the main verb keeps its simple form.

Practice 2

In the left column, each sentence contains a verb made up of some form of *to have* (the changeable helping verb) and a past participle (the main verb).

Each sentence in the right column contains a fixed-form helping verb and a blank. Write the form of the main verb from the left column that correctly completes each sentence.

Have + Past Participle	**Fixed-Form Helping Verb +** **Simple Form**

EXAMPLES: I have talked to him.   I may _____talk_____ to him.

She has flown to Ireland.   She will _____fly_____ to Ireland.

1. Irena has written a song.   1. Irena must _____ a song.

2. We have begun.   2. We can _____.

3. Joy has visited Graceland.   3. Joy will _____ Graceland.

4. He has slept all day.   4. He could _____ all day.

5. I have run three miles.   5. I will _____ three miles.

6. We have seen an eclipse.   6. We might _____ an eclipse.

7. It has drizzled.   7. It may _____.

8. Fred has gone on vacation.   8. Fred could _____ on vacation.

9. Has he studied?   9. Should he _____?

10. Della has been promoted.   10. Della might _____ promoted.

PART C   *Using CAN and COULD*

> (1) He said that I *can* use any tools in his garage.
> (2) He said that I *could* use any tools in his garage.

● What is the tense of sentence (1)? _____

● What is the tense of sentence (2)? _____

● What is the helping verb in (1)? _____

● What is the helping verb in (2)? _____

● As you can see, *could* may be used as the past tense of *can*.

> **Present tense:** Today, I *can* touch my toes.
> **Past tense:** Yesterday, I *could* touch my toes.

Can **means** *am/is/are able.* **It may be used to show present tense.**
Could **means** *was/were able* **when it is used to show the past tense of** *can.*

(3) If I went on a diet, I *could* touch my toes.

(4) Rod wishes he *could* touch his toes.

- In sentence (3), the speaker *could* touch his toes *if* . . . Touching his toes is a possibility, not a certainty.

- In sentence (4), Rod *wishes* he *could* touch his toes, but probably he cannot. Touching his toes is a wish, not a certainty.

Could **also means** *might be able,* **a possibility or a wish.**

Practice 3

Fill in the present tense helper *can* or the past tense *could,* whichever is needed. To determine whether the sentence is present or past, look at the other verbs in the sentence, or look for words like *now* and *yesterday.*

1. When I am rested, I _____ study for hours.

2. When I was rested, I _____ study for hours.

3. George insists that he _____ play the trumpet.

4. George insisted that he _____ play the trumpet.

5. A year ago, Zora _____ jog for only five minutes at a time.

6. Now Zora _____ jog for nearly an hour at a time.

7. If you're so smart, how come you _____ never find your own socks?

8. If you were so smart, how come you _____ never find your own socks?

9. When the air was clear, you _____ see the next town.

10. When the air is clear, you _____ see the next town.

Practice 4

Circle either *can* or *could.*

1. Sue thinks that she (can, could) carry a tune.

2. Yesterday, we (can, could) not go to the town meeting.

3. I wish I (can, could) pitch like Pedro Martinez.

4. You should meet Tony: he (can, could) lift a two-hundred-pound weight.

5. Everyone I meet (can, could) do a cartwheel.

6. Until the party, everyone thought that Harry (can, could) cook.

7. She (can, could) ice skate better now than she (can, could) last year.

8. On the night that Smithers disappeared, the butler (can, could) not be found.

9. When my brother was younger, he (can, could) name every car on the road.

10. I hope that the snow leopards (can, could) survive in captivity.

Practice 5

On separate paper, write five sentences using *can* to show present tense and five sentences using *could* to show past tense.

PART D *Using WILL and WOULD*

> (1) You know you *will* do well in that class.
> (2) You knew you *would* do well in that class.

● Sentence (1) says that *you know* now (present tense) that you *will* do well in the future. *Will* points to the future from the present.

● Sentence (2) says that *you knew* then (past tense) that you *would* do well after that. *Would* points to the future from the past.

Would **may be used as the past tense of** *will,* **just as** *could* **may be used as the past tense of** *can.*

> (3) *If* you studied, you *would* pass physics.
> (4) Juanita wishes she *would* get an A in French.

● In sentence (3), the speaker *would* pass physics *if* . . . Passing physics is a possibility, not a certainty.

● In sentence (4), Juanita *wishes* she *could* get an A, but this is a wish, not a certainty.

Would **can also express a possibility or a wish.**

Practice 6

Fill in the present tense *will* or the past tense *would.*

1. The meteorologist predicts that it _____ snow Friday.

2. The meteorologist predicted that it _____ snow Friday.

3. Hernan said that he _____ move to Colorado.

4. Hernan says that he _____ move to Colorado.

5. Roberta thinks that she _____ receive financial aid.

6. Roberta thought that she _____ receive financial aid.

7. I _____ marry you if you propose to me.

8. Unless you stop adding salt, no one _____ want to eat that chili.

9. Hugo thinks that he _____ be a country western star someday.

10. Because she wanted to tell her story, she said that she _____ write an autobiography.

Practice 7

Circle either *will* or *would*.

1. You (will, would) find the right major once you start taking courses.

2. When the house is painted, you (will, would) see how lovely the old place looks.

3. Yolanda wishes that her neighbor (will, would) stop raising ostriches.

4. The instructor assumed that everyone (will, would) improve.

5. They insisted that they (will, would) pick up the check.

6. The whole town assumed that they (will, would) live happily ever after.

7. When we climb the tower, we (will, would) see for miles around.

8. If I had a million dollars, I (will, would) buy a big house on the ocean.

9. Your flight to Mars (will, would) board in fifteen minutes.

10. Because we hated waiting in long lines, we decided that we (will, would) shop somewhere else.

PART E   *Writing Infinitives*

Every verb can be written as an *infinitive.* An infinitive has two parts: *to* + the simple form of the verb—*to kiss, to gaze, to sing, to wonder, to help.* Never add endings to the infinitive form of a verb: no *-ed,* no *-s,* no *-ing.*

(1) Erin has *to take* a course in clinical dental hygiene.
(2) Neither dictionary seems *to contain* the words I need.

- In sentences (1) and (2), the infinitives are *to take* and *to contain.*
- *To* is followed by the simple form of the verb: *take, contain.*

Don't confuse an infinitive with the preposition *to* followed by a noun or a pronoun.

(3) Robert spoke *to Sam.*
(4) I gave the award *to her.*

- In sentences (3) and (4), the preposition *to* is followed by the noun *Sam* and the pronoun *her.*
- *To Sam* and *to her* are prepositional phrases, not infinitives.*

---

*For more work on prepositions, see Chapter 6, Part C, and Chapter 23.

Practice 8

Find the infinitives in the following sentences, and write them in the blanks at the right.

Infinitive

EXAMPLE: Many people don't realize how hard it is to write a funny essay.

to write

1. Our guests started to leave at midnight. _____

2. Barbara has decided to run for mayor. _____

3. Hal has to get a *B* on his final exam, or he will not transfer to Wayne State. _____

4. It is hard to think with that radio blaring! _____

5. The man wanted to buy a silver watch to give to his son. _____

Practice 9

Write an infinitive in each blank in the following sentences. Use any verb that makes sense. Remember that the infinitive is made up of *to* plus the simple form of the verb.

1. They began _____ in the cafeteria.

2. Few people know how _____ well.

3. Would it be possible for us _____ again later?

4. She tried _____ the old toaster.

5. I enjoy people who like _____.

6. He hopes _____ an operating-room nurse.

7. They wanted _____ a better relationship.

8. _____ or not _____: this is the question.

9. Len figured out how _____ his VCR.

10. It will be easy _____ _____.

Practice 10

The verbs below are listed in the present, past, past participle, or *-ing* form. Put each one in the infinitive form. Then create a sentence using the infinitive.

	Word	Infinitive	Sentence
EXAMPLE:	helping	_to help_	_I want to help you_
1.	leaving	_____	_____
2.	drove	_____	_____

3. brings   _____   _____

4. heard   _____   _____

5. tried   _____   _____

6. found   _____   _____

7. directing   _____   _____

8. rumble   _____   _____

9. decided   _____   _____

10. discovers   _____   _____

PART F   *Revising Double Negatives*

The most common *negatives* are *no, none, not, nowhere, no one, nobody, never,* and *nothing.*

The negative *not* is often joined to a verb to form a contraction: *can't, didn't, don't, hasn't, haven't,* and *won't,* for example.

However, a few negatives are difficult to spot. Read these sentences:

> (1) There are hardly any beans left.
> (2) By noon, we could scarcely see the mountains on the horizon.

- The negatives in these sentences are *hardly* and *scarcely.*

- They are negatives because they imply that there are *almost* no beans left and that we *almost couldn't* see the mountains.

  Use only one negative in each idea. The double negative is an error you should avoid.

> (3) **Double negative:** I *can't* eat *nothing.*

- There are two negatives in this sentence—*can't* and *nothing*—instead of one.

- Double negatives cancel each other out.

  To revise a double negative, simply drop one of the negatives.

> (4) **Revised:** I *can't* eat anything.
> (5) **Revised:** I can eat *nothing.*

- In sentence (2), the negative *nothing* is changed to the positive *anything.*

- In sentence (3), the negative *can't* is changed to the positive *can.*

  When you revise double negatives that include the words *hardly* and *scarcely,* keep those words and change the other negatives to positives.

> (6) **Double negative:** They couldn't hardly finish their papers on time.

- The two negatives are *couldn't* and *hardly.*

(5) **Revised:** They could hardly finish their papers on time.

● Change *couldn't* to *could*.

Practice 11

Revise the double negatives in the following sentences.

EXAMPLE: I don't have no more homework to do.

Revised: I don't have any more homework to do.

1. I can't hardly wait for Christmas vacation.

   Revised: _____

2. Ms. Chandro hasn't never been to Los Angeles before.

   Revised: _____

3. Fido was so excited that he couldn't scarcely sit still.

   Revised: _____

4. Nat won't talk to nobody until he's finished studying.

   Revised: _____

5. Yesterday's newspaper didn't contain no ads for large-screen television sets.

   Revised: _____

6. Alice doesn't have no bathing suit with her.

   Revised: _____

7. If Harold were smart, he wouldn't answer no one in that tone of voice.

   Revised: _____

8. Kylie claimed that she hadn't never been to a rodeo before.

   Revised: _____

9. Some days, I can't seem to do nothing right.

   Revised: _____

10. Umberto searched, but he couldn't find his gold bow tie nowhere.

    Revised: _____

Practice 12   Writing Assignment

Review this chapter briefly. What part was most difficult for you? Write a paragraph in which you explain that difficult material to someone who is having the same trouble you had. Your purpose is to make the lesson crystal clear to him or her.

✔ Chapter Highlights

- **Fixed-form verbs do not change, no matter what the subject is:**

  I *can.*

  He *can.*

  They *can.*

- **The main verb after a fixed-form helping verb keeps the simple form:**

  I will *sleep.*

  She might *sleep.*

  Sarita should *sleep.*

- **An infinitive has two parts, *to* + the simple form of a verb:**

  to drive

  to exclaim

  to read

- **Do not write double negatives:**

  I didn't order no soup. *(incorrect)*

  I didn't order any soup. *(correct)*

  They couldn't hardly see. *(incorrect)*

  They could hardly see. *(correct)*

Chapter Review

Proofread the following essay for errors in fixed-form verbs, infinitives, and double negatives. Cross out each incorrect word, and correct the error above the line.

The Great Houdini

(1) Harry Houdini began to study magic as a child. (2) He became very famous as an escape artist. (3) He could free himself from ropes, chains, and locked containers. (4) Nobody couldn't keep Houdini where he didn't want to be. (5) He could get out of any jail. (6) Once, the head of Scotland Yard handcuffed Houdini's arms around a thick post and then locked him in a prison cell. (7) Houdini managed free himself immediately. (8) Another time, some of the best locksmiths in Europe attempted to trick him with a foolproof lock. (9) Houdini was able open it in seconds. (10) In one of the master's favorite stunts, the police

will first put him in a straitjacket and bind him with ropes and chains; then they would hang him by his feet. (11) Even in that position, Houdini can wriggle free.

(12) Houdini continued to amazing people with his incredible feats. (13) He once jumped in midair from one airplane to another while handcuffed. (14) He leaped from a bridge into San Francisco Bay with his hands tied behind his back and a seventy-five-pound ball and chain tied to his feet. (15) People expected to found him dead, but he survived the ordeal. (16) In the most daring feat of all, he asked to be sealed in a coffin and lowered into a swimming pool. (17) He stayed locked up underwater for ninety minutes and then emerged in perfect health. (18) No doubt, Houdini's fame would last. (19) Probably, we won't never see another escape artist as daring as he.

UNIT 3 *Review*

Transforming

A. Rewrite this paragraph, changing every *I* to *she*, every *me* to *her*, and so forth. Keep all verbs in the present tense. Be sure all verbs agree with the new subjects, and make any other necessary changes.

(1) The race is about to begin. (2) My heart pounds as I peel off my sweatpants and jacket and drop them on the grass. (3) I step onto the new, all-weather track and enter my assigned lane. (4) Next, I check my track shoes for loose laces. (5) By now, the athletes around me are stretching backwards, forwards, and sideways. (6) I extend one leg, then the other, and bend low, giving my hamstrings a final stretch. (7) Although I never come eye to eye with my opponents, I feel their readiness as they exhale loudly. (8) Their energy charges the air like electricity. (9) I plant my feet in the blocks. (10) Off to one side, a coach starts to speak. (11) My mind is flashing. (12) How will my opponents kick off? (13) How will they start? (14) The seconds swell, thick and dreamlike. (15) The gun sounds.

Sheila Grant, student

B. Rewrite this paragraph, changing the verbs from present tense to past tense.

(1) It is the morning of April 18, 1906. (2) Alfred Hunt sleeps peacefully in the Palace Hotel in San Francisco. (3) At 5:12, a violent jolt suddenly shakes his room and sends him rolling from bed. (4) The shaking lasts for forty-five seconds. (5) During the calm of the next ten seconds, Hunt staggers to the window. (6) Another tremor rocks the city for twenty-five more seconds. (7) Hunt watches in terror. (8) The whole city looks like breaking waves. (9) Buildings reel and tumble to the ground. (10) Then fires break out and start to spread. (11) Hunt quickly dresses, throws open his door, and runs downstairs into the street. (12) Crowds of rushing people block his path. (13) Some people carry screaming children while others struggle under loads of furniture and other valuable objects. (14) It takes Hunt four hours to push through the four blocks from his hotel to the safety of the Oakland ferry. (15) Later, he will learn that the great San Francisco earthquake has destroyed 520 city blocks and has killed more than seven hundred people.

Proofreading

The following essay contains both past tense errors and past participle errors. First, proofread for verb errors, underlining all the incorrect verbs. Then correct the errors above the lines. (You should find a total of thirteen errors.)

Protector of the Chimps

(1) Jane Goodall has did more than anyone else to understand the life of chimpanzees. (2) Always an animal lover, Goodall was too poor to go to college to study animals. (3) She worked as a waitress until the age of twenty-five. (4) Then she fufilled a lifelong dream and gone to East Africa. (5) There she was thrilled by the beauty of the land and the wild animals.

(6) In Africa, she meet Louis Leakey, a famous naturalist. (7) Leakey recognize Goodall's curiosity, energy, and passion for the natural world. (8) He hired her for a six-month study of the wild chimpanzees in a national park in Tanzania.

(9) Despite malaria, primitive living conditions, and hostile wildlife, Goodall followed the activities of a group of chimps in the Gombe forest. (10) For months, she watch the chimps through binoculars. (11) She moved closer and closer until she eventually become part of their lives. (12) Goodall named the chimps and recorded their daily activities.

(13) She learned that chimps was capable of feeling happiness, anger, and pain. (14) They formed complex societies with leaders, politics, and tribal wars. (15) One of her most important discoveries were that chimps made and used tools.

(16) Goodall expected to stay in Gombe for six months; instead she studied the chimps there for almost forty years. (17) Her studies lead to a totally new understanding of chimps, and she became world famous.

(18) However, her life changed completely in 1986. (19) She attend a conference in Chicago, where she heard horrible stories about the fate of chimps outside Gombe. (20) She learned about the destruction of the forests and the wildlife of Africa. (21) From that day on, Goodall committed herself to education and conservation. (22) Since 1986, she has traveled, lectured, gave interviews, and met with people constantly. (23) She established both the Jane Goodall Institute and a young people's group, Roots & Shoots. (24) These worldwide organizations have already carry out many important conservation and educational projects. (25) The author of remarkable books and the subject of inspiring television specials, Jane Goodall is knowed for her total commitment to chimps and to a healthy natural world.

Tell a Lively Story

A *narrative* tells a story. It presents the most important events in the story, usually in time order. Here, a student explains her main idea with a single example, a childhood narrative.

In your group or class, read this narrative essay aloud if possible. As you read, underline any words or details that strike you as vivid or powerful.

Happy in Butterfly Heaven

(1) When I was a child on our farm in South Carolina, my family always supported my expansive imagination. For example, one year, I had a favorite butterfly named Mr. Jonce Browne, and I named his wife Mrs. Sadie Caesar. I would play with them in the fields, flapping my arms and darting my head until I felt I had turned into a butterfly. One day I found Mr. Jonce Browne stiff and brittle in a spider web next to the barn. When I told Papa the tragic news, he said, "Give him a proper burial because Mrs. Sadie Caesar will be too busy taking care of her children."

(2) Mama gave me a wooden matchbox for a casket. Two of my sisters and three brothers made funeral arrangements. They dug a tiny grave, and we all picked wildflowers. My brother Emiza gave the eulogy from a milk crate. "We gather here today to put to rest a good butterfly papa." My sisters Gertrude and Jeanie jumped up and down flinging their arms and yelling, "Yes! He was a good papa!"

(3) The preacher started clapping his hands and flinging his arms. He rolled his eyes upward and raised his voice two octaves as he went on about the deceased's great qualities. "He never failed to bring home pretzels for his children!" I started waving my arms as I told how he always brought me balloons. "And yo-yos for me," my brother Jeff hollered.

(4) By this time, sweat was rolling down the preacher's face. He yelled and screamed, shaking his head. Spit was flying everywhere. Suddenly he squealed a high note that made my ears ring. My brother James started singing, "When the saints go marching in." We all sang as we covered the grave and put flowers on top. I felt assured that Mr. Jonce Browne was happy in butterfly heaven, knowing how much we all liked him.

Stelline Hill, student

1. How effective is Stelline Hill's essay?

_____ Clear thesis statement?   _____ Rich supporting details?

_____ Logical organization?   _____ Effective conclusion?

2. Underline the thesis statement (main idea sentence) for the whole essay. The rest of the paper—a childhood narrative—develops this idea.

3. How would you describe the writer's tone? Is she totally serious, or is she having some fun here? Do you find this subject appropriate for a college paper, or is it too childish?

4. On paper, as in life, this student shows a lively imagination. Discuss your underlinings with a group or with the class. How many of the words you liked are verbs or verb forms? Hill uses many different action verbs to help the reader see and hear the story, especially in paragraphs (3) and (4). Can you identify them?

5. Would you suggest any changes or revisions?

6. Proofread for grammar and spelling. Do you notice any error patterns (two or more errors of the same type) that this student should watch out for?

Writing and Revising Ideas

1. Write a lively story about one way your family supported you (or failed to).

2. Use narration to develop this topic or thesis sentence: Country (or city) living has great advantages (or disadvantages).

For help writing your paragraph or essay, see Chapters 4 and 5. As you revise, make sure your main idea is clear and that your paper explains it. To add punch to your writing as you revise, replace *is, was, has,* and *had* with action verbs whenever possible.

UNIT 3 *Writing Assignments*

As you complete each writing assignment, remember to perform these steps:

- Write a clear, complete topic sentence.

- Use freewriting, brainstorming, or clustering to generate ideas for the body of your paragraph, essay, or letter.

- Arrange your best ideas in a plan.

- Revise for support, unity, coherence, and exact language.

- Proofread for grammar, punctuation, and spelling errors.

Writing Assignment 1: *Write about a book or a film.* Summaries of books and films are often written in the present tense. Choose a book you know well or a film you saw recently and describe it. You could focus on the story itself, the characters, the setting, or—if you are writing about a film—the special effects. Whichever aspect you choose, write your paragraph using only present tense verbs. You may want to let a classmate read your paper and offer suggestions before you write your final draft. Check all verb endings for subject-verb agreement.

Writing Assignment 2: *Describe the moments just before a big event.* Reread paragraph A on page 183, which uses lively verbs to describe a runner's intense moments just before a race. This writer uses the present tense, as if the action is happening now. Describe the moments just before some important event—the birth of a child, the opening of an important letter, the arrival of a blind date, the verdict of a jury (or of the person to whom you just proposed). Decide whether present or past tense would be best, and choose varied, interesting verbs. As you revise, make sure the verbs are correct.

Writing Assignment 3: *Tell a family story.* Many of us heard family stories as we were growing up—how our great-grandmother escaped from Poland, how Uncle Chester took his sister for a joy ride in the Ford when he was six. Assume that you have been asked to write such a story for a scrapbook that will be given to your grandmother on her eightieth birthday. Choose a story that reveals something important about a member of your family. As you revise, make sure that all your verbs are correct.

Writing Assignment 4: *Write to Abby.* Think of a problem with love, marriage, parents, or school that might prompt you or someone you know to write to "Dear Abby." Then as if you are the person with the problem, write a letter. In your first sentence, state the problem clearly. Then explain it. Remember, you are confused and don't know what to do. You want to give Abby enough information so that she can answer you wisely. Proofread your letter carefully. Don't let grammatical errors or incorrect verbs stand between you and happiness!

UNIT 4

Joining Ideas Together

Too many short, simple sentences can make your writing sound monotonous. This unit will show you five ways to create interesting sentences. In this unit, you will

- Join ideas through *coordination* and *subordination*

- Spot and correct run-ons or comma splices

- Use semicolons and conjunctive adverbs correctly

- Join ideas with *who, which,* and *that*

- Join ideas by using *-ing* modifiers

Spotlight on Writing

Here, writer Brent Staples uses several methods of joining ideas as he describes his first passionate kiss (at least, *he* was passionate). If possible, read the paragraph aloud.

I stepped outside and pulled the door closed behind me, and in one motion encircled her waist, pulled her to me, and whispered breathlessly that I loved her. There'd been no rehearsing this; the thought, deed, and word were one. "You do? You love me?" This amused her, but that didn't matter; I had passion enough for the two of us. When I closed in for the kiss, she turned away her lips and offered me her cheek. I kissed it feverishly and with great force. We stood locked this way until I came up for air. Then she peeled me from her and went inside for the flour.

Brent Staples, *Parallel Time*

- Brent Staples mixes simple sentences with sentences that join ideas in different ways. Sentences 1, 2, and 5, for example, combine ideas in ways you will learn in this unit.

- How do you think the writer now feels about this incident from his youth? Does his tone seem angry, frustrated, or amused? Which sentences tell you?

 **Writing Ideas**
- Your first crush or romantic encounter
- A time you discovered that your loved one's view of the relationship was very different from your view

Coordination

As a writer, you will sometimes want to join short, choppy sentences to form longer sentences. One way to join two ideas is to use a comma and a *coordinating conjunction.*

> (1) This car has many special features, and it costs less than $15,000.
>
> (2) The television picture is blurred, but we will watch the football game anyway.
>
> (3) She wants to practice her Italian, so she is going to Italy.

- Can you break sentence (1) into two complete and independent ideas or thoughts? What are they? Underline the subject and verb in each.

- Can you do the same with sentences (2) and (3)? Underline the subjects and verbs.

- In each sentence, circle the word that joins the two parts of the sentence together. What punctuation mark comes before that word?

- *And, but,* and *so* are called *coordinating conjunctions* because they coordinate, or join together, ideas. Other coordinating conjunctions are *for, nor, or,* and *yet.*

To join two complete and independent ideas, use a coordinating conjunction preceded by a comma.

Now let's see just how coordinating conjunctions connect ideas:

Coordinating Conjunctions		
and	*means*	in addition
but, yet	*mean*	in contrast
for	*means*	because
nor	*means*	not either
or	*means*	either, a choice
so	*means*	as a result

BE CAREFUL: *Then, also,* and *plus* are not coordinating conjunctions. By themselves, they cannot join two ideas.

Incorrect: He studied, then he went to work.
Correct: He studied, and then he went to work.

Practice 1

Read these sentences for meaning. Then punctuate them correctly, and fill in the coordinating conjunction that best expresses the relationship between the two complete thoughts. REMEMBER: Do you want to *add, contrast, give a reason, show a result,* or *indicate a choice?*

1. President John F. Kennedy established the Peace Corps in 1961 _____ he didn't live long enough to see the program grow.

2. The first group of Peace Corps volunteers was made up of fifty-two people in their early twenties _____ the group was both small and young.

3. Since then, more than 161,000 people of all ages have participated in the program _____ they have worked in more than 134 different countries.

4. The Peace Corps has grown greatly _____ its goals have remained the same.

5. Americans and people in other countries learn about each other's cultures _____ Peace Corps volunteers help improve living conditions.

6. In the early days, most volunteers taught school _____ they worked on health projects.

7. However, many different kinds of projects have been added _____ nations now need new kinds of assistance.

8. For example, Eastern European countries are developing free markets _____ Peace Corps volunteers are helping them run small businesses.

9. Businesspeople in former Soviet Union provinces learn how to prepare budgets _____ meeting Americans interests them too.

10. Between October 2000 and September 2001, the Peace Corps celebrated its fortieth anniversary _____ many returned volunteers shared their experiences with their local communities.

Practice 2

Every one of these thoughts is complete by itself, but you can join them together to make more interesting sentences. Combine pairs of these thoughts, using *and, but, for, nor, or, so,* or *yet,* and write six new sentences on the lines that follow. Punctuate correctly.

babies need constant supervision

Rico overcame his disappointment

in the 1840s, American women began to fight for the right to vote

I will write my essay at home tonight

the ancient Chinese valued peaches

he decided to try again

they are the best Ping-Pong players on the block

you should never leave them by themselves

I will write it tomorrow in the computer lab

they did not win that right until 1920

they can't beat my cousin from Cleveland

they believed that eating peaches made a person immortal

1. _____

_____

2. _____

_____

3. _____

_____

4. _____

_____

5. _____

_____

6. _____

_____

Practice 3

Finish these sentences by adding a second complete idea after the coordinating conjunction.

1. She often interrupts me, but _____

_____

2. Please sign up for dancing lessons today, or _____

_____

3. Yuri has lived in the United States for ten years, so _____

_____

4. Len has been married three times, and _____

_____

5. These are my favorite sneakers, for _____

_____

6. He loves to tell people what to do, so _____

_____

7. She carries her math book everywhere, yet _____

_____

8. This curry had better be hot, or _____

_____

9. I like owning a car, for _____

_____

10. I like owning a car, but _____

_____

Practice 4

On separate paper, write seven sentences of your own using each of the coordinating conjunctions—*and, but, for, nor, or, so,* and *yet*—to join two independent ideas. Punctuate correctly.

Practice 5   Writing Assignment

Whether you are a teenager, a young adult, middle-aged, elderly, single, or part of a couple, there are characters in TV sitcoms who are supposed to represent you. Do these characters correctly portray the kind of person you are, or are you seeing one or more irritating exaggerations?

Write a letter of praise or complaint to a network that broadcasts one of these sitcoms. Make clear why you think a certain character does or does not correctly portray someone like you. Use examples and specific details. As you write, avoid choppy sentences by joining ideas with coordinating conjunctions.

✔ Chapter Highlights

- A comma and a coordinating conjunction join two independent ideas:

  The fans booed, *but* the umpire paid no attention.

  | Independent idea | {, and / , but / , for / , nor / , or / , so / , yet} | independent idea. |

- Note: *Then, also,* and *plus* are not coordinating conjunctions.

Chapter Review

Read this paragraph of short, choppy sentences. Then rewrite it, using different coordinating conjunctions to combine some pairs of sentences. Keep some short sentences for variety. Copy your revised paragraph on a fresh sheet of paper. Punctuate with care.

(1) In 1929, Alice Orr answered a want ad for bronco riders for a Wild West show. (2) She was hired immediately. (3) Her new job launched a remarkable career. (4) Orr became an international rodeo star. (5) She was an expert in every rodeo event. (6) Her specialty was saddle bronc riding. (7) That tough competition has since been dropped from women's rodeos. (8) Orr won four world championships in it. (9) Orr was also concerned about working conditions for rodeo competitors. (10) She helped establish a professional rodeo association. (11) In the 1940s, Orr and her husband put on rodeos themselves. (12) She would demonstrate her world-famous saddle bronc riding. (13) Orr retired from rodeos in her fifties. (14) She did movie stunt work until she was eighty. (15) When Alice Orr died in 1995 at the age of 93, many people still remembered her as queen of the bronco riders.

Chapter 14

Subordination

PART A *Defining and Using Subordinating Conjunctions*

PART B *Punctuating Subordinating Conjunctions*

PART A *Defining and Using Subordinating Conjunctions*

Another way to join ideas together is with a *subordinating conjunction*.
Read this paragraph:

> A great disaster happened in 1857. The SS *Central America* sank. This steamship was carrying six hundred wealthy passengers from California to New York. Many of them had recently struck gold. Battered by a storm, the ship began to flood. Many people on board bailed water. Others prayed and quieted the children. Thirty hours passed. A rescue boat arrived. Almost two hundred people were saved. The rest died. Later, many banks failed. Three tons of gold had gone down with the ship.

This could have been a good paragraph, but notice how dull the writing is because the sentences are short and choppy.
Here is the same paragraph rewritten to make it more interesting:

> A great disaster happened in 1857 *when* the SS *Central America* sank. This steamship was carrying six hundred wealthy passengers from California to New York. Many of them had recently struck gold. Battered by a storm, the ship began to flood. Many people on board bailed water *while* others prayed and quieted the children. *After* thirty hours passed, a rescue boat arrived. Almost two hundred people were saved *although* the rest died. Later, many banks failed *because* three tons of gold had gone down with the ship.

● Note that the paragraph now reads more smoothly and is more interesting because the following words were used to join some of the choppy sentences: *when, while, after, although,* and *because.*

● *When, while, after, although,* and *because* are part of a large group of words called *subordinating conjunctions.* As you can see from the paragraph, these conjunctions join ideas.

BE CAREFUL: Once you add a subordinating conjunction to an idea, that idea can no longer stand alone as a complete and independent sentence. It has become a subordinate or dependent idea; it must rely on an independent idea to complete its meaning.*

(1) Because he is tired, _____

(2) As I left the room, _____

(3) If you know Spanish, _____

● Note that each of these ideas is dependent and must be followed by something else—a complete and independent thought.

● Sentence (1), for example, could be completed like this: Because he is tired, *he won't go out.*

● Add an independent idea to complete each dependent idea on the lines above.

Below is a partial list of subordinating conjunctions.

Common Subordinating Conjunctions

after	even though	when
although	if	whenever
as	since	where
as if	so that	whereas
as though	though	wherever
because	unless	whether
before	until	while

Practice 1

Read these sentences for meaning. Then fill in the subordinating conjunction that best expresses the relationship between the two ideas.

1. _____ the animal world is filled with exciting journeys, perhaps none is more amazing than the flight of monarch butterflies.

2. _____ monarchs are only five inches across and weigh only a fiftieth of an ounce, they travel thousands of miles: north to south and back again.

---

*For more work on sentence fragments of this type, see Chapter 7, Part C.

3. _____ summer changes to fall, millions of these beautiful black-and-orange butterflies begin to migrate to warmer climates.

4. Monarchs have to migrate _____ they need warm sunshine to stay alive.

5. The monarch butterflies that live west of the Rocky Mountains fly to the California coast _____ those that live east of the Rockies go south.

6. For years, scientists wondered where eastern monarchs went _____ they left Canada and the northern United States.

7. Researchers at the University of Toronto eventually began tagging the butterflies _____ the monarchs migrated south.

8. Volunteers throughout the United States and Mexico would contact the university _____ they saw a tagged monarch.

9. People continued to search _____ they finally tracked the butterflies to several sites in the forests of central Mexico.

10. At those sites, millions of butterflies cover the giant fir trees _____ no green from the trees is visible.

11. _____ the butterflies leave the trees to find water, they fill the sky, sometimes blocking out the sun completely.

12. _____ visitors from all over the world arrive at the monarch sanctuary in El Rosario, they marvel at the incredible beauty of this butterfly world.

13. Unfortunately, _____ an unusual cold spell in Mexico in 1995 killed up to 15 percent of the monarch population, monarchs have been in danger.

14. Another threat to their existence is logging _____ monarchs need the fir trees to keep themselves warm and dry.

15. Some experts have predicted that these wonderful butterflies will be extinct within twenty years _____ logging in the Mexican forests continues at recent levels.

Practice 2

Now that you understand how subordinating conjunctions join thoughts together, try these sentences. Here you have to supply one idea. Make sure that the ideas you add have subjects and verbs.

1. The cafeteria food improved when _____

_____

2. Because Mark and Joel both love basketball, _____

_____

3. If _____
   Mike plans to get legal advice.

4. Whenever _____
   she eats a huge lunch.

5. The history class seemed sad after _____

   _____

6. I was repairing the roof while _____

   _____

7. Before _____
   you had better get all the facts.

8. After _____
   I always feel wonderful.

PART B — *Punctuating Subordinating Conjunctions*

As you may have noticed in the preceding exercises, some sentences with subordinating conjunctions use a comma while others do not. Here is how it's done.

> (1) Because it rained very hard, we had to leave early.
> (2) We had to leave early because it rained very hard.

- Sentence (1) has a comma because the dependent idea comes before the independent idea.

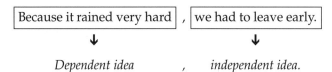

Dependent idea   ,   independent idea.

- Sentence (2) has no comma because the dependent idea follows the independent idea.

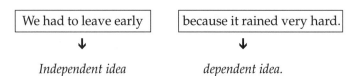

Independent idea   dependent idea.

Use a comma after a dependent idea; do not use a comma before a dependent idea.

Practice 3

If a sentence is punctuated correctly, write *C* in the blank. If not, punctuate it correctly by adding a comma.

1. Whenever Americans get hungry they want to eat quickly. _____

2. When McDonald's opened in 1954 it started a trend that still continues. _____

3. Whether you are talking about hamburgers or pizza fast food is big business—more than $113 billion a year. _____

4. Fast food is appealing because it is cheap, tasty, and—of course—fast. _____

5. Although it has many advantages fast food also presents some health hazards. _____

6. While the industry is booming many people are worried about the amount of fat in fast foods. _____

7. Although some nutritionists recommend only thirty-five grams of fat a day you often eat more than that in just one fast-food meal. _____

8. If you order a Big Mac, fries, and a chocolate shake you take in forty-five grams of fat. _____

9. That goes up to sixty-three grams whenever you go for a Burger King double whopper with cheese. _____

10. Fortunately, fast-food restaurants are now providing low-fat items so that they can attract health-conscious customers. _____

11. For instance, a McGrilled Chicken Classic has only three grams of fat while a Burger King chunky chicken salad has only four. _____

12. Whereas Wendy's provides salad bars in all its locations Taco Bell offers light Mexican entrées. _____

13. If you like seafood you can eat baked lemon crumb fish with only one gram of fat at Long John Silver's. _____

14. Although you may not think of baked potatoes or fresh vegetables as fast food many fast-food restaurants are offering these dishes. _____

15. However, restaurants will continue to offer low-fat meals only if people will continue to order them. _____

Practice 4

Combine each pair of sentences by using a subordinating conjunction. Write each combination two ways: once with the subordinating conjunction at the beginning of the sentence and once with the subordinating conjunction in the middle of the sentence. Punctuate correctly.

EXAMPLE: Marriage exists in all societies.
Every culture has unique wedding customs.

Although marriage exists in all societies, every culture has unique

wedding customs.

Every culture has unique wedding customs although marriage exists

in all societies.

1. Young couples in India marry.
   The ceremony may last for days.

   _____

   _____

   _____

   _____

2. The wedding takes place at the bride's home.
   Everyone travels to the groom's home for more celebrating.

   _____

   _____

   _____

   _____

3. They are often included in Korean wedding processions.
   Ducks mate for life.

   _____

   _____

   _____

   _____

4. Iroquois brides gave grain to their mothers-in-law.
   Mothers-in-law gave meat to the bride.

   _____

   _____

   _____

   _____

5. The food was exchanged.
   The bride and groom were considered married.

   _____

   _____

   _____

   _____

6. The tradition went out of style.
   Finnish brides and grooms used to exchange wreaths.

   _____

   _____

   _____

   _____

7. The bride, groom, and bridal party dance special dances.
   A Zulu wedding is not complete.

   _____

   _____

   _____

   _____

8. The bride dances wildly and gloriously.
   She stabs at imaginary enemies with a knife.

   _____

   _____

   _____

   _____

9. The wedding ring is a very old symbol.
   The elaborate wedding cake is even older.

   _____

   _____

   _____

   _____

10. The ring symbolizes the oneness of the new couple.
    The cake represents fertility.

    _____

    _____

    _____

    _____

Practice 5

Now try writing sentences of your own. Fill in the blanks, being careful to punctuate correctly. Do not use a comma before a dependent idea.

1. _____ because

   _____.

2. Although _____

   _____.

3. Since _____

   _____.

4. _____ whenever

   _____.

5. Unless _____

   _____.

Practice 6 Writing Assignment

Imagine that you are a teacher planning a lesson on courtesy for a class of young children. Use a personal experience, either positive or negative, to illustrate your point. Brainstorm, freewrite, or cluster to generate details for the lesson. Then write what—and how—you plan to teach. Keeping in mind that you are trying to reach young children, make sure that the significance of the experience you will describe is clear. Join ideas together with subordinating conjunctions, being careful about punctuation.

Form small groups to discuss one another's lessons. Which are most convincing? Why? Would children learn more from examples of good behavior or from examples of bad behavior?

✔ Chapter Highlights

● **A subordinating conjunction joins a dependent idea and an independent idea:**

When I registered, all the math courses were closed.

All the math courses were closed *when* I registered.

● **Use a comma after a dependent idea.**

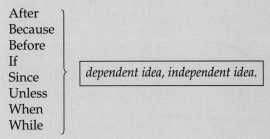

After
Because
Before
If
Since
Unless
When
While

dependent idea, independent idea.

● **Do not use a comma before a dependent idea.**

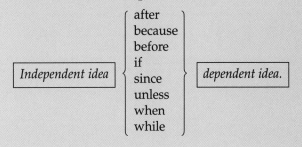

Independent idea

after
because
before
if
since
unless
when
while

dependent idea.

Chapter Review

Read this paragraph of short, choppy sentences. Then rewrite it on the blank lines, using different subordinating conjunctions to combine pairs of sentences. Keep some short sentences for variety. Punctuate with care.

(1) Bill Gates is known for his technological and business skills. (2) The chairman of Microsoft Corporation was born in 1955 in Seattle, Washington. (3) He started a computer company. (4) He was fourteen years old. (5) The successful company lost business. (6) Clients learned that it was run by high school students. (7) Gates attended Harvard University for two years. (8) He dropped out to create computer software. (9) In 1975, he and a friend established Microsoft. (10) The new company attracted attention. (11) It produced an operating system for IBM's personal computer. (12) By 1997, eight out of ten computers were starting up with Microsoft operating systems. (13) Microsoft Corporation is now embroiled in a huge antitrust battle. (14) Many people believe that the old antitrust laws cannot be applied to an information economy. (15) Meanwhile, Bill Gates is a billionaire several times over.

_____

_____

_____

_____

_____

_____

_____

_____

_____

_____

_____

_____

CHAPTER 15

Avoiding Run-Ons and Comma Splices

Now that you have had practice in joining ideas together, here are two errors to watch out for: the *run-on* and the *comma splice*.

Run-on: Herb talks too much nobody seems to mind.

● There are two complete ideas here: *Herb talks too much* and *nobody seems to mind*.

● A run-on incorrectly runs together two complete ideas without using a conjunction or punctuation.

Comma splice: Herb talks too much, nobody seems to mind.

● A comma splice incorrectly joins two complete ideas with a comma but no conjunction.

Here are three ways to correct a run-on and a comma splice.

1. Write two separate sentences, making sure that each is complete.

Herb talks too much. Nobody seems to mind.

2. Use a comma and a coordinating conjunction (*and, but, for, nor, or, so, yet*).*

Herb talks too much, *but* nobody seems to mind.

*For more work on coordinating conjunctions, see Chapter 13.

3. Use a subordinating conjunction (for example, *although, because, if, since,* or *when*).*

Although Herb talks too much, nobody seems to mind.

Practice 1

Many of these sentences contain run-ons or comma splices. If a sentence is correct, write *C* in the right-hand column. If it contains a run-on or a comma splice, write either *RO* or *CS*. Then correct the error in any way you wish. Use each method at least once.

EXAMPLE: ~~Several~~ celebrities have admitted their ~~addictions~~ public awareness of addiction has increased.   *Because several*   *addictions,*   RO

1. Many famous people have struggled with alcoholism or drug abuse some have overcome those problems.   _____

2. Often politicians, athletes, and actors hide their addiction and their recovery, they do not want to risk ruining their careers.   _____

3. Other celebrities choose to go public in their battles with alcohol or drugs.   _____

4. They feel that their struggles may help others, they want to act as positive role models.   _____

5. One such person is Betty Ford, a former First Lady with her family's help, she became sober at age sixty.   _____

6. Her recovery was successful she agreed to help several friends create a treatment center.   _____

7. The center opened in 1982 in Rancho Mirage, California.   _____

8. At the Betty Ford Center, alcoholics and addicts receive counseling and support for their new way of life, thousands have been treated there.   _____

9. Film star Elizabeth Taylor first entered the Betty Ford Center in 1983 to deal with alcohol dependency, she returned in 1988 to deal with painkiller dependency.   _____

10. NBA forward Lloyd Daniels was forced by his coach to admit his drinking and drug problems now he takes his recovery very seriously.   _____

*For more work on subordinating conjunctions, see Chapter 14.

11. Today people may become addicted when they are very young the
    actress Drew Barrymore is just one example. _____

12. At age six, Barrymore acted in *E.T.: The Extra-Terrestrial* by age nine
    she was addicted to drugs and alcohol. _____

13. Her mother forced her into treatment when she was thirteen, the
    two tried to keep Drew's problems a secret. _____

14. When a gossip magazine ran a story about her drug treatment,
    Barrymore decided to write a book about her addiction. _____

15. Alcohol and drugs harm millions of Americans, when someone
    recovers, his or her triumph can give others the courage to seek help. _____

Practice 2

Correct each run-on or comma splice in two ways. Be sure to punctuate correctly.

EXAMPLE: Technology will change the way we shop will we like the new way?

a. *Technology will change the way we shop. Will we like the new way?*

b. *Technology will change the way we shop, but will we like the new way?*

1. For instance, you want to purchase a car, you may walk up to an outdoor booth.

   a. _____

   _____

   b. _____

   _____

2. You select the options on a computer screen, you press an order entry key.

   a. _____

   _____

   b. _____

   _____

3. A factory assembles your car it is later delivered to your local dealer.

   a. _____

   _____

   b. _____

   _____

4. You go to a store to buy jeans, none are on the shelf.

   a. _____

   _____

   b. _____

   _____

5. Instead, you look at different styles on-screen you make your choice.

   a. _____

   _____

   b. _____

   _____

6. Taking measurements is not new now they can be taken by a three-dimensional camera.

   a. _____

   _____

   b. _____

   _____

7. Your measurements have been taken electronically your jeans will fit perfectly.

   a. _____

   _____

   b. _____

   _____

8. Your selection and measurements are transmitted to a factory your jeans are made to order.

   a. _____

   _____

   b. _____

   _____

9. You want to experiment with changing your hairstyle, a computer screen will show you with long, short, or differently colored hair.

a. _____

_____

b. _____

_____

10. You can leave the way you came in you can leave with a new look.

a. _____

_____

b. _____

_____

Practice 3   Writing Assignment

On the first day of the term, teachers generally announce their rules: rules about how homework should be handed in or how many absences are allowed. This writing assignment is your chance to think about rules that *students* might expect *instructors* to follow. In small groups, discuss what rules instructors should follow in order to help students learn. List at least five rules.

Then let each group member choose one rule to write about, using examples from his or her classroom experiences to explain why that rule is important. Finally, exchange papers with another group member, and check each other's work for run-ons and comma splices.

✔ Chapter Highlights

Avoid run-ons and comma splices:

Her house faces the ocean the view is breathtaking. *(run-on)*

Her house faces the ocean, the view is breathtaking. *(comma splice)*

Use these techniques to avoid run-ons and comma splices.

● **Write two complete sentences:**

Her house faces the ocean. The view is breathtaking.

● **Use a coordinating conjunction:**

Her house faces the ocean, *so* the view is breathtaking.

● **Use a subordinating conjunction:**

Because her house faces the ocean, the view is breathtaking.

Chapter Review

Run-ons and comma splices are most likely to occur in paragraphs or longer pieces of writing. Proofread each paragraph for run-ons and comma splices. Correct them in any way that makes sense: Make two separate sentences, add a coordinating conjunction, or add a subordinating conjunction. Make your corrections above the lines. Punctuate with care.

A. (1) Nearly one million people traveled to Graceland last year it is the most visited home in America except for the White House. (2) In case you didn't know, Graceland was the home of rock-and-roll legend Elvis Presley he bought it in 1957 at the age of twenty-two when he suddenly became rich and famous. (3) It was opened to the public in 1982, five years after Elvis died there. (4) The eighteen-room Memphis mansion was Elvis's home for twenty years, visitors can see what was considered luxury living in the 1960s and '70s. (5) Vinyl beanbag chairs, mirrored ceilings, and shag carpeting were high fashion then. (6) However, many visitors travel to the singer's home to honor the man rather than to see the house. (7) For some, a trip to Graceland has become a spiritual experience during Elvis Presley's "Death Week," tens of thousands arrive from all over the world to honor their idol.

B. (1) José Clemente Orozco was a brilliant twentieth-century Mexican painter. (2) He became interested in art when he was seven years old, on his way to school, Orozco watched printmaker José Guadalupe Posada. (3) He begged his mother to let him take art classes. (4) Orozco became the youngest student to study drawing at the Academia de San Carlos, he was soon able to draw better than older students. (5) At seventeen, Orozco lost his left hand in an accident the young artist continued to take classes. (6) In his late thirties, he began to paint large, colorful murals on building walls, these murals made him famous. (7) Although Orozco was driven out of Mexico several times for publicly criticizing the government, he won praise and awards, his work helped draw international attention to Mexican art.

C. (1) What do you do every night before you go to sleep and every morning when you wake up? (2) You probably brush your teeth, most people in the United States did not start brushing their teeth until after the 1850s. (3) People living in the nineteenth century did not have toothpaste, Dr. Washington Wentworth Sheffield developed a tooth-cleaning substance, which soon became widely available. (4) With the help of his son, this Connecticut dentist changed our daily habits by making the first toothpaste it was called Dr. Sheffield's Creme Dentifrice. (5) The product was not marketed cleverly enough, the idea of using toothpaste caught on slowly. (6) Then toothpaste was put into tin tubes everyone wanted to try this new product. (7) Think of life without tubes of mint-flavored toothpaste then thank Dr. Sheffield for his idea.

D. (1) The first semester of college is difficult for many students they must take on many new responsibilities. (2) For instance, they must create their own schedules. (3) New students get to select their courses in addition, they have to decide when they will take them. (4) Students also must purchase their own textbooks, colleges do not distribute textbooks each term as high schools do. (5) No bells ring to announce when classes begin and end students are supposed to arrive on time. (6) Furthermore, many professors do not call the roll they expect students to attend classes regularly and know the assignments. (7) Above all, new students must be self-disciplined. (8) No one stands over them telling them to do their homework or to visit the writing lab for extra help, they must balance the temptation to have fun and the desire to build a successful future.

E. (1) Languages are disappearing in countries on every continent. (2) North America has two hundred Native American languages, only about fifty now have more than a thousand speakers. (3) The Celtic languages of northwest Europe also have been declining for many generations. (4) However, the death of languages is most noticeable in isolated communities in Asia and Australia. (5) A different language is spoken in each tiny community sometimes only ten people speak it.

(6) In such small communities, a whole language can die if one village perishes. (7) Westerners explored a rain forest in Venezuela in the 1960s they carried a flu virus into a tiny community. (8) The virus killed all the villagers, their language disappeared with them. (9) However, most languages fade out when a smaller community comes into close contact with a larger, more powerful one, people begin to use the "more important" language. (10) A language that gives better access to education, jobs, and new technology usually prevails over a native mother tongue.

(11) According to scholars who study languages, almost half of the world's 6,500 languages are in danger of extinction. (12) That statistic represents more than the loss of specific languages, every language represents a way of looking at the world. (13) Whenever a language disappears, we lose a unique point of view. (14) No other language can really take its place.

CHAPTER 16

Semicolons

So far you have learned to join ideas together in two ways.

Coordinating conjunctions *(and, but, for, nor, or, so, yet)* can join ideas:

> (1) This is the worst food we have ever tasted, *so* we will never eat in this restaurant again.

Subordinating conjunctions (for example, *although, as, because, if,* and *when*) can join ideas:

> (2) *Because* this is the worst food we have ever tasted, we will never eat in this restaurant again.

Another way to join ideas is with a semicolon:

> (3) This is the worst food we have ever tasted; we will never eat in this restaurant again.

A *semicolon* joins two related independent ideas without a conjunction; do not capitalize the first word after a semicolon.

Use the semicolon for variety. In general, use no more than one or two semicolons in a paragraph.

Practice 1

Each independent idea below is the first half of a sentence. Add a semicolon and a second complete idea, one that can stand alone.

EXAMPLE: Ken was a cashier at Food City *; now he manages the store.* _____

1. My cat spotted a mouse _____

   _____

2. The garage became an art studio _____

   _____

3. Beatrice has an unlisted phone number _____

   _____

4. The man browsed through the items for sale _____

   _____

5. I felt sure someone had been in the room _____

   _____

6. Bruno is learning to rollerblade _____

   _____

7. Roslyn's first car had a stick shift _____

   _____

8. The batter takes a hard swing at the ball _____

   _____

   BE CAREFUL: Do not use a semicolon between a dependent idea and an independent idea.

   Although he is never at home, he is not difficult to reach at the office.

- You cannot use a semicolon in this sentence because the first idea (*although he is never at home*) cannot stand alone.

- The word *although* requires that another idea be added in order to make a complete sentence.

Practice 2

Which of these ideas can be followed by a semicolon and an independent thought? Check them (✔).

1. When Molly peered over the counter _____

2. The library has installed new computers _____

3. After he finishes cleaning the fish _____

4. She suddenly started to laugh _____

5. My answer is simple _____

6. I cannot find my car keys _____

7. The rain poured down in buckets _____

8. Before the health fair is over _____

9. Unless you arrive early _____

10. Because you understand, I feel better _____

Now copy the sentences you have checked, add a semicolon, and complete each sentence with a second independent idea. You should have checked sentences 2, 4, 5, 6, 7, and 10.

2. _____

_____

4. _____

_____

5. _____

_____

6. _____

_____

7. _____

_____

10. _____

_____

Practice 3   Writing Assignment

Many people find that certain situations make them nervous or anxious—for example, giving a speech or meeting strangers at a social gathering. Have you ever conquered such an anxiety yourself or even learned to cope with it successfully?

Write to someone who has the same fear you have had; encourage him or her with your success story, explaining how you managed the anxiety. Describe what steps you took.

Use one or two semicolons in your paper. Make sure that semicolons join together two independent ideas.

✔ Chapter Highlights

● **A semicolon joins two independent ideas:**

   I like hiking; she prefers fishing.

● **Do not capitalize the first word after a semicolon.**

| Independent idea | ; | independent idea. |

Chapter Review

Proofread for incorrect semicolons or capital letters. Make your corrections above the lines.

(1) The Swiss Army knife is carried in the pockets and purses of millions of travelers, campers, and just plain folks. (2) Numerous useful gadgets are folded into its famous red handle; These include knife blades, tweezers, scissors, toothpick, screwdriver, bottle opener, fish scaler, and magnifying glass. (3) Because the knife contains many tools; it is also carried by explorers, mountain climbers, and astronauts. (4) Lives have been saved by the Swiss Army knife. (5) It once opened the iced-up oxygen system of someone climbing Mount Everest; It saved the lives of scientists stranded on an island who used the tiny saw on the knife to cut branches for a fire. (6) The handy Swiss Army knife was created for Swiss soldiers in 1891; and soon became popular all over the world. (7) It comes in many models and colors many people prefer the classic original. (8) The Swiss Army knife deserves its reputation for beautiful design and usefulness; a red one is on permanent display in New York's famous Museum of Modern Art.

CHAPTER 17

Conjunctive Adverbs

PART A *Defining and Using Conjunctive Adverbs*

PART B *Punctuating Conjunctive Adverbs*

PART A *Defining and Using Conjunctive Adverbs*

Another excellent method of joining ideas is to use a semicolon and a special kind of adverb. This special adverb is called a *conjunctive adverb* because it is part *conjunction* and part *adverb*.

(1) (a) He received an *A* on his term paper; *furthermore,*

(b) the instructor exempted him from the final.

- *Furthermore* adds idea (b) to idea (a).

- The sentence might have been written, "He received an *A* on his term paper, *and* the instructor exempted him from the final."

- However, *furthermore* is stronger and more emphatic.

- Note the punctuation.

(2) (a) Jane has never studied finance; *however,*

(b) she plays the stock market like a pro.

- *However* contrasts ideas (a) and (b).

- The sentence might have been written, "Jane has never studied finance, *but* she plays the stock market like a pro."

- However, the word *however* is stronger and more emphatic.
- Note the punctuation.

> (3) (a) The complete dictionary weighs thirty pounds; *therefore*,
> (b) I bring my pocket edition to school.

- *Therefore* shows that idea (a) is the cause of idea (b).
- The sentence might have been written, "*Because* the complete dictionary weighs thirty pounds, I bring my pocket edition to school."
- However, *therefore* is stronger and more emphatic.
- Note the punctuation.

A *conjunctive adverb* may be used with a semicolon only when both ideas are independent and can stand alone.

Here are some common conjunctive adverbs and their meanings:

Common Conjunctive Adverbs		
consequently	*means*	as a result
furthermore	*means*	in addition
however	*means*	in contrast
instead	*means*	in place of
meanwhile	*means*	at the same time
nevertheless	*means*	in contrast
otherwise	*means*	as an alternative
therefore	*means*	for that reason

Conjunctive adverbs are also called *transitional expressions*. They help the reader see the transitions, or changes in meaning, from one idea to the next.

Practice 1

Add an idea after each conjunctive adverb. The idea you add must make sense in terms of the entire sentence, so keep in mind the meaning of each conjunctive adverb. If necessary, refer to the chart.

EXAMPLE: Several students had questions about the final; therefore, *they stayed after class to chat with the instructor.*

1. Aunt Bessie did a handstand; meanwhile,_____

_____

2. Anna says whatever is on her mind; consequently,_____

_____

3. I refuse to wear those red cowboy boots again; furthermore,_____

_____

4. Travis is a good role model; otherwise, _____

_____

5. Kim wanted to volunteer at the hospital; however, _____

_____

6. My mother carried two bulky pieces of luggage off the plane; furthermore,____

_____

7. I have many chores to do today; nevertheless,_____

_____

8. The gas gauge on my car does not work properly; therefore, _____

_____

PART B	*Punctuating Conjunctive Adverbs*

Notice the punctuation pattern:

Complete idea; conjunctive adverb, complete idea.

- The conjunctive adverb is preceded by a semicolon.
- It is followed by a comma.

Practice 2

Punctuate these sentences correctly.

1. In this new millennium, a new economy will replace the old one therefore we have to prepare for change.

2. The good news is that unemployment is low however a very low unemployment rate is a threat to prosperity.

3. Eighteen million new jobs may be created over the next eight years meanwhile twenty-four million people will either retire from their jobs or die.

4. The result will be a shortage of 4.6 million workers furthermore 3.5 million will need college-level skills to tackle the jobs of the new economy.

5. New economic policies should include lifelong education and retraining consequently both companies and employees need to take responsibility.

6. The workplace needs to be flexible therefore telecommuting, flexible hours, and time off instead of overtime should be encouraged.

7. Workers between the ages of eighteen and thirty-four now hold nine jobs during that time period nevertheless they usually cannot carry benefits over from job to job.

8. The information technology industry is short thousands of workers consequently that problem also must be addressed.

9. For more information about the job market, go to your college library otherwise you can go to your town library.

10. Studying books like the *Occupational Outlook Handbook* can give you valuable career information furthermore it may help you find a rewarding career.

Adapted from Edward E. Potter, "Labor Day 2000," *Cape Cod Times*

Practice 3

Combine each set of sentences into one, using a conjunctive adverb. Choose a conjunctive adverb that expresses the relationship between the two ideas. Punctuate with care.

1. (a) Marilyn fell asleep on the train.

   (b) She missed her stop.

   Combination: _____

   _____

2. (a) Last night, Channel 20 televised a special about gorillas.

   (b) I did not get home in time to see it.

   Combination: _____

   _____

3. (a) Roberta writes her nephew every week.

   (b) She sends a gift with every letter.

   Combination: _____

   _____

4. (a) It takes me almost an hour to get to school each morning.

   (b) The scenery makes the drive a pleasure.

   Combination: _____

   _____

5. (a) Luke missed work on Monday.

(b) He did not proofread the quarterly report.

Combination: _____

_____

BE CAREFUL: Never use a semicolon and a conjunctive adverb when the conjunctive adverb does not join two independent ideas.

(1) *However,* I don't climb mountains.
(2) I don't, *however,* climb mountains.
(3) I don't climb mountains, *however.*

● Why aren't semicolons used in sentences (1), (2), and (3)?

● These sentences contain only one independent idea; therefore, a semicolon cannot be used.

Never use a semicolon to join two ideas if one of the ideas is subordinate to the other.

(4) If I climbed mountains, *however,* I would hike in the Rockies.

● Are the two ideas in sentence (4) independent?

● *If I climbed mountains* cannot stand alone as an independent idea; therefore, a semicolon cannot be used.

Practice 4

On separate paper, write four sentences, using a different conjunctive adverb in each one. Make sure both ideas in each sentence are independent.

Practice 5   Writing Assignment

Reread Practice 2, and choose a career or a general area of work that interests you. Then assume that you are writing to a job counselor requesting information. You want him or her to get a clear sense of who you are and what kind of work might be right for you. Mention any relevant past experience you have had or even family members or friends who are doing similar work and have encouraged you.

Use one or two semicolons with conjunctive adverbs in your letter. Be sure that the semicolons and the conjunctive adverbs join two independent ideas.

✔ Chapter Highlights

● **A semicolon and a conjunctive adverb join two independent ideas:**

We can't go rowing now; *however,* we can go on Sunday.

Lou earned an 83 on the exam; *therefore,* he passed physics.

$$\boxed{\textit{Independent idea}} \left\{ \begin{array}{l} \text{; consequently,} \\ \text{; furthermore,} \\ \text{; however,} \\ \text{; instead,} \\ \text{; meanwhile,} \\ \text{; nevertheless,} \\ \text{; therefore,} \end{array} \right\} \boxed{\textit{independent idea.}}$$

● **Use a semicolon *only* when the conjunctive adverb joins two independent ideas:**

I wasn't sorry; however, I apologized. *(two independent ideas)*

I apologized, however. *(one independent idea)*

If you wanted to go, however, you should have said so. *(one dependent idea + one independent idea)*

Chapter Review

Proofread the following paragraph for conjunctive adverb errors and punctuation errors. Correct each error above the line.

(1) You might not know that the largest museum of Native American culture in the world is in New York City however, it is. (2) The National Museum of the American Indian houses more than one million items furthermore, it has more than eighty thousand photographs and forty thousand books. (3) The collection includes objects from such tribes as the Navajo, Algonquin, Hopi, Creek, Cherokee, and Seminole. (4) Among the items are textiles from Peru, baskets from the American Southwest, gold work from Colombia, and painted garments from the North American Plains tribes. (5) Many objects in the collection are on display nevertheless the museum needs more space in which to exhibit its treasures. (6) It will be moved; therefore, to Washington, D.C. (7) In 2002, it will open on a site between the National Air and Space Museum and the U.S. Capitol.

CHAPTER 18

Relative Pronouns

PART A *Defining and Using Relative Pronouns*

PART B *Punctuating Ideas Introduced by WHO, WHICH, or THAT*

PART A   *Defining and Using Relative Pronouns*

To add variety to your writing, you sometimes may wish to use *relative pronouns* to combine two sentences.

> (1) My grandfather is eighty years old.
>
> (2) He collects stamps.

- Sentences (1) and (2) are grammatically correct.
- They are so short, however, that you may wish to combine them.

> (3) My grandfather, who is eighty years old, collects stamps.

- Sentence (3) is a combination of (1) and (2).
- *Who* has replaced *he*, the subject of sentence (2). *Who* introduces the rest of the idea, *is eighty years old.*
- *Who* is called a *relative pronoun* because it *relates* "is eighty years old" to "my grandfather."*

   BE CAREFUL: An idea introduced by a relative pronoun cannot stand alone as a complete and independent sentence. It is dependent; it needs an independent idea (like "My grandfather collects stamps") to complete its meaning.

---

*For work on subject-verb agreement with relative pronouns, see Chapter 8, Part G.

Here are some more combinations:

(4) He gives great singing lessons.

(5) All his pupils love them.

(6) He gives great singing lessons, *which* all his pupils love.

(7) I have a large dining room.

(8) It can seat twenty people.

(9) I have a large dining room *that* can seat twenty people.

● As you can see, *which* and *that* also can be used as relative pronouns.

● In sentence (6), what does *which* relate or refer to? _____

● In sentence (9), what does *that* relate or refer to? _____

When *who, which,* and *that* are used as relative pronouns, they usually come directly after the words they relate to.

My father, who . . .

. . . singing lessons, which . . .

. . . dining room that . . .

BE CAREFUL: *Who, which,* and *that* cannot be used interchangeably.

Who **refers to people.**

Which **refers to things.**

That **refers to people or things.**

Practice 1

Combine each set of sentences into one sentence. Make sure to use *who, which,* and *that* correctly.

EXAMPLE: a. The garden is beginning to sprout.

b. I planted it last week.

Combination: The garden that I planted last week is beginning to sprout.

1. a. My uncle is giving me diving lessons.

   b. He was a state champion.

   Combination: _____

   _____

2. a. Our marriage ceremony was quick and sweet.

   b. It made our nervous parents happy.

   Combination: _____

   _____

3. a. The manatee is a sea mammal.

   b. It lives along the Florida coast.

   Combination: _____

   _____

4. a. Donna bought a new backpack.

   b. The backpack has thickly padded straps.

   Combination: _____

   _____

5. a. This walking tour has thirty-two stops.

   b. It is a challenge to complete.

   Combination: _____

   _____

6. a. Hockey is a fast-moving game.

   b. It often becomes violent.

   Combination: _____

   _____

7. a. Andrew Jackson was the seventh U.S. president.

   b. He was born in South Carolina.

   Combination: _____

   _____

8. a. At the beach, I always use sunscreen.

   b. It prevents burns and lessens the danger of skin cancer.

   Combination: _____

   _____

PART B   *Punctuating Ideas Introduced by WHO, WHICH, or THAT*

Ideas introduced by relative pronouns can be one of two types, either *restrictive* or *nonrestrictive*. Punctuating them must be done carefully.

Restrictive

> Never eat peaches *that are* green.

- A *relative clause* has (1) a subject that is a relative pronoun and (2) a verb.
- What is the relative clause in the sentence in the box? _____
- Can you leave out *that are green* and still keep the basic meaning of the sentence?
- No! You are not saying *don't eat peaches;* you are saying don't eat *certain kinds* of peaches—*green* ones.
- Therefore, *that are green* is *restrictive;* it restricts the meaning of the sentence.

A *restrictive clause* is not set off by commas; it is necessary to the meaning of the sentence.

Nonrestrictive

> My guitar, *which is a Martin,* was given to me as a gift.

- In this sentence, the relative clause is _____.
- Can you leave out *which is a Martin* and still keep the basic meaning of the sentence?
- Yes! *Which is a Martin* merely adds a fact. It does not change the basic idea of the sentence, which is *my guitar was given to me as a gift.*
- Therefore, *which is a Martin* is *nonrestrictive;* it does not restrict or change the meaning of the sentence.

A *nonrestrictive clause* is set off by commas; it is not necessary to the meaning of the sentence.

Note: *Which* **is often used as a nonrestrictive relative pronoun.**

Practice 2

Punctuate correctly. Write a *C* next to each correct sentence.

1. People who need help are often embarrassed to ask for it. _____

2. Ovens that clean themselves are the best kind. _____

3. Paint that contains lead can be dangerous to children. _____

4. The anaconda which is the largest snake in the world can

   weigh 550 pounds.   _____

5. Edward's watch which tells the time and the date was a

   gift from his wife.   _____

6. Carol who is a flight attendant has just left for Pakistan. _____

7. Joel Upton who is a dean of students usually sings in the

   yearly talent show.   _____

8. Exercise that causes severe exhaustion is dangerous.   _____

Practice 3

Complete each sentence by completing the relative clause.

EXAMPLE: Boxing is a sport that ___upsets me_____ .

1. My aunt, who _____ , rescued a cat last week.

2. A family that _____
   can solve its problems.

3. I never vote for candidates who _____ .

4. This T-shirt, which _____ , was a gift.

5. Paris, which _____ ,
   is an exciting city to visit.

6. James, who _____ ,
   just enlisted in the Air Force.

7. I cannot resist stores that _____ .

8. This company, which _____ , provides health
   benefits and retirement plans for employees.

Practice 4

On separate paper, write four sentences using restrictive relative clauses and four
using nonrestrictive relative clauses. Punctuate with care.

Practice 5   Writing Assignment

In a small group, discuss a change that you would like to see made in your neighborhood—an additional traffic light or more police patrols. Your task is to write a
flier that will convince neighbors that this change is important; your purpose is to
win them over to your side. The flier might note, for instance, that a child was
killed at a certain intersection or that you know of several burglaries that could
have been prevented.

   Each member of the group should write his or her own flier, including one or two
sentences with relative pronouns and correct punctuation. Then read the fliers aloud;
decide which are effective and why. Be prepared to defend your choices. Finally,
exchange papers with a partner and check for the correct use of relative pronouns.

✔ Chapter Highlights

- **Relative pronouns** (*who, which,* **and** *that*) **can join two independent ideas:**

  We met Krizia Stone, *who* runs an advertising agency.

  Last night, I had a hamburger *that* was too rare.

  My favorite radio station, *which* is WQDF, plays mostly jazz.

- **Restrictive relative clauses change the meaning of the sentence. They are not set off by commas:**

  The uncle *who is helping me through college* lives in Texas.

  The car *that we saw Ned driving* was not his.

- **Nonrestrictive relative clauses do not change the meaning of the sentence. They are set off by commas:**

  My uncle, *who lives in Texas,* owns a supermarket.

  Ned's car, *which is a 1992 Mazda,* was at the repair shop.

Chapter Review

Proofread the following paragraph for relative pronoun errors and punctuation errors. Correct each error above the line.

(1) Charles Anderson is best known as the trainer of the Tuskegee Airmen who were the first African-American combat pilots. (2) During a time when African Americans were prevented from becoming pilots, Anderson was fascinated by planes. (3) He learned about flying from books. (4) At age twenty-two, he bought a used plane which, became his teacher. (5) Eventually he met someone, who helped him become an expert flyer. (6) Battling against discrimination, Anderson became the first African American to earn an air transport pilot's license. (7) He and another pilot made the first round-trip flight across America by black Americans. (8) In 1939, Anderson started a civilian pilot training program at Tuskegee Institute, in Alabama. (9) One day Eleanor Roosevelt, which was First Lady at the time insisted on flying with him. (10) Soon afterward, Tuskegee Institute was chosen by the Army Air Corps for a special program. (11) Anderson who was chief flight instructor gave America's first African American World War II pilots their initial training. (12) During the war, the Tuskegee Airmen showed great skill and heroism which were later recognized by an extraordinary number of honors and awards.

CHAPTER 19

-ING Modifiers

PART A *Using -ING Modifiers*

PART B *Avoiding Confusing Modifiers*

PART A — *Using -ING Modifiers*

Another way to join ideas together is with an *-ing* modifier, or present participle.

> (1) Beth was learning to ski. She broke her ankle.
>
> (2) Learning to ski, Beth broke her ankle.

- It seems that *while* Beth was learning to ski, she had an accident. Sentence (2) emphasizes this time relationship and also joins two short sentences in one longer one.

- In sentence (2), *learning* without its helping verb, *was,* is not a verb. Instead, *learning to ski* refers to or modifies *Beth,* the subject of the new sentence.

Learning to ski, Beth broke her ankle.

- Note that a comma follows the introductory *-ing* modifier, setting it off from the independent idea.

Practice 1

Combine the two sentences in each pair, using the *-ing* modifier to connect them. Drop unnecessary words. Draw an arrow from the *-ing* word to the word or words to which it refers.

EXAMPLE: Tom was standing on the deck. He waved good-bye to his family.

Standing on the deck, Tom waved good-bye to his family.

1. Kyla was searching for change. She found her lost earring.

   _____

2. The children worked all evening. They completed the jigsaw puzzle.

   _____

3. They were hiking cross-country. They made many new friends.

   _____

4. She was visiting Santa Fe. She decided to move there.

   _____

5. You are loading your camera. You spot a grease mark on the lens.

   _____

6. Seth was mumbling to himself. He named the fifty states.

   _____

7. Judge Smithers was pounding his gavel. He called a recess.

   _____

8. The masons built the wall carefully. They were lifting huge rocks and cementing them in place.

   _____

   _____

PART B   *Avoiding Confusing Modifiers*

Be sure that your -*ing* modifiers say what you mean!

(1) Hanging by the toe from the dresser drawer, Joe found his sock.

- Probably the writer did not mean that Joe spent time hanging by his toe. What, then, was hanging by the toe from the dresser drawer?

- *Hanging* refers to the *sock,* of course, but the order of the sentence does not show this. We can clear up the confusion by turning the ideas around.

Joe found his sock hanging by the toe from the dresser drawer.

    Read your sentences in the previous exercise to make sure the order of the ideas is clear, not confusing.

(2) Visiting my cousin, our house was robbed.

- Does the writer mean that *our house* was visiting my cousin? To whom or what, then, does *visiting my cousin* refer?

- *Visiting* seems to refer to *I*, but there is no *I* in the sentence. To clear up the confusion, we would have to add or change words.

Visiting my cousin, I learned that our house was robbed.

Practice 2

Rewrite the following sentences to clarify any confusing *-ing* modifiers.

1. Biking and walking daily, Cheryl's commuting costs were cut.

   Rewrite: _____

2. Leaping from tree to tree, Professor Fernandez spotted a monkey.

   Rewrite: _____

3. Painting for three hours straight, the bathroom and the hallway were finished by Theresa.

   Rewrite: _____

   _____

4. My son spotted our dog playing baseball in the schoolyard.

   Rewrite: _____

5. Lying in the driveway, Tonia discovered her calculus textbook.

   Rewrite: _____

Practice 3

On separate paper, write three sentences of your own, using *-ing* modifiers to join ideas.

Practice 4   Writing Assignment

Some people feel that much popular music degrades women and encourages drug abuse and violence. Others feel that popular songs expose many of the social ills we suffer from today. What do you think?

Prepare to take part in a debate to defend or criticize popular music. Your job is to convince the other side that your view is correct. Use specific song titles and artists as examples to support your argument.

Use one or two *-ing* modifiers to join ideas together. Remember to punctuate correctly.

✔ Chapter Highlights

- **An -*ing* modifier can join two ideas:**

  (1) Sol was cooking dinner.

  (2) He started a small fire.

  (1) + (2) *Cooking* dinner, Sol started a small fire.

- **Avoid confusing modifiers:**

  I finally found my cat riding my bike. *(incorrect)*

  Riding my bike, I finally found my cat. *(correct)*

Chapter Review

Proofread the following paragraph for comma errors and confusing modifiers. Correct each error above the line.

(1) What happened in the shed behind Patrick O'Leary's house to start the Great Chicago Fire of 1871? (2) No one knows for sure. (3) Smoking in the shed, some people say the fire was started by careless boys. (4) In another story, poker-playing youngsters accidentally kicked over an oil lamp. (5) However, the blame usually is placed on Mrs. O'Leary's cow. (6) At 8:45 p.m., swinging a lantern at her side Mrs. O'Leary went out to milk the unruly cow. (7) The cow tipped the lantern switching its tail. (8) Recalling the incident Mrs. Nellie Hayes branded the cow theory "nonsense." (9) In fact, she said that the O'Learys' neighbors were having a party on the hot night of October 7. (10) Looking for some fresh milk a thirsty guest walked into the shed and dropped a lighted candle along the way. (11) Whatever happened, the fire was the greatest calamity of nineteenth-century America. (12) Killing three hundred people and destroying more than three square miles of buildings it left ninety thousand people homeless.

UNIT 4 *Review*

Five Useful Ways to Join Ideas

In this unit, you have combined simple sentences by means of a **coordinating conjunction,** a **subordinating conjunction,** a **semicolon,** and a **semicolon** and **conjunctive adverb.** Here is a review chart of the sentence patterns discussed in this unit.

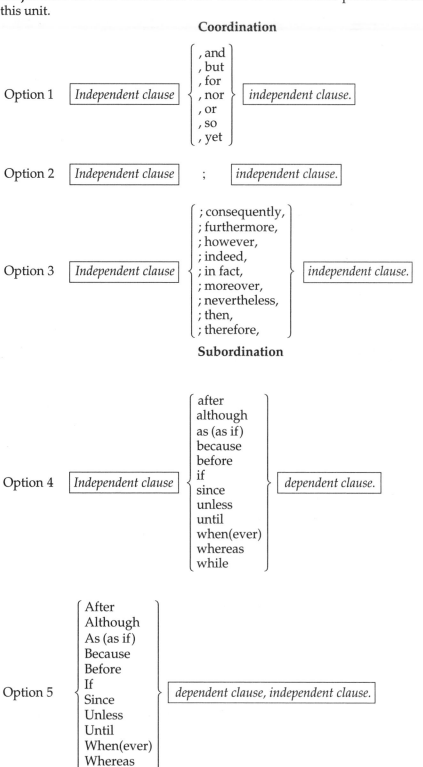

Coordination

Option 1 | Independent clause | { , and / , but / , for / , nor / , or / , so / , yet } | independent clause.

Option 2 | Independent clause | ; | independent clause.

Option 3 | Independent clause | { ; consequently, / ; furthermore, / ; however, / ; indeed, / ; in fact, / ; moreover, / ; nevertheless, / ; then, / ; therefore, } | independent clause.

Subordination

Option 4 | Independent clause | { after / although / as (as if) / because / before / if / since / unless / until / when(ever) / whereas / while } | dependent clause.

Option 5 | { After / Although / As (as if) / Because / Before / If / Since / Unless / Until / When(ever) / Whereas / While } | dependent clause, independent clause.

Proofreading

We have changed the student composition below so that it contains run-ons, comma splices, and misused semicolons. Proofread for these errors. Then correct them above the lines in any way you choose. (You should find eight errors.)

Managing Time in College

(1) When I started college, time was a problem. (2) I was always desperately reading an assignment just before class or racing to get to work on time. (3) The stress became too much. (4) It took a while now I know how to manage my time. (5) The secret of my success is flexible planning.

(6) At the beginning of each semester, I mark a calendar with all the due dates for the term these include deadlines for assignments, papers, and tests. (7) I also write in social events and obligations, therefore; I know at a glance when I need extra time during the next few months.

(8) Next, I make out a model weekly study schedule. (9) First, I block in the hours when I have to sleep, eat, work, go to class, and tend to my family then I decide what time I will devote to study and relaxation. (10) Finally, I fill in the times I will study each subject, making sure I plan at least one hour of study time for each hour of class time. (11) Generally, I plan some time just before or after a class that way I can prepare for a class or review my notes right after a lecture.

(12) In reality, I don't follow this schedule rigidly, I vary it according to the demands of the week and day. (13) In addition, I spend more time on my harder subjects and less time on the easy ones. (14) I also try to study my harder subjects in the morning; when I am most awake.

(15) I find that by setting up a model schedule but keeping it flexible, I can accomplish all I have to do with little worry. (16) This system may not help everyone, it has certainly worked for me.

Jesse Rose, student

Combining

Read each pair of sentences below to determine the relationship between them. Then join each pair in *two* different ways, using the conjunctions shown. Punctuate correctly.

1. The tide had not yet come in.
   We went swimming.

   (although) _____

   _____

   (but) _____

   _____

2. Michael enjoys drinking coffee.
   He needs to limit his caffeine intake.

   (yet) _____

   _____

   (nevertheless) _____

   _____

3. Alexis plays the trumpet very well.
   She hopes to have her own band someday.

   (and) _____

   _____

   (furthermore) _____

   _____

4. The lecture starts in five minutes.
   We had better get to our seats.

   (because) _____

   _____

   (so) _____

   _____

5. He knows how to make money.
   He doesn't want to start another company.

   (although) _____

   _____

   (however) _____

   _____

Revising

Read through this essay of short, choppy sentences. Then revise it, combining some sentences. Use one coordinating conjunction, one subordinating conjunction, and any other ways you have learned to join ideas together. Keep some short sentences for variety. Make your corrections above the lines, and punctuate with care.

Start Now!

(1) You may be young. (2) You are never too young to save money. (3) Save as much as you can. (4) Start as early as you can. (5) Invest your money well. (6) Compound interest earns money on your investment. (7) It also earns money on the interest you earn.

(8) Start investing at an early age. (9) You will see amazing results. (10) Perhaps you'd like to have a million dollars by the age of sixty-five. (11) Look at the difference in the money you would have to put away, depending on the age at which you get started. (12) You start at age twenty. (13) You would need to invest $1,391 a year to reach your goal. (14) You could start at age thirty. (15) You would then need to invest $3,690 a year. (16) You wait until age forty. (17) You would need to invest $10,168 a year. (18) Starting at age fifty is not too late. (19) You would have to save $31,474 a year to reach your goal. (20) You can see the advantage of starting at a young age.

(21) We can look at the power of compound interest from another perspective. (22) Let's imagine that you've saved $1,000 a year from age twenty until age thirty. (23) Your total investment would be $10,000. (24) You received 10 percent interest on your investment. (25) You would now have a total of $15,937. (26) Your interest earnings would be $5,937. (27) You let the total amount sit in the bank, continuing to earn 10 percent interest. (28) You don't add another dime to that amount. (29) By age sixty-five, you'd have $447,869. (30) That's a total of $437,869 in interest! (31) Now you can see why it's never too early to start saving!

Adapted from Cheryl Richardson, *Take Time for Your Life*

UNIT 4 *Writers' Workshop*

Describe a Detour off the Main Highway

When a writer really cares about a subject, often the reader will care too. In your group or class, read this student's paragraph, aloud if possible. As you read, underline any words or details that strike you as vivid or powerful.

> Sometimes detours off the main highway can bring wonderful surprises, and last week this happened to my husband and me. On the Fourth of July weekend, we decided to drive home the long way, taking the old dirt farm road. Pulling over to admire the afternoon light gleaming on a field of wet corn we saw a tiny farm stand under a tree. No one was in sight, but a card table covered with a red checked cloth held pints of tomatoes, jars of jam, and a handwritten price list. Next to these was a vase full of red poppies and tiny American flags. We bought tomatoes, leaving our money in the tin box stuffed with dollar bills. Driving home we both felt so happy—as if we had been given a great gift.
>
> *Kim Lee, student*

1. How effective is Kim Lee's paragraph?

   _____ Clear topic sentence?   _____ Rich supporting details?

   _____ Logical organization?   _____ Effective conclusion?

2. Discuss your underlinings with one another, explaining as specifically as possible why a particular word or sentence is effective. For instance, the "red poppies and tiny American flags" are so exact that you can see them.

3. This student supports her topic sentence with a single *example*, one brief story told in detail. If you were to support the same topic sentence, what example from your own life might you use?

4. The concluding sentence tells the reader that she and her husband felt they had been given "a great gift." What was that gift? Is it clear?

5. Proofread for grammar and spelling. Do you notice any error patterns (two or more errors of the same type) that this student should watch out for?

About her writing process, Kim Lee says:

I wrote this paper in my usual way—I sort of plan, and then I freewrite on the subject. I like freewriting—I pick through it for certain words or details, but of course it is also a mess. From my freewriting I got "light gleaming on a field of wet corn" and the last sentence, about the gift.

Writing and Revising Ideas

1. Develop the topic sentence "Sometimes detours off the main highway can bring wonderful [disturbing] surprises."

2. Use one example to develop the topic sentence *The best (worst) gifts are often* _____.

As you plan your paragraph, try to angle the subject toward something that interests *you*—chances are, it will interest your readers too. Consider using one good example to develop your paragraph. As you revise, make sure that the body of your paragraph perfectly fits the topic sentence.

UNIT 4 *Writing Assignments*

As you complete each writing assignment, remember to perform these steps:

- Write a clear, complete topic sentence.

- Use freewriting, brainstorming, or clustering to generate ideas for the body of your paragraph, essay, or letter.

- Arrange your best ideas in a plan.

- Revise for support, unity, coherence, and exact language.

- Proofread for grammar, punctuation, and spelling errors.

Writing Assignment 1: *Be a witness.* You have just witnessed a fender-bender involving a car and an ice cream truck. No one was hurt, but the insurance company has asked you to write an eyewitness report. First, visualize the accident and how it occurred. Then jot as many details as possible to make your description of the accident as vivid as possible. Use subordinating conjunctions that indicate time (*when, as, before, while,* and so on) to show the order of events. Use as many techniques for joining ideas as you can, being careful about punctuation. Proofread for run-ons and comma splices.

Writing Assignment 2: *Write a letter to the editor.* Suppose that a newspaper has asked readers to respond to the question "Has television programming gone too far?" Consider the marriage of Darva Conger and Rick Rockwell—who had never met before—on *Who Wants to Marry a Multi-Millionaire?* or think about *Survivor* or about court programs during which viewers vote on the defendant's innocence or guilt. If you prefer, respond in terms of violence or sexual explicitness on television. Write a letter to the editor, stating that television programming has or has not gone too far. Explain why you feel as you do, and give examples to support your view. Use as many techniques as you can for joining ideas effectively. Proofread for run-ons and comma splices.

Writing Assignment 3: *Define a person of faith.* How would you define a person of faith? Is it someone who goes regularly to a house of worship? Perhaps you feel it is someone who always volunteers for community service—in day-care centers or nursing homes. Use a person in the news, a friend, or a family member as an example of a person of faith. Give specific instances from his or her life and activities that show faith at work. Use as many techniques for joining ideas as you can. Proofread for run-ons and comma splices.

Writing Assignment 4: *React to a quotation.* From the "Work and Success" section of the Quotation Bank at the end of this book, choose a quotation that you strongly agree or disagree with. For instance, is it true that "most of us are looking for a calling, not a job" or that "money is like manure"? What do you think? In your first sentence, repeat the entire quotation, explaining whether you do or do not agree with it. Then brainstorm, freewrite, or cluster to generate examples and facts supporting your view. Use your own or other people's experiences to strengthen your argument. Use as many techniques for joining ideas as you can. Proofread for run-ons and comma splices.

UNIT 5

Choosing the Right Noun, Pronoun, Adjective, Adverb, or Preposition

Choosing the right *form* of many words in English can be tricky. This unit will help you avoid some common errors. In this unit, you will

- Learn about singular and plural nouns
- Choose correct pronouns
- Use adjectives and adverbs correctly
- Choose the right prepositions

Spotlight on Writing

Here, two researchers set forth new findings about happiness. If possible, read the paragraph aloud.

In study after study, four traits characterize happy people. First, especially in individualistic Western cultures, they like themselves. They have high self-esteem and usually believe themselves to be more ethical, more intelligent, less prejudiced, better able to get along with others, and healthier than the average person. Second, happy people typically feel personal control. Those with little or no control over their lives—such as prisoners, nursing home patients, severely impoverished groups or individuals, and citizens in totalitarian regimes—suffer lower morale and worse health. Third, happy people are usually optimistic. Fourth, most happy people are extroverted. Although one might expect that introverts would live more happily in the serenity of their less stressed . . . lives, extroverts are happier—whether alone or with others.

David G. Myers and Ed Diener, "The Pursuit of
Happiness," *Scientific American*

- This well-organized paragraph tells us that happy people think they are "more *ethical*, more *intelligent*, less *prejudiced*, better *able* . . . , and *healthier* . . ." Do you know why these words—adjectives—are correct as written?

- If you don't know the meaning of the words *extrovert* and *introvert*, look them up. Which refers to you?

Writing Ideas
- Analyze how happy you are, based on the four traits above.
- Describe an extrovert or an introvert you have observed.

CHAPTER 20

Nouns

PART A **Defining Singular and Plural**

PART B **Signal Words: Singular and Plural**

PART C **Signal Words with OF**

PART A   Defining Singular and Plural

A *noun* names a person, a place, a thing, or an idea. Nouns may be singular or plural.

Singular **means one.** *Plural* **means more than one.**

Singular	Plural
a reporter	the reporters
a pear	the pears
the couch	the couches

● Nouns usually add *-s* or *-es* to form the plural.

Some nouns form their plurals in other ways. Here is a partial list:

Singular	Plural
child	children
foot	feet
goose	geese
man	men
mouse	mice
tooth	teeth
woman	women

● Many nouns ending in *-f* or *-fe* change their endings to *-ves* in the plural:

Singular	Plural
half	halves
knife	knives
leaf	leaves
life	lives
scarf	scarves
shelf	shelves
wife	wives
wolf	wolves

Add *-es* to most nouns that end in *o*.

echo + *es* = echoes	potato + *es* = potatoes
hero + *es* = heroes	veto + *es* = vetoes

Here are some exceptions to memorize:

pianos	solos
radios	sopranos

Other nouns do not change at all to form the plural. Below is a partial list:

Singular	Plural
deer	deer
fish	fish
moose	moose
sheep	sheep

Hyphenated nouns usually form plurals by adding *-s* or *-es* to the first word:

Singular	Plural
brother-in-law	brothers-in-law
maid-of-honor	maids-of-honor
mother-in-law	mothers-in-law
runner-up	runners-up

If you are ever unsure about the plural of a noun, check a dictionary. For example, if you look up the noun *woman* in the dictionary, you will find an entry like this:

woman / women

The first word listed, *woman*, is the singular form of the noun; the second word, *women*, is the plural.

Some dictionaries list the plural form of a noun only if the plural is unusual. If no plural is listed, the noun probably adds -s or -es.

Practice 1

Make the following nouns plural.* If you are not sure of a particular plural, check the charts on the previous pages.

Singular	Plural
1. notebook	_____
2. hero	_____
3. man	_____
4. half	_____
5. bridge	_____
6. deer	_____
7. runner-up	_____
8. woman	_____
9. radio	_____
10. tooth	_____
11. brother-in-law	_____
12. birdcage	_____
13. shelf	_____
14. potato	_____
15. mouse	_____
16. child	_____
17. shirt	_____
18. wife	_____
19. place	_____
20. maid-of-honor	_____

REMEMBER: Do not add an -s **to words that form plurals by changing an internal letter or letters. For example, the plural of** man **is** men, **not** mens; **the plural of** woman **is** women, **not** womens; **the plural of** foot **is** feet, **not** feets.

---

*For help with spelling, see Chapter 31.

Practice 2

Proofread the following paragraph for incorrect plural nouns. Cross out the errors, and correct them above the lines.

(1) Last summer, my friend Jake and I took our families, including our mother-in-laws, to Yellowstone National Park. (2) While the adults looked forward to seeing hot springs and geysers, the childs were most excited about seeing the wildlife. (3) Yellowstone, which is located primarily in Wyoming, is one of the world's greatest wildlife sanctuaries. (4) The animals that live there include wolfes, sheeps, mooses, and deers. (5) Yellowstone's streams are filled with fishs. (6) Among its two hundred species of birds are Canada gooses. (7) Our sister-in-laws were most impressed by Old Faithful, the geyser that erupts almost hourly. (8) Our wifes enjoyed fishing in many of Yellowstone's lakes and streams. (9) We easily understood why so many mens and womans go to this beautiful place. (10) However, most of the three million tourists who visit each year arrive in cars and race through the park's 2.2 million acres in just three days. (11) Those with more time in their lifes and more willingness to experience discomfort can avoid being passer bys. (12) They can leave the cars, crowds, and hotels behind, camp in the wild, and have an even deeper experience of this gorgeous wilderness.

PART B   *Signal Words: Singular and Plural*

A *signal word* **tells you whether a singular or a plural noun usually follows.**

These signal words tell you that a *singular noun* usually follows:

Signal Words

a(n)
another
a single
each   } motorboat
every
one

These signal words tell you that a *plural noun* usually follows:

Signal Words

all
both
few
many } motorboats
several
some
two (or more)

Practice 3

In the blank following each signal word, write either a singular or a plural noun. Use as many different nouns as you can think of.

EXAMPLES: a single _stamp_____

most _fabrics_____

1. a(n) _____   7. each _____

2. some _____   8. another _____

3. few _____   9. a single _____

4. nine _____   10. every _____

5. one _____   11. both _____

6. all _____   12. many _____

Practice 4

Read the following essay for incorrect singular or plural nouns following signal words. Cross out the errors, and correct them above the lines.

The Best Medicine

(1) Many researcher believe that laughter is good for people's health. (2) In fact, some doctor have concluded that laughter actually helps patients heal faster. (3) To put this theory into practice, several hospital have introduced humor routines into their treatment programs. (4) One programs is a children's clown care unit that operates in seven New York City hospitals. (5) Thirty-five clown from the Big Apple Circus go to the hospitals three times every weeks. (6) Few child can keep from laughing at the "rubber chicken soup" and "red nose transplant" routines.

(7) Although the program hasn't been studied scientifically, many observer have witnessed its positive effects. (8) However, some specialist are conducting strictly scientific research on health and laughter. (9) One study, carried out at Loma Linda University in California, has shown the positive effects of laughter on the immune system. (10) Another tests, done at the College of William and Mary in Virginia, has confirmed the California findings. (11) Other studies in progress are suggesting that all physiological system may be affected positively by laughter. (12) Finally, research also is backing up a claims made by Norman Cousins, author of the book *Anatomy of an Illness.* (13) While he was fighting a life-threatening diseases, Cousins maintained that hearty laughter took away his pain. (14) Several recent study have shown that pain does become less intense when the sufferer responds to comedy.

Practice 5

On separate paper, write three sentences using signal words that require singular nouns. Then write three sentences using signal words that require plural nouns.

PART C   *Signal Words with OF*

Many signal words are followed by *of . . .* or *of the . . .* Usually, these signal words are followed by a *plural* noun (or a collective noun) because you are really talking about one or more from a larger group.*

many of the ⎫
a few of the ⎬ houses are . . .
lots of the ⎭

one of the ⎫
each of the ⎬ houses is . . .

BE CAREFUL: The signal words *one of the* and *each of the* are followed by a *plural* noun, but the verb is *singular* because only the signal word *(one, each)* is the real subject.**

---

*For more work on collective nouns, see Chapter 21, Part C.
**For more work on this type of construction, see Chapter 8, Part G.

> (1) *One* of the apples *is* spoiled.
> (2) *Each* of the trees *grows* quickly.

- In sentence (1), *one* is the subject, not *apples*.

- In sentence (2), *each* is the subject, not *trees*.

Practice 6

Fill in your own nouns in the following sentences. Use a different noun in each sentence.

1. Many of the _____ enrolled in Chemistry 202.

2. Larry lost one of his _____ at the beach.

3. This is one of the _____ that everyone liked.

4. Each of the _____ carried a sign.

5. You are one of the few _____ who can do somersaults.

6. Few of the _____ produced calves.

Practice 7

Use a different noun in each sentence. Write five sentences using signal words with *of.*

EXAMPLE: (many of those . . .) I planted many of those flowers myself. _____

1. (one of my . . .) _____

_____

2. (many of the . . .) _____

_____

3. (lots of the . . .) _____

_____

4. (each of these . . .) _____

_____

5. (a few of your . . .) _____

_____

Practice 8

Read the following essay for correct plural nouns after signal words with *of*. Cross out the errors, and correct them above the lines.

The Fender Sound

(1) If you are a fan of popular music or blues, the guitar sound you have been listening to was created by Leo Fender. (2) Leo Fender invented the modern amplified guitar, the instrument of choice for many of today's pop star. (3) The instrument that Fender introduced in the 1940s had an incredible sound—clear, crisp, and clean. (4) Buddy Holly, the Beatles, Jimi Hendrix, and B. B. King were just a few of the performer who bought and loved a Fender guitar.

(5) Unfortunately, by the time Fender sold his invention to CBS, the famous Fender guitars had declined in quality and were selling very poorly. (6) William Schultz, who worked for CBS at the time, felt that he could turn things around; however, few of the musician who had played the original Fenders believed he could succeed. (7) He did.

(8) The Telecaster and the Stratocaster have become two of the most famous instruments in music history. (9) Approximately 335,000 are sold a year; each of these instrument is considered a classic. (10) The next time you attend a concert, listen for the Fender sound.

Practice 9   Writing Assignment

For some families, shopping—whether for food, clothing, or a television set—is a delightful group outing, a time to be together and share. For other families, it is an ordeal, a time of great stress, with arguments about what to purchase and how much to spend.

Describe a particularly delightful or awful family shopping experience. Your first sentence might read, "Shopping for _____ was (is) a(n) _____ experience." Explain what made it so good or so bad: Was it what you were shopping for or where you were shopping? Were there arguments? Why?

Check your work for the correct use of singular and plural nouns. Be especially careful of nouns that follow signal words.

✔ Chapter Highlights

● **Most plural nouns are formed by adding -s or -es to the singular noun:**

egg/eggs   watch/watches

● **Some plurals are formed in other ways:**

child/children   woman/women   wolf/wolves

● **Some nouns ending in *o* add -es; others add -s:**

echo/echoes   solo/solos

● **Some nouns have identical singular and plural forms:**

fish/fish   deer/deer

● **Hyphenated nouns usually add -s or -es to the first word:**

sister-in-law/sisters-in-law

● **Signal words, with and without *of*, indicate whether a singular or a plural noun usually follows:**

another musician   *many of the* musicians

Chapter Review

Proofread the following essay for incorrect singular and plural nouns. Cross out the errors, and correct them above the lines.

The Effects of Alcohol on Pregnancy

(1) All mother-to-bes who drink alcohol run the risk of harming an innocent children. (2) When a pregnant women takes a drink, the alcohol goes straight from her bloodstream into the bloodstream of her child. (3) When she has several drink, the blood-alcohol level of her child rises as high as her own.

(4) Newborns can be harmed by alcohol in many way. (5) Some infant are born addicted to alcohol. (6) Other children are born mentally retarded. (7) In fact, most doctor believe that exposure to alcohol before birth is one of the major cause of mental retardation. (8) In the worst cases, babies are born with a disease called fetal alcohol syndrome. (9) These unfortunate children not only are mentally retarded but also can have many physical deformity as well. (10) In milder

cases, the children's problems don't show up until they go to school. (11) For instance, they may have poor memories and short attention spans. (12) Later, they may have trouble holding a jobs.

(13) Too many young life have been ruined before birth because of alcohol consumption. (14) All unborn child need and deserve a chance to have a healthy, normal futures. (15) If you are a women who is expecting a baby, stop drinking alcohol now!

CHAPTER 21

Pronouns

PART A Defining Pronouns and Antecedents

PART B Referring to Indefinite Pronouns

PART C Referring to Collective Nouns

PART D Referring to Special Singular Constructions

PART E Avoiding Vague and Repetitious Pronouns

PART F Using Pronouns as Subjects, Objects, and Possessives

PART G Choosing the Correct Case after AND or OR

PART H Choosing the Correct Case in Comparisons

PART I Using Pronouns with -SELF and -SELVES

PART A   Defining Pronouns and Antecedents

Pronouns take the place of or refer to nouns or other pronouns. The word or words that a pronoun refers to are called the *antecedent* of the pronoun.

(1) *Bob* said that *he* was tired.

252

© 2001 Houghton Mifflin Company

● *He* refers to *Bob.*

● *Bob* is the antecedent of *he.*

(2) *Sonia* left early, but I did not see *her* until later.

● *Her* refers to *Sonia.*

● *Sonia* is the antecedent of *her.*

(3) *Robert and Tyrone* have been good friends ever since *their* college days.

● *Their* refers to *Robert and Tyrone.*

● *Robert and Tyrone* is the antecedent of *their.*

A pronoun must agree with its antecedent. In sentence (1), the antecedent *Bob* requires the singular, masculine pronoun *he.* In sentence (2), the antecedent *Sonia* requires the singular, feminine pronoun *her.* In sentence (3), the antecedent *Robert and Tyrone* requires the plural pronoun *their.*

Practice 1

In each of the following sentences, circle the pronoun. In the columns on the right, write the pronoun and its antecedent as shown in the example.

	Pronoun	Antecedent
EXAMPLE: Susan B. Anthony promoted women's rights before (they) were popular.	they	rights
1. Susan B. Anthony deserves praise for her accomplishments.	_____	_____
2. Anthony became involved in the antislavery movement because of her principles.	_____	_____
3. She helped President Lincoln develop his plans to free the slaves during the Civil War.	_____	_____
4. Eventually, Anthony realized that women wouldn't be fully protected by law until they could vote.	_____	_____
5. When Anthony voted in the presidential election of 1872, she was arrested.	_____	_____

6. She was found guilty and given a
    $100 fine, but she refused to pay it.   _____   _____

7. The judge did not sentence Anthony
    to jail because a sentence would have
    given her grounds for an appeal.   _____   _____

8. If the Supreme Court had heard her
    appeal, it might have ruled that women
    had the right to vote.   _____   _____

9. Audiences in England and Germany
    showed their appreciation of Anthony's
    work with standing ovations.   _____   _____

10. Unfortunately, women in the United
    States had to wait until 1920 before
    they could legally vote.   _____   _____

Practice 2

Read this paragraph for meaning; then circle each pronoun you find and write its antecedent above the pronoun.

(1) In 1935, a Hungarian journalist got tired of the ink blotches his fountain pen made. (2) So László Biro and his brother developed a pen with a rolling ball at the point. (3) It wrote without making blotches. (4) Their pen wasn't the first ballpoint, but it was the first one that worked well. (5) The new pens got a big boost during World War II. (6) Pilots needed a pen they could use at high altitudes. (7) Only ballpoints did the job. (8) In 1945, a department store in New York City introduced these pens to its shoppers. (9) The store sold ten thousand ballpoints the first day. (10) They cost $12.50 each! (11) Today, people buy almost two *billion* ballpoints a year, for as little as ten cents apiece.

PART B   *Referring to Indefinite Pronouns*

Indefinite pronouns do not point to a specific person.

> anybody
> anyone
> each
> everybody
> everyone   Indefinite pronouns are usually *singular*.
> no one   A pronoun that refers to an indefinite
> nobody   pronoun should also be singular.
> somebody
> someone

(1) *Everyone* should do what *he* or *she* can to help.

- *Everyone* is a singular antecedent and must be used with the singular pronoun *he* or *she*.

(2) *Each* wanted to read *his* or *her* composition aloud.

- *Each* is a singular antecedent and must be used with the singular pronoun *his* or *her*.

(3) If *someone* smiles at you, give *him* or *her* a smile in return.

- *Someone* is a singular antecedent and must be used with the singular pronoun *him* or *her*.

In the past, writers used *he, his,* or *him* to refer to both men and women. Now, however, many writers use *he or she, his or her,* or *him or her.* Of course, if *everyone* is a woman, use *she* or *her;* if *everyone* is a man, use *he, his,* or *him.**

Someone left *her* purse in the classroom.

Someone left *his* necktie on the bus.

Someone left *his or her* glasses on the back seat.

It is often best to avoid the repetition of *his or her* and *he or she* by changing the indefinite pronoun to a plural.

(4) *Everyone* in the club agreed to pay *his or her* dues on time.
or
(5) The club *members* agreed to pay *their* dues on time.

---

*For more work on pronoun reference, see Chapter 25, "Consistent Person."

Practice 3

Fill in the blanks with the correct pronouns. Then write the antecedent of each pronoun in the column on the right.

Antecedent

EXAMPLE: Everyone should do _____his or her_____ best.   _____everyone_____

1. The average citizen does not take _____ right to vote seriously enough.   _____

2. If a person chooses a career in accounting,

   _____ must enjoy working with numbers.   _____

3. Each player gave _____ best in the women's basketball finals.   _____

4. Anyone can learn to do research on the Internet if

   _____ will put the time into it.   _____

5. Fred and Nina always do _____ housecleaning on Tuesday.   _____

6. Someone left _____ fingerprints on the windshield.   _____

7. The sales managers asked me to attend _____ meeting tomorrow.   _____

8. Everyone should see _____ dentist at least once a year.   _____

9. Nobody wanted to waste _____ money on a singing stapler.   _____

10. Everybody is welcome to try _____ luck in the lottery.   _____

Practice 4

Some of the following sentences contain errors in pronoun reference. Revise the incorrect sentences. Write a *C* in the blank next to each correct sentence.

EXAMPLE: Everyone must provide ~~their~~ his or her lunch. _____

1. Somebody left their bag of popcorn on the seat. _____

2. A child should not carry heavy items in his or her backpack. _____

3. Everybody can take their choice of two dishes from column A and

   one from column B. _____

4. No one works harder at their paramedic job than my brother-in-law. _____

5. Each state has their own flag. _____

6. Anyone can conquer his or her fear of speaking in public. _____

Practice 5

On separate paper, write three sentences using indefinite pronouns as antecedents.

PART C   *Referring to Collective Nouns*

Collective nouns imply more than one person but are generally considered *singular.* Here is a partial list:

Common Collective Nouns

board	family	panel
class	flock	school
college	government	society
committee	group	team
company	jury	tribe

(1) The *jury* meets early today because *it* must decide on a verdict.

● *Jury* is a singular antecedent and is used with the singular pronoun *it.*

(2) *Society* must protect *its* members from violence.

● *Society* is a singular antecedent and is always used with the singular pronoun *it.*
● Use *it* or *its* when referring to collective nouns.
● Use *they* or *their* only when referring to collective nouns in the plural (*schools, companies,* and so forth).

Practice 6

Write the correct pronoun in the blank. Then write the antecedent of the pronoun in the column on the right.

Antecedent

EXAMPLE: The committee sent ____its____ recommendations to the president of the college.   ___committee___

1. Wanda's company will have _____ annual picnic next week.   _____

2. The two teams picked up _____ gloves and bats and walked off the field.   _____

3. My high school class will soon have _____ tenth reunion.   _____

4. The city is doing _____ best to build a new stadium. _____

5. Many soap operas count on _____ viewers' enjoyment of "a good cry." _____

6. Each band has _____ guitar player and drummer. _____

7. The panel made _____ report public. _____

8. This college plans to train _____ student teachers in classroom management. _____

Practice 7

Some of the following sentences contain errors in pronoun reference. Cross out the incorrect pronoun, and write the correct pronoun above the line. Write a *C* in the blank next to each correct sentence.

EXAMPLES: The committee will present ~~their~~ *its* report today. _____

The jury has reached its verdict. *C*

1. The computer company retrains their employees for new jobs. _____

2. Central Technical College wants to double their enrollment by 2005. _____

3. That rock group has changed their name for the third time. _____

4. The plumbing crew did its best to finish by 4 a.m. _____

5. The gas company plans to move their headquarters again. _____

6. The Robinson family held its yearly reunion last week. _____

Practice 8

On separate paper, write three sentences using collective nouns as antecedents.

PART D *Referring to Special Singular Constructions*

each of . . .

either of . . .

every one of . . .   Each of these constructions is *singular*.

Pronouns that refer to them must also

neither of . . .   be singular.

one of . . .

> (1) *Each* of the women did *her* work.

- *Each* is a singular antecedent and is used with the singular pronoun *her.*
- Do not be confused by the prepositional phrase *of the women.*

> (2) *Neither* of the men finished *his* meal.

- *Neither* is a singular antecedent and is used with the singular pronoun *his.*
- Do not be confused by the prepositional phrase *of the men.*

> (3) *One* of the bottles is missing from *its* place.

- *One* is a singular antecedent and is used with the singular pronoun *its.*
- Do not be confused by the prepositional phrase *of the bottles.**

Practice 9

Fill in the blanks with the correct pronouns. Then write the antecedent of each pronoun in the column on the right.

Antecedent

EXAMPLE: Each of my nephews did _____*his*_____ homework.   _____*each*_____

1. One of the hikers filled _____ canteen.   _____

2. Every one of the women scored high on _____
   entrance examination.   _____

3. Each of the puzzles has _____ own solution.   _____

4. Either of them should be able to learn _____ lines
   before opening night.   _____

5. One of my brothers does not have a radio in

   _____ car.   _____

6. Neither of the dental technicians has had _____
   lunch yet.   _____

7. Every one of the children sat still when _____
   photograph was taken.   _____

8. Lin Li and her mother opened _____ boutique
   in 1998.   _____

_____

*For more work on these special constructions, see Chapter 8, Part G.

Practice 10

Some of the following sentences contain errors in pronoun reference. Cross out the incorrect pronoun, and write the correct pronoun above it. Write a *C* in the blank next to each correct sentence.

EXAMPLE: One of my uncles made ~~their~~ *his* opinion known. _____

1. One of the women at the hardware counter hasn't made their purchase yet. _____

2. Each of the birds has their distinctive mating ritual. _____

3. Most public speakers rehearse their speeches beforehand. _____

4. I hope that neither of the men will change their vote. _____

5. Both supermarkets now carry Superfizz Carrot Juice for their health-conscious customers. _____

6. Neither of the women bought their toe ring at Toes R Us. _____

7. One of the televisions was still in its box. _____

8. Each of my grandchildren has their own bedroom. _____

Practice 11

On separate paper, write three sentences that use the special singular constructions as antecedents.

PART E *Avoiding Vague and Repetitious Pronouns*

Vague Pronouns

Be sure that all pronouns *clearly* refer to their antecedents. Be especially careful of the pronouns *they* and *it*. If *they* or *it* does not refer to a *specific* antecedent, change *they* or *it* to the exact word you have in mind.

(1) **Vague pronoun:** At registration, they said I should take Math 101.
(2) **Revised:** At registration, an adviser said I should take Math 101.

• In sentence (1), who is *they?* The pronoun *they* does not clearly refer to an antecedent.

• In sentence (2), the vague *they* has been replaced by *an adviser*.

(3) **Vague pronoun:** On the beach, it says that no swimming is allowed.

(4) **Revised:** On the beach, a sign says that no swimming is allowed.

- In sentence (3), what is *it?* The pronoun *it* does not clearly refer to an antecedent.

- In sentence (4), the vague *it* has been replaced by *a sign.*

Repetitious Pronouns

Don't repeat a pronoun directly after its antecedent. Use *either* the pronoun *or* the antecedent—not both.

(1) **Repetitious pronoun:** The doctor, she said that my daughter is in perfect health.

- The pronoun *she* unnecessarily repeats the antecedent *doctor,* which is right before it.

(2) **Revised:** *The doctor* said that my daughter is in perfect health.

or

She said that my daughter is in perfect health.

- Use either *the doctor* or *she,* not both.

Practice 12

Rewrite the sentences that contain vague or repetitious pronouns. If a sentence is correct, write C.

EXAMPLE: Dyslexia, it is a learning disorder that makes reading difficult.

Revised: _____Dyslexia is a learning disorder that makes reading difficult._____

1. Many dyslexic persons, they have achieved success in their chosen professions.

   Revised: _____

   _____

2. For example, Albert Einstein, he was dyslexic.

   Revised: _____

   _____

3. His biography, it says that he couldn't interpret written words the way others could.

   Revised: _____

   _____

4. His elementary school teachers, they claimed that he was a slow learner.

   Revised: _____

   _____

5. However, this slow learner, he changed the way science looked at time and space.

   Revised: _____

   _____

6. Even politics has had its share of dyslexic leaders.

   Revised: _____

   _____

7. American history, it teaches us that President Woodrow Wilson and Vice President Nelson Rockefeller, they were both dyslexic.

   Revised: _____

   _____

8. Authors can have this problem too; the well-known mystery writer Agatha Christie, she had trouble reading.

   Revised: _____

   _____

9. Finally, several magazines, they report that Cher, the famous singer and actress, is dyslexic.

   Revised: _____

   _____

10. This show-business personality, she wasn't able to read until she was eighteen years old.

   Revised: _____

   _____

PART F — Using Pronouns as Subjects, Objects, and Possessives

Pronouns have different forms, depending on how they are used in a sentence. Pronouns can be *subjects* or *objects* or *possessives*. They can be in the *subjective case*, *objective case*, or *possessive case*.

Pronouns as Subjects

A pronoun can be the *subject* of a sentence:

> (1) *He* loves the summer months.
> (2) By noon, *they* had reached the top of the hill.

- In sentences (1) and (2), the pronouns *he* and *they* are subjects.

Pronouns as Objects

A pronoun can be the *object* of a verb:

> (1) Graciela kissed *him*.
> (2) Sheila moved *it* to the corner.

- In sentence (1), the pronoun *him* tells whom Graciela kissed.
- In sentence (2), the pronoun *it* tells what Sheila moved.
- These objects answer the questions *kissed whom?* and *moved what?*

A pronoun can also be the *object* of a preposition, a word like *to, for,* or *at.**

> (3) The umpire stood between *us*.
> (4) Near *them*, the children played.

- In sentences (3) and (4), the pronouns *us* and *them* are the objects of the prepositions *between* and *near*.

Sometimes the prepositions *to* and *for* are understood, usually after words like *give, send, tell,* and *bring*.

> (5) I gave *her* the latest sports magazine.
> (6) Carver bought *him* a cowboy hat.

- In sentence (5), the preposition *to* is understood before the pronoun *her*: I gave *to* her . . .

- In sentence (6), the preposition *for* is understood before the pronoun *him*: Carver bought *for* him . . .

---

*See the list of prepositions on page 286.

Pronouns That Show Possession

A pronoun can show *possession* or ownership.

> (1) Bill took *his* report and left.
>
> (2) The climbers spotted *their* gear on the slope.

● In sentences (1) and (2), the pronouns *his* and *their* show that Bill owns *his* report and that the climbers own *their* gear.

The chart below can help you review all the pronouns discussed in this part.

Pronoun Case Chart

Singular Pronouns			Plural Pronouns		
Subjective	Objective	Possessive	Subjective	Objective	Possessive
1st person: I	me	my (mine)	we	us	our (ours)
2nd person: you	you	your (yours)	you	you	your (yours)
3rd person: he	him	his	they	them	their (theirs)
she	her	her (hers)			
it	it	its			

Practice 13

In the sentences below, underline the pronouns. Then, over each pronoun, write an *S* if the pronoun is in the subjective case, an *O* if it is in the objective case, and a *P* if it is in the possessive case.

EXAMPLE: We sent our résumés; then the company invited us to go for interviews.
<small>   S   P   O</small>

1. My best friend and I had our job interviews on the same day.

2. To prepare, we had attended a job interviewing workshop.

3. Until then, I hadn't realized the importance of a first impression.

4. Our workshop leader explained that we had to make a good first impression or we wouldn't get a chance to make a second.

5. A few days before my interview, I had my hair cut.

6. Tom helped me decide what to wear, and I helped him.

7. We looked very professional when we headed for the Astra Insurance Company.

8. I chew gum occasionally, and so does Tom, but we left our gum at home.

9. Tom was offered a job in customer service because he was polite and professional.

10. He asked thoughtful questions about the responsibilities of the job before he accepted it.

11. I was offered a trainee position in the accounting department.

12. To celebrate, we took our families out to dinner.

PART G   *Choosing the Correct Case after AND or OR*

When nouns or pronouns are joined by *and* or *or*, be careful to use the correct pronoun case after the *and* or the *or*.

> (1) **Incorrect:** *Bob* and *her* have to leave soon.

- In sentence (1), the pronoun *her* should be in the *subjective case* because it is part of the subject of the sentence.

> (2) **Revised:** *Bob* and *she* have to leave soon.

- Change *her* to *she.*

> (3) **Incorrect:** The dean congratulated *Charles* and *I.*

- In sentence (3), the pronoun *I* should be in the *objective case* because it is the object of the verb *congratulated.*

- The dean congratulated *whom?* The dean congratulated *me.*

> (4) **Revised:** The dean congratulated *Charles* and *me.*

- Change *I* to *me.*

> (5) **Incorrect:** Is that letter for *them* or *he?*

- In sentence (5), both objects of the preposition *for* must be in the *objective case.*

  What should *he* be changed to? _____

One simple way to make sure that you have the right pronoun case is to leave out the *and* or the *or*, and the word before it. You probably would not write these sentences:

(6) **Incorrect:** *Her* have to leave soon.

(7) **Incorrect:** The dean congratulated *I*.

(8) **Incorrect:** Is that letter for *he?*

These sentences look and sound strange, and you would know that they have to be corrected.

Practice 14

Circle the correct pronoun in the parentheses. If the pronoun is a *subject,* use the *subjective case.* If the pronoun is the *object* of a verb or a preposition, use the *objective case.*

1. Frieda and (I, me) were born in Bogotá, Colombia.

2. My brother gave Kylee and (I, me) a ride to the subway.

3. For (we, us), a swim in the ocean on a hot day is one of life's greatest joys.

4. If it were up to Angelo and (she, her), they would spend all their time searching for out-of-print LPs.

5. Our lab instructor expects Dan and (I, me) to hand in our report today.

6. I'm going to the movies tonight with Yolanda and (she, her).

7. The foreman chose Ellen and (he, him).

8. Between you and (I, me), I don't like spinach.

9. Robert and (he, him) have decided to go to Rocky Mountain National Park with Jacinto and (I, me).

10. Either (he, him) or (she, her) must work overtime.

Practice 15

Revise the sentences in which the pronouns are in the wrong case. Write a C in the blank next to each sentence that is correct.

1. Annie and me enjoy going to the gym every day. _____

2. Her and me have tried every class, from kickboxing to spinning. _____

3. Between you and I, I favor hydrobox, which is kickboxing in water. _____

4. Us and our friends also use the pool for water aerobics. _____

5. On cold days, however, they and I prefer step classes to keep warm. _____

6. Stationary cycling sometimes feels boring to Annie and I. _____

7. On the other hand, it is a good time for she and I to daydream. ____

8. Annie favors body pump classes, but I think she likes the instructor. ____

9. I am not sure whether him or weightlifting makes her sweat so much. ____

10. Talking day and night about our aching muscles gives her and me

    mouth and jaw exercise too. ____

PART H *Choosing the Correct Case in Comparisons*

Pronouns in comparisons usually follow *than* or *as*.

> (1) Ferdinand is taller *than* I.
> (2) These guidelines help you as much *as* me.

● In sentence (1), the comparison is completed with a pronoun in the subjective case, *I*.

● In sentence (2), the comparison is completed with a pronoun in the objective case, *me*.

> (1) Ferdinand is taller than I . . . (am tall).
> (2) These guidelines help you as much as . . . (they help) . . . me.

● A comparison is really a kind of shorthand that omits repetitious words.

By completing the comparison mentally, you can choose the correct case for the pronoun.

  BE CAREFUL: The case of the pronoun you place after *than* or *as* can change the meaning of the sentence.

> (3) Diana likes Tom more than *I* . . . (more than *I* like him).
>   *or*
> (4) Diana likes Tom more than *me* . . . (more than she likes *me*).

● Sentence (3) says that Diana likes Tom more than I like Tom.

● Sentence (4) says that Diana likes Tom more than she likes me.*

————

*For more work on comparisons, see Chapter 22, Part C.

Practice 16

Circle the correct pronoun in these comparisons.

1. You exercise more often than (I, me).

2. The movie scared us more than it did (he, him).

3. Diego eats dinner earlier than (I, me).

4. She ran a better campaign for the local school board than (he, him).

5. Stan cannot memorize vocabulary words faster than (he, him).

6. The ringing of a telephone disturbs her more than it disturbs (they, them).

7. They may think they are sharper than (she, her), but wait until they tangle with her and find out the truth.

8. I hate doing laundry more than (they, them).

9. Sometimes our children are more mature than (we, us).

10. Remembering birthdays seems easier for me than for (he, him).

Practice 17

Revise only those sentences in which the pronoun after the comparison is in the wrong case. Write a *C* in the blank next to each correct sentence.

1. Ben walked to Death Valley more slowly than us. _____

2. Jean can sing Haitian folk songs better than me. _____

3. Nobody, but nobody, can whistle louder than she. _____

4. Sarah was surprised that Joyce paid more than her for a ticket. _____

5. In a crisis, you can reach us sooner than you can reach them. _____

6. Before switching jobs, I wanted to know if Rose would be as good a

   supervisor as him. _____

7. The night shift suits her better than I. _____

8. Antoinette is six feet tall; no one on the loading dock is taller than her. _____

Practice 18

On separate paper, write three sentences using comparisons that are completed with pronouns. Choose each pronoun case carefully.

PART I   *Using Pronouns with -SELF and -SELVES*

Pronouns with *-self* and *-selves* are used in two ways.

> (1) José admired *himself* in the mirror.

● In sentence (1), José did something to *himself*; he admired *himself*. In this sentence, *himself* is called a *reflexive* pronoun.

> (2) The teacher *herself* thought the test was too difficult.

● In sentence (2), *herself* emphasizes the fact that the teacher—much to her surprise—found the test too hard. In this sentence, *herself* is called an *intensive* pronoun.

This chart will help you choose the right reflexive or intensive pronoun.

Antecedent		Reflexive or Intensive Pronoun
Singular	I	myself
	you	yourself
	he	himself
	she	herself
	it	itself
Plural	we	ourselves
	you	yourselves
	they	themselves

Note that in the plural *-self* is changed to *-selves*.

Practice 19

Write the correct reflexive or intensive pronoun in each sentence. Be careful to match the pronoun with the antecedent.

EXAMPLES: I should have stopped _____myself_____.

Roberta _____herself_____ made this bracelet.

1. We built all the cabinets _____.

2. He _____ was surprised to discover that he had a green thumb.

3. Did you give _____ a party after you graduated?

4. Rick, look at _____ in the mirror!

5. Don't bother; Don and André will hang the pictures _____.

6. The trainer _____ was amazed at the progress the athletes had made.

7. Sonia found _____ in a difficult situation.

8. These new lamps turn _____ on and off.

9. The oven cleans _____ .

10. Because he snores loudly, he wakes _____ up several times each night.

Practice 20

On separate paper, write three sentences, using either a reflexive or an intensive pronoun in each.

Practice 21   Writing Assignment

In a small group, discuss the factors that seem absolutely necessary for a successful marriage or long-term relationship. As a group, brainstorm for four or five key factors.

Now imagine that a friend with very little experience has asked you for written advice about relationships. Each member of the group should choose just one of the factors and write a letter to this person. Explain in detail why this factor—for example, honesty or mutual respect—is so important to a good relationship.

Read the finished letters to one another. Which letters give the best advice or are the most convincing? Why? Exchange letters with a partner, checking for the correct use of pronouns.

✔ Chapter Highlights

● **A pronoun takes the place of or refers to a noun or another pronoun:**

Louise said that *she* would leave work early.

● **The word that a pronoun refers to is its antecedent:**

I have chosen *my* seat for the concert.
(*I* is the antecedent of *my*.)

● **A pronoun that refers to an indefinite pronoun or a collective noun should be singular:**

Everyone had cleared the papers off *his* or *her* desk.

The *committee* will give *its* report Friday.

● **A pronoun after *and* or *or* is usually in the subjective or objective case:**

Dr. Smythe and *she* always work as a team. *(subjective)*

The bus driver wouldn't give the map to Ms. Tallon or *me*. *(objective)*

● **Pronouns in comparisons usually follow *than* or *as*:**

Frank likes Sally more than *I*.
(*subjective:* . . . more than I like Sally)

Frank likes Sally more than *me*.
(*objective:* . . . more than he likes me)

● **A pronoun ending in *-self* (singular) or *-selves* (plural) may be used as a reflexive or an intensive pronoun. A reflexive pronoun shows that someone did something to himself or to herself; an intensive pronoun is used for emphasis:**

On his trip, Martin bought nothing for *himself*.

The musicians *themselves* were almost late for the street fair.

Proofread the following essay for pronoun errors. Cross out any incorrect, vague, or repetitious pronouns, and make your corrections above the lines. Use nouns to replace vague pronouns.

A New Beginning

(1) Martha Andrews, she was a good student in high school. (2) After graduation, she found a job as a bank teller in order to save money for college. (3) She liked her job because she knew her regular customers and enjoyed handling his or her business. (4) When she was nineteen, Patrick Kelvin, another teller, and her fell in love and married. (5) By the time she was twenty-two, she had become the mother of three children. (6) Martha's plans for college faded.

(7) As her fortieth birthday approached, Martha began thinking about going to college to study accounting; however, she had many fears. (8) Would she remember how to study after so many years? (9) Would the younger students be smarter than her? (10) Would she feel out of place with them? (11) Worst of all, her husband, he worried that Martha would neglect him. (12) He thought that everyone who went to college forgot their family. (13) He also feared that Martha would be more successful than him.

(14) One of Martha's children, who attended college hisself, encouraged her. (15) With his help, Martha got the courage to visit Middleton College. (16) In the admissions office, they told her that older students were valued at Middleton. (17) Older students often enriched classes because he or she brought a wealth of life experiences with them. (18) Martha also learned that the college had a special program to help their older students adjust to school.

(19) Martha enrolled in college the next fall. (20) To their credit, her and her husband soon realized that they had made the right decision.

Adjectives and Adverbs

PART A	Defining and Writing Adjectives and Adverbs
PART B	A Troublesome Pair: GOOD/WELL
PART C	Writing Comparatives
PART D	Writing Superlatives
PART E	Troublesome Comparatives and Superlatives
PART F	Demonstrative Adjectives: THIS/THAT and THESE/THOSE

PART A   Defining and Writing Adjectives and Adverbs

Adjectives and adverbs are two kinds of descriptive words. An *adjective* describes a noun or a pronoun. It tells *which one, what kind,* or *how many.*

> (1) The *red* coat belongs to me.
>
> (2) He looks *healthy.*

- In sentence (1), the adjective *red* describes the noun *coat.*
- In sentence (2), the adjective *healthy* describes the pronoun *he.*

An *adverb* describes a verb, an adjective, or another adverb. Adverbs often end in *-ly*. They tell *how, to what extent, why, when,* or *where.*

> (3) Laura sings *loudly.*
> (4) My biology instructor is *extremely* short.
> (5) Lift this box *very* carefully.

● In sentence (3), *loudly* describes the verb *sings.* How does Laura sing? She sings *loudly.*

● In sentence (4), *extremely* describes the adjective *short.* How short is the instructor? *Extremely* short.

● In sentence (5), *very* describes the adverb *carefully.* How carefully should you lift the box? *Very* carefully.

Practice 1

Complete each sentence with an appropriate adjective from the list below.

funny	orange	sarcastic	energetic
old	tired	bitter	little

1. Janet is _____.

2. He often wears a(n) _____ baseball cap.

3. _____ remarks will be his downfall.

4. My daughter collects _____ movie posters.

5. This coffee tastes _____.

Practice 2

Complete each sentence with an appropriate adverb from the list below.

quietly	loudly	wildly	convincingly
madly	quickly	constantly	happily

1. The waiter _____ cleaned the table.

2. Mr. Huff whistles _____.

3. The lawyer spoke _____.

4. They charged _____ down the long hallway.

5. _____, he entered the rear door of the church.

Many adjectives can be changed into adverbs by adding an *-ly* ending. For example, *glad* becomes *gladly, thoughtful* becomes *thoughtfully,* and *wise* becomes *wisely.*

Be especially careful of the adjectives and adverbs in this list; they are easily confused.

Adjective	Adverb	Adjective	Adverb
awful	awfully	quiet	quietly
bad	badly	real	really
poor	poorly	sure	surely
quick	quickly		

(6) This chair is a *real* antique.
(7) She has a *really* bad sprain.

- In sentence (6), *real* is an adjective describing the noun *antique.*

- In sentence (7), *really* is an adverb describing the adjective *bad.* How bad is the sprain? The sprain is *really* bad.

Practice 3

Change each adjective in the left-hand column into its adverb form.*

Adjective	Adverb

EXAMPLE: You are polite.   You answer _____ politely _____.

1. She is honest.   1. She responds _____.

2. They are loud.   2. They sing _____.

3. It is easy.   3. It turns _____.

4. We are careful.   4. We decide _____.

5. He is creative.   5. He thinks _____.

6. She was quick.   6. She acted _____.

7. It is perfect.   7. It fits _____.

8. It is real.   8. It is _____ hot.

9. He is eager.   9. He waited _____.

10. We are joyful.   10. We watch _____.

*If you have questions about spelling, see Chapter 31, Part F.

Practice 4

Circle the adjective or adverb form of the word in parentheses.

EXAMPLE: The office is (quiet, quietly) on a snowy Sunday afternoon.

1. On the couch, a young man snores (noisy, noisily).

2. A (tired, tiredly) young woman slumps in a chair.

3. (Sudden, Suddenly), the telephone rings.

4. Grunting (sleepy, sleepily), the man rolls over.

5. By the time he answers the phone, he is (full, fully) awake.

6. He takes notes (hasty, hastily) and nods to his partner.

7. She puts on her (official, officially) jacket and grabs her bag of tools.

8. This is another (typical, typically) call for two (high, highly) skilled technicians.

9. The man rereads his notes aloud while the panel truck moves (quick, quickly) through the streets.

10. In a (calm, calmly) voice, the man describes the problem to his partner.

11. Sam and Terri Phillips have been (anxious, anxiously) awaiting their arrival.

12. They point (sad, sadly) to the blank TV screen and say, "The game starts in exactly one hour."

13. The technicians examine the set (careful, carefully); the problem is not a (serious, seriously) one.

14. In fifty-five minutes, the screen is (bright, brightly) lit, and the game is about to begin.

15. "Another job well done," they whisper (happy, happily) to each other as they leave.

Practice 5

On separate paper, write sentences using the following adjectives and adverbs:
quick/quickly, bad/badly, glad/gladly, real/really, easy/easily.

EXAMPLES: (*cheerful*) You are cheerful this morning.

(*cheerfully*) You make breakfast cheerfully.

PART B   *A Troublesome Pair: GOOD/WELL*

Unlike most adjectives, *good* does not add *-ly* to become an adverb; it changes to *well*.

> (1) **Adjective:** Peter is a *good* student.
> (2) **Adverb:** He writes *well*.

● In sentence (1), the adjective *good* describes or modifies *student*.

● In sentence (2), the adverb *well* describes or modifies *writes*.

Note, however, that *well* can be used as an adjective to mean *in good health*—for example, *He felt well after his long vacation.*

Practice 6

Write either *good* or *well* in each sentence.

EXAMPLE: Charles plays ball very _____ well _____.

1. Lorelle is a _____ pilot.

2. She handles a plane _____.

3. How _____ do you understand virtual reality?

4. Pam knows my bad habits very _____.

5. It is a _____ thing we ran into each other.

6. Brian works _____ with other people.

7. How _____ or how badly did you do at the tryouts?

8. Were the cherry tarts _____ or tasteless?

9. Denzel Washington is not just a _____ actor; he's a great one.

10. These plants don't grow very _____ in the sunlight.

11. Carole doesn't look as though she takes _____ care of herself.

12. He asked _____ questions at the meeting, and she

    answered them _____.

PART C   *Writing Comparatives*

> (1) John is *tall.*
> (2) John is *taller* than Mike.

● Sentence (1) describes John with the adjective *tall,* but sentence (2) *compares* John and Mike in terms of how tall they are: John is the *taller* of the two.

Taller **is called the** *comparative* **of** *tall.*

Use the comparative when you want to compare two people or things.

To Form Comparatives

Add *-er* to adjectives and adverbs that have *one syllable:**

short	shorter
fast	faster
thin	thinner

Place the word *more* before adjectives and adverbs that have *two or more syllables:*

foolish	more foolish
rotten	more rotten
happily	more happily

Practice 7

Write the comparative form of each word. Either add *-er* to the word or write *more* before it. Never add both *-er* and *more!*

EXAMPLES: _____ fresh *er* _____

_____*more*_____ willing _____

1. _____ fast _____   5. _____ thick _____

2. _____ interesting _____   6. _____ foolish _____

3. _____ hopeful _____   7. _____ valuable _____

4. _____ sweet _____   8. _____ cold _____

Here is one important exception to the rule that two-syllable words use *more* to form the comparative:

_____

*For questions about spelling, see Chapter 31, Part D.

> To show the comparative of two-syllable adjectives ending in -*y*, change the
> *y* to *i* and add -*er*.*
>
> cloudy   cloudier
>
> sunny   sunnier

Practice 8

Write the comparative form of each adjective.

EXAMPLE: happy _____*happier*_____

1. shiny _____   5. fancy _____
2. friendly _____   6. lucky _____
3. lazy _____   7. lively _____
4. easy _____   8. crazy _____

Practice 9

The following incorrect sentences use both *more* and -*er*. Decide which one is correct, and write your revised sentences on the lines provided.

REMEMBER: Write comparatives with either *more* or -*er*—not both!

EXAMPLES: Jan is more younger than her brother.

Jan is younger than her brother.

I feel more comfortabler in this chair than on the couch.

I feel more comfortable in this chair than on the couch.

1. Her new boss is more fussier than her previous one.

   _____

2. The trail was more rockier than we expected.

   _____

3. The people in my new neighborhood are more friendlier than those in my old one.

   _____

4. Magda has a more cheerfuler personality than her sister.

   _____

5. I have never seen a more duller TV program than this one.

   _____

*For questions about spelling, see Chapter 31, Part G.

6. The audience at this theater is more noisier than usual.

_____

7. His jacket is more newer than Rudy's.

_____

8. If today is more warmer than yesterday, we'll picnic on the lawn.

_____

Practice 10

On separate paper, write sentences using the comparative form of the following adjectives or adverbs: *dark, cloudy, fortunate, slowly, wet.*

EXAMPLE: (*funny*) This play is funnier than the one we saw last week.

PART D *Writing Superlatives*

> (1) Tim is the *tallest* player on the team.
> (2) Juan was voted the *most useful* player.

● In sentence (1), Tim is not just *tall* or *taller than* someone else; he is the *tallest* of all the players on the team.

● In sentence (2), Juan was voted the *most useful* of all the players.

Tallest **and** *most useful* **are called** *superlatives.*

Use the superlative when you wish to compare more than two people or things.

> ### To Form Superlatives
>
> Add *-est* to adjectives and adverbs of *one syllable:*
>
> short   shortest
>
> Place the word *most* before adjectives and adverbs that have *two or more syllables:*
>
> foolish   most foolish
>
> *Exception:* With two-syllable adjectives ending in *-y*, change the *y* to *i* and add *-est.**
>
> happy   happiest

_____

*For questions about spelling, see Chapter 31, Part G.

Practice 11

Write the superlative form of each word. Either add *-est* to the word or write *most* before it; do not do both.

EXAMPLES: _____ tall _est_____

    _most____ ridiculous _____

1. _____ loud _____   6. _____ wild _____

2. _____ colorful _____   7. _____ practical _____

3. _____ brave _____   8. _____ frightening _____

4. _____ strong _____   9. _____ green _____

5. _____ brilliant _____   10. _____ hazy _____

Practice 12

The following incorrect sentences use both *most* and *-est*. Decide which one is correct, and write your revised sentences on the lines provided.
REMEMBER: Write superlatives with either *most* or *-est*—not both!

EXAMPLES: Jane is the most youngest of my three children.

Jane is the youngest of my three children.

He is the most skillfulest guitarist in the band.

He is the most skillful guitarist in the band.

1. My nephew is the most thoughtfulest teenager I know.

   _____

2. The World Trade Center towers are the most tallest buildings in New York City.

   _____

3. This baby makes the most oddest gurgling noises we have ever heard.

   _____

4. Jackie always makes us laugh, but she is most funniest when she hasn't had enough sleep.

   _____

   _____

5. When I finally started college, I was the most eagerest student on campus.

   _____

6. Ms. Dross raises the most strangest reptiles in her basement.

   _____

7. This peach is the most ripest in the basket.

_____

8. He thinks that the most successfulest people are just lucky.

_____

PART E   *Troublesome Comparatives and Superlatives*

These comparatives and superlatives are some of the trickiest you will learn:

		Comparative	Superlative
Adjective:	good	better	best
Adverb:	well	better	best
Adjective:	bad	worse	worst
Adverb:	badly	worse	worst

Practice 13

Fill in the correct comparative or superlative form of the word in parentheses. REMEMBER: *Better* and *worse* compare *two* persons or things. *Best* and *worst* compare three or more persons or things.

EXAMPLES: Is this report _____*better*_____ (good) than my last one?
(Here two reports are compared.)

It was the _____*worst*_____ (bad) movie I have ever seen.
(Of *all* movies, it was the *most* awful.)

1. He likes jogging _____ (well) than running.

2. I like country and western music _____ (well) of all.

3. Bob's motorcycle rides _____ (bad) now than it did last week.

4. That is the _____ (bad) joke Molly has ever told!

5. The volleyball team played _____ (badly) than it did last year.

6. He plays the piano _____ (well) than he plays the guitar.

7. The traffic is _____ (bad) on Fridays than on Mondays.

8. That was the _____ (bad) cold I have had in years.

9. Sales are _____ (good) this year than last.

10. He is the _____ (good) mechanic in the shop.

11. Last year's drought was the _____ (bad) one in decades.

12. Do you take this person for _____ (good) or for

_____ (bad)?

PART F   *Demonstrative Adjectives: THIS/THAT and THESE/THOSE*

This, that, these, and *those* are called *demonstrative adjectives* because they point out, or demonstrate, which noun is meant.

> (1) I don't trust *that* wobbly front wheel.
> (2) *Those* toys are not as safe as their makers claim.

● In sentence (1), *that* points to a particular wheel, the wobbly front one.

● In sentence (2), *those* points to a particular group of toys.

Demonstrative adjectives are the only adjectives that change to show singular and plural:

Singular	Plural
this book	these books
that book	those books

This and *that* are used before singular nouns; *these* and *those* are used before plural nouns.

Practice 14

In each sentence, circle the correct form of the demonstrative adjective in parentheses.

1. (This, These) corn flakes taste like cardboard.

2. Mr. Lathorpe is sure (this, these) address is correct.

3. You can find (that, those) maps in the reference room.

4. Can you catch (that, those) waiter's eye?

5. I can't imagine what (that, those) gadgets are for.

6. We prefer (this, these) tennis court to (that, those) one.

7. The learning center is in (that, those) gray building.

8. (These, This) biography tells the story of Charles Curtis, the first Native

American elected to the Senate.

Practice 15   Writing Assignment

Sports figures and entertainers can be excellent role models. Sometimes, though, they can be bad examples and teach the wrong lessons. For example, some athletes and entertainers have been convicted of drug possession, spousal abuse, or assault.

Assume that you are concerned that your child or sibling is being negatively influenced by one of these figures. Write a "fan letter" to this person explaining the bad influence he or she is having on young people—in particular, your child or sibling. Convince him or her that being in the spotlight is a serious responsibility and that a positive change in behavior could help many young fans.

Brainstorm, freewrite, or cluster to generate ideas and examples to support your concern. Check your letter for the correct use of adjectives and adverbs.

Chapter Highlights

- **Most adverbs are formed by adding -*ly* to an adjective:**

  quick/quickly   bright/brightly   *but* good/well

- **Comparative adjectives and adverbs compare two persons or things:**

  I think that Don is *happier* than his brother.

  Laura can balance a checkbook *more quickly* than I can.

- **Superlative adjectives and adverbs compare more than two persons or things:**

  Last night, Ingrid had the *worst* headache of her life.

  That was the *most carefully* prepared speech I have ever heard.

- **The adjectives *good* and *bad* and the adverbs *well* and *badly* require special care in the comparative and the superlative:**

  good/better/best
  bad/worse/worst

  well/better/best
  badly/worse/worst

- **Demonstrative adjectives can be singular or plural:**

  this/that (chair)

  these/those (chairs)

Chapter Review

Proofread these paragraphs for adjective and adverb errors. Cross out the errors, and correct them above the lines.

A. (1) The most famousest comet, Halley's comet, appears regular every seventy-six years. (2) This mass of gas and dust has caused panic and fear because its appearance has often coincided with the baddest events in history. (3) During the Middle Ages, people believed that Halley's comet was a surely omen of destruction. (4) The most silly notions about Halley's comet came about during its 1910 appearance when people bought pills and bottled oxygen to protect themselves. (5) Although that sounds real foolish, they believed that poisonous gas was contained in the comet's brilliantly tail. (6) Despite the most wildest superstitions, Halley's comet has given us more better information about comets and our solar system.

B. (1) One of the real inspirational stories of our times is the story of Lance Armstrong. (2) In 1993, Armstrong became the World Cycling champion. (3) In 1999, he won the 2,287-mile Tour de France, the world's most greatest bike race. (4) Between those two events, however, he won something that was even more importanter.

(5) In 1996, Lance Armstrong was diagnosed with testicular cancer. (6) The cancer spread to his brain, abdomen, and lungs. (7) He was given only a 40 percent chance of surviving and even worser odds of ever returning to biking. (8) According to his doctors, however, he approached his cancer with the same skills he used for competitive sports: discipline, persistence, sacrifice. (9) Armstrong courageous went through brain surgery and incredibly painful chemotherapy, but he also continued training. (10) Two years later, he became only the second American to win the twenty-one-day Tour de France. (11) More stronger than ever, Armstrong finished seven minutes and thirty-seven seconds ahead of his most nearest competitor. (12) Astonishingly enough, he went on to win the Tour de France the following year and an Olympic bronze in 2000.

(13) Although some people believe that cancer is the worstest thing that can happen, Armstrong maintains that cancer is the most best thing that ever happened to him. (14) In his book, *It's Not about the Bike,* he writes that without those disease he would not have married or had a child. (15) When you face death, he says, your focus becomes really clear.

CHAPTER 23

Prepositions

PART A *Defining Prepositions*

PART B *Troublesome Prepositions: IN, ON, and LIKE*

PART C *Prepositions in Common Expressions*

PART A — Defining Prepositions

A preposition is a word like *at, from, in,* or *of.* Below is a partial list of common prepositions:*

Common Prepositions		
about	beside	off
above	between	on
across	by	over
after	during	through
against	except	to
along	for	toward
among	from	under
around	in	until
at	into	up
before	like	with
behind	of	without

A preposition is usually followed by a noun or pronoun. The noun or pronoun is called the *object* of the preposition. Together, the preposition and its object are called a *prepositional phrase.*

---

*For more work on prepositions, see Chapter 6, Part C.

Here are some prepositional phrases:

Prepositional Phrase	=	Preposition	+	Object
after the movie		after		the movie
at Kean College		at		Kean College
beside them		beside		them
between you and me		between		you and me

The preposition shows a relationship between the object of the preposition and some other word in the sentence. Below are some sentences with prepositional phrases:

(1) Ms. Kringell arrived *at noon.*

(2) A man *in a gray suit* bought three lottery tickets.

(3) The huge moving van sped *through the tunnel.*

● In sentence (1), the prepositional phrase *at noon* tells when Ms. Kringell arrived. It describes *arrived.*

● In sentence (2), the prepositional phrase *in a gray suit* describes how the man was dressed. It describes *man.*

● What is the prepositional phrase in sentence (3)? _____

Which word does it describe? _____

Practice 1

Underline the prepositional phrases in the following sentences.

1. Bill collected some interesting facts about human biology.

2. Human eyesight is sharpest at midday.

3. In extreme cold, shivering produces heat, which can save lives.

4. A pound of body weight equals 3,500 calories.

5. Each of us has a distinguishing odor.

6. Fingernails grow fastest in summer.

7. One of every ten people is left-handed.

8. The human body contains approximately ten pints of blood.

9. Beards grow more rapidly than any other hair on the human body.

10. Most people with an extra rib are men.

PART B — Troublesome Prepositions: IN, ON, and LIKE

IN/ON for Time

Use *in* before seasons of the year, before months not followed by specific dates, and before years that do not include specific dates.

> (1) *In the summer,* some of us like to laze around in the sun.
>
> (2) No classes will meet *in January.*
>
> (3) Rona was a student at Centerville Business School *in 2001.*

Use *on* before days of the week, before holidays, and before months if a date follows.

> (4) *On Thursday,* the gym was closed for renovations.
>
> (5) The city looked deserted *on Christmas Eve.*
>
> (6) We hope to arrive in Burlington *on October 3.*

Practice 2

Writer either *in* or *on* in the following sentences.

EXAMPLE: _____*In*_____ the fall of 1999, eleven people who were escaping from Cuba to the United States died when their small boat overturned.

1. The only survivor, six-year-old Elián González, was rescued off the Florida coast _____ Thanksgiving Day.

2. _____ November 26, with his mother dead at sea and his father in Cuba, Elián went to live with Cuban relatives in Miami.

3. Elián's father arrived in the United States _____ April, but Elián's relatives would not give up the child to return to Cuba.

4. _____ Saturday, April 29, in a frightening raid by federal agents, Elián was taken from his relatives to be reunited with his father.

5. Elián and his father returned to Cuba _____ the summer, but in terms of both political and personal consequences, the story does not end there.

IN/ON for Place

In means *inside of.*

> (1) My grandmother slept *in the spare bedroom.*
>
> (2) The exchange student spent the summer *in Sweden.*

On means *on top of* or *at a particular place.*

> (3) The spinach pie *on the table* is for tonight's book discussion group.
> (4) Dr. Helfman lives *on Marblehead Road*.

Practice 3

Write either *in* or *on* in the following sentences.

EXAMPLE: Here's how you can make raspberry sherbet right _____*in*_____ your own kitchen.

1. Set out all the ingredients you need _____ a counter top: $\frac{3}{4}$ cup of sugar, 1 cup warm water, $\frac{1}{2}$ cup light corn syrup, $\frac{1}{4}$ cup lemon juice, 1 container of strained raspberries, and 2 egg whites.

2. Dissolve the sugar _____ the warm water; then add the corn syrup, lemon juice, and raspberries, and freeze the mixture until the edges are hard.

3. _____ a separate container, beat the egg whites until they are stiff.

4. Whip the partly frozen mixture _____ a chilled bowl so that it is smooth but not melted.

5. After folding in the egg whites quickly, place the mixture _____ a

   shelf _____ your refrigerator freezer until the sherbet is firm.

LIKE

Like is a preposition that means *similar to*. Therefore, it is followed by an object (usually a noun or a pronoun).

> (1) *Like you*, I prefer watching films on a VCR rather than going to a crowded movie theater.

Do not confuse *like* with *as* or *as if*. *As* and *as if* are subordinating conjunctions.*
They are followed by a subject and a verb.

> (2) *As the instructions explain*, insert flap B into slit B before folding the bottom in half.
> (3) Robert sometimes acts *as if he has never made a mistake*.

---

*For more work on subordinating conjunctions, see Chapter 14.

Practice 4

Write *like, as,* or *as if* in the following sentences.

EXAMPLE: George grinned _____*as*_____ he approached the door.

1. _____ his friends, Kirk plays basketball at least once a week.

2. Joyce came home _____ I was leaving, but she persuaded me to stay a bit longer.

3. Those children are behaving _____ they are lost.

4. Penny's voice sounds _____ her mother's.

5. _____ the weather forecaster predicted, six inches of snow fell overnight.

PART C — *Prepositions in Common Expressions*

Prepositions often are combined with other words to form certain expressions—groups of words, or phrases, in common use. These expressions can sometimes be confusing. Below is a list of some troublesome expressions. If you are in doubt about others, consult a dictionary.

Common Expressions with Prepositions

Expression	Example
acquainted with	He became *acquainted with* his duties.
addicted to	I am *addicted to* chocolate.
agree on (a plan)	They finally *agreed on* a sales strategy.
agree to (another's proposal)	Did she *agree to* their demands?
angry about or at (a thing)	The subway riders are *angry about* (or *at*) the delays.
angry with (a person)	The manager seems *angry with* Jake.
apply for (a position)	You should *apply for* this job.
approve of	Does he *approve of* the proposed budget?
consist of	The plot *consisted of* both murder and intrigue.
contrast with	The red lettering *contrasts* nicely *with* the gray stationery.
convenient for	Is Friday *convenient for* you?
correspond with (write)	My daughter *corresponds with* a pen pal in India.
deal with	How do you *deal with* friends who always want to borrow your notes?
depend on	He *depends on* your advice.

Common Expressions with Prepositions (*continued*)

Expression	Example
differ from (something)	A diesel engine *differs from* a gasoline engine.
differ with (a person)	On that point, I *differ with* the medical technician.
different from	His account of the accident is *different from* hers.
displeased with	She is *displeased with* all the publicity.
fond of	We are all *fond of* Sam's grandmother.
grateful for (something)	Jim was *grateful for* the two test review sessions.
grateful to (someone)	We are *grateful to* the plumber for repairing the leak on Sunday.
identical with	This watch is *identical with* hers.
interested in	George is *interested in* modern art.
interfere with	Does the party *interfere with* your study plans?
object to	She *objects to* the increase in the state sales tax.
protect against	This vaccine *protects* people *against* the flu.
reason with	Don't *reason with* a hungry pit bull.
reply to	Did the newspaper editor *reply to* your letter?
responsible for	Omar is *responsible for* marketing.
shocked at	We were *shocked at* the damage to the buildings.
similar to	That popular song is *similar to* another one I know.
specialize in	The shop *specializes in* clothing for large men.
succeed in	Gandhi *succeeded in* freeing India from British rule.
take advantage of	Let's *take advantage of* that two-for-one paperback book sale.
worry about	I no longer *worry about* my manager's moods.

Practice 5

Circle the correct expressions in these sentences.

1. The amazing career of Albert Goodwill Spalding (consisted of, consisted in) baseball and business success.

2. At first, his mother did not (approve in, approve of) his playing professional ball.

3. Spalding obeyed his mother and (applied for, applied to) a "regular" job.

4. Eventually (displeased with, displeased at) the work he found, Spalding signed up with the Boston Red Stockings in 1871.

5. Over the next five years, the Boston team came to (depend on, depend with) his unusual underhand pitching style.

6. In fact, he was the first pitcher ever to (succeed in, succeed on) winning two hundred games.

7. Spalding soon became more (interested in, interested with) designing baseballs than in playing.

8. Pitchers were (grateful for, grateful to) him for marketing the ball he had designed for his own pitching use; it became the official ball of the National League.

9. Spalding became (fond for, fond of) designing other kinds of balls; for example, he designed the first basketball.

10. He also (dealt on, dealt with) the problem of what to use as goals in this new ball game.

11. He (took advantage of, took advantage for) peach baskets, and the new game was called basketball.

12. By the 1890s, Spalding had been (responsible for, responsible to) developing one of the world's largest sporting goods companies.

Practice 6   Writing Assignment

A friend or relative of yours has come to spend a holiday week in your city. He or she has never been there before and wants advice on sightseeing. In complete sentences, write directions for one day's sightseeing. Make sure to explain why you think this person would enjoy visiting each particular spot.

Organize your directions according to time order: that is, what to do first, second, and so on. Use transitional expressions like *then*, *after*, and *while* to indicate time order.

Be especially careful of the prepositions *in* and *on*. Try to work in a few of the expressions listed in Part C.

✔ Chapter Highlights

● Prepositions are words like *at, from, in,* and *of.* A prepositional phrase contains a preposition and its object:

The tree *beneath my window* has lost its leaves.

● Be careful of the prepositions *in, on,* and *like:*

I expect to graduate *in* June.
I expect to graduate *on* June 10.

The Packards live *in* Tacoma.
The Packards live *on* Farnsworth Avenue.

Like my father, I am a Dodgers fan.

● Prepositions are often combined with other words to form fixed phrases:

convenient for, different from, reason with

Chapter Review

Proofread this essay for preposition errors. Cross out the errors, and correct them above the lines.

Taking a Stand

(1) Important events often begin with a person who decides to take a stand. (2) At Thursday, December 1, 1955, Rosa Parks helped inspire the civil rights movement simply by sitting down.

(3) On 1955, city buses in Montgomery, Alabama, were segregated. (4) African-American riders had to sit in the back of the bus. (5) The African-American community and its leaders were angry with segregation. (6) They also knew that the city depended at its African-American riders for income. (7) They were waiting to take advantage about the right occasion to organize a bus boycott. (8) Rosa Parks gave them that occasion.

(9) Rosa Parks was a forty-two-year-old tailor's assistant. (10) At that December afternoon, she was returning home from work. (11) When she was told to give her seat to a white man, she objected from moving. (12) She was arrested.

(13) African-American community leaders organized a boycott, and the buses stayed empty for more than a year. (14) To deal about the lack of transportation,

African Americans organized a system of car pools or just walked. (15) At last, in December 20, 1956, an order from the United States Supreme Court declared Montgomery's bus laws unconstitutional. (16) The next day, Rosa Parks was photographed inside one of the first integrated buses on the city. (17) Her simple act of courage helped change the course of American history.

Proofreading

Proofread the following essay for the incorrect use of nouns, pronouns, adjectives, adverbs, and prepositions. Cross out errors, and correct them above the lines. (You should find twenty-six errors.)

The Last Frontier

(1) When the government of Brazil opened the Amazon rain forest for settlement on the 1970s, they created the last frontier on earth. (2) Many concerned man and woman everywhere now fear that the move has been a disasters for the land and for the people.

(3) The most large rain forest in the world, the Amazon rain forest has been hit real hard. (4) The government built highways to make it more easy for poor people to get to the land, but the roads also made investors interested to the forest. (5) Lumber companies chopped down millions of tree. (6) Ranchers and settlers theirselves burned the forest to make room for cattle and crops. (7) All this activities have taken their toll: in one area, which is the size of Colorado, three-quarters of the rain forest has already been destroyed. (8) Many kinds of plants and animals have been lost forever.

(9) The Indians of the rain forest, they are also threatened by this wholesale destruction. (10) Ranchers, miners, loggers, and settlers have moved onto Indian lands. (11) Contact with the outside world has changed the Indians' traditional way of life. (12) A few Indian tribe have made economic and political gains; however, many tribes have totally disappeared.

(13) Many of the settler are not doing very good either. (14) People have poured into the region too rapid, and the government is unable to provide the needed services. (15) Small villages have become crowded cities, diseases (especially malaria) have spread, and lawlessness is common. (16) Worse of all, the soil beneath the rain forest is not fertile. (17) After a few years, the settlers' land, it is worthless. (18) As the settlers go into debt, businesses take advantage for the situation by buying land quick and exploiting it bad.

(19) Can the situation in the rain forest improve? (20) Although the Brazilian government has been trying to preserve those forest, thousands of fires are still

set every year to clear land for cattle grazing, planting, and building. (21) On the more hopeful side, however, scientists have discovered fruits in the rain forest that are extreme high in vitamins and proteins. (22) Those fruits would be much better crops for the rain forest than the corn, rice, and beans that farmers are growing now. (23) The world watches nervous. (24) Will the Earth's preciousest rain forest survive?

Transforming

Change the subject of this paragraph from singular (the Saint Bernard) to plural (Saint Bernards), changing every *the dog* to *dogs*, every *it* to *they*, and so forth. Make all necessary verb and other changes. Write your revisions above the lines.

(1) The Saint Bernard is a legendary dog famous for its many acts of bravery. (2) Bred in the wild mountains of Switzerland, it can find paths in the worst snowstorms, smell human beings buried in snow, and detect avalanches before they occur. (3) This powerful yet sensitive creature works in rescue patrols. (4) When a Saint Bernard finds a hurt traveler, it lies down next to the sufferer to keep him or her warm and licks the person's face to restore consciousness. (5) Another dog goes back to headquarters to sound the alarm and guide a rescue party to the scene. (6) In all, the Saint Bernard has saved more than two thousand lives. (7) Oddly enough, though this dog has been known for about three hundred years, the Saint Bernard did not get its name until about a hundred years ago. (8) The Saint Bernard was named for a shelter in the Swiss Alps. (9) Monks of the shelter of Saint Bernard used this dog in rescue patrols.

Tell How Someone Changed Your Life

Strong writing flows clearly from point to point so that a reader can follow easily. In your class or group, read this essay, aloud if possible. As you read, pay special attention to organization.

Stephanie

(1) There are many people who are important to me. However, the most important person is Stephanie. Stephanie is my daughter. She has changed my life completely. She has changed my life in a positive way.

(2) Stephanie is only five years old, but she has taught me the value of education. When I found out that I was pregnant, my life changed in a positive way. Before I got pregnant, I didn't like school. I went to school just to please my mom, but I wasn't learning anything. When I found out that I was pregnant, I changed my mind about education. I wanted to give my baby the best of this world. I knew that without a good education, I wasn't going anywhere, so I decided to get my life together.

(3) Stephanie taught me not to give up. I remember when she was trying to walk, and she fell down. She didn't stop but kept on going until she learned how to walk.

(4) In conclusion, you can learn a lot from babies. I learned not to give up. Stephanie is the most important person in the whole world to me. She has changed me in the past, and she will continue to change me in the future.

Claudia Huezo, student

1. How effective is this essay?

   _____ Clear thesis statement?   _____ Good support?

   _____ Logical organization?   _____ Effective conclusion?

2. Claudia Huezo has organized her essay very well: introduction and thesis statement, two supporting paragraphs, conclusion. Is the main idea of each supporting paragraph clear? Does each have a good topic sentence?

3. Is each supporting paragraph developed with enough facts and details? If not, what advice would you give the writer for revising, especially paragraph (3)?

4. This student has picked a wonderful subject and writes clearly—two excellent qualities. However, did you find any places where short, choppy, or repetitious sentences could be improved?

   If so, point out one or two places where Huezo might cross out or rewrite repetitious language (where she says the same thing twice in the same words). Point out one or two places where she might combine short sentences for variety.

5. Proofread for grammar and spelling. Do you spot any error patterns this student should watch out for?

Writing and Revising Ideas

1. Tell how someone changed your life.

2. Discuss two reasons why education is (is not) important.

Before you write, plan or outline your paragraph or essay so that it will be clearly organized (see Chapter 3, Part E, and Chapter 4, Part B). As you revise, pay special attention to the order of ideas and to clear, concise writing without needless repetition (see Chapter 4, Part C).

UNIT 5 *Writing Assignments*

As you complete each writing assignment, remember to perform these steps:

- Write a clear, complete topic sentence.

- Use freewriting, brainstorming, or clustering to generate ideas for the body of your paragraph, essay, or speech.

- Arrange your best ideas in a plan.

- Revise for support, unity, coherence, and exact language.

- Proofread for grammar, punctuation, and spelling errors.

Writing Assignment 1: *Explain your job.* Explain what you do—your duties and responsibilities—to someone who knows nothing about your kind of work but is interested in it. In your first sentence, sum up the work you do. Then name the equipment you use and tell how you spend an average working day. Explain the rewards and drawbacks of your job. Finally, proofread for the correct use of nouns, pronouns, adjectives, adverbs, and prepositions.

Writing Assignment 2: *Give an award.* When we think of awards, we generally think of awards for the most home runs or the highest grade average. However, Cal Ripkin, Jr., of the Baltimore Orioles, became famous because he played in a record number of consecutive games. In other words, his award was for *showing up,* for *being there,* for *constancy.* Write a speech for an awards dinner in honor of someone who deserves recognition for this kind of constancy. Perhaps your parents deserve the award, or your spouse, or the law enforcement officer on the beat in your neighborhood. Be specific in explaining why this person deserves the award. You might try a humorous approach. Proofread your speech for the correct use of nouns, pronouns, adjectives, adverbs, and prepositions.

Writing Assignment 3: *Discuss your future.* Imagine yourself ten years from now; how will your life be different? Pick one major way in which you expect it will have changed. You may want to choose a difference in your income, your marital status, your idea of success, or anything else that is important to you. Your first sentence should state this expected change. Then explain why this change will be important to you. Proofread for the correct use of nouns, pronouns, adjectives, adverbs, and prepositions.

Writing Assignment 4: *Respond to a natural setting.* Have you ever felt especially connected to the natural world? Did a special place (a specific mountain, forest, garden, beach, body of water, and so on) or a specific experience (a particular incident while you were camping, hiking, biking, skiing, and so on) make you feel that way? If so, describe the experience, including the setting. Explain how or why your response was different from your usual one. Proofread for the correct use of nouns, pronouns, adjectives, adverbs, and prepositions.

UNIT 6

Revising for Consistency and Parallelism

This unit will teach you some easy but effective ways to add style to your writing. In this unit, you will

- Make sure your verbs and pronouns are consistent

- Use a secret weapon of many writers— parallel structure

- Vary the lengths and types of your sentences

Spotlight on Writing

This writer uses balanced sentences to make her point about date rape. If possible, read her paragraph aloud.

Women charge that date rape is the hidden crime; men complain it is hard to prevent a crime they can't define. Women say it isn't taken seriously; men say it is a concept invented by women who like to tease but not take the consequences. Women say the date-rape debate is the first time the nation has talked frankly about sex; men say it is women's unconscious reaction to the excesses of the sexual revolution. Meanwhile, men and women argue among themselves about the "gray area" that surrounds the whole murky arena of sexual relations, and there is no consensus in sight.

Nancy Gibbs, "When Is It Rape?" *Time*

- This writer presents the differing ideas of many men and women by balancing their points of view in sentence after sentence, a technique you will learn in this unit.

- Note that she increases the force of the paragraph by placing the topic sentence last.

Writing Ideas
- Date rape
- Another issue on which men and women may disagree

CHAPTER 24

Consistent Tense

Consistent tense means using the same verb tense whenever possible within a sentence or paragraph. As you write and revise, avoid shifting from one tense to another—for example, from present to past—without a good reason for doing so.

(1)	**Inconsistent tense:**	We *were* seven miles from shore. Suddenly, the sky *turns* dark.
(2)	**Consistent tense:**	We *were* seven miles from shore. Suddenly, the sky *turned* dark.
(3)	**Consistent tense:**	We *are* seven miles from shore. Suddenly, the sky *turns* dark.

- The sentences in (1) begin in the past tense with the verb *were* but then shift into the present tense with the verb *turns.* The tenses are inconsistent because both actions are occurring at the same time.

- The sentences in (2) are consistent. Both verbs, *were* and *turned,* are in the past tense.

- The sentences in (3) are also consistent. Both verbs, *are* and *turns,* are in the present tense.

Of course, you should use different verb tenses in a sentence or paragraph if they convey the meaning you want to convey.

(4) Two years ago, I *wanted* to be a chef, but now I *am studying* forestry.

- The verbs in sentence (4) accurately show the time relationship: In the past, I *wanted* to be a chef, but now I *am studying* forestry.

As you proofread your papers for tense consistency, ask yourself: Have I unthinkingly moved from one tense to another, from past to present, or from present to past?

Practice 1

Underline the verbs in these sentences. Then correct any inconsistencies above the line.

EXAMPLE:
As soon as I get out of bed, I did fifty pushups.
got

or

As soon as I get out of bed, I did fifty pushups.
do

1. We were walking near the lake when a large moose appears just ahead.

2. When Bill asks the time, the cab driver told him it was after six.

3. The woman on the red bicycle was delivering newspapers while she is enjoying the morning sunshine.

4. Dr. Choi smiled and welcomes the next patient.

5. The Oklahoma prairie stretches for miles, flat and rusty red. Here and there, an oil rig broke the monotony.

6. They were strolling down Main Street when the lights go out.

7. My cousins questioned me for hours about my trip. I describe the flight, my impressions of Paris, and every meal I ate.

8. We started cheering as he approaches the finish line.

9. If Terry takes short naps during the day, she didn't feel tired in the evening.

10. Yesterday, we find the book we need online. We ordered it immediately.

Practice 2   Writing Assignment

Suppose that you have been asked for written advice on what makes a successful family. Your adult child, an inexperienced friend, or a sibling has asked you to write down some words of wisdom on what makes a family work. Using your own family as an example, write your suggestions for making family life as nurturing, cooperative, and joyful as possible. You may draw on your family's experience to give examples of pitfalls to avoid or of positive behaviors and attitudes.

Revise for consistent tense.

✔ Chapter Highlights

● **In general, use the same verb tense within a sentence or a paragraph:**

She *sings* beautifully, and the audience *listens* intently.

or

She *sang* beautifully, and the audience *listened* intently.

● **However, at times different verb tenses are required because of meaning:**

He *is* not *working* now, but he *spent* sixty hours behind the counter last week.

Chapter Review

Read each of these paragraphs for consistent tense. Correct any inconsistencies by changing the tense of the verbs. Write your corrections above the lines.

A. (1) Self-confidence is vital to success both in childhood and in adulthood. (2) With self-confidence, children knew that they are worthwhile and that they have important goals. (3) Parents can teach their children self-confidence in several ways. (4) First, children needed praise. (5) When they drew, for example, parents can tell them how beautiful their drawings are. (6) The praise lets them know they had talents that other people admire. (7) Second, children required exposure to many different experiences. (8) They soon found that they need not be afraid to try new things. (9) They realized that they can succeed as well at chess as they do at basketball. (10) They discovered that a trip to a museum to examine medieval armor is fascinating or that they enjoy taking a class in pottery. (11) Finally, it was very important to treat children individually. (12) Sensitive parents did not compare their children's successes or failures with those of their brothers or sisters, relatives, or friends. (13) Of course, parents should inform children if their behavior or performance in school needs improvement. (14) Parents helped children do better, however, by showing them how much they have accomplished so far and by suggesting how much they can and will accomplish in the future.

B. (1) Last summer, we visited one of the world's oddest museums, the home of someone who never existed. (2) Early one afternoon, we walked along the real Baker Street in London, England. (3) Suddenly, it looms in front of us: number 221B, Mrs. Hudson's boarding house, home of the famous but fictitious detective Sherlock Holmes. (4) Once inside the perfect reproduction of Holmes' rooms, we are astonished to find all of Holmes' belongings, including his violin, his walking stick, and his chemistry set. (5) We learn that the founders of the museum had searched the country for Victorian objects and furniture like those in the Holmes stories. (6) They succeed beyond any Sherlock Holmes fan's wildest dreams. (7) They locate a Persian slipper like the one in which Holmes' stored pipe tobacco. (8) They even uncover a gold and emerald tie pin like the one Queen Victoria gave Holmes. (9) The museum also had quarters for Holmes' friend and assistant, Dr. Watson. (10) For him, the founders buy nineteenth-century medical supplies and surgical instruments. (11) After we return home that summer, I reread several Sherlock Holmes stories. (12) In my mind's eye, I see Holmes' rooms and belongings more vividly than ever before. (13) Of course, Holmes would have predicted that. (14) "Elementary," he would have said.

C. (1) Almost every major city in the world has a subway system. (2) Underground trains speed through complex networks of tunnels and carried millions of passengers every day.

(3) Subway systems sometimes differ because of their locations. (4) In Mexico City, for example, subway cars traveled through suspended tunnels capable of absorbing earthquake shocks. (5) Residents of Haifa, Israel, use an unusually short, straight subway that ran up and down inside a mountain. (6) The train brought people from Haifa's lower port city up—a thousand feet—to the upper residential city. (7) In Hong Kong, the world's first completely air-conditioned subway system offered relief from extremely hot and humid outdoor temperatures. (8) Cities like San Francisco, of course, expand the definition of subway to cover underwater as well as underground transportation. (9) The San Francisco Bay Area Rapid Transit (BART) system included several miles of track under San Francisco Bay.

(10) Some subway systems are famous for their artwork. (11) With paintings and walls of precious marble, many Moscow subway stations looked like muse-

ums. (12) Several stations in Stockholm, Sweden, seemed like elegant caverns because of granite carvings and rock in its natural state. (13) With colorful designs and all kinds of special effects, subways stations from Montreal to Tokyo resembled modern art galleries.

(14) Subways, therefore, did more than provide an efficient means of public transportation. (15) They are creative solutions to special problems as well as expressions of art and culture.

CHAPTER 25

Consistent Person

Consistent person means using the same person or personal pronoun throughout a sentence or a paragraph. As you write and revise, avoid confusing shifts from one person to another. For example, don't shift from *first person (I, we)* or *third person (he, she, it, they)* to *second person (you).**

(1) **Inconsistent person:**		College *students* soon see that *you* are on *your* own.
(2) **Consistent person:**		College *students* soon see that *they* are on *their* own.
(3) **Consistent person:**		In college, *you* soon see that *you* are on *your* own.

- Sentence (1) shifts from the third person plural *students* to the second person *you* and *your*.

- Sentence (2) uses the third person plural consistently. *They* and *their* now clearly refer to *students*.

- Sentence (3) is also consistent, using the second person *you* and *your* throughout.

Practice 1

Correct any inconsistencies of person in these sentences. If necessary, change the verbs to make them agree with any new subjects. Make your corrections above the lines.

EXAMPLE: Each hiker should bring ~~your~~ his or her own lunch.

1. Belkys treats me like family when I visit her. She always makes you feel at home.

---

*For more work on pronouns, see Chapter 21.

2. I love to go dancing. You can exercise, work off tension, and have fun, all at the same time.

3. If a person has gone to a large high school, you may find a small college a welcome change.

4. When Lee and I drive to work at 6 a.m., you see the city waking up.

5. Every mechanic should make sure they have a good set of tools.

6. People who want to buy cars today are often stopped by high prices. You aren't sure how to get the most for your money.

7. Do each of you have his or her own e-mail address?

8. Many people mistakenly think that your vote doesn't really count.

9. A teacher's attitude affects the performance of their students.

10. It took me three years to decide to enroll in college; in many ways, you really didn't know what you wanted to do when you finished high school.

Practice 2   Writing Assignment

In small groups, write as many endings as you can think of for this sentence: "You can (cannot) tell much about a person by . . ." You might write, "the way he or she dresses," "the way he or she styles his or her hair," or "the kind of movies he or she likes." Each group member should write down every sentence.

Then choose one sentence and write a short paragraph supporting it. Let each group member write about a different sentence. Use people in the news or friends as examples to prove your point. As you write, be careful to use the first, second, or third person correctly. When everyone is finished, exchange papers, checking each other's work for consistent person.

 ## Chapter Highlights

● **Use the same personal pronoun throughout a sentence or a paragraph:**

When *you* apply for a driver's license, *you* may have to take a written test and a driving test.

When a *person* applies for a driver's license, *he or she* may have to take a written test and a driving test.

Chapter Review

Correct the inconsistencies of person in these paragraphs. Then make any other necessary changes. Write your corrections above the lines.

A. (1) When exam time comes, do you become anxious because you aren't sure how to study for tests? (2) They may have done all the work for their courses, but you still don't feel prepared. (3) Fortunately, he can do some things to make taking tests easier. (4) They can look through the textbook and review the material one has underlined. (5) You might read the notes you have taken in class and high-light or underline main points. (6) A person can think about some questions the professor may ask and then try writing answers. (7) Sometimes, they can find other people from your class and form a study group to compare class notes. (8) The night before a test, they shouldn't drink too much coffee. (9) They should get a good night's sleep so that your mind will be as sharp for the exam as your pencil.

B. (1) The sport of mountain biking began in northern California in the 1970s. (2) Some experienced cyclists began using his or her old one-speed fat-tire bikes to explore dirt roads and trails. (3) You began by getting car rides up one of the mountains and pedaling their bikes down. (4) Then they began cycling farther up the mountain until he and she were pedaling to the top. (5) Those cyclists eventu-ally started designing bikes to fit our sport. (6) By the end of the 1970s, road bike manufacturers decided you would join the action. (7) By the mid-1980s, mountain biking had become a national craze, and sales of mountain bikes were exceeding sales of road bikes.

(8) Today, mountain bikers pay about $1,000 for bikes that have everything we need for riding on rough trails: front-wheel shock absorbers, twenty-four gears that shift easily, a lightweight frame, flexible wheels, and even a full sus-pension frame. (9) Cyclists ride your bikes everywhere; some of their favorite places are South Dakota's Badlands, Colorado's ski resorts, and Utah's Canyon-lands National Park. (10) You compete in mountain bike races all over the world. (11) To top this off, in 1996 some of you competed in the first Olympic mountain bike race, outside Atlanta, Georgia. (12) The course, which had tightly spaced trees and large rocks, included steep climbs and sharp descents with surprise jumps. (13) What were those early "inventors" thinking as he and she watched that first Olympic race?

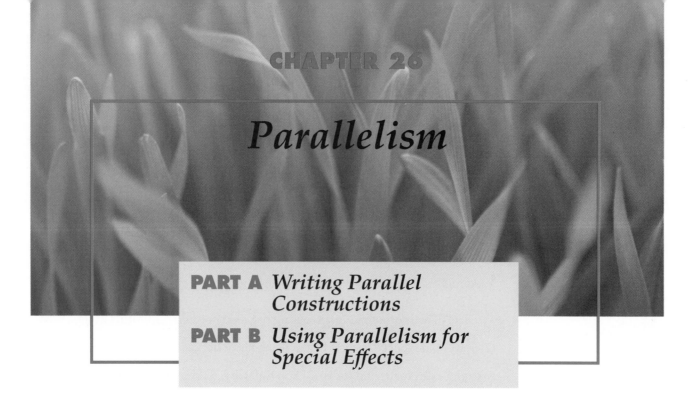

CHAPTER 26

Parallelism

PART A *Writing Parallel Constructions*

PART B *Using Parallelism for Special Effects*

PART A — Writing Parallel Constructions

Which sentence in each pair sounds better to you?

> (1) Jennie is an artist, spends time at athletics, and flies planes.
>
> (2) Jennie is *an artist, an athlete,* and *a pilot.*
>
> (3) He slowed down and came sliding. The winning run was scored.
>
> (4) He *slowed* down, *slid,* and *scored* the winning run.

- Do sentences (2) and (4) sound smoother and clearer than sentences (1) and (3)?

- Sentences (2) and (4) balance similar words or phrases to show similar ideas.

This technique is called *parallelism* **or** *parallel structure.* **The italicized parts of (2) and (4) are** *parallel.* **When you use parallelism, you repeat similar grammatical constructions in order to express similar ideas.**

- In sentence (2), can you see how *an artist, an athlete,* and *a pilot* are parallel? All three words in the series are singular nouns.

- In sentence (4), can you see how *slowed, slid,* and *scored* are parallel? All three words in the series are verbs in the past tense.

Now let's look at two more pairs of sentences. Note which sentence in each pair contains parallelism.

> (5) The car was big, had beauty, and it cost a lot.
>
> (6) The car was *big, beautiful,* and *expensive.*
>
> (7) They raced across the roof, and the fire escape is where they came down.
>
> (8) They raced *across the roof* and *down the fire escape.*

● In sentence (6), how are *big, beautiful,* and *expensive* parallel words?

_____

● In sentence (8), how are *across the roof* and *down the fire escape* parallel phrases?

_____

Certain special constructions require parallel structure:

> (9) The room is *both* light *and* cheery.
>
> (10) You *either* love geometry *or* hate it.
>
> (11) Tanya *not only* plays the guitar *but also* sings.
>
> (12) Richard would *rather* fight *than* quit.

Each of these constructions has two parts:

both . . . and	not only . . . but also
(n)either . . . (n)or	rather . . . than . . .

The words, phrases, or clauses following each part must be parallel:

light . . . cheery	plays . . . sings
love . . . hate	fight . . . quit

Parallelism is an excellent way to add smoothness and power to your writing. Use it in pairs or in a series of ideas, balancing a noun with a noun, an *-ing* verb with an *-ing* verb, a prepositional phrase with a prepositional phrase, and so on.

Practice 1

Circle the element that is *not* parallel in each list.

EXAMPLE: blue

red

colored like rust

purple

1. broiling	2. my four dogs
frying	out the door
baker	across the yard
cooking	under the fence

3. painting the kitchen

   cans of paint

   several brushes

   one roller

4. persistent

   strong-willed

   work

   optimistic

5. standing on tiptoes

   toward the audience

   smiling with anticipation

   leaning against the table

6. music shops

   clothing stores

   buying a birthday present

   gift boutiques

7. topped with whipped cream

   bananas and ice cream

   sprinkled with pecans

   covered with chocolate sauce

8. We shop for fruits at the market.

   We buy enough to last all week.

   We are baking a cake tonight.

   We cook special meals often.

Practice 2

Rewrite each sentence, using parallelism to accent the similar ideas.

EXAMPLE: How can you recognize and you can be helpful to someone who is on drugs?

Rewrite: _How can you recognize and help someone who is on drugs?_

1. A person on drugs may become unusually nervous, irritable, or there may be anger.

   Rewrite: _____

   _____

2. He or she might neglect chores, be forgetting dates, and the person might skip work or classes also.

   Rewrite: _____

   _____

3. New friends may appear whose names and where they are living are kept secret.

   Rewrite: _____

   _____

4. Other signs include reckless driving. Health may become poor, and sloppy physical appearance is also a sign.

Rewrite: _____

_____

5. Heavy drug users may experience deep depression and are having wild hallucinations.

Rewrite: _____

_____

6. Many drug users will deny their problem rather than admitting to having it.

Rewrite: _____

_____

7. However, wisely and thoughtful friends and relatives can try to help.

Rewrite: _____

_____

8. They can approach the person with compassion rather than accusingly.

Rewrite: _____

_____

9. They might not only express their concern but also be making suggestions about treatment programs.

Rewrite: _____

_____

10. Groups that use the twelve-step method or when the program uses the "tough love" approach have the most successful programs.

Rewrite: _____

_____

Practice 3

Fill in the blanks in each sentence with parallel words or phrases of your own. Be creative. Take care that your sentences make sense and that your parallels are truly parallel.

E X A M P L E :   I feel _____rested_____ and _____happy_____.

1. Ethan's favorite colors are _____ and
   _____.

2. The day of the storm, we _____, and they
   _____.

3. Her attitude was strange. She acted as if _____
   and as if _____.

4. I like people who _____ and who
   _____.

5. Some married couples _____ while others
   _____.

6. Harold _____, but I just
   _____.

7. To finish this project, work _____ and
   _____.

8. _____ and _____
   relax me.

9. We found _____, _____,
   and _____ on the beach.

10. They might want to _____ or to
    _____.

PART B — *Using Parallelism for Special Effects*

By rearranging the order of a parallel series, you can sometimes add a little drama or humor to your sentences. Which of these two sentences is more dramatic?

(1) Bharati is a wife, a mother, and a black belt in karate.
(2) Bharati is a wife, a black belt in karate, and a mother.

- If you chose sentence (1), you are right. Sentence (1) saves the most surprising item—*a black belt in karate*—for last.

- Sentence (2), on the other hand, does not build suspense but gives away the surprise in the middle.

    You can also use parallelism to set up your readers' expectations and then surprise them with humor.

> (3) The handsome cowboy saddled up, leaped on his horse, and slid off.

Practice 4

On separate paper, write five sentences of your own, using parallel structure. In one or two of your sentences, arrange the parallel elements to build toward a dramatic or humorous conclusion. For ideas, look at Practice 3, but create your own sentences.

Practice 5   Writing Assignment

Write a one-paragraph newspaper advertisement to rent or sell your house or apartment. Using complete sentences, let the reader know the number of rooms, their size, and their appearance, and why someone would be happy there. Emphasize your home's good points, such as "lots of light" or "closet space galore," but don't hide the flaws. If possible, minimize them while still being honest.

    You may want to begin with a general description, such as "This apartment is a plant lover's dream." Be careful, though: if you describe only the good features or exaggerate, readers may think, "It's too good to be true." Use parallel structure to help your sentences read more smoothly.

✔ Chapter Highlights

- **Parallelism balances similar words or phrases to express similar ideas:**

    He left the gym *tired, sweaty,* and *satisfied.*

    Tami not only *finished the exam in record time* but also *answered the question for extra credit.*

    To celebrate his birthday, Roger *took in a show, went to a dance,* and *ate a late dinner.*

Chapter Review

This essay contains both correct and faulty parallel constructions. Revise the faulty parallelism. Write your corrections above the lines.

Chinese Medicine in the United States

(1) When diplomatic relations between the United States and mainland China were restored in 1972, acupuncture was one import that sparked America's imagination and made people interested. (2) In the United States today, the most popular form of Chinese medicine is acupuncture.

(3) Acupuncture involves the insertion of thin, sterile, made of stainless steel needles at specific points on the body. (4) Chinese medical science believes that the *chi,* or life force, can be redirected by inserting and by the manipulation of these needles. (5) They are inserted to just below the skin and are either removed quickly or leave them in for up to forty minutes. (6) In addition, the acupuncturist can twirl them, heat them, or charging them with a mild electrical current. (7) Acupuncture can reduce pain for those suffering from allergies, arthritis, backache, or with a toothache. (8) It also has helped in cases of chronic substance abuse, anxiety, and for depressed people.

(9) Chinese medicine has grown in popularity and become important in America. (10) Thirty-five schools in the United States teach Chinese acupuncture. (11) Forty-four states have passed laws that regulate or for licensing the practice of acupuncture. (12) Since 1974, the government has authorized several studies of acupuncture's effectiveness and how reliable it is. (13) Although research has failed to explain how acupuncture works, it has confirmed that it does work. (14) The studies also suggest that acupuncture should continue to be tested and using it.

Proofreading

A. We have changed this student's composition so that it contains inconsistent tense and faulty parallelism. Proofread for these errors, and correct them above the lines. (You should find twelve errors.)

Inspiration

(1) When I was a freshman in high school, I have a serious problem with English. (2) All day long, my head was filled with ideas for compositions, but when I arrived in English class, my mind goes blank. (3) I feared that my teacher thought I was just another lazy student. (4) In fact, I almost gave up; thank goodness, I didn't!

(5) Then, by the strangest twist of fate, I find out why my mind goes blank and why my compositions were never finished. (6) One day, the English class moved from the basement to the third floor of the building. (7) The moment I stepped into the new room and the window was seen, I know what had bothered me all semester—no light, no fresh air, and the fact that there wasn't a sense of space. (8) I select a seat near the window and looked over my shoulder at the tall oak tree that stretched past the third-floor window. (9) When I pick up my pen, the writing began to flow. (10) If I ran out of things to say, I just glance over my shoulder at the tree and at the sky—and I would be inspired to continue my essay.

Chistopher Moore, student

B. Proofread the following essay for inconsistent person and faulty parallelism. Correct the errors above the lines. (You should find nine errors.)

Opening Up the Workplace

(1) New technology is helping people with disabilities enter the workforce in record numbers. (2) With the latest products, blind workers can see a computer screen, and deaf workers can be hearing a telephone call. (3) People who cannot speak can talk to others. (4) People can do word processing even if your fingers cannot type. (5) Pitney Bowes, Toshiba, Apple Computer, and other companies are doing it too are creating a workforce revolution with "assistive technology."

(6) For example, if workers cannot move their arms or legs, he or she can use an eye-gaze program. (7) They can direct a laser beam to points on his or her computer screen just by *looking* at control keys. (8) The laser sets off commands for the computer to follow. (9) Users need only keep their head still and controlling one eye is also necessary.

(10) There are computers that display information in Braille for blind people or the print is in extremely large print for those with vision problems. (11) Some software programs convert written text into speech so that blind workers can hear it. (12) Other products convert speech into written text so that deaf workers can see it.

(13) Assistive technology will also benefit the country's aging workforce. (14) Experts estimate that nearly two-thirds of the population will eventually suffer partial or it may be total hearing loss. (15) Glaucoma and cataracts will threaten vision. (16) Stroke victims may find ourselves unable to communicate or function independently. (17) The new technology will bring people into the workforce *and* keep them there.

Shift Your Audience and Purpose

Playing with the idea of audience and purpose can produce some interesting writing—such as writing to your car to persuade it to keep running until finals are over. Likewise, writing as if you are someone else can be a learning experience.

In your class or group, read this unusual essay, aloud if possible.

A Fly's-Eye View of My Apartment

(1) Hey, are you guys ready? Today is Armageddon!* When you enter this door, remember, you're not getting out alive. She's a pretty tough lady. Oh, and don't forget to eat all you can. The kids are always dropping crumbs. You can make it through the night if you stay on the ceilings. Whatever you do, stay out of the peach room that is always humid. Once the door is shut, you're trapped. Try not to be noticed on the cabinets in the room where the smells come from. There is nothing interesting in the room with the big screen, but the room with the large bed can be rather stimulating if you stay on the walls.

(2) She won't get tired of us until about 6 p.m.; that is usually around dinnertime. She switches around, using different swatters, so you never really know what to look for. When you hear the gospel music, start looking out. She gets an enormous amount of energy from this music, and her swats are accurate, which means they're deadly. It kills me how she becomes so baffled about how we get in since she has screens on the windows. Little does she know that it's every time she opens the front door.

(3) Well, I think she's ready to leave for work. I hear the lock. To a good life, fellows. See you in heaven—and remember to give her hell!

Tanya Peck, student

1. How effective is Tanya Peck's essay?

   _____ Interesting subject?   _____ Good supporting details?

   _____ Logical organization?   _____ Effective conclusion?

2. This writer cleverly plays with the notions of speaker, audience, and purpose. Who is Peck pretending to be as she writes? Whom is she addressing and for what purpose?

---

*Armageddon: a final battle between forces of good and evil.

3. The writer/speaker refers to the "pretty tough lady" of the house. Who is that lady? How do you know?

4. Peck divides her essay into two main paragraphs and a brief conclusion. Because of her unusual subject, the paragraphs do not have topic sentences. However, does each paragraph have a clear main idea? What is the main idea of paragraph (1)? of paragraph (2)?

5. Underline any details or sentences that you especially liked—for example, in paragraph (2), the clever idea that the fly realizes that gospel music (for some mysterious reason) energizes the woman with the swatter. Can you identify the rooms described in paragraph (1)?

6. The essay concludes by playing with the terms *heaven* and *hell.* Do you find this effective—or offensive? Are these words connected to *Armageddon* in the introduction? How?

7. Proofread for any grammar or spelling errors.

Writing and Revising Ideas

1. Write a _____ 's-eye view (dog, cat, flea, canary, goldfish, ant, roach) of your home.

2. Describe an important moment in history as if you were there.

Before you write, read about audience and purpose in Chapter 1. Prewrite and plan to get an engaging subject. As you revise, pay special attention to keeping a consistent point of view; really try to imagine what that person (or other creature) would say in those circumstances.

UNIT 6 *Writing Assignments*

As you complete each writing assignment, remember to perform these steps:

- Write a clear, complete topic sentence.
- Use freewriting, brainstorming, or clustering to generate ideas for the body of your paragraph, essay, or speech.
- Arrange your best ideas in a plan.
- Revise for support, unity, coherence, and exact language.
- Proofread for grammar, punctuation, and spelling errors.

Writing Assignment 1: *Explain your attitude toward writing.* From the "Writing" section of the Quotation Bank at the end of this book, pick a quotation that accurately describes how you feel about writing. For example, do you "think best with a pencil in your hand," or is writing "the hardest work in the world not involving heavy lifting"? Use the complete quotation as your first sentence; then explain how and why it describes your experience of writing. Refer to papers or letters you have written to illustrate your explanation. Revise for consistent tense and person; use parallelism to make your sentences smooth.

Writing Assignment 2: *Review a restaurant.* You have been asked to review the food, service, and atmosphere at a local restaurant. Your review will appear in a local newspaper and will have an impact on the success or failure of this eating establishment. Name what you ordered, how it tasted, and why you would or would not recommend this dish. Note the service: was it slow, efficient, courteous, rude, or generally satisfactory? Is the restaurant one in which customers can easily carry on a conversation, or is there too much noise? Is the lighting good or poor? Include as much specific detail as you can. Revise for consistent tense and person.

Writing Assignment 3: *Voice your opinion on land use.* Choose an issue involving land use that is of genuine significance for your city or town. You may live in a rural community, for example, that is concerned with growing while not sacrificing its rural quality of life. You may live in a suburban neighborhood that is affected by business development in or around established communities. You may live in an urban area where rental property is being taken over by condominiums. Concerned residents have been asked to present their viewpoint at a community meeting. Write a speech in which you voice your opinion. Present reasons why the land should be used in one way or the other. Use your experience or the experience of others to support your points. Revise for consistent tense and person; use parallelism to make your sentences smooth.

Writing Assignment 4: *Evaluate a textbook.* A publisher has asked you to evaluate this textbook, *Grassroots,* or a text you use in a different course. The publisher wants an honest evaluation so that the new edition can be even better than the present one. Rate the textbook on clarity and organization: that is, does it explain the subject matter well, and does one chapter naturally follow from another? You also might want to consider whether the material is shown in a way that is pleasing to the eye. Most important, does the book help you learn? Revise for consistent tense and person; use parallelism to make your sentences smooth.

UNIT 7

Mastering Mechanics

Even the best ideas may lose their impact if the writer doesn't know how to capitalize and punctuate correctly. In this unit, you will

- Learn when—and when not—to capitalize

- Recognize when—and when not—to use commas

- Find out how to use apostrophes

- Learn how to quote the words of others in your writing

Spotlight on Writing

Adolescence is a cruel word. Its cruelty lies hidden in its vaguely official, diagnostic air. To say people are "adolescent," "going through adolescence," or worse, "being adolescent" is to dismiss their feelings, minimize their troubles, and (if you're the parent) protect yourself from their uncompromising rage. The words *teenager* and *teen* are worse. They reek of cuteness. But we all know that being a teen doesn't feel cute.

People that age hardly ever use those words. They tend to call themselves "kids" when pushed, as in, "What makes you think you know so much about kids—you sure don't know much about *me!*" Or they dress up and act out and give themselves better words: "punk," "gothic," "rapper," . . . "low-rider," "homeboy," "soc," "hippie," "freak"—words to remind us just how volatile, how dangerous, how "freaked out," "awesome," "bummed," "bitchin'," "groovy," "wasted," and "bad" those years really are.

Michael Ventura, "The Age of Endarkenment," *UTNE Reader*

- This writer contrasts two sets of names for the same period of life: the first paragraph looks at the "cruel" adult words, and the second paragraph looks at the colorful—and disturbing—words that young people use about themselves.

- Do you think that teenagers have more rage than people of other ages?

Writing Ideas
- A term currently used by teenagers

- Any jargon—specialized words—from your job: for instance, terms from sales, fast food, computer or car repair, or patient care

CHAPTER 27

Capitalization

Here are the basic rules of capitalization:

1. nationality, race,
   language, religion   →Capitalize→   American, African American, French, English, Protestant, Jewish, Catholic, Muslim, Buddhist, and so forth

This group is *always capitalized*.

2. names of persons,
   countries, states, cities,
   places, streets, bodies of
   water, and so forth   Bill Morse, New Zealand, California, Denver, Central Park, Jones Street, Pacific Ocean, and so forth

   but →   a large state, a town, the lake, and so forth

If you name a specific person, state, city, street, or body of water, *capitalize;* if you don't, use small letters.

3. buildings, organizations,
   institutions   World Trade Center, Paradise Theater, National Organization for Women, Johnson City Library, Smithson University, and so forth

   but →   a tall building, an expensive theater, a feminist group, an old school, and so forth

If you name a specific building, group, or institution, *capitalize;* if you don't, use small letters.

4. historical events, periods, documents *Capitalize* → the Spanish-American War, the Renaissance, the Constitution, and so forth

but → a terrible war, a new charter, and so forth

If you name a specific historical event, period, or document, *capitalize;* if you don't, use small letters.

5. months, days, holidays *Capitalize* → June, Monday, the Fourth of July, and so forth

but → summer, fall, winter, spring

Always capitalize months, days, and holidays; use small letters for the seasons.

6. professional and civil titles *Capitalize* → Dr. Smith, Professor Greenstein, Judge Alvarez, and so forth

but → the doctor, the professor, the judge, and so forth

If you name the doctor, judge, and so forth, *capitalize;* if you don't, use small letters.

7. family names *Capitalize* → Uncle Joe, Grandmother Stein, Cousin Beverly, Mother, Grandfather, and so forth

but → an uncle, the aunt, our cousin, my mother, her grandfather, and so forth

If you name a relative or use *Mother, Father, Grandmother,* or *Grandfather* as a name, *capitalize;* however, if these words are preceded by the word *a, an,* or *the,* a possessive pronoun, or an adjective, use small letters.

8. brand names *Capitalize* → Greaso hair oil, Quick drafting ink, and so forth

Capitalize the brand name but not the type of product.

9. geographic locations *Capitalize* → the East, the Northwest, the South, and so forth

but → east on the boulevard

If you mean a geographic location, *capitalize;* if you mean a direction, use small letters.

10. academic subjects

Capitalize → Mathematics 51, Sociology 11, English Literature 210, and so forth

but → a tough mathematics course, an *A* in sociology, a course in English literature, and so forth

If you use the course number, *capitalize;* if you don't, use small letters. However, always capitalize languages and countries.

11. titles of books, poems, plays, films

Capitalize → *A Farewell to Arms,* "Ode to a Bat," *Major Barbara, Almost Famous,* and so forth

Capitalize titles except for *a, an,* and *the;* prepositions; and coordinating conjunctions. However, always capitalize the *first* and *last* words of the title.

Practice 1

Capitalize where necessary.

EXAMPLE: The smithsonian consists of many museums and the national zoological park.

1. Judy and I took the children and aunt mae to washington last summer during the week of independence day.

2. We spent one full day visiting the museums.

3. Carl and Luke liked the national air and space museum best.

4. They thought that the tiny craft flown by orville and wilbur wright at kitty hawk, north carolina, in 1903 looked like a model plane.

5. We all marveled that charles lindbergh would dare to fly a plane as small as the *spirit of saint louis* across the atlantic ocean.

6. There was a great difference between those early planes and the model of the *voyager* spacecraft; this modern spacecraft was designed to explore jupiter, saturn, and uranus.

7. Next, we walked along constitution avenue to the national museum of american history.

8. There I saw my favorite car, the 1903 winton that made the first trip across the united states.

9. We also saw the flag that inspired francis scott key to write "the star spangled banner."

10. This was the same flag that mrs. pickersgill sewed to fly over Fort McHenry in chesapeake bay during 1812.

11. Some of the other treasures we viewed there were president washington's wooden false teeth, a pair of ruby slippers from the film *the wizard of oz,* and a copy of thomas paine's book *common sense.*

12. Finally, my family and I went to the national museum of natural history to stare at the african bull elephant and bengal tiger on display.

13. Exhausted, we returned to the ramada inn, flopped into bed, and watched a rerun of *star trek.*

14. The next day, thursday, we visited the white house and the library of congress.

15. We never saw any of the art museums that are also part of the smithsonian.

Practice 2   Writing Assignment

Is your vacation usually a disaster or a success? Describe a particularly memorable vacation—either bad or good—in which you learned something about how to plan or enjoy a vacation.

In your first sentence, tell what you learned. Explain what went right and what went wrong. Be sure to name the places you visited and the sights you saw. You will probably want to arrange events in time order. Proofread for correct capitalization.

✔ Chapter Highlights

- **Capitalize nationalities, languages, races, and religions:**

  Asian, French, Caucasian, Baptist

- **Capitalize specific countries, states, cities, organizations, and buildings:**

  Belgium, Utah, Akron, United Nations, the White House

- **Capitalize months, days, and holidays, but not seasons:**

  November, Friday, Labor Day, summer

- **Capitalize professional titles only when a person is named:**

  Mayor Alexander, the mayor, Superintendent Alicia Morgan

- **Capitalize brand names, but not the type of product:**

  Dawn dishwashing detergent

- **Capitalize geographic locations, but not directions:**

  the West, west of the city

- **Capitalize academic subjects only when they are followed by a course number:**

  History 583, psychology

- **Capitalize titles of books, poems, plays, and films:**

  Lord of the Flies, "The Raven," *Rent, The Perfect Storm*

Proofread the following essay for errors in capitalization; correct the errors above the lines.

The Strange Career of Deborah Sampson

(1) Few Soldiers have had a stranger army career than Deborah Sampson. (2) Sampson disguised herself as a man so that she could fight in the revolutionary war. (3) Born on december 17, 1760, she spent her early years in a Town near plymouth, massachusetts. (4) Her Father left his large family, however, and went to sea when Sampson was seven years old. (5) After living with a Cousin and then with the widow of a Minister, sampson became a servant in a wealthy family.

(6) Household tasks and hard outdoor work built up her physical strength. (7) She was taller than the average Man and more muscular than the average Woman. (8) Therefore, she was able to disguise herself successfully. (9) Sampson enlisted in the continental army on may 20, 1782, under the name of robert shurtleff.

(10) Sampson fought in several Battles and was wounded at least twice. (11) One story says that she took a bullet out of her own leg with a penknife to avoid seeing a Doctor. (12) However, after the surrender of the british, Sampson's regiment was sent to philadelphia, where she was hospitalized with a high fever and lost consciousness. (13) At the Hospital, dr. Barnabas Binney made the discovery that ended Sampson's army life. (14) She was honorably discharged by general henry knox at west point on october 28, 1783.

(15) Officially female again, Sampson returned to Massachusetts and eventually married a Farmer named benjamin gannett. (16) The story of Sampson's adventures spread; in 1797, a book titled *the female review* was published about her. (17) When Sampson decided to earn money by telling her own story, she became the first american woman to be paid as a Public Speaker. (18) She gave her first talk at the federal street theatre in boston in march 1802 and toured until september. (19) Her health was poor, however, and she could not continue her appearances.

(20) In 1804, paul revere, who was a neighbor of the gannetts, wrote to a member of the united states congress. (21) He asked for a pension for this Soldier

who had never been paid and was still suffering from her war wounds. (22) Congress granted deborah sampson gannett a pension of four dollars a month.

(23) Deborah Sampson died in sharon, Massachusetts, in april 1827. (24) Her story inspired the People of her own time and continues to inspire People today. (25) Two plays have been written about her: *she was there* and *portrait of deborah.* (26) On veterans day in 1989, a life-size bronze statue was dedicated in front of the sharon public library to honor her.

CHAPTER 28

Commas

PART A Commas after Items in a Series

PART B Commas after Introductory Phrases

PART C Commas for Direct Address

PART D Commas to Set Off Appositives

PART E Commas for Parenthetical Expressions

PART F Commas for Dates

PART G Commas for Addresses

PART H Commas for Coordination and Subordination

The comma is a pause. It gives your reader a chance to stop for a moment to think about where your sentence has been and where it is going, and to prepare to read on.

Although this chapter will cover some basic uses of the comma, always keep this generalization in mind: If there is no reason for a comma, leave it out!

PART A   Commas after Items in a Series

(1) I like apples, oranges, and pears.

● What three things do I like? _____, _____, and

_____

Use commas to separate three or more items in a series.

> (2) We will walk through the park, take in a film, and visit a friend.

● What three things will we do? _____,

_____, and _____

> (3) She loves to explore new cultures sample different foods and learn foreign
>   languages.

● In sentence (3), what are the items in the series?

_____, _____,

and _____

● Punctuate sentence (3).

However, if you want to join three or more items with *and* or *or* between the items, do not use commas.

> (4) She plays tennis *and* golf *and* softball.

● Note that commas are not used in sentence (4).

Practice 1

Punctuate these sentences correctly.

1. I can't find my shoes my socks or my hat!

2. Sylvia Eric and James have just completed a course in welding.

3. Over lunch, they discussed new accounts marketing strategy and motherhood.

4. Frank is in Florida Bob is in Brazil and I am in the bathtub.

5. On Sunday, we repaired the porch cleaned the basement and shingled the roof.

6. The exhibit will include photographs diaries and love letters.

7. Spinning kickboxing and Tai Chi have become very popular recently.

8. Paula hung her coat on the hook Henry draped his jacket over her coat and

   Sonia threw her scarf on top of the pile.

Practice 2

On separate paper, write three sentences, each containing three or more items in a series. Punctuate correctly.

PART B — *Commas after Introductory Phrases*

> (1) By the end of the season, our local basketball team will have won thirty games straight.

● *By the end of the season* introduces the sentence.

An introductory phrase is usually followed by a comma.

> (2) On Thursday we left for Hawaii.

However, a very short introductory phrase, like the one in sentence (2), need not be followed by a comma.

Practice 3

Punctuate these sentences correctly. One sentence is already punctuated correctly.

1. During the rainstorm we huddled in a doorway.

2. Every Saturday at 9 p.m. she carries her telescope to the roof.

3. After their last trip Fred and Nita decided on separate vacations.

4. The first woman was appointed to the U.S. Supreme Court in 1981.

5. By the light of the moon we could make out a dim figure.

6. During the coffee break George reviewed his psychology homework.

7. In the deep end of the pool he found three silver dollars.

8. In almost no time they had changed the tire.

Practice 4

On separate paper, write three sentences using introductory phrases. Punctuate correctly.

PART C — *Commas for Direct Address*

> (1) Bob, you must leave now.
> (2) You must, Bob, leave now.
> (3) You must leave now, Bob.
> (4) Don't be surprised, old buddy, if I pay you a visit very soon.

● In sentences (1), (2), and (3), Bob is the person spoken to; he is being *addressed directly*.

● In sentence (4), *old buddy* is being *addressed directly*.

The person addressed directly is set off by commas wherever the direct address appears in the sentence.

Practice 5

Circle the person or persons directly addressed, and punctuate the sentences correctly.

1. I am happy to inform you Mr. Forbes that you are the father of twins.

2. We expect to return on Monday Miguel.

3. It appears my friend that you have won two tickets to the opera.

4. Get out of my roast you mangy old dog.

5. Tom it's probably best that you sell the old car at a loss.

6. If I were you Hilda I would put off the phone call until we are off the highway.

7. Bruce it's time you learned to operate the lawn mower!

8. I am pleased to announce ladies and gentlemen that Madonna is our surprise guest tonight.

Practice 6

On separate paper, write three sentences using direct address. Punctuate correctly.

PART D   *Commas to Set Off Appositives*

(1) The Rialto, a new theater, is on Tenth Street.

● *A new theater* describes *the Rialto*.

(2) An elderly man, my grandfather walks a mile every day.

● What group of words describes *my grandfather?* _____

(3) They bought a new painting, a rather beautiful landscape.

● What group of words describes *a new painting?*

_____

● *A new theater, an elderly man,* and *a rather beautiful landscape* are called *appositives*.

An *appositive* **is usually a group of words that renames a noun or pronoun and gives more information about it. The appositive can appear at the beginning, middle, or end of a sentence. An appositive is usually set off by commas.**

Practice 7

Circle the appositive, and punctuate correctly.

1. That door the one with the X on it leads backstage.

2. A short man he decided not to pick a fight with the basketball player.

3. Hassim my friend from Morocco will be staying with me this week.

4. My nephew wants to go to Mama's Indoor Arcade a very noisy place.

5. George Eliot a nineteenth-century novelist was a woman named Mary Ann Evans.

6. A very close race the election for mayor wasn't decided until 2 a.m.

7. On the Fourth of July my favorite holiday my high school friends get together for an all-day barbecue.

8. Dr. Simpson a specialist in ethnic music always travels with a tape recorder.

Practice 8

On separate paper, write three sentences using appositives. Punctuate correctly.

PART E   *Commas for Parenthetical Expressions*

(1) By the way, I think that you're beautiful.
(2) I think, by the way, that you're beautiful.
(3) I think that you're beautiful, by the way.

● *By the way* modifies or qualifies the entire sentence or idea.

● It is called a *parenthetical expression* because it is a side remark, something that could be placed in parentheses: *(By the way) I think that you're beautiful.*

Set off a parenthetical expression with commas.

Below is a partial list of parenthetical expressions:

as a matter of fact	in fact
believe me	it seems to me
I am sure	it would seem
I assure you	to tell the truth

Practice 9

Circle the parenthetical expressions in the sentences below; then punctuate correctly.

1. Believe me Sonia has studied hard for her driver's test.

2. She possesses it would seem an uncanny gift for gab.

3. It was I assure you an accident.

4. To tell the truth I just put a treadmill in your basement.

5. His supervisor by the way will never admit when he is wrong.

6. A well-prepared résumé as a matter of fact can help you get a job.

7. He is in fact a black belt.

8. To begin with you need a new carburetor.

Practice 10

On separate paper, write three sentences using parenthetical expressions. Punctuate them correctly.

PART F   *Commas for Dates*

(1) I arrived on Monday, March 20, 2000, and found that I was in the wrong city.

● Note that commas separate the different parts of the date.
● Note that a comma follows the last item in the date.

(2) She saw him on Wednesday and spoke with him.

However, a one-word date (*Wednesday* or *1995*) **preceded by a preposition** (*in, on, near,* or *from,* **for example) is not followed by a comma unless there is some other reason for it.**

Practice 11

Punctuate these sentences correctly. Not every sentence requires additional punctuation.

1. By Tuesday October 6 he had outlined the whole history text.

2. Thursday May 8 is Hereford's birthday.

3. She was born on January 9 1945 in a small New England town.

4. He was born on July 4 1976 the two-hundredth anniversary of the Declaration of Independence.

5. Do you think we will have finished the yearbook by May?

6. On January 24 1848 James Wilson Marshall found gold in California.

7. My aunt is staying with us from Tuesday to Friday.

8. Charles Schulz's final *Peanuts* comic strip was scheduled for February 13 2000 the day on which he died.

Practice 12

On separate paper, write three sentences using dates. Punctuate correctly.

PART G   *Commas for Addresses*

> (1)   We just moved from 11 Landow Street, Wilton, Connecticut, to 73 James Street, Charleston, West Virginia.

- Commas separate different parts of an address.
- A comma generally follows the last item in an address, usually a state (*Connecticut*).

> (2)   Julio Smith *from* Queens was made district sales manager.

However, a one-word address preceded by a preposition (*in, on, at, near,* or *from,* for example) is not followed by a comma unless there is another reason for it.

> (3)   Julio Smith, Queens, was made district sales manager.

Commas are required to set off a one-word address if the preposition before the address is omitted.

Practice 13

Punctuate these sentences correctly. Not every sentence requires additional punctuation.

1. Their address is 6 Great Ormond Street London England.

2. Seattle Washington faces the Cascade Mountains.

3. That package must be sent to 30 West Overland Street Phoenix Arizona.

4. We parked on Marble Lane, across the street from the bowling alley.

5. His father now lives in Waco Texas but his sister has never left Vermont.

6. How far is Kansas City Kansas from Independence Missouri?

7. The old watch factory at 43 North Oak Street Scranton Pennsylvania has been condemned by the building inspector.

8. Foster's Stationery 483 Heebers Street Plainview sells special calligraphy pens.

Practice 14

On separate paper, write three sentences using addresses. Punctuate correctly.

PART H   *Commas for Coordination and Subordination*

Chapters 13 and 14 cover the use of commas with coordinating and subordinating conjunctions. Below is a brief review.

> (1) Enzio enjoys most kinds of music, but heavy metal gives him a headache.
> (2) Although the weather bureau had predicted rain, the day turned out bright and sunny.
> (3) The day turned out bright and sunny although the weather bureau had predicted rain.

- In sentence (1), a comma precedes the coordinating conjunction *but,* which joins together two independent ideas.

- In sentence (2), a comma follows the dependent idea because it precedes the independent idea.

- Sentence (3) does not require a comma because the independent idea precedes the subordinate one.

Use a comma before coordinating conjunctions—*and, but, for, nor, or, so,* or *yet*— that join two independent ideas.

Use a comma after a dependent idea only when the dependent idea precedes the independent one; do not use a comma if the dependent idea follows the independent one.

Practice 15

Punctuate correctly. Not every sentence requires additional punctuation.

EXAMPLE: Because scrapped cars create millions of tons of ~~waste~~ *waste,* recycling auto parts has become an important issue.

1. Today new cars are made from many old parts and manufacturers are trying to increase the use of recycled materials from old cars.

2. Scrapped cars can be easily recycled because they consist mostly of metals.

3. After these cars are crushed magnets draw the metals out of them.

4. However, the big problem in recycling cars is the plastic they contain.

5. Although plastic can be recycled the average car contains about twenty different kinds of plastic.

6. Separating the different types of plastic takes much time but companies are developing ways to speed up the process.

7. Still, new cars need to be made differently before recycling can truly succeed.

8. Their parts should detach easily and they should be made of plastics and metals that can be separated from each other.

9. As we develop more markets for the recycled auto parts new cars may soon be 90 percent recycled and recyclable.

10. Our environment will benefit and brand-new cars will really be more than fifty years old!

Practice 16

On separate paper, write three sentences, one with a coordinating conjunction, one beginning with a subordinating conjunction, and one with the subordinating conjunction in the middle.

Practice 17   Writing Assignment

With the twentieth century, we entered what is often called the age of invention because of rapid advances in technology, communication, and medicine. Which modern invention has meant the most to you *personally,* and why? You might choose something as common as disposable diapers or as sophisticated as a special feature of a personal computer.

In the first sentence, name the invention. Then, as specifically as possible, discuss why it means so much to you. Proofread for the correct use of commas.

✔ Chapter Highlights

- **Commas separate three or more items in a series:**

  He bought a ball, a bat, and a fielder's glove.

- **Unless it is very short, an introductory phrase is followed by a comma:**

  By the end of January, I'll be in Australia.

- **Commas set off the name of a person directly addressed:**

  I think, Aunt Betty, that your latest novel is a winner.

- **Commas set off appositives:**

  My boss, the last person in line in the cafeteria, often forgets to eat lunch.

- **Commas set off parenthetical expressions:**

  My wife, by the way, went to school with your sister.

- **Commas separate the parts of a date or an address, except for a one-word date or address preceded by a preposition:**

  On April 1, 1997, I was in a terrible blizzard.

  I live at 48 Trent Street, Randolph, Michigan.

  She works in Tucson as a plumber.

- **A comma precedes a coordinating conjunction that joins two independent ideas:**

  We had planned to see a movie together, but we couldn't agree on one.

- **If a dependent idea precedes the independent idea, it is followed by a comma; if the independent idea comes first, it is not followed by a comma:**

  Although I still have work to do, my project will be ready on time.

  My project will be ready on time although I still have work to do.

Chapter Review

Proofread the following essay for comma errors—either missing commas or commas used incorrectly. Correct the errors above the lines.

Lovely as a Tree

(1) On December 18, 1999 Julia Butterfly Hill's feet touched ground for the first time in more than two years. (2) She had just climbed down from the top, of an ancient tree, in Humboldt County California. (3) The tree a thousand-year-old redwood was named Luna. (4) Hill had climbed 180 feet up Luna on December 10 1997 for what she thought would be a protest of two or three weeks.

(5) Hill's action was intended to stop Pacific Lumber a division of the Maxxam Corporation from cutting down old-growth forests. (6) The area immediately next to Luna, had already been stripped of trees. (7) Because nothing was left to hold the soil to the mountain a huge part of the hill had slid into the town of Stafford California. (8) Many homes had been totally destroyed.

(9) During her unimaginably long tree-sit, Hill endured incredible hardships. (10) For more than two years she lived, on a tiny platform eighteen stories off the ground. (11) El Niño storms almost destroyed her with ferocious winds razor-sharp rain and numbing cold. (12) She once wore two pairs of socks booties two pairs of thermal ski pants two thermal shirts a wool sweater two windbreakers a raincoat gloves and two hats to keep from freezing to death during a storm. (13) In addition to enduring nature's hardships Hill withstood life-threatening torment from the logging company. (14) She was harassed by helicopters various sieges and interference with receiving supplies. (15) Of course she also endured great loneliness sometimes paralyzing fear and always deep sorrow for the destruction around her.

(16) Only twenty-three at the beginning of her tree-sit Hill eventually became both world famous and very knowledgeable about ancient forests. (17) At the top of Luna she would use a cell phone a pager and a daily engagement planner. (18) She was trying to protect the tree itself to slow down all logging in the area and to bring about public awareness. (19) She gave hundreds of phone interviews and answered hundreds of letters.

(20) Hill's action was dramatically successful; Luna was eventually saved from destruction. (21) When Hill returned to normal life she wrote a book *The Legacy of Luna: The Story of a Tree, a Woman, and the Struggle to Save the Redwoods.* (22) Julia Butterfly Hill is now a writer a poet and an activist. (23) She is a frequent speaker at environmental conferences she helped found the Circle of Life Foundation for preserving all life and she has received many honors and awards.

Adapted from Julia Butterfly Hill, *The Legacy of Luna*

CHAPTER 29

Apostrophes

PART A   *Using the Apostrophe for Contractions*

A *contraction* **is a way of combining two words and making one word out of them.**

$$do + not = don't$$

- Note that the *o* of *not* is omitted in the contraction. An apostrophe (') replaces the omitted letter *o*.

$$should + not = shouldn't \ (o \text{ omitted})$$

$$I + have = I've \ (ha \text{ omitted})$$

BE CAREFUL: *Won't* is an odd contraction because it cannot be broken into parts in the same way the previous contractions can.

$$will + not = won't$$

Practice 1

Write these words as contractions.

1. you + are = _____
2. who + is = _____
3. was + not = _____
4. they + are = _____

5. can + not = _____
6. it + is =   _____
7. I + am =   _____
8. will + not = _____

Practice 2

Insert the missing apostrophes in these contractions.

1. Wont you go with us?
2. Whats in the locked box?
3. Ive called home twice.
4. Youre gorgeous.
5. Whos appearing at the Blue Bongo?
6. Arent we early?
7. Now were in trouble.

8. They just cant agree.
9. Its too early to leave.
10. Lets have lunch now.
11. Didnt he mention his name?
12. She doesnt like blues; they
    dont like classical music.

Practice 3

On separate paper, write five sentences using an apostrophe in a contraction.

PART B   *Defining the Possessive*

A *possessive* **is a word that shows that someone or something owns someone or something else.**

Practice 4

In the following phrases, who owns what?

EXAMPLE: "The hat of the man" means <u>the man owns the hat</u>.

1. "The camera of Judson" means _____.
2. "The hopes of the people" means _____.
3. "The thought of the woman" means _____.
4. "The trophies of the home team" means _____.
5. "The ideas of that man" means _____.

PART C — Using the Apostrophe to Show Possession (in Words That Do Not Already End in -S)

| (1) the hands of my father | becomes | (2) my father's hands |

- In phrase (1), who owns what? _____
- In phrase (1), what is the *owner word?* _____
- How does the owner word show possession in phrase (2)?

  _____

- Note that what is owned, *hands,* follows the owner word.

If the *owner word* (possessive) does not end in -*s*, add an apostrophe and an -*s* to show possession.

Practice 5

Change these phrases into possessives with an apostrophe and an -*s*. (Note that the owner words do not already end in -*s*.)

EXAMPLE: the friend of my cousin = _____ *my cousin's friend* _____

1. the eyes of Rona = _____
2. the voice of the coach = _____
3. the ark of Noah = _____
4. the technology of tomorrow = _____
5. the jacket of someone = _____

Practice 6

Add an apostrophe and an -*s* to show possession in these phrases.

1. Judy briefcase
2. the diver tanks
3. Murphy Law
4. Bill decision
5. somebody umbrella

6. everyone dreams
7. your daughter sandwich
8. last month prices
9. that woman talent
10. anyone guess

Practice 7

On separate paper, write five sentences. In each, use an apostrophe and an -*s* to show ownership. Use owner words that do not already end in -*s*.

PART D — Using the Apostrophe to Show Possession (in Words That Already End in -S)

(1) the uniforms of the pilots	becomes	(2) the pilots' uniforms

- In phrase (1), who owns what? _____
- In phrase (1), what is the owner word? _____
- How does the owner word show possession in phrase (2)?

  _____

- Note that what is owned, *uniforms*, follows the owner word.

If the *owner word* (possessive) ends in -s, add an apostrophe after the -s to show possession.*

Practice 8

Change these phrases into possessives with an apostrophe. (Note that the owner words already end in -s.)

EXAMPLE: the helmets of the players = the players' helmets _____

1. the farm of my grandparents = _____
2. the kindness of my neighbors = _____
3. the dunk shots of the basketball players = _____
4. the music of The Smashing Pumpkins = _____
5. the trainer of the horses = _____

Practice 9

Add either 's or ' to show possession in these phrases. BE CAREFUL: Some of the owner words end in -s and some do not.

1. the models faces
2. the model face
3. the pilot safety record
4. the children room
5. the runner time
6. Boris radio

7. my niece CDs
8. your parents anniversary
9. the men locker room
10. three students exams
11. several contestants answers
12. Mr. Jones band

_____

*Some writers add an 's to one-syllable proper names that end in -s: *James's book*.

Practice 10

Rewrite each of the following pairs of short sentences as *one* sentence by using a possessive.

EXAMPLE: Joan has a friend. The friend comes from Chile.

Joan's friend comes from Chile.
_____

1. Rusty has a motorcycle. The motorcycle needs new brakes.

   _____

2. Nurse Johnson had evidence. The evidence proved that the doctor was not careless.

   _____

3. Ahmad has a salary. The salary barely keeps him in peanut butter.

   _____

4. Lee has a job. His job in the Complaint Department keeps him on his toes.

   _____

5. José has a bad cold. It makes it hard for him to sleep.

   _____

6. Jessie told a joke. The joke did not make us laugh.

   _____

7. John Adams had a son. His son was the first president's son to also become president of the United States.

   _____

   _____

8. My sisters have a day-care center. The day-care center is open seven days a week.

   _____

9. The twins have a goal. Their goal is to learn synchronized swimming.

   _____

10. Darren has a thank-you note. The thank-you note says it all.

   _____

Practice 11

On separate paper, write six sentences that use an apostrophe to show ownership—three using owner words that do not end in *-s* and three using owner words that do end in *-s*.

BE CAREFUL: Apostrophes show possession by nouns. As the following chart indicates, possessive pronouns do not have apostrophes.

Possessive Pronouns	
Singular	**Plural**
my book, mine	our book, ours
your book, yours	your book, yours
his book, his	their book, theirs
her book, hers	
its book, its	

Do not confuse *its* (possessive pronoun) with *it's* (contraction for *it is* or *it has*) or *your* (possessive pronoun) with *you're* (contraction for *you are*).*

REMEMBER: Use apostrophes for contractions and possessive nouns only. Do not use apostrophes for plural nouns (*four marbles*), verbs (*he hopes*), or possessive pronouns (*his, hers, yours, its*).

Practice 12   Writing Assignment

Assume that you are writing to apply for a position as a teacher's aide. You want to convince the school principal that you would be a good teacher, and you decide to do this by describing a time that you taught a young child—your own child, a younger sibling, or a friend's child—to do something new.

In your topic sentence, briefly state who the child was and what you taught him or her. What made you want to teach this child? Was the experience easier or harder than you expected? How did you feel afterward? Proofread for the correct use of apostrophes.

✔ Chapter Highlights

- **An apostrophe can indicate a contraction:**

  We're glad you could come.

  They *won't* be back until tomorrow.

- **A word that does not end in -*s* takes an *'s* to show possession:**

  Is that *Barbara's* coat on the sofa?

  I like *Clint Eastwood's* movies.

- **A word that ends in -*s* takes just an *'* to show possession:**

  That store sells *ladies'* hats with feathers.

  I depend on my *friends'* advice.

*See Chapter 32 for work on words that look and sound alike.

Chapter Review

Proofread this essay for apostrophe errors—missing apostrophes and apostrophes used incorrectly. Correct the errors above the lines.

The Magic Fastener

(1) Its hard to remember the world without Velcro. (2) Shoelaces had to be tied; jackets' had to be zipped and did'nt make so much noise when they were loosened. (3) We have a Swiss engineers' curiosity to thank for todays changes.

(4) On a hunting trip in 1948, Georges de Mestral became intrigued by the seedpods that clung to his clothing. (5) He knew that they we're hitching rides to new territory by fastening onto him, but he could'nt tell how they were doing it. (6) He examined the seedpods to find that their tiny hooks were catching onto the threads of his jacket.

(7) The idea of Velcro was born, but the actual product wasnt developed overnight. (8) It took eight more years' before Georges de Mestrals invention was ready for the market. (9) Today, Velcro is used on clothing, on space suits, and even in artificial hearts. (10) Velcro can not only help keep a skier warm but can also save a persons' life.

CHAPTER 30

Direct and Indirect Quotations

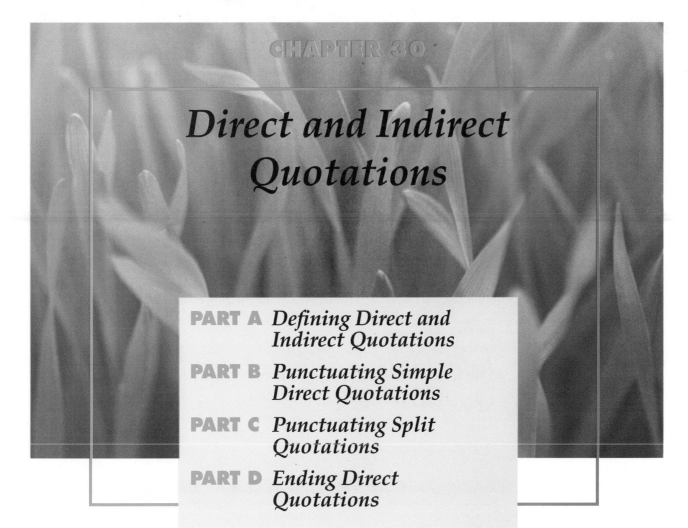

PART A   Defining Direct and Indirect Quotations

(1) John said that he was going.

(2) John said, "I am going."

● Which sentence gives the *exact words* of the speaker, John?

_____

● Why is sentence (2) called a *direct quotation?*

_____

● Why is sentence (1) called an *indirect quotation?*

_____

● Note that the word *that* introduces the *indirect quotation.*

Practice 1

Write *D* in the blank at the right if the sentence uses a *direct quotation.* Write *I* in the blank at the right if the sentence uses an *indirect quotation.*

1. She said that she was thirsty. _____

2. Rita asked, "Which is my chair?" _____

3. Ruth insisted that one turkey would feed the whole family. _____

4. The students shouted, "Get out of the building! It's on fire!" _____

5. "This is silly," she said, sighing. _____

6. I suggested that Rod's future was in the catering business. _____

PART B — *Punctuating Simple Direct Quotations*

Note the punctuation:

(1) Rafael whispered, "I'll always love you."

- Put a comma before the direct quotation.
- Put quotation marks around the speaker's exact words.
- Capitalize the first word of the direct quotation.
- Put the period *inside* the end quotation marks.

  Of course, the direct quotation may come first in the sentence:

(2) "I'll always love you," Rafael whispered.

- List the rules for a direct quotation written like the sentence above:

_____

_____

_____

Practice 2

Rewrite these simple direct quotations, punctuating them correctly.

1. He yelled answer the phone!

   Rewrite: _____

2. The usher called no more seats in front.

   Rewrite: _____

3. My back aches she repeated dejectedly.

    Rewrite: _____

4. Examining the inside cover, Bob said, this book was printed in 1879.

    Rewrite: _____

5. Something is doing the backstroke in my soup the man said.

    Rewrite: _____

PART C   *Punctuating Split Quotations*

Sometimes one sentence of direct quotation is split into two parts:

> (1) "Because it is 2 a.m.," he said, "you had better go."

- *He said* is set off by commas.
- The second part of the quotation—*you had better go*—begins with a small letter because it is part of one directly quoted sentence.

> (2) "Because it is 2 a.m. . . . you had better go."

A direct quotation can also be broken into separate sentences:

> (3) "It is a long ride to San Francisco," he said. "We should leave early."

- Because the second part of the quotation is a separate sentence, it begins with a capital letter.
- Note the period after *said.*

    BE CAREFUL: If you break a direct quotation into separate sentences, be sure that both parts of the quotation are complete sentences.

Practice 3

Rewrite these split direct quotations, punctuating them correctly.

1. Before the guests arrive she said let's relax.

    Rewrite: _____

2. Don't drive so fast he begged I get nervous.

    Rewrite: _____

3. Although Mort is out shellfishing Fran said his hip boots are on the porch.

    Rewrite: _____

    _____

4. Being the youngest in the family she said has its advantages.

   Rewrite: _____

5. This catalog is fantastic the clerk said and you can have it for free.

   Rewrite: _____

   _____

Practice 4

On separate paper, write three sentences using split quotations.

PART D   *Ending Direct Quotations*

A sentence can end in any of three ways:

- with a period (.)
- with a question mark (?)
- with an exclamation point (!)

The period is *always* placed inside the end quotation marks:

(1) He said, "My car cost five thousand dollars."

The question mark and the exclamation point go before or after the quotation marks—depending on the sense of the sentence.

(2) He asked, "Where are you?"
(3) Did he say, "I am thirty-two years old"?
(4) She yelled, "Help!"

- The question mark in sentence (2) is placed before the end quotation marks because the direct quotation is a question.

- The question mark in sentence (3) is placed after the end quotation marks because the direct quotation itself *is not a question.*

   Note that sentence (2) can be reversed:

(5) "Where are you?" he asked.

- Can you list the rules for the exclamation point used in sentence (4)?

   _____

   _____

   Note that sentence (4) can be reversed:

(6) "Help!" she yelled.

Practice 5

Rewrite these direct quotations, punctuating them correctly.

1. Barbara asked is that your SUV.

   Rewrite: _____

2. Did Shenoya make the team he inquired.

   Rewrite: _____

3. Be careful with that mirror she begged the movers.

   Rewrite: _____

4. The truck driver shouted give me a break.

   Rewrite: _____

5. Did she say I wouldn't spend my money on that pet rock.

   Rewrite: _____

Practice 6   Writing Assignment

Write a note to someone with whom you have had an argument. Your goal is to get back on friendly terms with this person. In your first sentence, state this goal, asking for his or her open-minded attention. Then tell him or her why you think a misunderstanding occurred, and explain how you think conflict might be avoided in the future. Refer to the original argument by using both direct and indirect quotations. Check for the correct use of quotation marks; be careful with *all* punctuation.

✔ Chapter Highlights

- **A direct quotation requires quotation marks:**

  Benjamin Franklin said, "There never was a good war or a bad peace."

- **Both parts of a split quotation require quotation marks:**

  "It isn't fair," she argued, "for us to lose the money for the after-school programs."

- **When a direct quotation is split into separate sentences, begin the second sentence with a capital letter:**

  "It's late," he said. "Let's leave in the morning."

- **Always place the period inside the end quotation marks:**

  He said, "Sometimes I talk too much."

- **A question mark or an exclamation point can be placed before or after the end quotation marks, depending on the meaning of the sentence:**

  She asked, "Where were you when we needed you?"

  Did she say, "Joe looks younger without his beard"?

Chapter Review

Proofread this essay for direct and indirect quotations. Punctuate the quotations correctly, and make any other necessary changes above the lines.

Satchel Paige

(1) Some people say that the great pitcher Leroy Paige was called Satchel because of his big feet. (2) Paige himself said I got the nickname as a boy in Mobile before my feet grew. (3) He earned money by carrying bags, called satchels, at the railroad station. (4) I figured out a way to make more money by carrying several bags at a time on a pole he said. (5) Other boys began shouting at him that he looked like a satchel tree. (6) The name stuck.

(7) Unfortunately, for most of Paige's long pitching career, major league baseball excluded African-American players. (8) However, Satchel Paige pitched impressively in the black leagues and in tours against white teams. (9) In 1934, he won a thirteen-inning, one-to-nothing pitching duel against the white pitcher Dizzy Dean and a team of major league all-stars. (10) My fast ball admitted Dean looks like a change of pace alongside of that little bullet old Satchel shoots up to the plate!

(11) After Jackie Robinson broke the major league color barrier in 1948, Satchel Paige took his windmill windup to the Cleveland Indians. (12) He became the oldest rookie in major league history. (13) Some people said that he was too old, but his record proved them wrong. (14) His plaque in the Baseball Hall of Fame reads he helped pitch the Cleveland Indians to the 1948 pennant.

(15) Satchel Paige pitched off and on until he was sixty years old. (16) When people asked how he stayed young, he gave them his famous rules. (17) Everyone remembers the last one. (18) Don't look back he said. (19) Something might be gaining on you.

UNIT 7 *Review*

Proofreading

A. Proofread the following business letter for incorrect or missing capitals, commas, apostrophes, and quotation marks. Correct all errors above the lines. (You should find thirty-two individual errors.)

99 somers street

Northfield, ohio 44056

february 28, 1996

weird walts Discount Store

Main office

akron, Ohio 44313

Dear sir or Madam:

On february 20 1996 I ordered a Zenith nineteen-inch color television with remote control from your store at 1101, Lakeland avenue medina ohio. The model number is 19K44P. When the delivery man brought the set to my home yesterday, he seemed impatient. He urged me to sign before I had a chance to open the box unpack it or examine the equipment. In fact, he said, "Listen, mister Im leaving now whether you open this box or not. To my dismay I later discovered that the handheld remote control was missing.

As soon as possible please send me this remote control. I want to use my new zenith properly. For years now I have been a loyal customer of Weird walt's and would appreciate your prompt attention in this matter. thank You.

Sincerely your's,

Milton rainford

B. Proofread the following essay for incorrect or missing capitals, commas, apostrophes, and quotation marks. Correct the errors above the lines. (You should find thirty-nine individual errors.)

The Liberator of South America

(1) One day in 1805 Simón Bolívar made a vow. (2) He vowed that he wouldnt rest until South America was free from spanish oppression. (3) This promise changed his life and Latin American history (4) Bolívar surprisingly enough spent the first twenty-two years of his life as a rich aristocrat. (5) When he died at fifty-seven he was known as the george Washington of south america.

(6) Bolívar was born in caracas, Venezuela on July 24 1783. (7) after he became an orphan at the age of nine his uncle provided him with a tutor Simón Rodriguez (8) A fierce patriot Rodriguez wanted South American's to rule themselves. (9) However young Simón Bolívar was'nt very interested in his tutors ideas about independence. (10) Bolívars uncle sent Simón to europe to help further the young mans education. (11) during his travels in Spain, Bolívar realized that Latin America was destined to be independent of Spain.

(12) Bolívar returned to Venezuela and joined those fighting Spain. (13) His troops were defeated but Bolívar would not admit to failure. (14) In a famous letter that he wrote in 1814, he declared, "the bonds that unite us to Spain have been cut". (15) Finally, the tide turned against Spain. (16) The spaniards were driven out of Colombia Venezuela Ecuador Peru, and Bolivia (17) Bolívar, leader of much of South America wanted to unite the people under one government. (18) His idea may have been a good one yet each area preferred to become a separate nation. (19) Although his plan for a united country failed Bolívar is still remembered as South Americas greatest hero.

Explain a Cause or an Effect

Examining causes and effects is a useful skill, both in college and at work. This student's thoughtful essay looks at the effects of school pressure to "speak like an American." In your group or class, read it aloud if possible. As you read, pay attention to the causes and effects he describes.

In America, Speak Like an American

(1) Many teachers tell immigrant students to lose their accents and "speak like an American." They mean well. They want the children to succeed. However, this can also encourage children to be ashamed of who they are and give up their heritage.

(2) When I was in fourth grade, I was sent to a class for "speech imperfections." Apparently, I had a Spanish accent. The class wasn't so bad, it taught us to say "chair" instead of "shair" and "school" instead of "eschool." It was so important for me to please the teacher, I did practically everything she asked. She told us things like "The bums on the street have accents, that's why they're not working." I abandoned my roots and my culture and embraced "America." I learned about Stonewall Jackson and William Shakespeare. Soon Ponce de León and Gonzalo de Barca were just memories at the back of my mind. I listened to country music and rock because this was "American."

(3) I can't remember when it happened, but suddenly I found myself listening to Spanish love songs. They were great! They were so sincere, the lyrics were beautiful. While turning the radio dial one day, I stopped at a Hispanic radio station. It was playing salsa. Holy smokes, I thought to myself. All the instruments were synchronized so tightly. The horn section kept accenting the singer's lines. All of a sudden, my hips started swaying, my feet started tapping, and I stood up. And then the horror. I couldn't dance to this music, I had never learned how. There I was, a Puerto Rican boy, listening to Puerto Rican music, but unable to dance the typical Puerto Rican way.

(4) Anger flared through me as I remembered my fourth grade teacher. I was also upset with my parents, in their zeal to have me excel, they kept me from my roots as a first-generation Hispanic American. But that was years ago. I have searched for my Latin heritage. I've

found beautiful music, wonderful literature, and great foods. I now associate with "my people" as well as with everyone else, and I am learning the joys of being Sam Rodriguez, Puerto Rican.

Sam Rodriguez, student

1. How effective is Sam Rodriguez's essay?

   _____ Clear main idea?   _____ Good supporting details?

   _____ Logical organization?   _____ Effective conclusion?

2. Does the essay have a *thesis statement,* one sentence that states the main idea of the entire essay? Which sentence is it?

3. In paragraph (2), the writer says that he "abandoned [his] roots." In his view, what caused him to do this?

4. Underline the lines and ideas you find especially effective, and share them with your group or class. Try to understand exactly why you like a word or sentence. For example, in paragraph (3), we can almost experience the first time the writer really *hears* salsa—the instruments, the horns accenting the singer's lines, his tapping feet and swaying hips.

5. As the writer gets older, he realizes he has lost too much of his heritage. At first he is angry (short-term effect), but what long-term effect does this new understanding have on him?

6. What order does this writer follow throughout the essay?

7. This fine essay is finished and ready to go, but the student makes the same punctuation error four different times. Can you spot and correct the error pattern that he needs to watch out for?

Writing and Revising Ideas

1. What does it mean to "become American"?

2. Write about something important that you gave up and why you did so.

Plan carefully, outlining your paragraph or essay before you write. State your main idea clearly, and plan your supporting ideas or paragraphs. As you revise, pay special attention to clear organization and convincing, detailed support.

As you complete each writing assignment, remember to perform these steps:

- Write a clear, complete topic sentence.

- Use freewriting, brainstorming, or clustering to generate ideas for the body of your paragraph, essay, letter, or commercial.

- Arrange your best ideas in a plan.

- Revise for support, unity, coherence, and exact language.

- Proofread for grammar, punctuation, and spelling errors.

Writing Assignment 1: *Write a letter to compliment or to complain.* Write a letter to a store manager or a dean, praising an especially helpful salesperson or a particularly good teacher. If you are not feeling complimentary, write the opposite: a letter of complaint about a salesperson or an instructor. State your compliment or complaint, describing what occurred and explaining why you are pleased or displeased. Remember, how well your letter is written will contribute to the impression you make. Proofread carefully for the correct use of capitals, commas, apostrophes, and quotation marks.

Writing Assignment 2: *Write about an intergenerational friendship.* Write about a friendship you have had with someone who is not of the same generation as you. How did the friendship first come about? What did you share? What did you not share? Did the friendship change over time? How did the generation difference affect the friendship? Proofread carefully for the correct use of capitals, commas, apostrophes, and quotation marks.

Writing Assignment 3: *Write a TV or radio commercial.* Interested in a career in advertising, you have been asked to write a short commercial to show your skills. Pick a product or service that you really like. You might want to get other people to buy a particular kind of paper towel, athletic shoe, or weed killer. Your commercial can be serious or funny, using hard sell or soft. It is up to you. Proofread carefully for the correct use of capitals, commas, apostrophes, and quotation marks.

Writing Assignment 4: *Revise a quotation.* Pick a quotation from the Quotation Bank at the end of this book, and alter it to express something new. For example, you might want to change "Insanity is hereditary—you get it from your children" to "Insanity is learned—you get it from going to school." Be as serious or as humorous as you would like. Prove that your quotation is valid, arguing from your own or others' experience. Proofread carefully for the correct use of capitals, commas, apostrophes, and quotation marks.

UNIT 8

Improving Your Spelling

Some people are naturally better spellers than others, but anyone can *become* a better speller. In this unit, you will

- Master six basic spelling rules

- Learn to avoid common look-alike/sound-alike errors

Spotlight on Writing

No spelling errors mar this writer's memory of summer mornings years ago. If possible, read the paragraph aloud.

Summer, when I was a boy in Brooklyn, was a string of <u>intimacies</u>, a sum of small knowings, and almost none of them cost money. Nobody ever <u>figured</u> out a way to charge us for morning, and morning then was the <u>beginning</u> of everything. I was an altar boy in the years after the war, up in the morning before most other people for the long walk to the church on the hill. And I would watch the sun rise in Prospect Park—first a rumor, then a <u>heightened</u> light, something unseen and immense melting the hard early darkness; then suddenly there was a molten ball, <u>screened</u> by the trees, about to climb to a scalding noon. The sun would dry the dew on the grass of the park, soften the tar, bake the rooftops, brown us on the <u>beaches</u>, make us sweat, force us out of the tight small flats of the tenements.

Pete Hamill, "Spaldeen Summers"

- Through his choice and arrangement of words, this writer helps us see and feel the park at sunrise. He also has avoided the six most common types of spelling errors. The underlined words are all spelled correctly. If you don't know why, read on.

Writing Ideas

- Morning in a particular place (a desert, a suburb, an all-night bar, a mountaintop, and so forth)

- An experience of "awe" or wonder

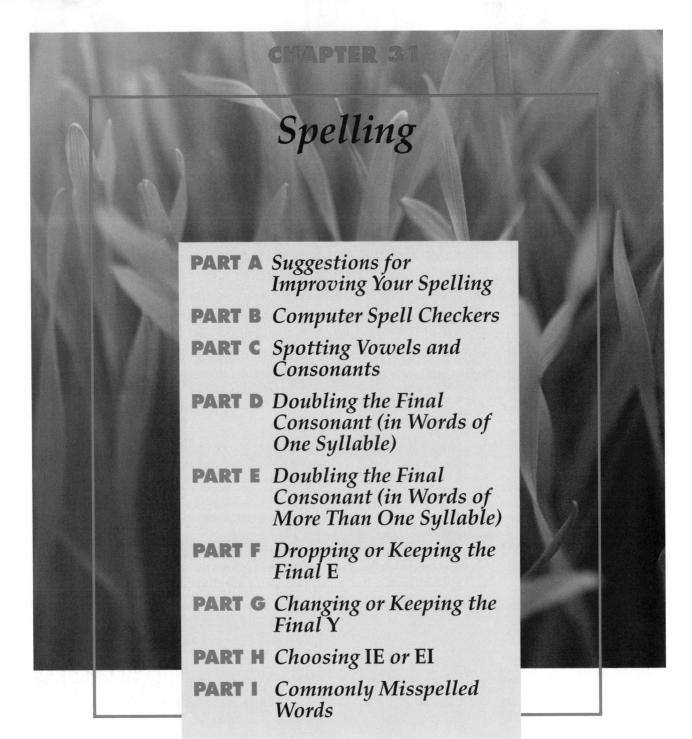

CHAPTER 31

Spelling

PART A   *Suggestions for Improving Your Spelling*

One important ingredient of good writing is accurate spelling. No matter how interesting your ideas are, your writing will not be effective if your spelling is incorrect.

Tips for Improving Your Spelling

1. **Look closely at the words on the page.** Use any tricks you can to remember the right spelling. For example, "The *a*'s in *separate* are separated by an *r*," or "*Dessert* has two *s*'s because you want two *desserts*."

2. **Use a dictionary.** Even professional writers frequently check spelling in a dictionary. As you write, underline the words you are not sure of, and look them up when you write your final draft. If locating words in the dictionary is a real problem for you, consider a "poor speller's dictionary." Ask your professor to recommend one.

3. **Use a spell checker.** If you write on a computer, make a habit of using the spell-check software. See Part B for tips and cautions about spell checkers.

4. **Keep a list of the words you misspell.** Look over your list whenever you can, and keep it handy as you write.

5. **Look over corrected papers for misspelled words** (often marked *sp*). Add these words to your list. Practice writing each word three or four times.

6. **Test yourself.** Use flash cards or have a friend dictate words from your list or from this chapter.

7. **Review the basic spelling rules explained in this chapter.** Take time to learn the material; don't rush through the entire chapter all at once.

8. **Study the spelling list on page 376,** and test yourself on those words.

9. **Read through Chapter 32, "Look-Alikes/Sound-Alikes,"** for commonly confused words (*their, there,* and *they're,* for instance). The practices in that chapter will help you eliminate some common spelling errors from your writing.

PART B   *Computer Spell Checkers*

Almost all word-processing programs are equipped with a spell checker. A spell checker picks up spelling errors and gives you alternatives for correcting them. Your word-processing program may highlight misspelled words as you type. If it does not, get in the habit of using the spell checker as your first and last proofreading task.

Depending on your software program and the paper you are writing, determine the best ways to use the spell checker. For example, if your paper repeats an unusual name, you could add the name to the spell-check dictionary so that the name does not continually appear as a misspelled word. Another approach is to use the "ignore all" feature. If the name suddenly appears as a misspelled word, you've spelled the name differently that time.

What a spell checker cannot do is think. If you've typed one correctly spelled word for another—*if* for *it*, for example—the spell checker cannot bring that error to your attention. If you've written *then* for *than*, the spell checker cannot help.* To find such errors, you need to proofread your paper after using the spell checker.

If your word-processing program does not highlight misspelled words as you type, run a spell check after you've made all your corrections. If you've introduced a new error, the spell checker will let you know.

---

*For questions about words that sound the same but are spelled differently, check Chapter 32, "Look-Alikes/Sound-Alikes."

In a small group, read this poem, which "passed" every spell check. Correct the errors that the spell check missed, and write them above the lines.

Eye halve a spelling check her,

It came with my pea see.

It clearly marques four my revue,

Miss steaks eye kin knot sea.

I strike a key and type a word

And weight four it two say

Weather eye am wrong oar write,

It shows me strait aweigh.

Whenever a mist ache is maid,

It nose bee fore two long,

And eye can put the error rite.

Its rare lea ever wrong.

I've run this poem threw it.

I'm shore your please too no.

Its letter perfect in it's weigh.

My checker tolled me sew.

PART C   *Spotting Vowels and Consonants*

To learn some basic spelling rules, you must know the difference between vowels and consonants.

The vowels are *a, e, i, o,* **and** *u.*

The consonants are *b, c, d, f, g, h, j, k, l, m, n, p, q, r, s, t, v, w, x,* **and** *z.*

The letter *y* **can be either a vowel or a consonant, depending on its sound.**

> happy, shy

● In each of these words, *y* is a vowel because it has a vowel sound: an *ee* sound in *happy* and an *i* sound in *shy.*

> young, yawn

● In each of these words, *y* is a consonant because it has the consonant sound of *y.*

Practice 2

Write *V* for vowel or *C* for consonant in the space over each letter. Be careful of the *y*.

EXAMPLES:

$$\frac{C}{h}\ \frac{V}{o}\ \frac{C}{p}\ \frac{V}{e}\ \frac{C}{d}$$

$$\frac{C}{s}\ \frac{C}{t}\ \frac{V}{a}\ \frac{C}{r}$$

1. __ __ __ __
  t h e r e

3. __ __ __ __
  r e l y

5. __ __ __ __ __ __
  h i d d e n

2. __ __ __ __
  j u m p

4. __ __ __ __
  y a m s

6. __ __ __ __ __ __
  s i l v e r

PART D — Doubling the Final Consonant (in Words of One Syllable)

When you add a suffix or ending that begins with a vowel (like *-ed, -ing, -er, -est*) to a word of one syllable, double the final consonant *if* the last three letters of the word are consonant-vowel-consonant, or *cvc*.

> mop + ed = mopped
>
> swim + ing = swimming
>
> thin + est = thinnest
>
> burn + er = burner

- *Mop, swim,* and *thin* all end in *cvc*; therefore, the final consonants are doubled.
- *Burn* does not end in *cvc*; therefore, the final consonant is not doubled.

Practice 3

Which of the following words double the final consonant? Check to see whether the word ends in *cvc*. Double the final consonant if necessary; then add the suffixes *-ed* and *-ing*.

Word	Last Three Letters	-ed	-ing
EXAMPLES: drop	cvc	dropped	dropping
boil	vvc	boiled	boiling
1. plan			
2. brag			
3. dip			
4. sail			

Word	Last Three Letters	-er	-est
5. stop	_____	_____	_____
6. peel	_____	_____	_____

Practice 4

Which of the following words double the final consonant? Check for *cvc*. Then add the suffixes *-er* or *-est*.

	Word	Last Three Letters	-er	-est
EXAMPLES:	hot	*cvc*	*hotter*	*hottest*
	cool	*vvc*	*cooler*	*coolest*
	1. tall	_____	_____	_____
	2. short	_____	_____	_____
	3. fat	_____	_____	_____
	4. slim	_____	_____	_____
	5. wet	_____	_____	_____
	6. dry	_____	_____	_____

Practice 5

Which of the following words double the final consonant? Check for *cvc*. Then add the suffixes *-ed* or *-ing*.

Basketball's Clown Princes

(1) The Harlem Globetrotters, organized in 1927, are the longest-

_____ exhibition basketball team, but success and recognition
    run + ing

did not come easily. (2) _____ red, white, and blue uniforms and
                 Don + ing

_____ over rough roads in an old beat-up car, the Globetrotters
    bump + ing

_____ the Midwest, picking up games against local amateur teams.
    tour + ed

(3) Although it had a _____ first season, _____ its oppo-
                win + ing   beat + ing

nents in 101 out of 117 games, the team _____ only about $75 a game.
                       earn + ed

(4) At first, it _____ just like the other touring teams of that day,
       look + ed

playing aggressive, straightforward basketball.

(5) When Inman Jackson joined it in 1929, however, he _____
_____
add + ed

his sense of humor to the team. (6) He introduced _____ the ball on the
_____
spin + ing

tip of one finger, _____ the ball between the players in outrageous fake-
_____
flip + ing

out plays, and drop-kicking the ball toward the basket. (7) The Globetrotters soon

_____ that if they could entertain and amuse as well as win, they could
_____
learn + ed

gain a _____ audience than any other team. (8) They _____
_____   _____
big + er   cap + ed

their fourteenth season by winning the world championship against the Chicago

Bruins in overtime after being five points behind late in the game. (9) From then

on, the Globetrotters were _____ into the best arenas, _____
_____   _____
book + ed   pair + ed

against the best teams, and treated like a first-class team.

(10) In recent years, the team has _____ in two feature films, faced
_____
star + ed

numerous college all-star teams, toured the world several times, raised a fortune

for charity, and been the subject of a children's animated TV series. (11) The key to

the Harlem Globetrotters' _____ success has been its determination
_____
great + est

in developing its unique style of brilliantly skillful basketball and hilarious

_____.
_____
clown + ing

PART E — Doubling the Final Consonant (in Words of More Than One Syllable)

When you add a suffix that begins with a vowel to a word of more than one syllable, double the final consonant *if*

(1) the last three letters of the word are *cvc, and*

(2) the accent or stress is on the *last* **syllable.**

> begin + ing = beginning
>
> patrol + ed = patrolled

● *Begin* and *patrol* both end in *cvc.*

● In both words, the stress is on the last syllable: *be-gin´, pa-trol´.* (Pronounce the words aloud, and listen for the correct stress.)

- Therefore, *beginning* and *patrolled* double the final consonant.

gossip + ing = gossiping	
visit + ed = visited	

- *Gossip* and *visit* both end in *cvc.*
- However, the stress is *not* on the last syllable: *gos-sip, vis-it.*
- Therefore, *gossiping* and *visited* do not double the final consonant.

Practice 6

Which of the following words double the final consonant? First, check for *cvc.* Then check for the final stress, and add the suffixes *-ed* and *-ing.*

Word	Last Three Letters	-ed	-ing
EXAMPLES: repel	cvc	repelled	repelling
enlist	vcc	enlisted	enlisting
1. occur	_____	_____	_____
2. happen	_____	_____	_____
3. polish	_____	_____	_____
4. commit	_____	_____	_____
5. offer	_____	_____	_____
6. prefer	_____	_____	_____
7. exit	_____	_____	_____
8. travel	_____	_____	_____
9. wonder	_____	_____	_____
10. omit	_____	_____	_____

Practice 7

Which of the following words double the final consonant? First check for *cvc.* Then check for the final stress, and add the suffixes *-ed* and *-ing.*

Martial Arts Magic

(1) Jackie Chan, the martial arts film star and director, _____ long
                                                                    labor + ed

and hard for his success in movies. (2) When he was a child, his parents

_____ him in the Peking Opera Academy. (3) Unlike Western opera,
enroll + ed

Chinese opera is more like a circus that features acrobats, jugglers, and contortion-

ists. (4) Throughout his film career, Chan has _____ on the tumbling

depend + ed

and gymnastic skills that he learned in those years at the academy. (5) When he

graduated from the academy, Chinese opera was out of fashion, and he was

_____ to take a job _____ stunts in martial arts films. (6)

compel + ed   perform + ing

He _____ small parts in two of Bruce Lee's films and much larger parts

obtain + ed

in many other, unsuccessful pictures.

(7) Following Lee's death, a producer _____ that Jackie Chan

predict + ed

would be the new Bruce Lee and signed him to a multipicture contract. (8) After

more unsuccessful films, Chan _____ to himself that he was getting

admit + ed

nowhere and considered retiring from movies entirely. (9) By a stroke of luck,

another producer _____ him to star in the martial arts comedy *Snake in*

borrow + ed

the Eagle's Shadow. (10) Instead of trying to turn Chan into a poor copy of Bruce Lee,

this producer _____ him to create a comic underdog character.

permit + ed

(11) The film was a huge success in Asia, and audiences _____ more

demand + ed

martial arts comedies and more Jackie Chan movies.

(12) Once Chan was a hit in the Far East, he _____ his time and

commit + ed

energy to breaking into the American film industry. (13) After several unsuccessful

attempts in the 1980s, he eventually had a worldwide crossover hit with *Rumble in*

the Bronx (with Toronto standing in for New York) in 1994.

(14) Following the success of *Rumble in the Bronx,* Chan announced that he

_____ to make films in Hollywood and _____ to leave the

prefer + ed   intend + ed

Far East. (15) Since that announcement, he has _____ audiences with hits

astonish + ed

such as *Operation Condor, Rush Hour,* and *Shanghai Noon.* (16) His performances have

been so extraordinary that he has been _____ "a human special effect."

proclaim + ed

PART F *Dropping or Keeping the Final* E

When you add a suffix that begins with a vowel (like *-able*, *-ence*, or *-ing*), drop the final *e*.

When you add a suffix that begins with a consonant (like *-less*, *-ment*, or *-ly*), keep the final *e*.

> write + ing = writing
>
> pure + ity = purity

● *Writing* and *purity* both drop the final *e* because the suffixes *-ing* and *-ity* begin with vowels.

> hope + less = hopeless
>
> advertise + ment = advertisement

● *Hopeless* and *advertisement* keep the final *e* because the suffixes *-less* and *-ment* begin with consonants.

Here are some exceptions to memorize:

argument	manageable
awful	noticeable
courageous	truly
judgment	

Practice 8

Add the suffix shown to each word.

EXAMPLES: come + ing = _____coming_____

rude + ness = _____rudeness_____

1. blame + less = _____
2. guide + ance = _____
3. debate + able = _____
4. motive + ation = _____
5. sincere + ly = _____
6. desire + able = _____
7. argue + ment = _____
8. home + less = _____

9. response + ible = _____
10. rejoice + ing = _____
11. awe + ful = _____
12. manage + er = _____
13. judge + ment = _____
14. fame + ous = _____
15. grieve + ance = _____

Practice 9

Add the suffix shown to each word in parentheses. Write the correctly spelled word in each blank.

A Precious Resource

(1) Many people have _____ memories of _____ their
    (pleasure + able)   (receive + ing)

first library card or _____ books for the first time at a local public
                      (choose + ing)

library. (2) _____ recognized as a _____ resource, the public
            (Wide + ly)   (price + less)

library is _____ just as you might expect: as a collection of books and
           (define + ed)

other materials supported by the public for public use.

(3) Several New England towns claim the honor of _____ the first
                                                 (contribute + ing)

public money for a library. (4) However, the first such library of meaningful size

and influence—the first _____ public library—_____ in
                        (fame + ous)   (originate + ed)

Boston, Massachusetts, in 1854. (5) The Boston Public Library, with its

_____ reference collection and its policy of _____ popular
(use + ful)   (circulate + ing)

books, set the pattern for all public libraries _____ _____ in
                                                (ultimate + ly)   (create + ed)

the United States and Canada. (6) By the end of the nineteenth century, many state

legislatures felt _____ for _____ taxes to support
                  (response + ible) (raise + ing)

libraries. (7) They _____ that public libraries had an _____
                    (recognize + ed)   (extreme + ly)

_____ role in _____ people with the best possible means of
(value + able)   (provide + ing)

_____ their education. (8) Although public libraries today have much
(continue + ing)

the same goal, they now offer a _____ _____ number of
                                (true + ly)   (admire + able)

resources and services. (9) These include story hours for children, book discus-

sion clubs for adults, lectures, art exhibits, literacy classes, and most recently,

_____ training and _____.
(compute + er)   (guide + ance)

(10) Technology, of course, has _____ transformed the
(complete + ly)

_____ of the public library, as well as the way the library is
(manage + ment)

_____ . (11) The most _____ changes— today's computerized
(use + ed)   (notice + able)

catalogs and searchable databases—would _____ have been beyond
(sure + ly)

the wildest dreams of even the most _____ enthusiastic early
(sincere + ly)

public library supporters.

PART G — *Changing or Keeping the Final Y*

When you add a suffix to a word that ends in -*y*, change the *y* to *i* if the letter before the *y* is a consonant.

> **Keep the final *y* if the letter before the *y* is a vowel.**

> happy + ness = happiness
>
> delay + ed = delayed

- The *y* in *happiness* is changed to *i* because the letter before the *y* is a consonant, *p*.

- However, the *y* in *delayed* is not changed to *i* because the letter before it is a vowel, *a*.

> **When you add -*ing* to words ending in *y*, always keep the *y*.**

> copy + ing = copying
>
> delay + ing = delaying

Here are some exceptions to memorize:

day + ly = daily	pay + ed = paid
lay + ed = laid	say + ed = said

When the final *y* is changed to *i*, add -*es* instead of -*s*.

> fly + es = flies
>
> marry + es = marries
>
> candy + es = candies

Practice 10

Add the suffix shown to each of the following words.

EXAMPLES: marry + ed = ____married____

buy + er = ____buyer____

1. cry + ed = _____
2. mercy + ful = _____
3. worry + ing = _____
4. say + ed = _____
5. juicy + er = _____

6. enjoy + able = _____
7. clumsy + ness = _____
8. wealthy + est = _____
9. day + ly = _____
10. merry + ly = _____

Practice 11

Add the suffixes in parentheses to each word.

1. lively   (er) _____
   (est) _____
   (ness) _____

2. beauty (fy) _____
   (ful) _____
   (es) _____

3. grumpy (er) _____
   (est) _____
   (ly) _____

4. study   (es) _____
   (ous) _____
   (ing) _____

5. busy   (ness) _____
   (er) _____
   (est) _____

6. try   (es) _____
   (ed) _____
   (al) _____

Practice 12

Add the suffix in parentheses to each word.

Winter Blues

(1) Although Kim _____ to ignore her feelings, she always felt
                        try (ed)

_____, _____, _____, and _____ during
   hungry (er)   sleepy (er)   angry (er)   lonely (er)

the winter months of the year. (2) As part of her _____, she would go
                                                      deny (al)

about her _____ as usual, but she knew that she was no longer
              busy (ness)

_____ her _____ surroundings or feeling _____.
  enjoy (ing)   beauty (ful)   happy (ness)

(3) Then one day she read a magazine article that discussed several

_____ of a medical condition called seasonal affective disorder, or
   study (es)

SAD. (4) Kim immediately _____ many _____ between
                      identify (ed)   similarity (es)

her own yearly mood changes and the symptoms that people with SAD

_____. (5) She learned that winter SAD is brought on _____
  display (ed)   primary (ly)

by a lack of exposure to light. (6) The article _____ that insufficient sun-
                                       say (ed)

shine, inadequate artificial light at home or at work, and even _____
                                                    mercy (lessly)

cloudy weather could trigger SAD.

    (7) _____, Kim discovered that three or four different kinds of
        Happy (ly)

treatment are available. (8) The most severe cases—people who sleep more than

fourteen hours a day and still feel fatigued, for example—are usually cured by

_____ light therapy, which can be administered by a light-therapy
  day (ly)

clinic or by the patient under a doctor's supervision. (9) Medication, exercise,

and changes in diet are also effective in many cases. (10) Although Kim had

_____ treatment for so long, she didn't waste any time _____
  delay (ed)   pity (ing)

herself. (11) She immediately telephoned the Center for Environmental

_____ in Colorado and the Depression and Related Affective Disorders
  Therapy (es)

Association in Maryland for a list of SAD clinics and for more information and

support. (12) Within a short time, she had received information from both

_____ about a light-therapy clinic near her, and she was beginning to
  agency (es)

experience her _____ winter in years.
           healthy (est)

PART H   *Choosing* IE *or* EI

Write *i* **before** *e,* **except after** *c,* **or in any** *ay* **sound like** *neighbor:*

> niece, believe
> conceive
> weigh

● *Niece* and *believe* are spelled *ie.*

● *Conceive* is spelled *ei* because of the preceding *c.*

● *Weigh* is spelled *ei* because of its *ay* sound.

However, words with a *shen* sound are spelled with an *ie* after the *c: ancient, conscience, efficient, sufficient.*

Here are some exceptions to memorize:

either	seize
foreign	society
height	their
neither	weird

Practice 13

Pronounce each word out loud. Then fill in the blanks with either *ie* or *ei.*

1. f __ __ ld
2. w __ __ ght
3. n __ __ ther
4. w __ __ rd
5. ch __ __ f

6. s __ __ ze
7. rec __ __ ve
8. br __ __ f
9. h __ __ ght
10. ach __ __ ve

Practice 14

In the following sentences, write either *ie* or *ei* in the blanks.

(1) The story is anc __ __ nt history, but I can't bel __ __ ve how easy it is for parents to rel __ __ ve a child's gr __ __ f. (2) My n __ __ ce Paula was staying with me while her mother and father took a br __ __ f vacation. (3) She was __ __ ght years old and a bundle of energy. (4) All day Saturday, we played baseball in a n __ __ ghbor's f __ __ ld, so we were tired at the end of the afternoon—at least I was! (5) That night there was a f __ __ rce storm. (6) My ch __ __ f fear was that the lights would go out because I knew that Paula was afraid of the dark. (7) At the h __ __ ght of the storm, I effic __ __ ntly got out a flashlight and candles. (8) That's all Paula needed to see! (9) She immediately burst into worr __ __ d tears. (10) I

tr __ __ d to calm her; I cut us each a p __ __ ce of p __ __. (11) However, n __ __ ther I nor my dog, who climbed into her lap, could console her. (12) Suddenly the phone rang; Paula ran to it and picked up the rec __ __ ver. (13) Her parents were calling, and just hearing th __ __ r voices made her feel much better. (14) Within seconds, she was her cheery, fr __ __ ndly self again. (15) I just stared in amazement.

PART I   *Commonly Misspelled Words*

Below is a list of commonly misspelled words. They are words that you probably use daily in speaking and writing. Each word has a trouble spot, the part of the word that is often spelled incorrectly. The trouble spot is in bold type.

Two tricks to help you learn these words are (1) to copy each word twice, underlining the trouble spot, and (2) to copy the words on flash cards and have someone else test you.

If possible, consult this list while or after you write.

1. across	26. gra**mm**ar	51. possible
2. ad**d**ress	27. hei**gh**t	52. **prefer**
3. ans**w**er	28. **ill**egal	53. preju**d**ice
4. argument	29. immed**iately**	54. privil**ege**
5. **a**thlete	30. import**ant**	55. pro**bab**ly
6. begi**nn**ing	31. inte**g**ration	56. **psychology**
7. beha**vior**	32. in**te**lligent	57. pursue
8. calen**dar**	33. in**te**rest	58. refe**r**ence
9. care**er**	34. inte**rf**ere	59. **rhy**thm
10. cons**cie**nce	35. jew**e**lry	60. ridiculous
11. crow**ded**	36. jud**gm**ent	61. separate
12. defi**nite**	37. knowle**dge**	62. simi**lar**
13. de**s**cribe	38. main**tain**	63. **since**
14. despe**rate**	39. mathematics	64. speech
15. di**ff**erent	40. meant	65. stren**gth**
16. dis**app**oint	41. nec**essa**ry	66. success
17. dis**app**rove	42. nerv**ous**	67. **surprise**
18. doesn't	43. occasion	68. **taught**
19. eig**ht**h	44. opin**ion**	69. temp**era**ture
20. embarrass	45. optimist	70. **thorough**
21. envir**on**ment	46. particular	71. **thought**
22. exa**gg**erate	47. **per**form	72. tire**d**
23. famil**iar**	48. **per**haps	73. until
24. finally	49. perso**nn**el	74. weight
25. government	50. posse**ss**	75. written

Personal Spelling List

In your notebook, keep a list of words that *you* misspell. Add words to your list from corrected papers and from the exercises in this chapter. First, copy each word as you misspelled it, underlining the trouble spot; then write the word correctly. Use the following form. Study your list often.

	As I Wrote It	Correct Spelling
1.	di<u>ss</u>apointed	disappointed
2.		
3.		
4.		
5.		

Practice 15   Writing Assignment

Success can be defined in many different ways. In a small group, discuss what the term *success* means to you. Is it a rewarding career, a happy family life, lots of money? Offer as many different definitions of success as you can.

Now pick the definition that most appeals to you and write a paragraph explaining what success is. You may wish to use people in the news or friends to support your main idea. Proofread your work for accurate spelling, especially the words covered in this chapter. Finally, exchange papers and read each other's work. Did your partner find any spelling errors that you missed?

✔ Chapter Highlights

- **Double the final consonant in one-syllable words that end in** *cvc:*

  hop/hopped   swim/swimming

- **Double the final consonant in words of more than one syllable if they end in** *cvc* **and if the stress is on the last syllable:**

  begin/beginning   prefer/preferred

- **Keep the final** *e* **when adding a suffix that begins with a consonant:**

  hope/hopeful   time/timely

- **Drop the final** *e* **when adding a suffix that begins with a vowel:**

  hope/hoping   time/timer

- **Keep the final** *y* **when adding a suffix if the letter before the** *y* **is a vowel:**

  buy/buying   delay/delayed

- **Change the** *y* **to** *i* **when adding a suffix if the letter before the** *y* **is a consonant:**

  happy/happiest   pity/pitiful

- **Write** *i* **before** *e,* **except after** *c,* **or in any** *ay* **sound like** *neighbor:*

  believe, niece, *but* receive, weigh

- **Remember that there are exceptions to all of these rules. Check a dictionary whenever you are uncertain.**

Chapter Review

Proofread this essay for spelling errors. Correct the errors above the lines.

The Magic of Dolphins

(1) According to most people who have done it, swiming with dolphins is an amazeing experience. (2) People report feeling magically uplifted or filled with joy. (3) They come away from the encounter feeling totally refreshed; supprisingly enough, some even feel reborn. (4) In fact, doctors and pychologists have maintaned for years that dolphin-assisted therapy greatly improves the

condition of thier pateints. (5) What is it about dolphins that seems to raise human beings to greater heigts?

(6) The anser probaly has to do with the animals' powerful sonar. (7) Dolphins use this sonar to scan the envirement around them. (8) The sonar is so precise that it can locate a shark half a mile away and determine whether its stomach is full or empty. (9) According to scientific studies, after someone swims with dolphins, the left and right sides of the person's brain are in much greater harmony. (10) The brain functions much more efficeintly than usual. (11) In the opinyin of many experts, the sonar boosts the production of infection-fighting cells and also releases deep-relaxation hormones.

(12) Some people have definately experienced the sonar. (13) They felt as if they were being zapped by electricity. (14) Some reported lightheadedness followed by deep calm. (15) For many people, however, playing in the water nose to nose or eye to eye with a dolphin and sensing that the animal is truely communicateing with them is an incredible high in itself, sonar or no sonar!

CHAPTER 32

Look-Alikes/ Sound-Alikes

A/An/And

A is used before a word beginning with a consonant or a consonant sound.

> (1) *a* man
> (2) *a* house
> (3) *a* union (the *u* in *union* is pronounced like the consonant *y*)

An is used before a word beginning with a vowel (*a, e, i, o, u*) or a silent *h*.

> (4) *an* igloo
> (5) *an* apple
> (6) *an* hour (the *h* in *hour* is silent)

And joins words or ideas together.

> (7) Edward *and* Ralph are taking the same biology class.
> (8) He is very honest, *and* most people respect him.

Practice 1

Fill in *a*, *an*, or *and*.

EXAMPLE: Choosing __*a*__ career is __*an*__ important step for __*a*__ college student.

1. Don Miller has used each summer vacation to try out _____ different career choice.

2. Last summer, he worked in _____ law office.

3. He filled in for _____ administrative assistant on leave.

4. He found the work _____ the atmosphere very stimulating.

5. In fact, he had never liked _____ job so much.

6. Because Don was eager to learn, _____ young lawyer let him proofread some important documents.

7. The lawyer was impressed by how carefully Don worked _____

   suggested that Don consider _____ law career.

8. Don returned to school in the fall _____ spent time researching his new career.

9. He talked to his adviser about becoming _____ paralegal.

10. _____ paralegal investigates the facts of cases, prepares documents, _____ does other background work for lawyers.

11. His adviser could see that Don had both _____ interest in law _____ the ability to succeed.

12. With his adviser's help, Don found _____ course of study to prepare for his career.

13. Next summer, he hopes to work for _____ public interest law firm

    _____ to learn about environmental law.

14. He is happy to have found _____ worthwhile career _____ looks forward to the future.

Practice 2

On separate paper, write two sentences using *a*, two using *an*, and two using *and*.

Accept/Except

Accept means "to receive."

(1) Please *accept* my apologies.
(2) I *accepted* his offer of help.

Except means "other than" or "excluding."

(3) Everyone *except* Ron thinks it's a good idea.

Practice 3

Fill in forms of *accept* or *except*.

1. Did Steve _____ the collect call from his brother?

2. Mr. Francis will _____ the package in the mailroom.

3. All of our friends attended the wedding _____ Meg.

4. The athlete proudly _____ his award.

5. Every toddler _____ my daughter enjoyed the piñata party.

6. _____ for Jean, we all had tickets for the movie.

7. The tornado left every building standing, _____ for the barn.

8. Everyone _____ Ranjan was willing to _____ the committee's decision.

Practice 4

On separate paper, write two sentences using some form of *accept* and two using *except*.

Been/Being

Been is the past participle form of *to be*. *Been* is usually used after the helping verb *have, has,* or *had.*

> (1) I *have been* to that restaurant before.
> (2) She *has been* in Akron for ten years.

● *Being* is the *-ing* form of *to be*. *Being* is usually used after the helping verbs *is, are, am, was,* and *were.*

> (3) They *are being* helped by the salesperson.
> (4) Rhonda *is being* courageous and independent.

Practice 5

Fill in *been* or *being*.

1. The children have _____ restless all day.

2. What good films are _____ shown on television tonight?

3. We have _____ walking in circles!

4. I haven't _____ in such a good mood for a week.

5. This building is _____ turned into a community center.

6. His last offer has _____ on my mind all day.

7. Which elevator is _____ inspected now?

8. Because you are _____ honest with me, I admit that I have

_____ in love with you for years.

Practice 6

On separate paper, write two sentences using *been* and two using *being*.

Buy/By

Buy means "to purchase."

(1) She *buys* new furniture every five years.

By means "near," "before," or "by means of."

(2) He walked right *by* and didn't say hello.
(3) *By* sunset, we had finished the harvest.
(4) We prefer traveling *by* bus.

Practice 7

Fill in *buy* or *by*.

1. Did you _____ that computer, or did you rent it?

2. These tracks on the trail were made _____ a deer.

3. He stood _____ the cash register and waited his turn to

_____ a cheeseburger.

4. She finds it hard to walk _____ a bookstore without going in to browse.

5. It's better to stick with your budget than to _____ that ten-seater couch.

6. Please answer this letter _____ October 10.

7. Pat trudged through the storm to _____ a Sunday paper.

8. The dishes _____ the sink need to be put away.

Practice 8

On separate paper, write two sentences using *buy* and two using *by*.

Fine/Find

Fine means "good" or "well." It can also mean "a penalty."

> (1) He wrote a *fine* analysis of the short story.
> (2) She paid a $10 *fine*.

Find means "to locate."

> (3) I can't *find* my red suspenders.

Practice 9

Fill in *fine* or *find*.

1. The library charges a large _____ for overdue videotapes.

2. As soon as we _____ your lost suitcase, we'll send it to you.

3. Can you _____ me one of these in an extra-large size?

4. Harold made a _____ impression on the assistant buyer.

5. By tonight, I will be feeling _____.

6. My father gave me good advice: "When you _____ good friends, stick with them."

Practice 10

On separate paper, write two sentences using *fine* and two using *find*.

It's/Its

It's is a contraction of *it is* or *it has*. If you cannot substitute *it is* or *it has* in the sentence, you cannot use *it's*.

> (1) *It's* a ten-minute walk to my house.
> (2) *It's* been a nice party.

Its is a possessive and shows ownership.

> (3) The bear cub rolled playfully on *its* side.
> (4) Industry must do *its* share to curb inflation.

Practice 11

Fill in *it's* or *its*.

1. If _____ not too much trouble, drop the package off on your way home.

2. _____ been hard for him to accept the fact that he can no longer play ball.

3. The *Daily News* reporter was lucky because the jury reached _____ verdict just before her deadline.

4. _____ been a long time since I had a real vacation.

5. _____ a chocolate cake with your social security number in pink frosting.

6. My family is at _____ best when there is work to be done.

7. _____ impossible to open this window.

8. Although I hate shoveling the walk, I am happy _____ been a good year for winter sports.

9. _____ sad to see that seagull huddled in the sand.

10. If _____ not flying, perhaps _____ wing is hurt.

Practice 12

On separate paper, write two sentences using *it's* and two using *its*.

Know/Knew/No/New

Know means "to have knowledge or understanding." *Knew* is the past tense of the verb *to know*.

(1) Carl *knows* he has to finish by 6 p.m.
(2) The police officer *knew* the quickest route to the pier.

No is a negative.

(3) He is *no* longer dean of academic affairs.

New means "fresh" or "recent."

(4) I like your *new* belt.

Practice 13

Fill in *know, knew, no,* or *new.*

1. We will need _____ wiring to handle those powerful air conditioners.

2. She didn't _____ the lid was loose.

3. Tim has _____ time to recheck his answers to the quiz.

4. I _____ I need to find _____ jokes because no one laughs when I tell my old ones.

5. Because she _____ the answer, she won a pool table and a complete set of china.

6. Gus tasted the _____ apples and accepted three more bushels.

7. Because you really _____ the _____ material, why don't you take the final early?

8. Charlene thinks there's _____ way we can do it, but I

   _____ we'll be speaking Italian by June.

9. Arnold _____ that he shouldn't have eaten the third dessert.

10. We have _____ way of knowing how well you scored on the civil service examination.

11. He didn't _____ whether the used equipment came with a guarantee.

12. I wish I _____ then what I _____ now.

Practice 14

On separate paper, write two sentences using *know,* two using *knew,* two using *no,* and two using *new.*

Lose/Loose

Lose means "to misplace" or "not to win."

> (1) Be careful not to *lose* your way on those back roads.
> (2) George hates to *lose* at cards.

Loose means "ill fitting" or "too large."

> (3) That's not my size; it's *loose* on me.

Practice 15

Fill in *lose* or *loose.*

1. Because the plug is _____ in the socket, the television keeps blinking on and off.

2. A professional team has to learn how to win and how to _____ gracefully.

3. If Irene doesn't tighten that _____ hubcap, she will _____ it.

4. I like wearing _____ clothing in the summer.

5. Before these pants shrank in the dryer, they were too_____ .

6. Act now, or you will _____ your opportunity to get that promotion.

7. She won't _____ those mittens again because I've clipped them onto her jacket.

8. I'm surprised you didn't _____ those _____ quarters.

Practice 16

On separate paper, write two sentences using *lose* and two using *loose*.

Mine/Mind

Mine is a possessive and shows ownership.

> (1) This is your umbrella, but where is *mine?*

Mind means "intelligence." It can also be a verb meaning "to object" or "to pay attention to."

> (2) What's on your *mind?*
> (3) I don't *mind* if you come late.

Practice 17

Fill in *mine* or *mind.*

1. Her road test is tomorrow; _____ was yesterday.

2. Will Doris _____ if we spend the evening talking about our days in boot camp?

3. Sherlock put his _____ to work and solved the mystery.

4. Please _____ your manners when we meet the king.

5. Please don't interrupt us; we really _____ when someone breaks our train of thought.

6. My _____ is made up; I want to switch my major from accounting to marketing.

7. Don't _____ him; he always snores in public.

8. "That toy is _____ ," whined Tim, "and I *do* _____ if you take it!"

Practice 18

On separate paper, write two sentences using *mine* and two using *mind.*

Past/Passed

Past is that which has already occurred; it is over with.

> (1) His *past* work has been satisfactory.
> (2) Never let the *past* interfere with your hopes for the future.

Passed is the past tense of the verb *to pass.*

> (3) She *passed* by and nodded hello.
> (4) The wild geese *passed* overhead.

Practice 19

Fill in *past* or *passed.*

1. He asked for the butter, but I absentmindedly _____ him the mayonnaise.

2. Forget about failures in the _____, and look forward to success in the future.

3. The police car caught up to the truck that had _____ every other car on the road.

4. I have _____ this same corner every Saturday morning for a year.

5. Wasn't that woman who just _____ us on a motorcycle your Aunt Sally?

6. In the _____, Frieda and Carolyn used to talk on the phone once a week.

7. Your _____ attendance record was perfect.

8. Don knew he had _____ the test, but he had never received such a

   high grade in the _____.

Practice 20

On separate paper, write two sentences using *past* and two using *passed.*

Quiet/Quit/Quite

Quiet means "silent, still."

> (1) The woods are *quiet* tonight.

Quit means "to give up" or "to stop doing something."

(2) Last year, I *quit* smoking.

Quite means "very" or "exactly."

(3) He was *quite* tired after playing handball for two hours.
(4) That's not *quite* right.

Practice 21

Fill in *quiet, quit,* or *quite.*

1. When it comes to expressing her feelings, Tonya is _____ vocal.

2. I can't concentrate when my apartment is too _____.

3. Selling belly chains can be _____ amusing.

4. Please be _____; I'm trying to listen to the news.

5. If she _____ now, she will risk losing her vacation pay.

6. Dwight asked the crew to be absolutely _____ while the magicians performed.

7. Don't _____ when the going gets rough; just increase your efforts and succeed.

8. I have the general idea, but I don't _____ understand all the details.

9. This usually _____ library is now _____ noisy.

10. She _____ whistling when people in the line began to stare at her.

Practice 22

On separate paper, write two sentences using *quiet,* two using *quit,* and two using *quite.*

Rise/Raise

Rise means "to get up by one's own power." The past tense of *rise* is *rose.* The past participle of *rise* is *risen.*

(1) The sun *rises* at 6 a.m.
(2) Daniel *rose* early yesterday.
(3) He *has risen* from the table.

Raise means "to lift an object" or "to grow or increase." The past tense of *raise* is *raised.* The past participle of *raise* is *raised.*

> (4) *Raise* your right hand.
> (5) She *raised* the banner over her head.
> (6) We *have raised* $1,000.

Practice 23

Fill in forms of *rise* or *raise*.

1. When the moon _____, we'll be able to see the path better.

2. During the meeting, she _____ the possibility of a strike.

3. The jet _____ off the runway and roared into the clouds.

4. Bud would like to _____ early, but usually he wakes, turns over, and goes back to sleep.

5. Can you _____ corn in this soil?

6. He couldn't _____ from his chair because of the chewing gum stuck to his pants.

7. My boss has unexpectedly _____ my salary.

8. I felt foolish when I accidentally _____ my voice in the quiet concert hall.

9. The loaves of homemade bread have _____.

10. He _____ to his feet and shuffled out the door.

Practice 24

On separate paper, write two sentences using some form of *rise* and two using some form of *raise*.

Sit/Set

Sit means "to seat oneself." The past tense of *sit* is *sat*. The past participle of *sit* is *sat*.

> (1) *Sit* up straight!
> (2) He *sat* down on the porch and fell asleep.
> (3) She has *sat* reading that book all day.

Set means "to place" or "to put something down." The past tense of *set* is *set*. The past participle of *set* is *set*.

> (4) Don't *set* your books on the dining room table.
> (5) She *set* the package down and walked off without it.
> (6) He had *set* the pot on the stove.

Practice 25

Fill in forms of *sit* or *set*.

1. Marcy _____ her glasses on the seat next to her.

2. Please _____ there; the dentist will see you in ten minutes.

3. _____ the cans of paint in the corner, please.

4. My grandfather always _____ in that overstuffed, red-and-blue plaid chair.

5. Please _____ that box of clothes by the door.

6. _____ down, and let me _____ this Hawaiian feast before you.

7. I would have _____ your bracelet on the counter, but I was afraid someone might walk off with it.

8. We have always _____ in the first row, but tonight I want to

   _____ at the back of the auditorium.

Practice 26

On separate paper, write two sentences using some form of *sit* and two using *set*.

Suppose/Supposed

Suppose means "to assume" or "to guess." The past tense of *suppose* is *supposed*. The past participle of *suppose* is *supposed*.

(1) Brad *supposes* that the teacher will give him an *A*.
(2) We all *supposed* she would win first prize.
(3) I had *supposed* Dan would win.

● *Supposed* means "should have"; it is followed by *to*.

(4) He is *supposed to* meet us after class.
(5) You were *supposed to* wash and wax the car.

REMEMBER: When you mean *ought* or *should*, always use the *-ed* ending— *supposed*.

Practice 27

Fill in *suppose* or *supposed*.

1. How do you _____ he will get himself out of this mess?

2. My father-in-law was _____ to arrive last night.

3. I _____ I'll find my car keys in my other pants.

4. Why do you _____ that cereal is so expensive?

5. You are not _____ to open the presents until your birthday.

6. Diane was _____ to check the bus schedule.

7. Where do you _____ he bought that gold lamé shirt?

8. What are we _____ to do with these three-by-five-inch cards?

9. Frank _____ that Meredith would meet him for dinner.

10. I _____ Ron is willing to shovel the snow this time.

Practice 28

On separate paper, write two sentences using *suppose* and two using *supposed to.*

Their/There/They're

Their is a possessive pronoun and shows ownership.

> (1) They couldn't find *their* wigs.
> (2) *Their* children are charming.

There indicates a location.

> (3) I wouldn't go *there* again.
> (4) Put the lumber down *there.*

There is also a way of introducing a thought.

> (5) *There* is a fly in my soup.
> (6) *There* are two ways to approach this problem.

They're is a contraction: *they + are = they're.* If you cannot substitute *they are* in the sentence, you cannot use *they're.*

> (7) *They're* the best poems I have read in a long time.
> (8) If *they're* coming, count me in.

Practice 29

Fill in *their, there,* or *they're.*

1. If you move over _____ , I can get everyone into the picture.

2. _____ are three ways to mix paint, all of which are messy.

3. If _____ here, we can set out the food.

4. Do you see the air balloon way up _____ ?

5. My uncle and aunt always helped _____ children with _____ homework.

6. _____ preparing for a hot, sticky summer.

7. Is _____ a faster route to Topeka?

8. _____ never on time when it comes to paying _____ phone bills.

9. _____ products contain no sugar and no preservatives.

10. Is _____ a wrench in the toolbox?

11. Because _____ so quiet, I suppose _____ asleep.

12. Isn't _____ a better way to organize _____ closets?

Practice 30

On separate paper, write two sentences using *their*, two using *there*, and two using *they're*.

Then/Than

Then means "next" or "at that time."

> (1) First, we went to the theater, and *then* we went for pizza.
> (2) I was a heavyweight boxer *then*.

Than is used in a comparison.

> (3) She is a better student *than* I.

Practice 31

Fill in *then* or *than*.

1. Carlos works harder _____ anyone else in this office.

2. San Francisco has colder winters _____ San Diego.

3. Get your first paycheck; _____ think about moving into your own apartment.

4. It's often better to forgive someone _____ to carry a grudge.

5. If you receive straight *A*'s this semester, will you _____ apply for a scholarship?

6. You asked me a question and _____ interrupted me before I could answer.

7. This red convertible gets more miles to the gallon _____ any other car on the lot.

8. Now I'm ready for marriage; _____, I was confused.

Practice 32

On separate paper, write two sentences using *then* and two using *than*.

Thought/Taught

Thought is the past tense of the verb *to think*. It can also mean "an idea."

(1) She *thought* it was an interesting idea.
(2) Now that's a strange *thought*!

Taught is the past tense of the verb *to teach*.

(3) Last summer, César *taught* his daughters how to swim.
(4) She once *taught* mathematics at Stanford Community College.

Practice 33

Fill in *thought* or *taught*.

1. Nora _____ me how to decipher her handwriting.

2. I _____ about the company's offer but decided to refuse it and wait for a better one.

3. Perry _____ that he could make extra money driving a cab.

4. Charlie _____ he could always borrow anything he needed.

5. Every great deed begins with a _____.

6. Who _____ you how to balance your checkbook?

7. When Joan _____ about the courses she had chosen, she knew she would have a challenging semester.

8. Louis _____ that if he _____ French, he wouldn't forget his native language.

Practice 34

On separate paper, write two sentences using *thought* and two using *taught*.

Threw/Through

Threw is the past tense of the verb *to throw.*

> (1) Charleen *threw* the ball into the bleachers.

Through means "in one side and out the other" or "finished."

> (2) He burst *through* the front door laughing.
> (3) If you are *through* eating, we can leave.

Practice 35

Fill in *threw* or *through.*

1. I went _____ my notes, but I couldn't find any reference to Guatemala.

2. He _____ the pillow on the floor and plopped down in front of the TV.

3. Gail _____ her raincoat over her head and ran out into the storm.

4. You go _____ that door to get to the dean's office.

5. If you are _____ with that reference material, I would like to take a look at it.

6. I am not sure why Sandra _____ a life preserver to that group of swimmers.

7. We can always see _____ their tricks.

8. It took Beverly more than an hour to go _____ airport security.

Practice 36

On separate paper, write two sentences using *threw* and two using *through.*

To/Too/Two

To means "toward."

> (1) We are going *to* the stadium.

To can also be combined with a verb to form an infinitive.

> (2) Where do you want *to go* for lunch?

Too means "also" or "very."

> (3) Roberto is going to the theater *too*.
> (4) They were *too* bored to stay awake.

Two is the number 2.

> (5) Ms. Palmer will teach *two* new accounting courses this term.

Practice 37

Fill in *to*, *too*, or *two*.

1. If you want _____ enroll in college this fall, you will need _____ letters of recommendation.

2. It will be _____ awkward _____ leave the dinner before the dessert is served.

3. She likes _____ eat sushi _____ .

4. It's _____ early _____ go _____ the football game.

5. That dance step may be _____ advanced for me right now.

6. No one is _____ old _____ learn the polka.

7. The _____ students worked all night preparing for the debate.

8. On the express bus, there were _____ many people in the front and _____ few in the back.

9. Even the students admitted that the test was _____ easy.

10. Jimmy and I have _____ build the drawers by Friday if we want _____ stain the chest on Monday.

11. Have you ever been _____ the Grand Canyon?

12. Tracey hates _____ complain, even when she is clearly right.

13. It's _____ much trouble to make my own salad dressing.

14. She _____ likes _____ watch professional wrestling.

15. We saw _____ undercover agents talking quietly _____ the bartender.

Practice 38

On separate paper, write two sentences using *to*, two using *too*, and two using *two*.

Use/Used

Use means "to make use of." The past tense of *use* is *used*. The past participle of *use* is *used*.

> (1) Why do you *use* green ink?
> (2) He *used* the wrong paint in the bathroom.
> (3) I have *used* that brand of toothpaste myself.

Used means "in the habit of" or "accustomed"; it is followed by *to*.

> (4) I am not *used to* getting up at 4 a.m.
> (5) They got *used to* the good life.

REMEMBER: When you mean *in the habit of* or *accustomed*, always use the *-ed* ending—*used*.

Practice 39

Fill in *use* or *used*.

1. Terry is _____ to long bus rides.

2. It may take a few days to get _____ to this high altitude.

3. Do you know how to _____ a buzz saw?

4. Vera hopes to get _____ to her grumpy father-in-law.

5. Please _____ the pink striped towel.

6. Carlotta and Roland still _____ the laundromat on the corner.

7. We _____ the self-service pump; the gas was cheaper.

8. Feel free to _____ my telephone if you need to make a call.

9. _____ your head!

10. Never _____ big words to try to impress people.

11. My grandmother does not _____ her microwave oven because

    she has never gotten _____ to it.

12. Never get _____ to failure; always expect success.

Practice 40

On separate paper, write two sentences using *use* and two using *used to*.

Weather/Whether

Weather refers to atmospheric conditions.

(1) In June, the *weather* in Spain is lovely.

Whether implies a question.

(2) *Whether* you pass is up to you.

Practice 41

Fill in *weather* or *whether*.

1. Rainy _____ makes me lazy.

2. Be sure to tell the employment agency _____ you plan to take the job.

3. You never know _____ Celia will be happy or sad.

4. Good _____ always brings joggers to the park.

5. Flopsy didn't know _____ to eat the carrot or the lettuce first.

6. Please check to see _____ the printer needs a new ink cartridge.

7. The real estate agent must know by 10 a.m. _____ you intend to rent the house.

8. _____ the _____ cooperates or not, we're going to the beach.

Practice 42

On separate paper, write two sentences using *weather* and two using *whether*.

Where/Were/We're

Where implies place or location.

(1) *Where* have you been all day?
(2) Home is *where* you hang your hat.

Were is the past tense of *are*.

(3) We *were* on our way when the hurricane hit.

We're is a contraction: *we* + *are* = *we're*. If you cannot substitute *we are* in the sentence, you cannot use *we're*.

(4) *We're* going to leave now.
(5) Because *we're* in the city, let's go to the zoo.

Practice 43

Fill in *where, were,* or *we're.*

1. The desk was scratched, but _____ not sure who did it.

2. _____ did you put the tape measure?

3. Ted and Gloria _____ childhood sweethearts. _____

4. When you _____ at your aunt's house, _____ did your cat stay?

5. Virginia is not _____ I was born.

6. The librarians _____ very helpful in showing us _____

   things _____.

7. _____ you surprised that _____ as good a team as we are?

8. The clouds _____ blocking the sun in exactly the spot

   _____ we _____ sitting.

9. Our children want a story every night, but sometimes _____ too tired to read them one.

10. Does Alissa remember _____ she hid her diary?

11. Everyone needs a little hideaway, a place _____ he or she can be absolutely alone.

12. _____ _____ going is a question _____ not about to answer.

Practice 44

On separate paper, write two sentences using *where,* two using *were,* and two using *we're.*

Whose/Who's

Whose implies ownership and possession.

> (1) *Whose* term paper is that?

Who's is a contraction of *who is* or *who has.* If you cannot substitute *who is* or *who has,* you cannot use *who's.*

> (2) *Who's* knocking at the window?
> (3) *Who's* seen my new felt hat with the green bows?

Practice 45

Fill in *whose* or *who's*.

1. _____ ready for an adventure?

2. _____ CDs are scattered all over the floor?

3. We found a puppy in the vacant lot, but we don't know _____ it is.

4. _____ tapping on the window?

5. He's a physician _____ diagnosis can be trusted.

6. Grace admires the late Marian Anderson, _____ singing always moved her.

7. I'm not sure _____ coming and _____ not.

8. _____ been eating all the chocolate chip cookies?

Practice 46

On separate paper, write two sentences using *whose* and two using *who's*.

Your/You're

Your is a possessive and shows ownership.

> (1) *Your* knowledge is astonishing!

You're is a contraction: *you + are = you're.* If you cannot substitute *you are* in the sentence, you cannot use *you're.*

> (2) *You're* the nicest person I know.

Practice 47

Fill in *your* or *you're*.

1. Is that _____ salad plate or mine?

2. If _____ tired, take a nap.

3. Does _____ daughter like her new school?

4. I hope _____ children haven't forgotten their notebooks.

5. If _____ in a rush, we can mail _____ scarves to you.

6. _____ foreman was just transferred.

7. Please keep _____ Saint Bernard out of my rose garden.

8. _____ in charge of _____ finances from now on.

9. When _____ optimistic about life, everything seems to go right.

10. Let me have _____ order by Thursday; if it's late, _____ not likely to receive the merchandise in time for the holidays.

Practice 48

On separate paper, write two sentences using *your* and two using *you're*.

Practice 49   Writing Assignment

While away from home—perhaps at school, in the service, or at an out-of-town job—you have met the person you wish to marry. Write a letter to introduce him or her to your parents. Since you want your parents to like your fiancé or fiancée, your letter should explain his or her most appealing qualities: career success, education, kindness, generosity, poise, friendliness, dependability, good looks, and so on. However, since you want to be realistic, show that you and this person have some differences that will have to be accepted or resolved.

Proofread your letter for accurate spelling.

✔ Chapter Highlights

Some words look and sound alike. Below are a few of them:

● **it's/its**

It's the neatest room I ever saw.

Everything is in *its* place.

● **their/they're/there**

They found *their* work easy.

They're the best actors I have ever seen.

Put the lumber down *there*.

● **then/than**

I was a heavyweight boxer *then*.

He is a better cook *than* I.

● **to/too/two**

We are going *to* the stadium.

No one is *too* old to learn.

I bought *two* hats yesterday.

● **whose/who's**

Whose Italian dictionary is this?

I'm not sure *who's* leaving early.

● **your/you're**

Is *your* aunt the famous mystery writer?

You're due for a promotion and a big raise.

Proofread this essay for look-alike/sound-alike errors. Write your corrections above the lines.

Arranging for Happiness and Success

(1) Feng shui (pronounced *fung shway*) is the Chinese art of creating harmony an balance in one's surroundings. (2) Ten years ago, this ancient Eastern tradition was not excepted by mainstream America. (3) Today, however, ordinary people are using feng shui to improve many aspects of there personal and work lives. (4) Established businesses, from Universal Studios to Merrill Lynch, have embraced it to increase they're success and prosperity. (5) Architects, builders, and real estate developers are using it to create places and spaces that enhance people's lives.

(6) Feng shui means "wind-water" in Chinese. (7) The system, which was once used only by the emperor of China, is more then four thousand years old. (8) It is based on the idea that everything has powerful positive energy, or *chi*. (9) Feng shui practitioners believe that *chi* connects a person's surroundings with what happens in the person's life. (10) The proper flow of *chi* in a home or a business is suppose to create an environment in which someone can become healthier, happier, and more successful. (11) Those who's lives have been improved by feng shui believe that arranging their surroundings so that *chi* flows freely leads to positive change.

(12) In the work environment, feng shui makes people aware of the color of walls, the placement of furniture, the lighting, the sound, the choice and location of art and plants, and so on. (13) A well-known feng shui principle has people set facing the door with a wall behind them in order to feel protected and powerful.

(14) However, other suggestions have being much more unusual. (15) One executive has twelve stones sitting on a windowsill to guard against negative forces from the surrounding buildings. (16) He also has sit sixty-nine small stones on the ledge of an inside window to push away the heat and negative energy from fax machines and computers on the other side. (17) A store owner was told that the direct path from the front entrance too the rear exit of her shop would tempt customers to walk into and than directly out of her store without buying anything. (18) She was advised to hang a mirror above the back door so that the

energy would flow back into the store. (19) In the too locations were this owner paid special attention to the flow of *chi* by careful placement of cash tables, fitting rooms, and even toilets, her profits increased buy 20 percent.

(20) On the home front, people have become use to promoting they're health, comfort, peace, good fortune, prosperity, and relationships threw feng shui. (21) Feng shui experts sometimes use a *bagua,* a kind of map, to help people evaluate their homes. (22) Each *bagua* has eight areas, or "corners," each representing a different aspect of life. (23) Interestingly enough, if a house is missing the wealth corner, the family often has difficulty getting ahead financially. (24) Creating a wealth corner usually brings about a raise in income. (25) Standard remedies for house problems include placing furniture differently or sitting objects like mirrors, crystals, wind chimes, plants, water fountains, and aquariums in strategic locations to redirect the *chi*.

(26) Weather your looking to improve your personal life or your job success, you can find feng shui guidelines to help you. (27) Their are many books, magazines, TV shows, videos, workshops, and websites about feng shui. (28) A good place to begin is by fining something that is quiet easy for you to do—for example, attacking clutter. (29) According to feng shui, clutter—things from the passed that you don't love, use, or need—blocks *chi* and exhausts your energy. (30) Getting rid of clutter in backpacks, book bags, purses, and closets helps free *chi* and sends your energy soaring!

Proofreading

The following essay contains a number of spelling and look-alike/sound-alike errors. First, underline the misspelled or misused words. Then write each correctly spelled word above the line. (You should find twenty-eight errors.)

Nature's Own Weed Whackers

(1) If you raise goats mostly for milk and wool, you might be intrested in this new idea. (2) Your goats can earn a liveing just buy eating! (3) Parks, citys, and other businesses are now using goats in three seperate but similer ways. (4) Goats are reduceing forest fires, clearing overgrown feilds, and protecting native plants—all threw eating.

(5) Goats like nothing better then chomping on tons of weeds and branchs. (6) They are lawnmowers with legs, and, unlike human workers, they don't mind thorns or poisonous plants. (7) They scale steep hills easily an get into places were mowers can't go. (8) They work without the noise of chain saws. (9) Finaly, goats fertilize the land as they work.

(10) When goats reduce the vegetation in an area, they greatly reduce the intensity of fires. (11) If grasses are three feet tall, they create a fifteen-foot-high fire wall that moves at fifteen miles an hour. (12) If grasses are only too inchs tall, they create a one-foot fire wall that moves at three miles an hour.

(13) Goats have been hired to eat foriegn weeds and plants that have no natural enemys. (14) These plants, which were brought from other countrys, are completely takeing over the native plants of some areas. (15) The use of goats avoids the nesessity for poisonous herbicides or for cuting and triming by hand.

(16) However, unless goats are managed carefuly, they can turn the thickest forest or countryside into a desert. (17) If you accept this importent new work for youre goats, you must prevent them from purforming their job to well!

Examine Positive (or Negative) Values

One good way to develop a paragraph or essay is by supporting the topic sentence or the thesis statement with three points. A student uses this approach in the following essay. In your group or class, read her work, aloud if possible.

Villa Avenue

(1) The values I learned growing up on Villa Avenue in the Bronx have guided me through thirty-five years and three children. Villa Avenue taught me the importance of having a friendly environment, playing together, and helping people.

(2) Villa Avenue was a three-block, friendly environment. I grew up on the middle block. The other ones were called "up the block" and "down the block." Mary's Candy Store was up the block. It had a candy counter and soda fountain on the left and on the right a jukebox that played three songs for twenty-five cents. My friends and I would buy candy, hang out, and listen to the Beatles and other music of the sixties. A little down from Mary's on the corner was Joey's Deli. When you walked into Joey's, different aromas would welcome you to a world of Italian delicacies. Fresh mozzarella in water always sat on the counter, with salami, pepperoni, and imported provolone cheese hanging above. On Sundays at Joey's, my father would buy us a black-and-white cookie for a weekly treat.

(3) On Villa Avenue, everyone helped everyone else. Everybody's doors were open, so if I had to go to the bathroom or needed a drink of water, I could go to a dozen different apartments. If my parents had to go somewhere, they would leave me with a friend. When people on the block got sick, others went to the store for them, cleaned for them, watched their kids, and made sure they had food to eat. If someone died, everyone mourned and pitched in to help with arrangements. When I reflect on those days, I realize that the way the mothers looked out for each other's children is like your modern-day play group. The difference is that our play area was "the block."

(4) The whole street was our playground. We would play curb ball at the intersection. One corner was home plate, and the other ones were

the bases. Down the block where the street was wide, we would play Johnny on the Pony with ten to fifteen kids. On summer nights, it was kick the can or hide and seek. Summer days we spent under an open fire hydrant. Everyone would be in the water, including moms and dads. Sometimes the teenagers would go to my Uncle Angelo's house and get a wine barrel to put over the hydrant. With the top and bottom of the barrel off, the water would shoot twenty to thirty feet in the air and come down on us like a waterfall.

Loretta M. Carney, student

1. How effective is Loretta Carney's essay?

   _____ Clear main idea?   _____ Good supporting details?

   _____ Logical organization?   _____ Effective conclusion?

2. What is the main idea of the essay? Can you find the thesis statement, one sentence that states this main idea?

3. The writer states that Villa Avenue taught her three values. What are they? Are these clearly explained in paragraphs 2, 3, and 4? Are they discussed in the same order in which the thesis statement presents them? If not, what change would you suggest?

4. Does this essay *conclude,* or just stop? What suggestions would you make to the writer for a more effective conclusion?

5. Proofread Carney's essay. Do you see any error patterns that she should watch out for?

Writing and Revising Ideas

1. Describe a place or person that taught you positive (or negative) values.

2. Do places like Villa Avenue exist anymore? Explain why you do or do not think so.

See Chapter 5 for help with planning and writing. You might wish to present your topic with three supporting points, the way Loretta Carney does. As you revise, pay close attention to writing a good thesis sentence and supporting paragraphs that contain clear, detailed explanations.

As you complete each writing assignment, remember to perform these steps:

- Write a clear, complete topic sentence.

- Use freewriting, brainstorming, or clustering to generate ideas for the body of your paragraph, essay, letter, or review.

- Arrange your best ideas in a plan.

- Revise for support, unity, coherence, and exact language.

- Proofread for grammar, punctuation, and spelling errors.

Writing Assignment 1: *Write a letter.* You have identified what you consider to be a problem in your place of employment. When you go to your supervisor, you are asked to write up your concerns and to suggest a solution. Begin by describing the problem and then by giving background information, including what you suspect are the causes of the problem. Then give suggestions for solving it. End with some guidelines for evaluating the success of the changes. In your concluding sentence, thank your supervisor for his or her consideration of your letter. Don't allow your letter to become less effective because of typos or mistaken look-alikes/sound-alikes. Proofread for accurate spelling!

Writing Assignment 2: *Discuss giving and getting advice.* We all give advice to and get advice from others. Sometimes that advice can have a great impact. Have you received advice that changed your life? Were you advised to return to school, marry, or change careers? Did you give advice to others that changed their lives? In your first sentence, explain who advised whom to do what. What happened? What were the consequences of the advice? End with advice to others about giving or receiving advice. Proofread for accurate spelling.

Writing Assignment 3: *Review a movie.* Your college newspaper has asked you to review a movie. Pick a popular film that you especially liked or disliked. In your first sentence, name the film, and state whether or not you recommend it. Explain your evaluation by discussing two or three specific reasons for your reactions to the picture. Describe as much of the film as you need to, to make your point, but do not retell the plot. Proofread for accurate spelling.

Writing Assignment 4: *Describe a family custom.* Most families have customs that they perform together. These customs often help strengthen the bond that the members of the family feel toward each other. A custom might be eating Sunday dinner together, going to religious services, celebrating holidays in a special way, or even holding a family council to discuss difficulties and concerns. Write about a custom in your family that was especially meaningful. Of what value was this custom to you or other members of the family? Proofread for accurate spelling.

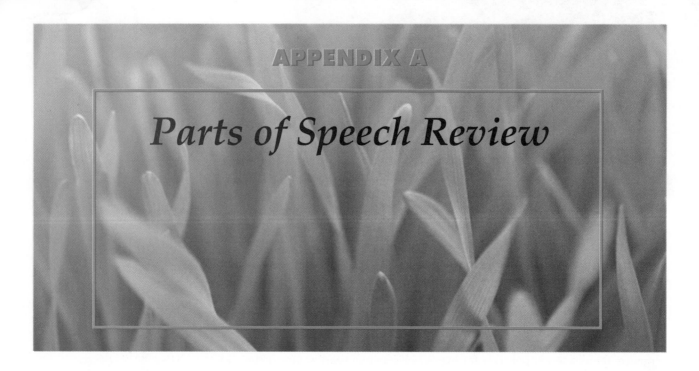

Parts of Speech Review

A knowledge of basic grammar terms will make your study of English easier. Throughout this book, these key terms are explained as needed and are accompanied by ample practice. For your convenience and reference, below is a short review of the eight parts of speech.

Nouns

Nouns are the names of persons, places, things, animals, activities, and ideas.*

Persons:	Ms. Caulfield, Mike, secretaries
Places:	Puerto Rico, Vermont, gas station
Things:	sandwich, Sears, eyelash
Animals:	whale, ants, Lassie
Activities:	running, discussion, tennis
Ideas:	freedom, intelligence, humor

Pronouns

Pronouns replace or refer to nouns or other pronouns. The word that a pronoun replaces is called its *antecedent*.**

My partner succeeded; *she* built a better mousetrap!

These computers are amazing; *they* alphabetize and index.

Everyone should do *his* or *her* best.

All students should do *their* best.

---

*For more work on nouns, see Chapter 20.
**For more work on pronouns, see Chapter 21.

Pronouns take different forms, depending on how they are used in a sentence. They can be the subjects of sentences (*I, you, he, she, it, we, they*) or the objects of verbs and prepositions (*me, you, him, her, it, us, them*). They also can show possession (*my, mine, your, yours, his, her, hers, its, our, ours, their, theirs*).

Subject:	*You* had better finish on time.
	Did *someone* leave a red jacket?
Object of verb:	Robert saw *her* on Thursday.
Object of preposition:	That VCR is for *her.*
Possessive:	Did Tom leave *his* sweater on the dresser?

Verbs

Verbs can be either action verbs or linking verbs. Verbs can be single words or groups of words.*

Action verbs show what action the subject of the sentence performs.

Sonia *bought* a French dictionary.

Jack *has opened* the letter.

Linking verbs link the subject of a sentence with a descriptive word or words. Common linking verbs are *be, act, appear, become, feel, get, look, remain, seem, smell, sound,* and *taste.*

This report *seems* well organized and complete.

You *have been* quiet this morning.

The *present participle* of a verb is its *-ing* form. The present participle can be combined with some form of the verb *to be* to create the progressive tenses, or it can be used as an adjective or a noun.

Pat *was waiting* for the report.	(*past progressive tense*)
The *waiting* taxis lined up at the curb.	(*adjective*)
Waiting for trains bores me.	(*noun*)

The *past participle* of a verb can be combined with helping verbs to create different tenses, it can be combined with forms of *to be* to create the passive voice, or it can be used as an adjective. Past participles regularly end in *-d* or *-ed,* but irregular verbs take other forms (*seen, known, taken*).

He *has edited* many articles for us.	(*present perfect tense*)
This report *was edited* by the committee.	(*passive voice*)
The *edited* report reads well.	(*adjective*)

---

*For more work on verbs, see Unit 3.

Every verb can be written as an *infinitive: to* plus the *simple form* of the verb.

She was surprised *to meet* him at the bus stop.

Adjectives

Adjectives describe or modify nouns or pronouns. Adjectives can precede or follow the words they describe.*

Several green chairs arrived today.

Gordon Lake is *dangerous* and *deep*.

Adverbs

Adverbs describe or modify verbs, adjectives, or other adverbs.**

Anita reads *carefully*.	*(adverb describes verb)*
She is *extremely* tired.	*(adverb describes adjective)*
He wants a promotion *very* badly.	*(adverb describes adverb)*

Prepositions

A preposition begins a *prepositional phrase*. A prepositional phrase contains a preposition (a word such as *at, in, of,* or *with*), its object (a noun or pronoun), and any adjectives modifying the object.†

Preposition	Object
after	*work*
on	the blue *table*
under	the broken *stairs*

Conjunctions

Conjunctions are connector words.

Coordinating conjunctions (and, but, for, nor, or, so, yet) join two equal words or groups of words.††

---

*For more work on adjectives, see Chapter 22.

**For more work on adverbs, see Chapter 22.

†For more work on prepositions, see Chapter 23.

††For more work on conjunctions, see Chapters 13 and 14.

> James is quiet *but* sharp.
>
> Ms. Chin *and* Mr. Warburton attended the Ice Capades.
>
> He printed out the report, *and* Ms. Helfman faxed it immediately.
>
> She will go to Norfolk Community College, *but* she will also continue working at the shoe store.

Subordinating conjunctions (after, because, if, since, unless, and so on) join an independent idea with a dependent idea.

> *Whenever* Ken comes to visit, he takes the family out to dinner.
>
> I haven't been sleeping well *because* I've been drinking too much coffee.

Interjections

Interjections are words such as *ouch* and *hooray* that express strong feeling. They are rarely used in formal writing.

If the interjection is the entire sentence, it is followed by an exclamation point. If the interjection is attached to a sentence, it is followed by a comma.

> *Hey!* You left your wallet in the phone booth.
>
> *Oh,* she forgot to send in her tax return.

A Reminder

REMEMBER: The same word may be used as a different part of speech.

> Harry *thought* about the problem. *(verb)*
>
> Your *thought* is a good one. *(noun)*

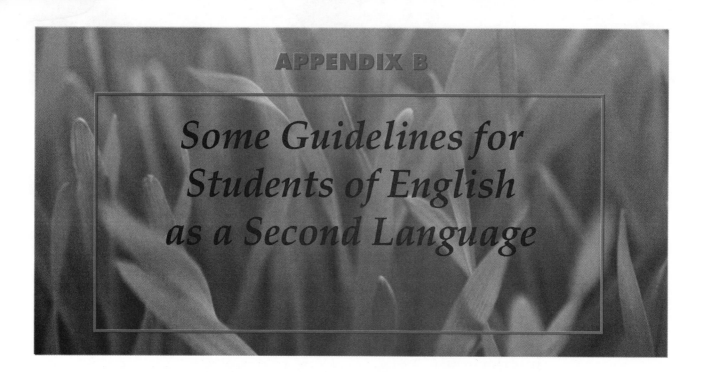

Some Guidelines for Students of English as a Second Language

Count and Noncount Nouns

Count nouns refer to people, places, or things that are separate units. You can often point to them, and you can always count them.

Count Noun	Sample Sentence
computer	The writing lab has four *computers*.
dime	There are two *dimes* under your chair.
professor	All of my *professors* are at a conference today.
notebook	I carry three *notebooks* in my backpack.
child	Why is your *child* jumping on the table?

Noncount nouns refer to things that are wholes. You cannot count them separately. Noncount nouns may refer to ideas, feelings, and other things that you cannot see or touch. Noncount nouns may refer to food or beverages.

Noncount Noun	Sample Sentence
courage	It takes *courage* to study a new language.
warmth	The *warmth* of your smile makes me feel welcome.
happiness	We wish the bride and groom much *happiness*.
bread	Who will slice this loaf of *bread*?
meat	Do you eat *meat*, or are you a vegetarian?
coffee	The *coffee* turned cold as we talked.

Plurals of Count and Noncount Nouns

Most count nouns form the plural by adding *-s* or *-es*. Some count nouns have irregular plurals.*

---

*For work on singular and plural nouns, see Chapter 20.

Plurals of Count Nouns

ship/ships	newspaper/newspapers
flower/flowers	nurse/nurses
library/libraries	knife/knives
child/children	woman/women

Noncount nouns do not usually form the plural at all. We do not speak of *courages*, *warmths*, or *happinesses*.

Practice 1

Write the plural for every count noun. If the noun is a noncount noun, write "no plural."

1. mountain _____
2. wealth _____
3. forgiveness _____
4. student _____
5. generosity _____
6. man _____
7. assignment _____
8. homework _____
9. knowledge _____
10. bravery _____

Some nouns have both a count meaning and a noncount meaning. Usually, the count meaning is concrete and specific. Usually, the noncount meaning is abstract and general.

Count meaning: All the *lights* in the classroom went out.
Noncount meaning: What is the speed of *light*?

Count meaning: Odd *sounds* came from the basement.
Noncount meaning: The speed of *sound* is slower than the speed of light.

Food and beverages, which are usually noncount nouns, may also have a count meaning.

Noncount meaning: Would you like some more *fruit, pie,* or *tea*?
Count meaning: This store sells *fruits, pies,* and *teas* from different countries.

Articles with Count and Noncount Nouns

Indefinite Articles

The words *a* and *an* are indefinite articles. They refers to one *nonspecific* (indefinite) thing. For example, "a man" refers to *any* man, not to a specific, particular man. The article *a* or *an* is used before a singular count noun.*

Singular Count Noun	**With Indefinite Article**
question	a question
textbook	a textbook
elephant	an elephant
umbrella	an umbrella

*For when to use *an* instead of *a*, see Chapter 32.

The indefinite article *a* or *an* is never used before a noncount noun.

Noncount Noun	Sample Sentence
music	*Incorrect:* I enjoy a music.
	Correct: I enjoy music.
health	*Incorrect:* Her father is in a poor health.
	Correct: Her father is in poor health.
patients	*Incorrect:* Good teachers have a patience.
	Correct: Good teachers have patience.
freedom	*Incorrect:* We have a freedom to choose our courses.
	Correct: We have freedom to choose our courses.

Practice 2

The indefinite article *a* or *an* is italicized in each sentence. Write *correct* or *incorrect* after each sentence to indicate whether the *a* or *an* is used correctly or incorrectly.

1. My friends give me *a* help when I need it.   _____

2. He is in *a* love with that singer.   _____

3. *An* honesty is the best policy.   _____

4. We have *an* answer to your question.   _____

5. They have *an* information for us.   _____

Definite Articles

The word *the* is a definite article. It refers to one (or more) *specific* (definite) thing (or things). For example, "the man" refers not to *any* man but to a specific, particular man. "The men" (plural) refers to specific, particular men. The article *the* is used before singular and plural count nouns.

Definite (*The*) and Indefinite Articles (*A/An*) with Count Nouns

I saw *the* film. (singular; refers to a specific film)
I saw *the* films. (plural; refers to more than one specific film)
I saw *a* film. (refers to any film; nonspecific)
I enjoy seeing *a* good film. (refers to any good film; nonspecific)
I like *a* film that has an important message. (refers to any film that has an important message; nonspecific)
The film that I saw last night had an important message. (refers to a specific film)

The definite article *the* is used before a noncount noun only if the noun is specifically identified.

Noncount Noun	Sample Sentence
fitness	*Incorrect:* He has *the* fitness. (not identified)
	Correct: He has *the* fitness of a person half his age. (identified)
	Incorrect: The fitness is a goal for many people. (not identified)
	Correct: Fitness is a goal for many people. (not identified, so no *the*)
art	*Incorrect:* I do not understand *the* art. (not identified)
	Correct: I do not understand *the* art in this show. (identified)
	Correct: I do not understand *the* art that you have created. (identified)
	Incorrect: The art touches our hearts and minds. (not identified)
	Correct: Art touches our hearts and minds. (not identified, so no *the*)

Practice 3

The definite article *the* is italicized whenever it appears below. Cross it out if it is used incorrectly. If the sentence is correct, write *correct* on the line provided.

1. This building has *the* beauty.   _____

2. *The* beauty of this building surprises me.   _____

3. This building has *the* beauty of a work of art.   _____

4. *The* beauty created by that architect is astonishing.   _____

5. A thing of beauty is a joy forever.   _____

Verb + Gerund

A gerund is a noun that is made up of a verb plus *-ing*. The italicized words below are gerunds.

> *Playing* solitaire on the computer helps some students relax.
>
> I enjoy *hiking* in high mountains.

In the first sentence, the gerund *playing* is the simple subject of the sentence.* In the second sentence the gerund *hiking* is the object of the verb enjoy.** Some common verbs are often followed by gerunds.

---

*For more on simple subjects, see Chapter 6, Part A.
**For more on objects of verbs, see Chapter 21, Part F, "Pronouns as Objects."

Some Common Verbs That Can Be Followed by a Gerund	
Verb	**Sample Sentence with Gerund**
consider	Would you *consider* **taking** a course in accounting?
discuss	Let's *discuss* **buying** a fax machine.
enjoy	I *enjoy* **jogging** in the morning before work.
finish	Sue *finished* **studying** for her nursing exam.
keep	*Keep* **trying** and you will succeed.
postpone	The Brookses *postponed* **visiting** their grandchildren.
quit	Three of my friends *quit* **smoking** this year.

The verbs listed above are *never* followed by an infinitive (*to* + the simple form of the verb)[†]

> Incorrect: Would you consider *to take* a course in journalism?
> Incorrect: Let's discuss *to buy* a fax machine.
> Incorrect: I enjoy *to jog* in the morning before work.

Practice 4

Write a gerund after each verb in the blank space provided.

1. Dave enjoys _____ television in the evening.

2. Have you finished _____ for tomorrow's exam?

3. Pat is considering _____ to Mexico next month.

4. I have postponed _____ until I receive the results of the test.

5. We are discussing _____ a car.

Preposition + Gerund

A preposition[††] may be followed by a gerund.

> I forgive you *for* **stepping** on my toe.
> Alice believes *in* **pushing** herself to her limits.
> We made the flight *by* **running** from one terminal to another.

A preposition is *never* followed by an infinitive (*to* + the simple form of the verb.)

> *Incorrect:* I forgive you *for* **to step** on my toe.
> *Incorrect:* Alice believes *in* **to push** herself to her limits.
> *Incorrect:* We made the flight *by* **to run** from one terminal to another.

[†]For more on infinitives, see Chapter 12, Part E.
[††]For more on prepositions, see Chapter 23.

Practice 5

Write a gerund after the preposition in each blank space provided.

1. We have succeeding in _____ the CD you wanted.

2. You can get there by _____ left at the next corner.

3. Thank you for _____ those striped socks for me.

4. I enjoy sports like _____ and _____ .

5. Between _____ to school and _____ , I have little time

   for _____ .

Verb + Infinitive

Many verbs are followed by the infinitive (*to* + the simple form of the verb).

Some Common Verbs That Can Be Followed by an Infinitive	
Verb	**Sample Sentence**
afford	Carla can *afford **to buy*** a new outfit whenever she wants.
agree	I *agree **to marry*** you a year from today.
appear	He *appears **to be*** happy in his new job.
decide	Will they *decide **to drive*** across the country?
expect	Jamal *expects **to graduate*** next year.
forget	Please do not *forget **to cash*** the check.
hope	My nephews *hope **to visit*** Santa Fe this year.
intend	I *intend **to study*** harder this semester than I did last semester.
mean	Did Frank *mean **to leave*** his lunch on the kitchen table?
need	Do you *need **to stop*** for a break now?
plan	Justin *plans **to go*** into advertising.
promise	Sharon has *promised **to paint*** this wall green.
offer	Did they really *offer **to babysit*** for a month?
refuse	Sean *refuses **to walk*** another step.
try	Let's *try **to set*** up this tent before dark.
wait	On the other hand, we could *wait **to camp*** out until tomorrow.

Write an infinitive after the verb in each blank space provided.

1. The plumber promised _____ the sink today.

2. My son plans _____ a course in electrical engineering.

3. We do not want _____ late for the meeting again.

4. They refused _____ before everyone was ready.

5. I expect _____ Jim next week.

Verb + Either Gerund or Infinitive

Some verbs can be followed by *either* a gerund or an infinitive.

Some Common Verbs That Can Be Followed by a Gerund or an Infinitive	
Verb	**Sample Sentence**
begin	They began to laugh. (infinitive)
	They began laughing. (gerund)
continue	Fran continued to giggle. (infinitive)
	Fran continued giggling. (gerund)
hate	Paul hates to drive in the snow. (infinitive)
	Paul hates driving in the snow. (gerund)
like	My daughter likes to surf the Net. (infinitive)
	My daughter likes surfing the Net. (gerund)
love	Phil loves to watch soccer games. (infinitive)
	Phil loves watching soccer games. (gerund)
start	Will you start to write the paper tomorrow? (infinitive)
	Will you start writing the paper tomorrow? (gerund)

Practice 7

For each pair of sentences, first write an infinitive in the space provided. Then write a gerund.

1. a. (infinitive)   Sue hates _____ in long lines.

   b. (gerund)   Sue hates _____ in long lines.

2. a. (infinitive)   When will we begin _____ dinner?

   b. (gerund)   When will we begin _____ dinner?

3. a. (infinitive)   Carmen loves _____ in the rain.

   b. (gerund)   Carmen loves _____ in the rain.

4. a. (infinitive)   The children continued _____ noisily.

   b. (gerund)   The children continued _____ noisily.

5. a. (infinitive)   Suddenly, the people started _____ .

   b. (gerund)   Suddenly, the people started _____ .

UNIT 9

Reading Selections and Quotation Bank

Unit 9 contains three parts:

● *Effective Reading: Strategies for the Writer*
This introduction to the readings section gives tips on how to get the most out of your reading.

● *The Readings*
Here you will find twenty-two readings on a range of interesting subjects. Discussion questions and writing assignments follow each reading.

● *Quotation Bank*
This section contains seventy-four brief quotations for you to read and enjoy, be inspired by, and use in your writing.

Reading Selections

Effective Reading: Strategies for the Writer

We hope that the reading selections that follow will interest you and make you think. Many deal with issues you face at college, at work, or at home. Your instructor may ask you to read a selection and be prepared to discuss it in class or to write a composition or journal entry about it. The more carefully you read these selections, the better you will be able to think, talk, and write about them. Below are seven strategies that can help you become a more careful and effective reader.

1. **Underline important ideas.** It is easy to forget what you have read, even though you have recently read it. Underlining or highlighting what you consider the main ideas will help you later—when you review the essay—to remember what you have read. Some students number the main points in order to understand the development of the author's ideas.

2. **Write your reactions in the margins.** If you strongly agree or disagree with an idea, write *yes* or *no* next to it. Record other questions and comments also, as if you were having a conversation with the author. Writing assignments will often ask you to respond to a particular idea or situation in a selection. Having already noted your reactions in the margins will help you focus your thinking and your writing.

3. **Prepare questions.** You will occasionally come across material that you cannot follow. Reread the passage. If rereading and further thinking do not help, place a question mark in the margin to remind you to ask a classmate or the instructor for an explanation.

4. **Circle unfamiliar words.** If you come across an unfamiliar word that makes it difficult to follow the sense of what the author is saying, look up the word immediately, write the definition in the margin, and continue reading. If, however, you are able to get a general sense of what the word means from the context—how it fits into the meaning of the sentence—do not break your reading "stride" to consult a dictionary. Circle it, and look it up when you have finished reading the entire selection.

5. **Note effective or powerful writing.** If a particular line strikes you as especially important or moving, underline or highlight it. You may wish later to quote it in your written assignment. Be selective, however, in what you mark. *Too much* annotation can turn a selection into a mass—or mess—of underlinings, circles, and highlighting. An overly annotated essay can make it hard to focus on what is important when the selection is discussed in class or when you write about it.

6. **Vary your pace.** Some selections can be read quickly because you already know a great deal about the subject or because you find the material simple and direct. Other selections may require you to read slowly, pausing between sentences. Guard against the tendency to skim when the going gets tough: more difficult material will usually reward your extra time and attention.

7. **Reread.** If you expect to discuss or write about a particular selection, one reading is usually not enough. Budget your time so you will be able to give the selection a second or third reading. You will be amazed at how much more you can get from the selection as you reread. You may understand ideas that were unclear the first time around. In addition, you may notice significant new points and details: perhaps you will change your mind concerning ideas you originally agreed or disagreed with. These benefits of rereading will help you

to discuss and write about the selection more intelligently. They will also increase your reading enjoyment.

The following essay has been marked by a student. Your own responses to this essay would, of course, be different. Examining how this essay was annotated may help you annotate other selections in this book and read more effectively in your other courses.

Women Are Missing from Newspaper Pages

ELLEN GOODMAN

bylines = a line identifying author of an article
Why "boys" and "girls"?

kindling = used to light fires
tabulation = list

In the press women almost invisible!

1. Women underrepresented in newspapers

Take last week's papers out of the pile in the corner of the kitchen. Check the 1
bylines. Check the photos. How many boys, how many girls?

Now put the papers back in the recycle bin, or in the bird cage, or in the 2
kindling box. Wherever. Compare your tabulation with the fourth annual report just released by the Women, Men and Media Project at the University of Southern California.

The folks there surveyed the front page and the local front page of 20 news- 3
papers for the month of February. They came to the unsurprising and unhappy conclusion that women—52 percent of the population—show up just 13 percent of the time in the prime news spots. Lest you think that this is just a reflection of reality, even the stories about breast implants quoted men more often than women.

The names in the stories

Women's names appear *on* the stories more often than *in* the stories. Even so, two- 4
thirds of the bylines on front pages were male and three-quarters of the opinions on op-ed pages were by men. To complete this, uh, picture, less than a third of the photographs on front pages feature women.

This small statistical reminder comes just in time for the American Society of 5
Newspaper Editors' [ASNE] annual convention. In Washington this week, editors will be talking about America and the World, economics and politics, readers and nonreaders. Which brings them back to gender.

emergence = coming into existence
gender gap = difference in attitudes between women and men
2. Women read papers less.

One of the less heralded facts of declining newspaper readership in the 1990s is 6
the emergence of a gender gap among people under 35 years old. Young women are seven to nine points less likely to be daily newspaper readers than men.

It would be nice to blame this on the infamous time crunch in young 7
women's lives. Nice to find yet another reason for men to lift the double burden: Share housework, save a newspaper. But full-time working women are more loyal newspaper readers than women who are part-time workers or homemakers.

No wonder! ———→

Too strong

It turns out that women across the board are more likely than men to feel that 8
the paper doesn't speak to them. Or about them. As Nancy Woodhull, a founding editor of *USA Today* who now runs her own consulting firm, says, "Women around the country really notice when the press doesn't report their existence. It's like walking into a room where nobody knows you're there. If you have choices, you don't go into that room anymore."

some history of trends in journalism

The search for a welcome sign to hang on the newspaper door has brought up 9
the question of "women's pages." Back in the 1960s, these pages were the ghetto to which women, children, food, home, and family were restricted. In the crest of the women's movement, many of us in the business embarked on a movement to integrate the whole paper.

3. "Women's pages" have become unisex.

What happened was a kind of premature equality. The old women's pages 10
became more or less "unisex." Lifestyle sections wrote about and to women and men. But the rest of the paper remained nearly as lopsided as ever (see Page One [of your newspaper]). The result has been a net loss in the news about women.

Going backward or back to the future

Now there is a lively debate about whether to bring back women's pages. Is that going backward or back to the future? Is that admitting defeat in the struggle to get women's concerns into the rest of the paper or is it some unabashed recognition that women retain separate interests? 11

Experiments abound and so do opinions. Some women worry that a marketing move to target female readers will inevitably "dumb down" and talk down to them. Others believe that these pages can create a strong forum for a woman's different voice. And still others wonder if you can win the women who are drifting away without offending the loyal female readers who write in to ask, Why is the story about Hillary Clinton in the Lifestyle section? 12

As someone who has been around this argument for a couple of decades, I have no problem with experiments in re-creating a woman's "place" in the paper IF—here comes the big if—the place doesn't become a ghetto again. And IF it doesn't take the pressure off changing the rest of the paper. 13

Men and women are more alike in their news interests than they are different. Moreover, the surveys on "difference" that I have seen suggest that what women really want are stories that go deep, that focus on matters close to their lives, that are less about institutional politics than about how institutions affect people. They want to read about families, relationships, health, safety, jobs, learning, the environment. That's a pretty good guide for any gender and any editor's story list. 14

News decisions rest with the editors and the number of women editors is even smaller than the number of women on the front pages (see masthead). The female membership of ASNE is at an all-time high: 9.7 percent. 15

So, if newspapers want to make women feel welcome, begin the way a reader begins. Start with Page One. And keep counting. 16

Montgomery, Alabama, 1955

ROSA PARKS

A refusal to give up her seat in a segregated bus pushed Rosa Parks into the spotlight of the civil rights movement. In this excerpt from *Rosa Parks: My Story*, the 1999 Medal of Freedom winner tells what really happened.

When I got off from work that evening of December 1, I went to Court Square as usual to catch the Cleveland Avenue bus home.[1] I didn't look to see who was driving when I got on, and by the time I recognized him, I had already paid my fare. It was the same driver who had put me off the bus back in 1943, twelve years earlier. He was still tall and heavy, with red, rough-looking skin. And he was still mean-looking. I didn't know if he had been on that route before—they switched the drivers around sometimes. I do know that most of the time if I saw him on a bus, I wouldn't get on it. 1

I saw a vacant seat in the middle section of the bus and took it. I didn't even question why there was a vacant seat even though there were quite a few people standing in the back. If I had thought about it at all, I would probably have figured maybe someone saw me get on and did not take the seat but left it vacant for me. There was a man sitting next to the window and two women across the aisle. 2

The next stop was the Empire Theater, and some whites got on. They filled up the white seats, and one man was left standing. The driver looked back and noticed the man standing. Then he looked back at us. He said, "Let me have those front seats," because they were the front seats of the black section. Didn't anybody move. We just sat right where we were, the four of us. Then he spoke a second time: "Y'all better make it light on yourselves and let me have those seats." 3

---

1. home: Parks lived in Montgomery, the capital of Alabama, when racial segregation was legal.

"The only tired I was, was tired of giving in."

The man in the window seat next to me stood up, and I moved to let him pass 4 by me, and then I looked across the aisle and saw that the two women were also standing. I moved over to the window seat. I could not see how standing up was going to "make it light" for me. The more we gave in and complied,[2] the worse they treated us.

I thought back to the time when I used to sit up all night and didn't sleep and my 5 grandfather would have his gun right by the fireplace, or if he had his one-horse wagon going anywhere, he always had his gun in the back of the wagon. People always say that I didn't give up my seat because I was tired, but that isn't true. I was not tired physically, or no more tired than I usually was at the end of a working day. I was not old, although some people have an image of me as being old then. I was forty-two. No, the only tired I was, was tired of giving in.

The driver of the bus saw me still sitting there, and he asked was I going to stand 6 up. I said, "No." He said, "Well, I'm going to have you arrested." Then I said, "You may do that." These were the only words we said to each other. I didn't even know his name, which was James Blake, until we were in court together. He got out of the bus and stayed outside for a few minutes, waiting for the police.

As I sat there, I tried not to think about what might happen. I knew that any- 7 thing was possible. I could be manhandled or beaten. I could be arrested. People have asked me if it occurred to me then that I could be the test case the NAACP[3] had been looking for. I did not think about that at all. In fact if I had let myself think too deeply about what might happen to me, I might have gotten off the bus. But I chose to remain.

Discussion and Writing Questions

1. How had Parks been treated on buses before this particular bus incident? How had she reacted before?

2. What does the bus driver mean by "make it light on yourselves" (paragraph 3)? What does Parks think about her seatmates' decision to stand up?

3. Paragraph 5 describes the actual moment of deliberation when Parks is decid- ing whether to stand up. What determined her decision? What factors were not important?

4. Why does the author conclude, "In fact if I had let myself think too deeply about what might happen to me, I might have gotten off the bus" (paragraph 7)? Parks takes full responsibility for her action, however. What two words indicate that?

Writing Assignments

1. Have you known someone who protested an injustice? What were the circum- stances? Describe the circumstances, along with your reaction. Then discuss how your view of the event has changed (or not changed) over time.

2. Parks maintains that the public's understanding of her motivation (she was old and tired) is simply not true. She thus draws attention to the difference between how others may see us and how we see ourselves. Have you ever acted in a specific way, only to have others describe your actions differently? Write about your experience.

3. Do you have a complaint about college life? In a letter to your school news- paper, try to imitate Parks' low-key style as you describe the problem and sug- gest a solution.

---

2. complied: acted in accordance with the rules

3. NAACP: National Association for the Advancement of Colored People

Just One More

LEONARD PITTS, JR.

Award-winning commentator, book author, and columnist Leonard Pitts, Jr., wrote four newspaper articles about Princess Diana's death. The first article, below, suggests that blaming the media for Diana's death is a cop-out. Pitts believes that people like us, who devour TV and newspaper coverage of celebrities, are to blame.

How many pictures of her do you suppose there were? Thousands? Hundreds of 1 thousands? A million?

How many do you suppose would have been enough? How many before 2 photographers and editors and people like us said: This is sufficient. This satisfies our need.

At this writing, the shock of Princess Diana's death in Paris is still fresh. There is 3 still a numbness from this latest cold reminder that life is chance, not guarantee. And yet already, one sorrow surfaces distinct from the others: the manner of her death.

The black Mercedes in which she rode led a high-speed motor chase to escape 4 pursuing photographers. It crashed. And just like that, she was gone. Just like that, she was dead.

It seems a grisly object lesson, its ironies sharp as razor blades. The paparazzi[1] 5 chased to death that which justified their existence, paid their bills and, not incidentally, made some of them wealthy. The goose who laid all those golden eggs lies dead, and there is blood on the hands of her exploiters.

And already, the people are righteous in their anger, outraged at this latest 6 excess of "the media"—a catch-all excoriation[2] that draws no distinction between the *National Enquirer* and *The New York Times*. A television newsperson doing a stand-up report hours after Diana's death was called a "scavenger"[3] by a passerby.

But the hypocrisy of the people is transparent. After all, the photographers 7 who chased Diana into that tunnel weren't badgering her on a whim, bore her no enmity.[4] Rather, their pursuit was based in the sure knowledge that any pictures they took would find favor with magazines and newspapers and thus with readers around the world who could not get enough of this woman.

"Fame makes scavengers of us all."

Fame makes scavengers of us all, then. Even Diana herself was in on the deal, 8 willing when necessary to use her celebrity toward her own ends. She used it to win sympathy, used it to mold public opinion in her battles with Prince Charles. And yes, she used it, too, to bring attention to the hungry, the sick and the suffering.

She used it, it used her. Her fame was symbiosis[5] and incest, a handshake 9 with the devil.

But she did her best with it, lived her life to the whir and click of the shutters. 10 She entered a room and brought with her a sudden electrical storm, flashes of light and patches of shadow with photographers yelling, leaning in, elbowing one another, trying to capture her. For us.

And you have to wonder, how much more of her did we really need? What 11 amount of pictures would have done the trick? How much closer did we want to be?

We'd attended her wedding, watched her bear children, seen her marriage 12 crumble, heard secrets she whispered to friends. We knew about her eating disorders, her infidelities and insecurities. We saw her sweating in the gym.

We were not this intimate with our own families and friends. Yet we wanted 13 more. Always more.

---

1. paparazzi: freelance photographers who try to capture celebrities in candid poses
2. excoriation: accusation
3. scavenger: one who feeds on the dead and dying
4. enmity: hatred
5. symbiosis: mutual dependency

Once upon a time, fame seemed one of life's nicer perks, something that raised you above the common run of women and men. Now it is a public body search, the camera lens a proctoscope.[6] We confuse fascination with intrusion, human interest with trespass. . . . We know everything about everybody. All it has cost is their dignity. And ours. 14

Now it seems to have cost one woman her life. 15

Yet one doubts the object lesson is learned even at that price, even as we remember how a shy, coquettish girl smiling on the arm of her husband became a woman always ducking, running, seeking a lonely place where voyeurs[7] could not intrude. Until finally she fled into a tunnel on the banks of the Seine, still racing for that lonely place she never quite found. 16

It is said that after the crash, with the vehicle twisted and steaming, with blood leaking, bodies torn and Diana dying, a photographer stood over the mess taking pictures. 17

Just one more, luv. One more before you go. 18

Discussion and Writing Questions

1. What does the author mean by describing Princess Diana's death as "a grisly object lesson" (paragraph 5)? Who found out what?

2. What is Pitts' point in paragraph 6? What distinction does he make between the *National Enquirer* and the *New York Times*? Does he agree with the person who called the TV reporter "a scavenger"?

3. What "deal" was Princess Diana "in on" (paragraph 8)? Why does Pitts use the expression "in on the deal"?

4. Does Pitts believe that the public and the media have learned their lesson? How can you tell?

Writing Assignments

1. How do you react to being photographed? Is it all right provided you're asked first—or if the photographer is a friend rather than a stranger? Do you enjoy *taking* photographs but not *being* photographed? Write a paragraph or an essay about your feelings on the subject. Examining photographs of yourself might offer clues about the image you try to project as well as about your need (or lack of it) for privacy.

2. Imagine that your favorite celebrity has gotten on an elevator with you. What do you do? What don't you do? Describe your behavior as well as the celebrity's.

3. How does celebrity appeal change after death? Is it different depending on the person? Consider Princess Diana or Elvis Presley or any other well-known figure. Has the person's popularity faded? Try to be accurate in describing the before and after, but don't focus your paragraph or essay on the death itself.

---

6. proctoscope: a medical instrument equipped with a light, used to examine the rectum
7. voyeurs: people who find excitement in watching others

One Man's Kids

DANIEL MEIER

A first-grade teacher describes his workday and reflects on his career—a career that crosses traditional gender boundaries. Daniel Meier raises questions for all of us to consider.

I teach first-graders. I live in a world of skinned knees, double-knotted shoelaces, riddles that I've heard a dozen times, stale birthday cakes, hurt feelings, wandering stories, and one lost shoe ("and if you don't find it my mother'll kill me"). My work is dominated by six-year-olds.

It's 10:45, the middle of snack, and I'm helping Emily open her milk carton. She has already tried the other end without success, and now there's so much paint and ink on the carton from her fingers that I'm not sure she should drink it at all. But I open it. Then I turn to help Scott clean up some milk he has just spilled onto Rebecca's whale crossword puzzle.

While I wipe my milk- and paint-covered hands, Jenny wants to know if I've seen that funny book about penguins that I read in class. As I hunt for it in a messy pile of books, Jason wants to know if there is a new seating arrangement for lunch tables. I find the book, turn to answer Jason, then face Maya, who is fast approaching with a new knock-knock joke. After what seems like the tenth "Who's there?" I laugh and Maya is pleased.

Then Andrew wants to know how to spell "flukes"[1] for his crossword. As I get to "u," I give a hand signal for Sarah to take away the snack. But just as Sarah is almost out the door, two children complain that "we haven't even had ours yet." I stop the snack mid-flight, complying with their request for graham crackers. I then return to Andrew, noticing that he has put "flu" for 9 Down, rather than 9 Across. It's now 10:50.

My work is not traditional male work. It's not a singular[2] pursuit. There is not a large pile of paper to get through or one deal to transact. I don't have one area of expertise or knowledge. I don't have the singular power over language of a lawyer, the physical force of a construction worker, the command over fellow workers of a surgeon, the wheeling and dealing transactions of a businessman. My energy is not spent in pursuing, climbing, achieving, conquering, or cornering some goal or object.

My energy is spent in encouraging, supporting, consoling, and praising my children. In teaching, the inner rewards come from without. On any given day, quite apart from teaching reading and spelling, I bandage a cut, dry a tear, erase a frown, tape a torn doll, and locate a long-lost boot. The day is really won through matters of the heart. As my students groan, laugh, shudder, cry, exult,[3] and wonder, I do too. I have to be soft around the edges.

A few years ago, when I was interviewing for an elementary-school teaching position, every principal told me with confidence that, as a male, I had an advantage over female applicants because of the lack of male teachers. But in the next breath, they asked with a hint of suspicion why I chose to work with young children. I told them that I wanted to observe and contribute to the intellectual growth of a maturing mind. What I really felt like saying, but didn't, was that I loved helping a child learn to write her name for the first time, finding someone a

> *"In teaching, the inner rewards come from without."*

---

1. flukes: the two divided ends of a whale's tail; also, strokes of luck or random accidents
2. singular: related to one thing; also, exceptional
3. exult: rejoice

new friend, or sharing in the hilarity of reading about Winnie the Pooh getting so stuck in a hole that only his head and rear show.

I gave that answer to those principals, who were mostly male, because I 8 thought they wanted a "male" response. This meant talking about intellectual matters. If I had taken a different course and talked about my interest in helping children in their emotional development, it would have been seen as closer to a "female" answer. I even altered my language, not once mentioning the word "love" to describe what I do indeed love about teaching. My answer worked; every principal nodded approvingly.

Some of the principals also asked what I saw myself doing later in my career. 9 They wanted to know if I eventually wanted to go into educational administration. Becoming a dean of students or a principal has never been one of my goals, but they seemed to expect me, as a male, to want to climb higher on the career stepladder. So I mentioned that, at some point, I would be interested in working with teachers as a curriculum coordinator. Again, they nodded approvingly.

If those principals had been female instead of male, I wonder whether their 10 questions, and my answers, would have been different. My guess is that they would have been.

At other times, when I'm at a party or a dinner and tell someone that I teach 11 young children, I've found that men and women respond differently. Most men ask about the subjects I teach and the courses I took in my training. Then, unless they bring up an issue such as merit pay, the conversation stops. Most women, on the other hand, begin the conversation on a more immediate and personal level. They say things like "those kids must love having a male teacher" or "that age is just wonderful, you must love it." Then, more often than not, they'll talk about their own kids or ask me specific questions about what I do. We're then off and talking shop.

Possibly, men would have more to say to me, and I to them, if my job had 12 more of the trappings and benefits of more traditional male jobs. But my job has no bonuses or promotions. No complimentary box seats at the ball park. No cab fare home. No drinking buddies after work. No briefcase. No suit. (Ties get stuck in paint jars.) No power lunches. (I eat peanut butter and jelly, chips, milk, and cookies with the kids.) No taking clients out for cocktails. The only place I take my kids is to the playground.

Although I could have pursued a career in law or business, as several of my 13 friends did, I chose teaching instead. My job has benefits all its own. I'm able to bake cookies without getting them stuck together as they cool, buy cheap sewing materials, take out splinters, and search just the right trash cans for useful odds and ends. I'm sometimes called "Daddy" and even "Mommy" by my students, and if there's ever a lull in the conversation at a dinner party, I can always ask those assembled if they've heard the latest riddle about why the turkey crossed the road. (He thought he was a chicken.)

Discussion and Writing Questions

1. What, besides reading, writing, and 'rithmetic, is Meier teaching his first graders?

2. Why do so few men teach in elementary schools? What reasons does the author seem to offer?

3. Meier confesses that during job interviews he "even altered [his] language" (paragraph 8). What does he mean? Why did he do that?

4. In paragraph 11, the author observes that outside of school "men and women respond differently" to him. In what ways? How does Meier account for the differences?

Writing Assignments

1. Write a letter to the school principal nominating Meier for Teacher of the Year, or nominate a teacher from your own school history. In either case, discuss what you think makes a good teacher.

2. Do you have any experience in a nontraditional role—perhaps in a club, on a team, or on a job? What prompted you to cross traditional boundaries? How did the experience differ from your expectations? Write about your experience. Conclude with a reflection on how the experience changed, or didn't change, your views on traditional roles.

3. Meier suggests that work, to be rewarding, must provide benefits other than status and salary. Agree or disagree, using examples from your own experience.

For a Parent, There's No Language Dilemma

ANA VECIANA-SUAREZ

The issue of bilingual education—the teaching of two languages in the public schools—has become an increasingly sensitive one in recent years. Some argue for the practice; others oppose it. Here, a concerned parent argues that two languages are better than one.

My son Christopher cannot roll his R's.[1]

I realize that on the seismic[2] chart of development this does not rate as high as a diagnosis of dyslexia,[3] but in my book of milestones it falls squarely between not being able to tie your shoelaces and repeated fighting with classmates.

In increasingly Latin Miami, rolling R's is a survival skill. In Christopher's future world, it will mean more money and better opportunities. It will allow him to communicate with his many older relatives, to connect with the culture of his heritage.

Having lived most of his life in Palm Beach County, Christopher can barely speak Spanish. He understands most everything especially if the conversation has to do with food or play. But ask him to complete a sentence or answer a question and his eyes grow wide and blank. He hesitates. His tongue proves to be as stubborn as a pack mule at the foot of a hill.

This causes him much stress, and it mortifies[4] me. I'm the one to blame. From the beginning, when he babbled his first words, I should have insisted on Spanish because eventually he would have learned, and preferred, English.

As a daughter of Cuban exiles, I grew up speaking Spanish at home. I learned to read and write it. At one time, the rules of where to place the accents were second nature when I put pen to paper. No more. I make my living in English, and English is the language that comes more easily. This saddens me. I am losing an important and valuable part of my personal history.

Not everyone feels this way. In fact, language is a volatile[5] issue in South Florida. It is the red flag that separates the "us" from "them," the rallying cry for those who feel that immigrants must melt in, not stay apart.

"From the beginning, when he babbled his first words, I should have insisted on Spanish."

---

1. roll his R's: pronounce the letter *R* like a native speaker of Spanish
2. seismic: like an earthquake
3. dyslexia: a reading disorder
4. mortifies: badly embarrasses
5. volatile: explosive

Spanish and English signs mingle on this American street.
(© Owen Franken/CORBIS)

I know both sides of the language argument. I've heard those complaints from 8 strangers as well as from those close and dear to my heart. A childhood friend, who moved north when she felt she could not compete in a job market that often required Spanish as well as English, confided that she wasn't sure people like me, people not willing to give up that part of their identity, would ever be American enough. These were not words of hate; they were of love and concern.

As a kid, I knew a few children in the neighborhood who spoke broken 9 Spanish, accented and irregular. They were teased and labeled "cubanos arrepentidos," which loosely translates into regretful Cubans.

My children, I vowed, would not grow up to be like them. They would speak 10 both languages fluently and, because I'm such a stickler for grammar, they would also learn them correctly.

But I have failed, and now the urgency of making up for lost years has become 11 as important for cultural reasons as economic and emotional ones. I want them to be able to speak to their grandparents as freely as they do with their neighbors. I want them to have an edge in what is quickly becoming a global village.

The two older ones, exposed to Spanish for a longer period, speak it well 12 enough to be acceptable. Their trouble lies in pronunciation and verb tenses.

But until our return to Miami, Christopher had spent more than half of his 13 seven years in a place where no one spoke Spanish. His exposure was limited to periodic visits with grandparents, when the communication between them was an odd amalgam[6] of sign language and Spanglish.[7]

Not so long ago in school a teacher read a story with a few words in Spanish. He was the only child able to translate those words for the rest of the class. He came home triumphant and demanding. He wanted to know more. 14

So now almost every night before bed, we sit together to make our way through an ancient reader his father's grandmother mailed page by page from Cuba in the early 1960s. 15

"Va, ve, vi, vo, vu," he repeats after me. "Una uva. Una uva en la mesa." 16

After the first lessons, the oldest two asked to read, too. "But not from a baby book," insisted the ten-year-old. "A real book." We got a real book. 17

Together we have begun a lifelong journey into a place whose doors open only when the R's are rolling. This is where history takes on a face and a name, where lilt[8] and inflection[9] suggest identity, culture, an unusual past that enriches and assures a hopeful future. 18

We are learning to double our L's and squiggle the top of our N's. We are learning from where we have come and where we are going, and perhaps more importantly, why the two cannot be separated. 19

I know that their lives, like mine, will sometimes appear fractured. "What do you dream in?" a boss once asked me. "Depends," I answered. 20

Their lives, like mine, will grow into a duality[10] of more than language, and they will be better for it. Rest assured, it will not make them any less American. 21

Discussion and Writing Questions

1. What reasons does Veciana-Suarez offer for wanting her boys to speak Spanish as well as English?

2. The author speaks of "us" and "them" (paragraph 7). What does she mean by these terms?

3. Why does the author discuss her own experiences with two languages (paragraphs 6 and 9)?

4. Why did Christopher suddenly want to learn more Spanish after he translated Spanish words for his class at school (paragraphs 14–15)? What changed his attitude?

Writing Assignments

1. Write about an aspect of your own cultural, racial, ethnic, or religious background that makes you proud, that you don't want to lose. Do you feel, like the author, that you can hold on to this identity and still be American?

2. Do you speak a language other than English at home? If so, describe where and how you learned, or are learning, English. If English is your first language, have you tried to learn a second? If you have, describe your experience.

3. Can the United States continue to be called the "melting pot" if people speak a language other than English at school or at work? Why or why not? Argue for one side of this issue or the other, or, if you prefer, discuss both sides.

---

6. amalgam: mixture
7. Spanglish: a mixture of Spanish and English
8. lilt: lightness in the voice
9. inflection: change in pitch or tone when speaking
10. duality: having two parts or sides

Papa, the Teacher

LEO BUSCAGLIA

Leo Buscaglia was the youngest of four children of Italian immigrants. In this selection, he describes how a father with only a fifth-grade education taught his children to respect—and even love—learning.

Papa had natural wisdom. He wasn't educated in the formal sense. When he was growing up at the turn of the century in a very small village in rural northern Italy, education was for the rich. Papa was the son of a dirt-poor farmer. He used to tell us that he never remembered a single day of his life when he wasn't working. The concept of doing nothing was never a part of his life. In fact, he couldn't fathom[1] it. How could one do nothing? 1

He was taken from school when he was in the fifth grade, over the protestations[2] of his teacher and the village priest, both of whom saw him as a young person with great potential for formal learning. Papa went to work in a factory in a nearby village, the very same village where, years later, he met Mama. 2

For Papa, the world became his school. He was interested in everything. He read all the books, magazines, and newspapers he could lay his hands on. He loved to gather with people and listen to the town elders and learn about "the world beyond" this tiny, insular[3] region that was home to generations of Buscaglias before him. Papa's great respect for learning and his sense of wonder about the outside world were carried across the sea with him and later passed on to his family. He was determined that none of his children would be denied an education if he could help it. 3

Papa believed that the greatest sin of which we were capable was to go to bed at night as ignorant as we had been when we awakened that day. The credo[4] was repeated so often that none of us could fail to be affected by it. "There is so much to learn," he'd remind us. "Though we're born stupid, only the stupid remain that way." To ensure that none of his children ever fell into the trap of complacency,[5] he insisted that we learn at least one new thing each day. He felt that there could be no fact too insignificant, that each bit of learning made us more of a person and insured us against boredom and stagnation. 4

So Papa devised a ritual. Since dinnertime was family time and everyone came to dinner unless they were dying of malaria, it seemed the perfect forum for sharing what new things we had learned that day. Of course, as children we thought this was perfectly crazy. There was no doubt, when we compared such paternal[6] concerns with other children's fathers, Papa was weird. 5

It would never have occurred to us to deny Papa a request. So when my brother and sisters and I congregated in the bathroom to clean up for dinner, the inevitable question was, "What did *you* learn today?" If the answer was "Nothing," we didn't dare sit at the table without first finding a fact in our much-used encyclopedia. "The population of Nepal is . . . ," etc. 6

Now, thoroughly clean and armed with our fact for the day, we were ready for dinner. I can still see the table piled high with mountains of food. So large were the mounds of pasta that as a boy I was often unable to see my sister sitting across from me. (The pungent[7] aromas were such that, over a half century later, even in memory they cause me to salivate.) 7

"The greatest sin . . . was to go to bed at night as ignorant as we had been when we awakened that day."

---

1. fathom: understand; get to the bottom of
2. protestations: objections
3. insular: like an island; isolated
4. credo: a statement of belief
5. complacency: a feeling of satisfaction or smugness
6. paternal: having to do with fathers
7. pungent: sharp, spicy

Dinner was a noisy time of clattering dishes and endless activity. It was also a [8] time to review the activities of the day. Our animated conversations were always conducted in Piedmontese dialect[8] since Mama didn't speak English. The events we recounted, no matter how insignificant, were never taken lightly. Mama and Papa always listened carefully and were ready with some comment, often profound and analytical, always right to the point.

"That was the smart thing to do." "*Stupido,* how could you be so dumb?" "*Cosi* [9] *sia,*[9] you deserved it." "*E allora,*[10] no one is perfect." "*Testa dura* ('hardhead'), you should have known better. Didn't we teach you anything?" "Oh, that's nice." One dialogue ended and immediately another began. Silent moments were rare at our table.

Then came the grand finale to every meal, the moment we dreaded most—the [10] time to share the day's new learning. The mental imprint of those sessions still runs before me like a familiar film clip, vital and vivid.

Papa, at the head of the table, would push his chair back slightly, a gesture [11] that signified the end of the eating and suggested that there would be a new activity. He would pour a small glass of red wine, light up a thin, potent Italian cigar, inhale deeply, exhale, then take stock of his family.

For some reason this always had a slightly unsettling effect on us as we stared [12] back at Papa, waiting for him to say something. Every so often he would explain why he did this. He told us that if he didn't take time to look at us, we would soon be grown and he would have missed us. So he'd stare at us, one after the other.

Finally, his attention would settle upon one of us. "*Felice,*"[11] he would say to [13] me, "tell me what you learned today."

"I learned that the population of Nepal is . . ." [14]

Silence. [15]

It always amazed me, and reinforced my belief that Papa was a little crazy, [16] that nothing I ever said was considered too trivial for him. First, he'd think about what was said as if the salvation of the world depended upon it.

"The population of Nepal. Hmmm. Well." [17]

He would then look down the table at Mama, who would be ritualistically fix- [18] ing her favorite fruit in a bit of leftover wine. "Mama, did you know that?"

Mama's responses were always astonishing and seemed to lighten the other- [19] wise reverential atmosphere. "Nepal," she'd say. "Nepal? Not only don't I know the population of Nepal, I don't know where in God's world it is!" Of course, this was only playing into Papa's hands.

"*Felice,*" he'd say. "Get the atlas so we can show Mama where Nepal is." And the [20] search began. The whole family went on a search for Nepal. This same experience was repeated until each family member had a turn. No dinner at our house ever ended without our having been enlightened by at least a half dozen such facts.

As children, we thought very little about these educational wonders and even [21] less about how we were being enriched. We couldn't have cared less. We were too impatient to have dinner end so we could join our less-educated friends in a rip-roaring game of kick the can.

In retrospect, after years of studying how people learn, I realize what a [22] dynamic educational technique Papa was offering us, reinforcing the value of continual learning. Without being aware of it, our family was growing together, sharing experiences, and participating in one another's education. Papa was, without knowing it, giving us an education in the most real sense.

By looking at us, listening to us, hearing us, respecting our opinions, affirming [23] our value, giving us a sense of dignity, he was unquestionably our most influential teacher.

---

8. Piedmontese dialect: the language spoken in the Piedmont region of north-western Italy
9. *Cosi sia:* Italian for "so be it"
10. *E allora:* Italian for "oh, well"
11. *Felice: Felice* is Buscaglia's real first name. The name *Leo* was taken from his middle name, *Leonardo.*

Discussion and Writing Questions

1. What does Buscaglia mean when he says that his father "wasn't educated in the formal sense" (paragraph 1)? In what way *was* his father educated?

2. How did Buscaglia's father and mother react to information that the children reported at dinnertime? How did their reaction affect Buscaglia as a child? As an adult?

3. Years later, Buscaglia realized that his father had offered the family "a dynamic educational technique" (paragraph 22). What does he mean?

4. What point does the author make by using the population of Nepal as an example in paragraph 14? Is it useful to know the population of Nepal? Why or why not?

Writing Assignments

1. Describe a typical dinnertime in your family as you were growing up. Was dinnertime a time for sharing? Fighting? Eating alone? What effect did this have on you? If you now live away from your birth family, are dinnertimes different?

2. Discuss your attitude toward education. Who or what shaped your point of view? Has your attitude changed since childhood? Why is education important?

3. Did *you* learn anything new today? If so, describe what you learned. If not, what got in the way of your learning?

One Human Hand

LI-YOUNG LEE

"How can we know the dancer from the dance?" asks the Irish poet W. B. Yeats in his 1923 masterpiece, "Among School Children." Generations later and continents removed, an Asian-born American poet, Li-Young Lee, seeks answers to a similar question about his father—who was once Mao Zedong's doctor, then a political prisoner in Indonesia, and later a painter intent on recreating traditional Chinese scrolls, as described below. How can we know the artist from the art?

I remember how on certain Sunday evenings my father would show us his best-loved possessions, unrolling across our dining-room table the hundred-year-old scrolls he'd carried over the sea from China. He showed them to us in the order he remembered having collected them, and the first one, unscrolled, revealed first the black claws, and then the long legs, and at last the whole height of a standing crane,[1] long-beaked, with coarse head and neck feathers, and one fierce eye. The second scroll was mostly white except for the blight-struck pine, and one bird perched at the tip: a shrike,[2] surviving, last carrier of seed and stones in his little gizzard. The scrolls in my father's house, stored in room after room, or hung in the halls, were so many any breeze could send their silk dancing and their bones all knocking against the walls. He spent every day in August, his vacation time, 5

10

---

1. crane: large, stately, long-necked wading bird, a central image in Chinese art
2. shrike: screeching hook-billed bird of prey

© 2001 Houghton Mifflin Company

A traditional Chinese hanging scroll.
(© 1950 by Lin Feng-Mien. Werner Forman Archive, Private Collection. ART RESOURCE)

"...he painted ... to make you see flying in a standing body."

painting from morning to evening, filling sheet after sheet of rice paper with washes of ink. I watched him lean over the table and his hand flee, or seem to flee, the ink running past the brush and into the very bird. It was birds he painted, one after another. To make you see flying in a standing body, he said, his arm moving 15 up and down to be flying, pushing backward to be drawing nigh,[3] backing up into the future in order to be coming into what's passed. One human hand, a bird, resigned to let time resolve it in paper and ink. It takes one bird to write the central action of the air, lending its wings to gravity, in order to be aloft.

Discussion and Writing Questions

1. Lee begins with the words "I remember." What is his memory of his father?

2. How do the two ancient Chinese scrolls differ? Why do you think Lee includes these detailed descriptions? Why doesn't he give any detailed descriptions of the scrolls created by his father?

3. Lee's father says that he paints birds "to make you see flying in a standing body" (line 15). What does he mean?

---

3. nigh: near

4. Lee observes parallels between the birds in the scrolls and his father in the act of painting. Find two. How does the last line, "It takes one bird to write the central action of the air," sum up his observations?

Writing Assignments

1. Is there an object prized in your household for its place of origin? Does it represent a cultural link to the past? Describe the object in detail so that your readers will be able to visualize it. Then discuss its origin and travels. End by explaining why the object holds a place of honor.

2. Family pastimes often become the basis for favorite childhood memories—as is the case of Sunday nights in Li-Young Lee's home when his father showed his prized possessions. Write about a similar pastime in your family, or write about a pastime you hope to introduce into your family's life in the future.

3. Have you ever attempted to understand someone's passion for an occupation or a hobby? Have you wondered why a person would devote so much energy and time to a single pursuit? Imitate Lee's style, beginning with "I remember." Then, through the use of examples, capture the person's passion and devotion.

Yolanda

Julia Alvarez

Living in a new country and learning a new language are challenges for anyone. For a young child, whose experience of the world is limited, the challenges may be even greater. This fictional selection by a writer from the Dominican Republic captures one child's fear and wonder in a new country.

Our first year in New York we rented a small apartment with a Catholic school 1 nearby, taught by the Sisters of Charity, hefty[1] women in long black gowns and bonnets that made them look peculiar, like dolls in mourning. I liked them a lot, especially my grandmotherly fourth grade teacher, Sister Zoe. I had a lovely name, she said, and she had me teach the whole class how to pronounce it. *Yo-lan-da.* As the only immigrant in my class, I was put in a special seat in the first row by the window, apart from the other children so that Sister Zoe could tutor me without disturbing them. Slowly, she enunciated the new words I was to repeat: *laundromat, corn flakes, subway, snow.*

Soon I picked up enough English to understand holocaust[2] was in the air. 2 Sister Zoe explained to a wide-eyed classroom what was happening in Cuba.[3] Russian missiles were being assembled, trained supposedly on New York City. President Kennedy, looking worried too, was on the television at home, explaining we might have to go to war against the Communists. At school, we

"*Slowly, she enunciated the new words I was to repeat: laundromat, corn flakes, subway, snow.*"

---

1. hefty: heavy
2. holocaust: total destruction
3. what was happening in Cuba: During the Cuban missile crisis of 1962, the United States discovered that the former Soviet Union was building nuclear missile launch sites on Cuba. After several weeks of great tension and the threat of nuclear war, the former Soviet Union withdrew. In return, President Kennedy agreed not to try again to overthrow the Castro government in Cuba.

had air-raid drills: an ominous[4] bell would go off and we'd file into the hall, fall to the floor, cover our heads with our coats, and imagine our hair falling out, the bones in our arms going soft. At home, Mami and my sisters and I said a rosary for world peace. I heard new vocabulary: *nuclear bomb, radioactive fallout, bomb shelter.* Sister Zoe explained how it would happen. She drew a picture of a mushroom on the blackboard and dotted a flurry of chalkmarks for the dusty fallout that would kill us all.

The months grew cold, November, December. It was dark when I got up in the 3 morning, frosty when I followed my breath to school. One morning as I sat at my desk daydreaming out the window, I saw dots in the air like the ones Sister Zoe had drawn—random at first, then lots and lots. I shrieked, "Bomb! Bomb!" Sister Zoe jerked around, her full black skirt ballooning as she hurried to my side. A few girls began to cry.

But then Sister Zoe's shocked look faded. "Why, Yolanda dear, that's snow!" 4 She laughed. "Snow."

"Snow," I repeated. I looked out the window warily. All my life I had heard 5 about the white crystals that fell out of American skies in the winter. From my desk I watched the fine powder dust the sidewalk and parked cars below. Each flake was different, Sister Zoe had said, like a person, irreplaceable and beautiful.

Discussion and Writing Questions

1. Yolanda tells us that the word *snow* is among the words she is supposed to learn (paragraph 1). What other words does she learn that she does not yet have the experience to understand?

2. In paragraph 3, Yolanda describes the scene outside her school window: "I saw dots in the air like the ones Sister Zoe had drawn—random at first, then lots and lots." What did she think she was seeing, and what was she actually seeing? When did you realize what was really happening outside her window that day?

3. Does Yolanda's mistake indicate that she pays attention in school and is a very bright child, or just the opposite? Explain your answer.

4. Yolanda likes her teacher, Sister Zoe, from the start. Is Sister Zoe a good teacher? How can you tell?

Writing Assignments

1. Did you ever have a teacher who was especially important in your life? What was that teacher like? What influence did he or she have on you?

2. Children and people learning languages sometimes draw wrong conclusions based on limited experience. A child, for example, might think that he or she has to learn to fly like a bird in order "to fly to Grandma's next week." Did you ever draw a mistaken conclusion because you misunderstood a word or words? How did you find out the correct (or generally accepted) meaning?

3. Did you (or anyone you know) ever leave home to live in a new country? What was it like to adjust to a new culture? Choose one or two incidents to write about that capture one aspect of the experience—wonder or frustration, for example. Your audience is a friend or family member from another country who is considering a move to your area.

---

4. ominous: threatening

Esperanto

RANBIR SIDHU

This excerpt from Ranbir Sidhu's prize-winning short story, "Neanderthal Tongues,"[1] captures the tensions that can affect almost any transplanted family. The story unfolds with an ironic twist. The domestic drama over control and language played out in the new home looks very much like the political drama that fractured the old country the family left behind.

When my parents moved to New York, my father already spoke English well, [1] though haltingly. My mother's English, she told me, was poor, and she was excited at the possibility of improving it. She wanted both of them to take ESL[2] classes at City College, but my father refused to listen to the idea. He said that they (meaning *him,* according to my mother) spoke English more than well enough to get by. He said they would both take classes in Esperanto,[3] which—my father claimed—was the language of the future; in a decade, everyone would be speaking it. It was language, he told my mother, that had ripped India apart, thrown it into the pool of communal[4] violence. How can a country persist—a world even—where people cannot speak to each other? This was his argument.

All this was when my mother was pregnant with me. Years later she told me [2] she almost took his head off with her fist. It was the pregnancy, the sudden mood swings, the new country. She was furious. She slammed her fist into his face, knocking him down onto the carpet, bloodying his nose.

See! he shouted from where he lay on the floor. Until we all speak one lan- [3] guage, we will always fight.

All argument fled my mother with that single blow. She was not a violent person [4] and was shocked at herself. It was not the weight of my father's belief but of her own violence that persuaded her to go along with him and learn Esperanto before she mastered English. When I was still small, I remember her voice, sometimes late at night, singing me songs and nursery rhymes in a language I barely remember, a language I have never since heard anyone else speak.

Still, she did stand firm on one point. She made sure I was never forced to speak [5] that language. I learned English and Hindi[5] instead, and only those few words of Esperanto that I picked up sometimes from the two of them. It was a strange household, all of us speaking different languages. My father clung to Esperanto, my mother to Hindi, and I managed a patois[6] of those two and English. It was the farthest thing from my father's dream of a common language that I can imagine.

One night, I remember, they were arguing—both shouting in Esperanto. I must [6] have been five at the time. I can see them clearly, the small shelf of books behind my father, the black-and-white TV flickering, the smell of milk on the stove in the kitchen. I don't know *what* they were saying to each other, but it was the last night my mother ever spoke Esperanto in the house. At one point my father was about to hit her. I could see his hand forming a fist. Just at that moment, my mother let out a scream— the only time I ever heard her scream, a scream in no language I knew. It wasn't a Hindi scream or an English scream—I have heard those—and I cannot imagine that it

---

1. Neanderthal: related to an extinct race of human beings; tongues: languages
2. ESL: English as a second language
3. Esperanto: an artificial language created by a Polish linguist, Ludwik Zamenhof (1859–1917). By selecting vocabulary from words common to several languages and developing standard pronunciation, he hoped Esperanto would become universally adopted; in fact, the word *Esperanto* means "one who hopes."
4. communal: group
5. Hindi: group of spoken languages native to northern India
6. patois: nontraditional, regional speech

was an Esperanto scream, because I cannot believe that my mother would resort to so foreign a language at such a moment. It was something else entirely, and it stopped my father's fist midair. Stunned, he stood motionless for a moment—then his body slumped, relaxed, and he put his arms around my mother, talking softly in Hindi.

Discussion and Writing Questions

1. What causes the parents' first argument (paragraphs 1–3)? What is at issue—language, dominance, something else? What brings about the end of the argument?

2. Why does the narrator say, "It was a strange household" (paragraph 5)? Do you agree?

3. Does the last argument (paragraph 6) differ significantly from the first argument? How (or how does it not)? In five years, does the family seem to have changed much?

4. The child cannot identify the language his mother uses to scream (paragraph 6). Why not? Why does her scream stop the father's violence? Do you think the mother will be calmed and comforted by the father's "talking softly in Hindi" (last line)?

Writing Assignments

1. "Until we all speak one language," the father argues, "we will always fight" (paragraph 3). Perhaps your family members speak more than one language, or perhaps they speak only one. In either case, different generations speak differently, each with its own special vocabulary (such as slang) and acceptable limits (to swearing, for example). Choose two or three examples from your family's experience, either with different languages or the same language used by different generations, to prove the father right or wrong.

2. From your childhood, do you recall overhearing a disagreement between adults—family members, teachers, shoppers, or bus riders, for example? How did you react? Give the key details. Then discuss the incident from two sides: what you made of the incident then from a child's point of view and what you conclude about the incident now.

3. Read or review Daniel Goleman's article, "Emotional Intelligence," on page 457. After surveying the five qualities that contribute to emotional success, rate the emotional IQ of each parent in Sidhu's story. Does either parent excel—or fail—in any one quality? Which one? Why? Which sentences in "Esperanto" helped you make your evaluation?

The Gift

COURTLAND MILLOY

> Help sometimes comes from unexpected places. This newspaper story describes the generosity of a friend whose gift saved someone's life—and baffled most people who knew him. As you read, ask yourself how you would have acted in his place.

When Jermaine Washington entered the barbershop, heads turned and clippers fell 1
silent. Customers waved and nodded, out of sheer respect. With his hands in the pockets of his knee-length, black leather coat, Washington acknowledged them with a faint smile and quietly took a seat.

"You know who that is?" barber Anthony Clyburn asked in a tone reserved for the most awesome neighborhood characters, such as ball players and ex-cons. 2

A year and a half ago, Washington did something that still amazes those who know him. He became a kidney donor, giving a vital organ to a woman he described as "just a friend." 3

"They had a platonic[1] relationship," said Clyburn, who works at Jake's Barber Shop in Northeast Washington. "I could see maybe giving one to my mother, but just a girl I know? I don't think so." 4

Washington, who is 25, met Michelle Stevens six years ago when they worked for the D.C. Department of Employment Services. They used to have lunch together in the department cafeteria and chitchat on the telephone during their breaks. 5

"It was nothing serious, romance-wise," said Stevens, who is 23. "He was somebody I could talk to. I had been on the kidney donor waiting list for 12 months and I had lost all hope. One day, I just called to cry on his shoulder." 6

Stevens told Washington how depressing it was to spend three days a week, three hours a day, on a kidney dialysis machine.[2] She said she suffered from chronic fatigue and blackouts and was losing her balance and her sight. He could already see that she had lost her smile. 7

"I saw my friend dying before my eyes," Washington recalled. "What was I supposed to do? Sit back and watch her die?" 8

Stevens's mother was found to be suffering from hypertension[3] and was ineligible to donate a kidney. Her 14-year-old sister offered to become a donor, but doctors concluded that she was too young. 9

Stevens's two brothers, 25 and 31, would most likely have made ideal donors because of their relatively young ages and status as family members. But both of them said no. 10

So did Stevens's boyfriend, who gave her two diamond rings with his apology. 11

"I understood," Stevens said. "They said they loved me very much, but they were just too afraid." 12

Joyce Washington, Jermaine's mother, was not exactly in favor of the idea, either. But after being convinced that her son was not being coerced,[4] she supported his decision. 13

The transplant operation took four hours. It occurred in April 1991, and began with a painful X-ray procedure in which doctors inserted a metal rod into Washington's kidney and shot it with red dye. An incision nearly 20 inches long was made from his groin to the back of his shoulder. After the surgery he remained hospitalized for five days. 14

Today, both Stevens and Washington are fully recovered. Stevens, a graduate of Eastern High School, is studying medicine at the National Educational Center. Washington still works for D.C. Employment Services as a job counselor. 15

"I jog and work out with weights," Washington said. "Boxing and football are out, but I never played those anyway." 16

A spokesman for Washington Hospital Center said the Washington-to-Stevens gift was the hospital's first "friend-to-friend" transplant. Usually, it's wife to husband, or parent to child. But there is a shortage of even those kinds of transplants. Today, more than 300 patients are in need of kidneys in the Washington area. 17

"A woman came up to me in a movie line not long ago and hugged me," Washington said. "She thanked me for doing what I did because no one had come forth when her daughter needed a kidney, and the child died." 18

About twice a month, Stevens and Washington get together for what they call a gratitude lunch. Since the operation, she has broken up with her boyfriend. 19

"'I had been on the kidney donor waiting list for 12 months and I had lost all hope. One day, I just called to cry on his shoulder.'"

---

1. platonic: nonromantic
2. kidney dialysis machine: a machine that filters waste material from the blood when the kidneys fail
3. hypertension: high blood pressure
4. coerced: pressured into doing something

Seven months ago, Washington got a girlfriend. Despite occasional pressure by friends, a romantic relationship is not what they want.

"We are thankful for the beautiful relationship that we have," Stevens said. 20 "We don't want to mess up a good thing."

To this day, people wonder why Washington did it. To some of the men gathered 21 at Jake's Barber Shop not long ago, Washington's heroics were cause for questions about his sanity. Surely he could not have been in his right mind, they said. 22

One customer asked Washington where he had found the courage to give away a kidney. His answer quelled[5] most skeptics[6] and inspired even more awe.

"I prayed for it," Washington replied. "I asked God for guidance and that's 23 what I got."

Discussion and Writing Questions

1. A year and a half after Jermaine Washington donated a kidney to Michelle Stevens, his friends are still amazed by what he did. Why do they find his action so surprising?

2. Washington says, "What was I supposed to do? Sit back and watch her die?" (paragraph 8). Yet Stevens' brothers and her boyfriend did not offer to donate a kidney. Do you blame them? Do you understand them?

3. In what ways has Stevens' life changed because of Washington's gift? Consider her physical status, her social life, her choice of profession, her "gratitude lunches" with Washington, and so on.

4. According to Washington, where did he find the courage to donate a kidney? How did his action affect his standing in the community? How did it affect other aspects of his life?

Writing Assignments

1. Have you ever been unusually generous—or do you know someone who was? Describe that act of generosity. Why did you—or the other person—do it? How did your friends or family react?

2. Do you have or does anyone you know have a serious medical condition? Describe the situation. How do or how can friends help? Can strangers help in any way?

3. Stevens and Washington do not have or want a romantic relationship. "We don't want to mess up a good thing," Stevens says (paragraph 21). Does romance "mess things up"? Write about a time when a relationship changed—either for better or for worse—because romance entered the picture.

A Link to the Living

PATSY GARLAN

Patsy Garlan has written poetry, stories, textbooks, and a musical play. In this article from the Atlantic Monthly, *she uses the setting of a horror story—dark night, cold underground, dead bodies—in an unusual way.*

You can imagine how startling it was when my daughter the medical student 1 inquired, "Would you like to see my cadaver?"[1] A glance at her eager young face

---

5. quelled: quieted
6. skeptics: people who doubt or question
1. cadaver: dead body

filled with cheerful expectancy made me soften the fervor[2] of my denial to "Oh, no, darling, no—I don't think so. No. No."

But then I thought. How often does a person, a lay person, have an opportunity like this—to look inside the body of another human being? You'll be forever sorry if you pass up this chance. I glanced at her again. She was waiting for me to come round. As she always did—as kids do. "Well," I said, "what would it be like?" 2

So off we went, in the warm dusk of the New Hampshire evening. I found myself fighting off my apprehension and hoping I would be able to control my queasiness.[3] As we descended the stairs heading deep into the cavernous basement of the medical-school building where the anatomy lab was housed, she began to prepare me. It will be cold, because—you know. And there will be a smell of formaldehyde[4]—don't mind it: you get used to it. 3

We entered the dimly lit lab. I want to say, we crossed the threshold—"Abandon all hope, ye who enter here." I put my trust in her, like Dante following Virgil[5] into the underworld. We wound our way among the sleek gurneys[6] with their sheet-shrouded burdens. Not another soul breathed in that vast space. The smell of formaldehyde was an assault. The silence was thick, as if the bodies had absorbed all the sound, like flannel, like blankets, like snow. 4

She showed me first the trays of parts, stainless-steel basins of raw things— one full of kidneys, another of livers—like offerings in a meat market. She spoke in hushed tones, as if we were in an intensive-care room or a nursery. We approached the gurney that bore the cadaver she had been dissecting. Slowly, gently, she turned back the cover from the thin white feet and legs. "We'll start here," she said. "The head is so very personal." I knew she was allowing me time to prepare for the intimacy of that encounter. 5

She pointed to a clipboard on a low wall where the history of the cadaver was detailed. He was an old man—and an old cadaver, having been in storage for many months. I don't remember why he died. She told me that in some medical-school labs the students make dark jokes and horse around, probably in an effort to handle their feelings. She was grateful that the attitude here was different. 6

She raised the sheet from the lower torso, which was laid open like a display package. I was astonished to see that our bodies' essential parts are all neatly organized, many in their own little membranes like plastic-wrapped leftovers in a well-maintained refrigerator. I had always assumed that the coils of intestines, the stomach, the liver, the spleen, would be jumbled up together. The tidy reality was strangely satisfying. 7

She had been working on a section of colon, I think it was. I watched in fascination as she carefully removed the covering from the head. She said, "It is so important to us students to have this experience. And if people are willing to donate their bodies for us, we must, must give them due respect." 8

I gazed at the small face of an old man, an old man who somehow linked my daughter and me and all human flesh together, in the semi-dark, in this timeless moment. 9

Outside, green, growing leaves were gleaming softly under a star-studded sky. Up into the freshness of evening we came, full of a sense of the enduring connectedness of all living things, and of the child who becomes the parent and the parent the child. 10

"The silence was thick, as if the bodies had absorbed all the sound, like flannel, like blankets, like snow."

---

2. fervor: passion
3. queasiness: nervous stomach
4. formaldehyde: preservation fluid
5. Dante following Virgil: a reference to Dante's *Divine Comedy* (c. 1300), in which the Roman poet Virgil escorts Dante through hell and purgatory
6. gurneys: wheeled stretchers

Discussion and Writing Questions

1. Why did Garlan change her mind about accepting her daughter's invitation? What made her feel that she'd be "forever sorry" (paragraph 2) if she didn't accept?

2. What was Garlan's reaction to the cadaver's body parts (paragraph 7)?

3. What is the mother's reaction to the old man's face (paragraph 9)? How does it differ from the daughter's reaction (paragraph 5)? What might account for the difference?

4. After coming out of the basement laboratory, the author remarks that "the child . . . becomes the parent and the parent the child" (paragraph 10). What does she mean? What has happened to her?

Writing Assignments

1. Imagine that you have been invited by someone who loves you to tour his or her medical school's anatomy lab. Write a letter giving your reasons for accepting or declining. Mention how Garlan's essay influenced your decision.

2. At first, Garlan has negative feelings about seeing a cadaver, but she changes her mind and seizes the opportunity. Has instinct ever prompted you to seize an unusual opportunity, perhaps overcoming a fear in the bargain? Describe the incident and explain its importance to you, then and now.

3. From relationships you know firsthand, select one to illustrate a time when a child became the parent and the parent became the child. What brought about the role reversal? What was special about the reversing of roles? Conclude by describing what both the child and the parent learned (or did not learn) from the experience.

A Homemade Education

Malcolm X

> Sometimes a book can change a person's life. In this selection, Malcolm X, the influential and controversial black leader who was assassinated in 1965, describes how, while he was in prison, a dictionary set him free.

It was because of my letters that I happened to stumble upon starting to acquire some kind of homemade education.

I became increasingly frustrated at not being able to express what I wanted to convey in letters that I wrote, especially those to Mr. Elijah Muhammad.[1] In the street, I had been the most articulate hustler out there—I had commanded attention when I said something. But now, trying to write simple English, I not only wasn't articulate, I wasn't even functional. How would I sound writing in slang, the way I would *say* it, something such as, "Look, daddy, let me pull your coat about a cat. Elijah Muhammad—"

Many who today hear me somewhere in person, or on television, or those who read something I've said, will think I went to school far beyond the eighth grade. This impression is due entirely to my prison studies.

It had really begun back in the Charlestown Prison, when Bimbi first made me feel envy of his stock of knowledge. Bimbi had always taken charge of any conver-

---

1. Elijah Muhammad: founder of the Muslim sect Nation of Islam

Malcolm X giving one of his many speeches
(Corbis-Bettman)

"I saw that the best thing I could do was get hold of a dictionary—to study, to learn some words."

sation he was in, and I had tried to emulate² him. But every book I picked up had few sentences which didn't contain anywhere from one to nearly all of the words that might as well have been in Chinese. When I just skipped those words, of course, I really ended up with little idea of what the book said. So I had come to the Norfolk Prison Colony still going through only book-reading motions. Pretty soon, I would have quit even these motions, unless I had received the motivation that I did.

I saw that the best thing I could do was get hold of a dictionary—to study, to learn some words. I was lucky enough to reason also that I should try to improve my penmanship. It was sad. I couldn't even write in a straight line. It was both ideas together that moved me to request a dictionary along with some tablets and pencils from the Norfolk Prison Colony school.

I spent two days just riffling³ uncertainly through the dictionary's pages. I'd never realized so many words existed! I didn't know *which* words I needed to learn. Finally, just to start some kind of action, I began copying.

In my slow, painstaking, ragged handwriting, I copied into my tablet everything printed on that first page, down to the punctuation marks.

———
2. emulate: copy
3. riffling: thumbing through

I believe it took me a day. Then, aloud, I read back, to myself, everything I'd writ- 8
ten on the tablet. Over and over, aloud, to myself, I read my own handwriting.

I woke up the next morning, thinking about those words—immensely proud to 9
realize that not only had I written so much at one time, but I'd written words that
I never knew were in the world. Moreover, with a little effort, I also could remember what many of these words meant. I reviewed the words whose meanings I
didn't remember. Funny thing, from the dictionary first page right now, that
"aardvark" springs to my mind. The dictionary had a picture of it, a long-tailed,
long-eared burrowing African mammal, which lives off termites caught by sticking
out its tongue as an anteater does for ants.

I was so fascinated that I went on—I copied the dictionary's next page. And the 10
same experience came when I studied that. With every succeeding page, I also
learned of people and places and events from history. Actually the dictionary is like
a miniature encyclopedia. Finally, the dictionary's A section had filled a whole
tablet—and I went on into the B's. That was the way I started copying what eventually became the entire dictionary. It went a lot faster after so much practice helped
me pick up handwriting speed. Between what I wrote in my tablet, and writing letters, during the rest of my time in prison I would guess I wrote a million words.

I suppose it was inevitable that as my word-base broadened, I could for the first 11
time pick up a book and read and now begin to understand what the book was saying. Anyone who has read a great deal can imagine the new world that opened. Let
me tell you something: from then until I left that prison, in every free moment I had,
if I was not reading in the library, I was reading on my bunk. You couldn't have gotten me out of books with a wedge. Between Mr. Muhammad's teachings, my corre-
spondence, my visitors—usually Ella and Reginald—and my reading of books,
months passed without my even thinking about being imprisoned. In fact, up to
then, I never had been so truly free in my life.

Discussion and Writing Questions

1. Malcolm X says that in the streets he had been the "most articulate hustler" of
   all, but that in writing English he "not only wasn't articulate, [he] wasn't even
   functional" (paragraph 2). What does he mean?

2. What motivated Malcolm X to start copying the dictionary? What benefits did
   he gain from doing this?

3. What does Malcolm X mean when he says that until he went to prison, he
   "never had been so truly free in [his] life" (paragraph 11)?

4. Have you ever seen the 1992 film *Malcolm X*? If so, do you think the film's
   prison scenes showed how strongly Malcolm X was changed by improving his
   writing skills?

Writing Assignments

1. Did you ever notice a difference between your speaking skills and your
   writing skills? Write about a time when you needed or wanted to write something important but felt that your writing skills were not up to the task. What
   happened?

2. Malcolm X's inner life changed completely because of the dictionary he
   copied. Write about a time when a book, a story, a person, or an experience
   changed your life.

3. Choose three entries on a dictionary page and copy them. Then describe your
   experience. What did you learn? Can you imagine copying the entire dictionary? How do you feel about what Malcolm X accomplished? Where do you
   think he got the motivation to finish the task?

Mrs. Flowers

Maya Angelou

Maya Angelou (born Marguerite Johnson) is widely known today as the poet who read her work at President Clinton's inauguration and as the author of *I Know Why the Caged Bird Sings*. In this book, her life story, she tells of being raped when she was eight years old. Her response to the traumatic experience was to stop speaking. In this selection, Angelou describes the woman who eventually threw her a "life line."

1 For nearly a year, I sopped around the house, the Store, the school and the church, like an old biscuit, dirty and inedible. Then I met, or rather got to know, the lady who threw me my first life line.

2 Mrs. Bertha Flowers was the aristocrat of Black Stamps. She had the grace of control to appear warm in the coldest weather, and on the Arkansas summer days it seemed she had a private breeze which swirled around, cooling her. She was thin without the taut[1] look of wiry people, and her printed voile[2] dresses and flowered hats were as right for her as denim overalls for a farmer. She was our side's answer to the richest white woman in town.

3 Her skin was a rich black that would have peeled like a plum if snagged, but then no one would have thought of getting close enough to Mrs. Flowers to ruffle her dress, let alone snag her skin. She didn't encourage familiarity. She wore gloves too.

4 I don't think I ever saw Mrs. Flowers laugh, but she smiled often. A slow widening of her thin black lips to show even, small white teeth, then the slow effortless closing. When she chose to smile on me, I always wanted to thank her. The action was so graceful and inclusively benign.[3]

5 She was one of the few gentlewomen I have ever known, and has remained throughout my life the measure of what a human being can be. . . .

6 One summer afternoon, sweet-milk fresh in my memory, she stopped at the Store to buy provisions. Another Negro woman of her health and age would have been expected to carry the paper sacks home in one hand but Momma said, "Sister Flowers, I'll send Bailey up to your house with these things."

7 She smiled that slow dragging smile, "Thank you, Mrs. Henderson. I'd prefer Marguerite though." My name was beautiful when she said it. "I've been meaning to talk to her, anyway." They gave each other age-group looks.

8 Momma said, "Well, that's all right then. Sister, go and change your dress. You going to Sister Flowers's." . . .

9 There was a little path beside the rocky road, and Mrs. Flowers walked in front swinging her arms and picking her way over the stones.

10 She said, without turning her head, to me, "I hear you're doing very good school work, Marguerite, but that it's all written. The teachers report that they have trouble getting you to talk in class." We passed the triangular farm on our left and the path widened to allow us to walk together. I hung back in the separate unasked and unanswerable questions.

11 "Come and walk along with me, Marguerite." I couldn't have refused even if I wanted to. She pronounced my name so nicely. Or more correctly, she spoke each word with such clarity that I was certain a foreigner who didn't understand English could have understood her.

---

1. taut: tight, tense
2. voile: a light, semi-sheer fabric
3. benign: kind, gentle

"Now no one is going to make you talk—possibly no one can. But bear in 12
mind, language is man's way of communicating with his fellow man and it is language alone which separates him from the lower animals." That was a totally new idea to me, and I would need time to think about it.

"Your grandmother says you read a lot. Every chance you get. That's good, 13
but not good enough. Words mean more than what is set down on paper. It takes the human voice to infuse[4] them with the shades of deeper meaning."

I memorized the part about the human voice infusing words. It seemed so 14
valid and poetic.

She said she was going to give me some books and that I not only must read 15
them. I must read them aloud. She suggested that I try to make a sentence sound in as many different ways as possible.

"I'll accept no excuse if you return a book to me that has been badly handled." 16
My imagination boggled at the punishment I would deserve if in fact I did abuse a book of Mrs. Flowers's. Death would be too kind and brief.

The odors in the house surprised me. Somehow I had never connected Mrs. 17
Flowers with food or eating or any other common experience of common people. There must have been an outhouse, too, but my mind never recorded it.

The sweet scent of vanilla had met us as she opened the door. 18

"I made tea cookies this morning. You see, I had planned to invite you for 19
cookies and lemonade so we could have this little chat. The lemonade is in the icebox."

It followed that Mrs. Flowers would have ice on an ordinary day, when most 20
families in our town bought ice late on Saturdays only a few times during the summer to be used in the wooden ice-cream freezers.

She took the bags from me and disappeared through the kitchen door. I looked 21
around the room that I had never in my wildest fantasies imagined I would see. Browned photographs leered or threatened from the walls and the white, freshly done curtains pushed against themselves and against the wind. I wanted to gobble up the room entire and take it to Bailey, who would help me analyze and enjoy it.

"Have a seat, Marguerite. Over there by the table." She carried a platter cov- 22
ered with a tea towel. Although she warned that she hadn't tried her hand at baking sweets for some time, I was certain that like everything else about her the cookies would be perfect.

They were flat round wafers, slightly browned on the edges and butter-yellow 23
in the center. With the cold lemonade they were sufficient for childhood's lifelong diet. Remembering my manners, I took nice little lady-like bites off the edges. She said she had made them expressly for me and that she had a few in the kitchen that I could take home to my brother. So I jammed one whole cake in my mouth and the rough crumbs scratched the insides of my jaws, and if I hadn't had to swallow, it would have been a dream come true.

As I ate she began the first of what we later called "my lessons in living." She 24
said that I must always be intolerant of ignorance but understanding of illiteracy. That some people, unable to go to school, were more educated and even more in-telligent than college professors. She encouraged me to listen carefully to what country people called mother wit. That in those homely sayings was couched the collective[5] wisdom of generations.

When I finished the cookies she brushed off the table and brought a thick, 25
small book from the bookcase. I had read *A Tale of Two Cities* and found it up to my standards as a romantic novel. She opened the first page and I heard poetry for the first time in my life.

"I was liked, and what a difference it made. I was respected not as Mrs. Henderson's grandchild or Bailey's sister but for just being Marguerite Johnson."

---

4. infuse: to fill or penetrate
5. collective: gathered from a group

"It was the best of times and the worst of times . . . " Her voice slid in and 26
curved down through and over the words. She was nearly singing. I wanted to look
at the pages. Were they the same that I had read? Or were there notes, music, lined
on the pages, as in a hymn book? Her sounds began cascading[6] gently. I knew from
listening to a thousand preachers that she was nearing the end of her reading, and I
hadn't really heard, heard to understand, a single word.

"How do you like that?" 27

It occurred to me that she expected a response. The sweet vanilla flavor was 28
still on my tongue and her reading was a wonder in my ears. I had to speak.

I said, "Yes ma'am." It was the least I could do, but it was the most also. 29

"There's one more thing. Take this book of poems and memorize one for me. 30
Next time you pay me a visit, I want you to recite."

I have tried often to search behind the sophistication of years for the 31
enchantment I so easily found in those gifts. The essence escapes but its aura[7] re-
mains. To be allowed, no, invited, into the private lives of strangers, and to share
their joys and fears, was a chance to exchange the Southern bitter wormwood[8]
for . . . a hot cup of tea and milk with Oliver Twist.[9]

I was liked, and what a difference it made. I was respected not as Mrs. Hen- 32
derson's grandchild or Bailey's sister but for just being Marguerite Johnson.

Childhood's logic never asks to be proved (all conclusions are absolute). I 33
didn't question why Mrs. Flowers had singled me out for attention, nor did it occur
to me that Momma might have asked her to give me a little talking to. All I cared
about was that she had made tea cookies for *me* and read to *me* from her favorite
book. It was enough to prove that she liked me.

Discussion and Writing Questions

1. Angelou vividly describes Mrs. Flowers' appearance and style (paragraphs
   2–5). What kind of woman is Mrs. Flowers? What words and details convey
   this impression?

2. What strategies does Mrs. Flowers use to reach out to Marguerite?

3. What does Marguerite's first "lesson in living" include (paragraph 24)? Do you
   think such a lesson could really help a young person live better or differently?

4. In paragraph 31, the author speaks of her enchantment at receiving gifts from
   Mrs. Flowers. Just what gifts did Mrs. Flowers give her? Which do you consider the most important gift?

Writing Assignments

1. Has anyone ever thrown you a life line when you were in trouble? Describe the
   problem or hurt facing you and just what this person did to reach out. What
   "gifts" did he or she offer you (attention, advice, and so forth)? Were you able
   to receive them?

   If you prefer, write about a time when you helped someone else. What
   seemed to be weighing this person down? How were you able to help?

2. Mrs. Flowers read aloud so musically that Marguerite "heard poetry for the
   first time in [her] life." Has someone ever shared a love—of music, gardening,

---

6. cascading: falling like a waterfall
7. aura: a special quality or air around something or someone
8. wormwood: something harsh or embittering
9. Oliver Twist: a character from a novel by Charles Dickens

or history, for example—so strongly that you were changed? What happened and how were you changed?

3. Many people have trouble speaking up—in class, at social gatherings, even to one other person. Can you express your thoughts and feelings as freely as you would like in most situations? What opens you up, and what shuts you up?

Barbie at 35

ANNA QUINDLEN

To what extent is the Barbie doll responsible for the poor self-image that afflicts so many women? Anna Quindlen—novelist, Pulitzer Prize–winning journalist, and mother—thinks that there's more to Barbie than meets a child's eye.

My theory is that to get rid of Barbie you'd have to drive a silver stake through her 1 plastic heart. Or a silver lamé[1] stake, the sort of thing that might accompany Barbie's Dream Tent.

This is not simply because the original Barbie, launched lo these 35 years ago, 2 was more than a little vampiric[2] in appearance, more Natasha of "Rocky and Bullwinkle" than the "ultimate girl next door" Mattel described in her press kit.

It's not only that Barbie, like Dracula, can appear in guises that mask her 3 essential nature: Surgeon, Astronaut, UNICEF Ambassador. Or that she is untouched by time, still the same parody[3] of the female form she's been since 1959. She's said by her manufacturers to be "eleven and one-half stylish inches" tall. If she were a real live woman she would not have enough body fat to menstruate regularly. Which may be why there's no PMS Barbie.

The silver stake is necessary because Barbie—the issue, not the doll—simply 4 will not be put to rest.

"Mama, why can't I have Barbie?" 5

"Because I hate Barbie. She gives little girls the message that the only thing 6 that's important is being tall and thin and having a big chest and lots of clothes. She's a terrible role model."

"Oh, Mama, don't be silly. She's just a toy." 7

It's an excellent comeback; if only it were accurate. But consider the recent 8 study at the University of Arizona investigating the attitudes of white and black teen-age girls toward body image.

The attitudes of the white girls were a nightmare. Ninety percent expressed dis- 9 satisfaction with their own bodies and many said they saw dieting as a kind of all-purpose panacea.[4] "I think the reason I would diet would be to gain self-confidence," said one. "I'd feel like it was a way of getting control," said another.

And they were curiously united in their description of the perfect girl. She's 10 5 feet 7 inches, weighs just over 100 pounds, has long legs and flowing hair. The researchers concluded: "The ideal girl was a living manifestation of the Barbie doll."

While the white girls described an impossible ideal, black teenagers talked about 11 appearance in terms of style, attitude, pride and personality. White respondents talked "thin," black ones "shapely." Seventy percent of the black teenagers said they were satisfied with their weight, and there was little emphasis on dieting. "We're all

"Barbie—the issue, not the doll—simply will not be put to rest."

---

1. lamé: fabric with metallic threads
2. vampiric: bloodsucking, in the manner of a vampire
3. parody: ridiculous imitation
4. panacea: cure-all; remedy for everything

brought up and taught to be realistic about life," said one, "and we don't look at things the way you want them to be. You look at them the way they are."

There's a quiet irony in that. While black women correctly complain that they are not sufficiently represented in advertisements, commercials, movies, even dolls, perhaps the scarcity of those idealized and unrealistic models may help in some fashion to liberate black teenagers from ridiculous standards of appearance. When the black teenagers were asked about the ideal woman, many asked: Whose ideal? The perfect girl projected by the white world simply didn't apply to them or their community, which set beauty standards from within. "White girls," one black participant in the Arizona study wrote, "have to look like Barbie dolls." 12

There are lots of reasons teenage girls have such a distorted fun-house mirror image of their own bodies, so distorted that one study found that 83 percent wanted to lose weight, although 62 percent were in the normal range. Fashion designers still showcase anorexia chic; last year the supermodel Kate Moss was reduced to insisting that, yes, she did eat. 13

But long before Kate and Ultra Slimfast came along, hanging over the life of every little girl born in the second half of the twentieth century was the impossibly curvy shadow (40-18-32 in life-size terms) of Barbie. That preposterous physique, we learn as kids, is what a woman looks like with her clothes off. "Two Barbie dolls are sold every second," says Barbie's résumé, which is more extensive than that of Hillary Rodham Clinton. "Barbie doll has had more than a billion pairs of shoes . . . has had over 500 professional makeovers . . . has become the most popular toy ever created." 14

Has been single-handedly responsible for the popularity of the silicone implant? 15

Maybe, as my daughter suggests while she whines in her Barbie-free zone, that's too much weight to put on something that's just a toy. Maybe not. Happy birthday, Babs. Have a piece of cake. Have two. 16

Discussion and Writing Questions

1. According to the author, why is it necessary to drive a silver stake through Barbie's heart? Why does Quindlen change her wording to "a silver lamé stake" (paragraph 1)?

2. Why does the author consider her daughter's argument that Barbie is "just a toy" (paragraph 7) a false statement?

3. What is the difference between the attitudes of white and black teenage girls toward body image, according to the University of Arizona study? In your experience or opinion, are the conclusions of the study accurate?

4. "Happy birthday, Babs. Have a piece of cake. Have two." What is the significance of these concluding lines of Quindlen's essay?

Writing Assignments

1. Quindlen believes that the fashion industry contributes to white girls' distorted body image (paragraph 13). Write a profile of a model or a designer who contributes to this distortion. Alternatively, choose a model or a designer who does not distort the female body. In either case, use specific examples of fashions to develop your paper.

2. Have you (or has someone you know well) ever dieted? Were the reasons for dieting similar to those described by the white girls in the Arizona study (to gain self-confidence, control, and so on)? Describe the experience. Include such details as when you dieted, how, why, for how long, and your success rate, both in terms of losing weight and gaining whatever you hoped to gain.

3. A local elementary school has invited you to participate in an updated "Show and Tell." For the children's enjoyment, you bring along a favorite childhood toy, book, or game. Write up your presentation for the students. Begin with an episode when you greatly enjoyed your toy, book, or game; then describe the object in detail. End with an explanation of why it meant (or still means) so much to you.

Sports Nuts

DAVE BARRY

Dave Barry is a Pulitzer Prize–winning humorist who writes a column for the *Miami Herald*. This essay, on men who are fanatic about sports, is written in Barry's usual tongue-in-cheek style.

Today, in our continuing series on How Guys Think, we explore the question: How come guys care so much about sports? 1

This is a tough one, because caring about sports is, let's face it, silly. I mean, suppose you have a friend who, for no apparent reason, suddenly becomes obsessed with the Amtrak Corporation. He babbles about Amtrak constantly, citing[1] obscure railroad statistics from 1978; he puts Amtrak bumper stickers on his car; and when something bad happens to Amtrak, such as a train crashes and investigators find that the engineer was drinking and wearing a bunny suit, your friend becomes depressed for weeks. You'd think he was crazy, right? "Bob," you'd say to him, as a loving and caring friend, "you're a moron. The Amtrak Corporation has *nothing to do with you.*" 2

But if Bob is behaving exactly the same deranged[2] way about, say, the Pittsburgh Penguins, it's considered normal guy behavior. He could name his child "Pittsburgh Penguin Johnson" and be considered only mildly eccentric. There is something wrong with this. And before you accuse me of being some kind of sherry-sipping ascot[3]-wearing ballet-attending MacNeil-Lehrer Report–watching wussy, please note that I am a sports guy myself, having had a legendary athletic career consisting of nearly a third of the 1965 season on the track team at Pleasantville High School ("Where The Leaders Of Tomorrow Are Leaving Wads Of Gum On The Auditorium Seats Of Today"). I competed in the long jump, because it seemed to be the only event where afterward you didn't fall down and throw up. I probably would have become an Olympic-caliber long-jumper except that, through one of those "bad breaks" so common in sports, I turned out to have the raw leaping ability of a convenience store. I'd race down the runway and attempt to soar into the air, but instead of going up I'd be seized by powerful gravity rays and yanked *downward* and wind up with just my head sticking out of the dirt, serving as a convenient marker for the other jumpers to take off from. 3

So, OK, I was not Jim Thorpe,[4] but I care as much about sports as the next guy. If you were to put me in the middle of a room, and in one corner was Albert Einstein, in another corner was Abraham Lincoln, in another corner was Plato, in another corner was William Shakespeare, and in another corner (this room is a pentagon) was a TV set showing a football game between teams that have no connection whatsoever with my life, such as the Green Bay Packers and the Indianapolis Colts, I would ignore the greatest minds in Western thought, gravitate toward the TV, and become far more concerned about the game than I am about my child's education. 4

" . . . I turned out to have the raw leaping ability of a convenience store. . . . but I care as much about sports as the next guy."

---

1. citing: offering examples of
2. deranged: crazed, insane
3. ascot: an English necktie
4. Jim Thorpe: famous Native-American athlete

And *so would the other guys.* I guarantee it. Within minutes Plato would be pounding Lincoln on the shoulder and shouting in ancient Greek that the receiver did *not* have both feet in bounds.

Obviously, sports connect with something deeply rooted in the male psyche,[5] dating back to prehistoric times, when guys survived by hunting and fighting, and they needed many of the skills exhibited by modern athletes—running, throwing, spitting, renegotiating their contracts, adjusting their private parts on nationwide television, etc. So that would explain how come guys like to *participate* in sports. But how come they care so much about games played by *other* guys? Does this also date back to prehistoric times? When the hunters were out hurling spears into mastodons,[6] were there also prehistoric guys watching from the hills, drinking prehistoric beer, eating really bad prehistoric hot dogs, and shouting "We're No. 1!" but not understanding what it meant because this was before the development of mathematics?

There must have been, because there is no other explanation for such bizarre phenomena as:

- Sports-talk radio, where guys who have never sent get-well cards to their own mothers will express heartfelt, near-suicidal anguish over the hamstring problems of strangers.

- My editor, Gene, who can remember the complete starting lineups for the New York Yankee teams from 1960 through 1964, but who routinely makes telephone calls wherein, after he dials the phone, he forgets who he's calling, so when somebody answers, Gene has to ask (a) who it is, and (b) does this person happen to know the purpose of the call.

- Another guy in my office, John, who appears to be a normal middle-aged husband and father until you realize that he spends most of his waking hours managing a *pretend baseball team.* This is true. He and some other guys have formed a league where they pay actual money to "draft" major-league players, and then they have their pretend teams play a whole pretend season, complete with trades, legalistic memorandums, and heated disputes over the rules. This is crazy, right? If these guys said they were managing herds of pretend caribou,[7] the authorities would be squirting lithium[8] down their throats with turkey basters, right? And yet we all act like it's *perfectly normal.* In fact, eavesdropping from my office, I find myself getting involved in John's discussions. That's how pathetic I am: I'm capable of caring about a pretend sports team that's not even my own pretend sports team.

So I don't know about the rest of you guys, but I'm thinking it's time I got some perspective in my life. First thing after the Super Bowl, I'm going to start paying more attention to the things that should matter to me, like my work, my friends, and above all my family, especially my little boy, Philadelphia Phillies Barry.

Discussion and Writing Questions

1. Barry often humorously exaggerates to make a point. Find several examples of exaggeration in his essay.

2. What details or points of the essay do you find particularly funny?

3. Why do you suppose Barry talks about Einstein, Lincoln, Plato, and Shakespeare in paragraph 4? Could he have chosen other famous men to make his point?

---

5. psyche: the mind
6. mastodons: prehistoric animals resembling elephants
7. caribou: a kind of Arctic deer
8. lithium: a drug used to treat mental illness

4. Do you think that "sports connect with something deeply rooted in the male psyche," as Barry states in paragraph 5? What is that "something"? What about the female psyche?

Writing Assignments

1. Fill in the blank in the following line: Today, in our continuing series on How Gals Think, we explore the question "_____

_____?"

   Then write a newspaper column exploring your topic. Be as humorous or as serious as you wish.

2. Reread Barry's description of his attempts at the long jump in paragraph 3. Then describe your own efforts in a sport you thought you might be good at but weren't.

3. Is there a sport you really like—either watching or playing? Describe your love of this sport, giving at least two reasons why the sport appeals to you. Your audience is a group of people who know little about this sport.

Four Directions

AMY TAN

Have you ever possessed a certain skill or strength, and then, as you grew, lost it? Amy Tan, a Chinese-American novelist who lives in San Francisco, writes about a young chess player who seemed unbeatable—at age ten.

I was ten years old. Even though I was young, I knew my ability to play chess was 1 a gift. It was effortless, so easy. I could see things on the chessboard that other people could not. I could create barriers to protect myself that were invisible to my opponents. And this gift gave me supreme confidence. I knew at exactly what point their faces would fall when my seemingly simple and childlike strategy would reveal itself as a devastating and irrevocable[1] course. I loved to win.

And my mother loved to show me off, like one of my many trophies she pol- 2 ished. She used to discuss my games as if she had devised the strategies.

"I told my daughter, Use your horses to run over the enemy," she informed 3 one shopkeeper. "She won very quickly this way." And of course, she had said this before the game—that and a hundred other useless things that had nothing to do with my winning.

To our family friends who visited she would confide, "You don't have to be so 4 smart to win chess. It is just tricks. You blow from the North, South, East, and West. The other person becomes confused. They don't know which way to run."

I hated the way she tried to take all the credit. And one day I told her so, 5 shouting at her on Stockton Street, in the middle of a crowd of people. I told her she didn't know anything, so she shouldn't show off. She should shut up. Words to that effect.

That evening and the next day she wouldn't speak to me. She would say stiff 6 words to my father and brothers, as if I had become invisible and she was talking about a rotten fish she had thrown away but which had left behind its bad smell.

I knew this strategy, the sneaky way to get someone to pounce back in anger and 7 fall into a trap. So I ignored her. I refused to speak and waited for her to come to me.

---

1. irrevocable: impossible to cancel or halt

After many days had gone by in silence, I sat in my room, staring at the sixty-[8] four squares of my chessboard, trying to think of another way. And that's when I decided to quit playing chess.

Of course I didn't mean to quit forever. At most, just for a few days. And I [9] made a show of it. Instead of practicing in my room every night, as I always did, I marched into the living room and sat down in front of the television with my brothers, who stared at me, an unwelcome intruder. I used my brothers to further my plan; I cracked my knuckles to annoy them.

"Ma!" they shouted. "Make her stop. Make her go away." [10]

But my mother did not say anything. [11]

Still I was not worried. But I could see I would have to make a stronger move. [12] I decided to sacrifice a tournament that was coming up in one week. I would refuse to play in it. And my mother would certainly have to speak to me about this. Because the sponsors and the benevolent associations[2] would start calling her, asking, shouting, pleading to make me play again.

And then the tournament came and went. And she did not come to me, cry-[13] ing, "Why are you not playing chess?" But I was crying inside, because I learned that a boy whom I had easily defeated on two other occasions had won.

I realized my mother knew more tricks than I had thought. But now I was [14] tired of her game. I wanted to start practicing for the next tournament. So I decided to pretend to let her win. I would be the one to speak first.

"I am ready to play chess again," I announced to her. I had imagined she [15] would smile and then ask me what special thing I wanted to eat.

But instead, she gathered her face into a frown and stared into my eyes, as if she [16] could force some kind of truth out of me.

"Why do you tell me this?" she finally said in sharp tones. "You think it is so [17] easy. One day quit, next day play. Everything for you is this way. So smart, so easy, so fast."

"I said I'll play," I whined. [18]

"No!" she shouted, and I almost jumped out of my scalp. "It is not so easy [19] anymore."

I was quivering, stunned by what she said, in not knowing what she [20] meant. And then I went back to my room. I stared at my chessboard, its sixty-four squares, to figure out how to undo this terrible mess. And after staring like this for many hours, I actually believed that I had made the white squares black and the black squares white, and everything would be all right.

And sure enough, I won her back. That night I developed a high fever, and she sat [21] next to my bed, scolding me for going to school without my sweater. In the morning she was there as well, feeding me rice porridge flavored with chicken broth she had strained herself. She said she was feeding me this because I had the chicken pox and one chicken knew how to fight another. And in the afternoon, she sat in a chair in my room, knitting me a pink sweater while telling me about a sweater that Auntie Suyuan had knit for her daughter June, and how it was most unattractive and of the worst yarn. I was so happy that she had become her usual self.

But after I got well, I discovered that, really, my mother had changed. She no [22] longer hovered over[3] me as I practiced different chess games. She did not polish my trophies every day. She did not cut out the small newspaper item that mentioned my name. It was as if she had erected[4] an invisible wall and I was secretly groping each day to see how high and how wide it was.

"I could no longer see the secret weapons of each piece, the magic within the intersection of each square."

---

2. benevolent associations: charities
3. hovered over: paid close attention to
4. erected: built

At my next tournment, while I had done well overall, in the end the points 23 were not enough. I lost. And what was worse, my mother said nothing. She seemed to walk around with this satisfied look, as if it had happened because she had devised this strategy.

I was horrified. I spent many hours every day going over in my mind what I 24 had lost. I knew it was not just the last tournament. I examined every move, every piece, every square. And I could no longer see the secret weapons of each piece, the magic within the intersection of each square. I could see only my mistakes, my weaknesses. It was as though I had lost my magic armor. And everybody could see this, where it was easy to attack me.

Over the next few weeks and later months and years, I continued to play, but 25 never with that same feeling of supreme confidence. I fought hard, with fear and desperation. When I won, I was grateful, relieved. And when I lost, I was filled with growing dread, and then terror that I was no longer a prodigy,[5] that I had lost the gift and had turned into someone quite ordinary.

When I lost twice to the boy whom I had defeated so easily a few years before, I 26 stopped playing chess altogether. And nobody protested. I was fourteen.

Discussion and Writing Questions

1. Why did the child and her mother fight? Do you think the mother really wanted "all the credit" for herself (paragraph 5)? Why did she refuse to speak to the child after their argument?

2. The mother and daughter almost seem locked in a chess match of their own after their argument. What do you think is happening between them? Does the daughter's age—adolescence—have anything to do with it?

3. Why do you suppose the author says she had lost more than the last tournament, she had lost her "magic armor" (paragraph 24)?

4. The author says that "nobody protested" when she gave up chess permanently at age fourteen (paragraph 26). Do you think people might have protested if she were a boy? Why or why not?

Writing Assignments

1. Did you possess a talent or strength as a young person that you later lost? What happened? What caused you to change?

2. Adolescence is for most people a time of enormous change, and change often produces great anxiety. Was there an incident in your adolescence that caused you such anxiety—because you or your surroundings were somehow changing? Describe this incident.

3. Research suggests that once they reach adolescence, many girls give up asserting themselves—in sports, in class, and in student government, for example—because they feel pressure to be "feminine." Do you think this is true? Discuss why or why not, using yourself or a young woman you know as an example.

---

5. prodigy: a person with enormous talents in a particular area

Forever

FRANCINE KLAGSBRUN

Francine Klagsbrun has written extensively on relationships between women and men. In this selection, she characterizes healthy marriage as a dynamic, ever-changing process between two people, one that begins only when romance wears off.

Probably every couple that ever existed has looked at one another at some point 1 during or after the honeymoon and wondered, "Who are you?" and "What am I doing here?" For every couple there are expectations and dreams that go unfulfilled. Those who remain married and satisfied with their marriages are willing to discard the fantasies and build a richer and deeper life beyond the illusions.

All marriages, not only those that fail, begin with unreal expectations that 2 color much of what happens between partners. Maggie and Robbie are a good example. They have known one another for years. They are not carried away in transports[1] of romantic blindness about one another, nor does either deny the other's faults. But they are so pleased about getting married, so wanting to be adults now, that they happily gloss over[2] those faults. "We're as different as two people can be, and we'll never change," Robbie says, as though his acknowledgment makes the differences unimportant. "We fight all the time," Maggie laughs, shoving aside the anger that must lie behind the constant bickering. "Of course I'll take off from work when we have a baby," Robbie asserts, denying to himself the drive of ambition that makes him spend every evening working at his desk, leaving little time for the two to be together. And Maggie accepts his assertion, pretending to herself and to him that he will be able to put aside his ambitions when the time comes.

There are many kinds of expectations with which people begin their marriages. 3 "I'll change him/her after we marry" is one of the most common of these—trite,[3] actually, because it is so widely known and often laughed at. The "I'll be happy once I'm married" illusion is also widely held, an anticipation that marriage will take care of all one's emotional needs. Then there is the illusion that "if she loved me, she'd know how I feel," which may begin before marriage and continue well into it. This is the expectation that in some fantasy land of love you never have to tell your partner how you feel or what you want.

"A marriage is a process . . . it never stays the same and it never completes itself."

Underlying all the other expectations is the expectation of perfection. All of us 4 begin marriages with such high hopes, it is hard to believe that anything about our life could be less than perfect. When imperfections appear (as they must), most couples look around at other marriages and wonder what is wrong with them. They are sure that everybody else's sex life is wonderful, while they have had trouble adjusting to one another; everybody else knows how to communicate feelings, while they have had vicious battles; everybody else is adept at handling finances, while theirs are in constant chaos. Since their marriage isn't perfect, as everybody else's is, they conclude that it is probably no good at all.

Marital therapist Carl Whitaker, who has written and lectured a great deal, 5 believes that a real marriage doesn't begin until that time when the illusions wear off, or wear thin. It takes a couple about ten years, says Whitaker, to realize that the expectations with which they began marriage and the assumptions they held about each other are not quite the way they seemed. At this point they see themselves as having "fallen out of love." He no longer thinks he can change her, and she no

---

1. transports: ecstasies
2. gloss over: not take seriously; treat superficially
3. trite: too often used

longer thinks he can understand her. The characteristics that had once seemed endearing—his fear of flying, her fear of failure—now drive them crazy. They have come to see each other as real people, neither saviors nor therapists, saints nor charming rogues.[4] Each knows the other's vulnerabilities, and knows well how to hurt the other. Now their marriage is at a crossroads. They can become locked onto a pattern of fighting and making each other miserable; they can become involved in outside affairs; they can decide that this is not what they bargained for and split; or they can create a true marriage. That is, they can come to accept the frailties and vulnerabilities each has, accept them and respect them, and in doing so, discover a much more profound love for the real person whom they married.

It may not take ten years for Whitaker's "ten-year-syndrome" to occur. It may 6 take three weeks or five months or two decades for the exaggerated expectations and fantasies to fall away and for a couple to find themselves face to face with one another, confronting the realities of their marriage.

If they make the decision to stay together, they will begin the real process of 7 marriage. Marriage is a process because it is always in flux;[5] it never stays the same and it never completes itself. It is a process of changing and accepting change, of settling differences and living with differences that will never be settled, of drawing close and pulling apart and drawing close again. Because it is a process that demands discipline and responsibility, it can bring frustration and pain, but it also can plumb[6] the depths of love and provide an arena for self-actualization as nothing else can.

If Maggie and Robbie stay married, their marriage will have a special kind of 8 romance. It will not be only the romance of loving one another and it will not be the romance of sexual excitement—although those will be part of their marriage. The romance of a marriage that lasts beyond the illusions comes in its incompleteness, and in the adventure of exploring the unfolding process together.

Discussion and Writing Questions

1. The author says that all marriages begin with unreal expectations (paragraph 2). Give some examples of unreal expectations. What does the author believe must happen to those expectations for a marriage to succeed?

2. What does the author think of the communication between Maggie and Robbie? Why?

3. The author believes that marriage "is a process" (paragraph 7). What does she mean by this? What predictable stages occur in this process?

4. Once the romantic illusions are gone, does the relationship become boring? What, according to Klagsbrun, is exciting about a long-term relationship?

Writing Assignments

1. Write about a relationship you have had or a relationship you are familiar with in which the couple found themselves "at a crossroads." How did they handle this turning point? What happened?

2. Write about a situation that you approached with high hopes. Did those early hopes change over time? Try to give your reader a sense of the events you

---

4. rogues: rascals
5. flux: change
6. plumb: examine deeply

experienced and feelings you had. Did you come to a more realistic understanding of the situation? Why or why not?

3. Klagsbrun describes the "real process of marriage" as one that "demands discipline and responsibility" (paragraph 7). What else do you think marriage, or any healthy relationship, demands? Describe the characteristics of a successful relationship, as you see them.

In This Arranged Marriage, Love Came Later

Shoba Narayan

Although arranged marriages are common in many parts of the world, most Americans believe that the best marriages start with falling in love. In this essay, an American-educated journalist from India discusses her decision to let her family find her a husband.

We sat around the dining table, my family and I, replete[1] from yet another home-cooked South Indian dinner. It was my younger brother, Shaam, who asked the question.

"Shoba, why don't you stay back here for a few months? So we can try to get you married."

Three pairs of eyes stared at me across the expanse of the table. I sighed. Here I was, at the tail end of my vacation after graduate school. I had an airplane ticket to New York from Madras, India, in ten days. I had accepted a job at an artists' colony in Johnson, Vermont. My car, and most of my possessions, were with friends in Memphis.

"It's not that simple," I said. "What about my car . . . ?"

"We could find you someone in America," my dad replied. "You could go back to the States."

They had thought it all out. This was a plot. I glared at my parents accusingly.

Oh, another part of me rationalized, why not give this arranged-marriage thing a shot? It wasn't as if I had a lot to go back to in the States. Besides, I could always get a divorce.

Stupid and dangerous as it seems in retrospect,[2] I went into my marriage at twenty-five without being in love. Three years later, I find myself relishing my relationship with this brilliant, prickly man who talks about the yield curve and derivatives,[3] who prays when I drive, and who tries valiantly to remember names like Giacometti, Munch, Kandinsky.[4]

My enthusiasm for arranged marriages is that of a recent convert. True, I grew up in India, where arranged marriages are common. My parents' marriage was arranged, as were those of my aunts, cousins and friends. But I always thought I was different. I blossomed as a foreign fellow in Mount Holyoke College where individualism was expected and feminism encouraged. As I experimented with being an American, I bought into the American value system.

I was determined to fall in love and marry someone who was not Indian. Yet, somehow, I could never manage to. Oh, falling in love was easy. Sustaining it was the hard part.

> "Stupid and dangerous as it seems in retrospect, I went into my marriage at twenty-five without being in love."

---

1. replete: filled to satisfaction
2. in retrospect: looking back
3. yield curve and derivatives: technical terms from finance
4. Giacometti, Munch, Kandinsky: great twentieth-century artists

Arranged marriages in India begin with matching the horoscopes of the man 11 and the woman. Astrologers look for balance . . . so that the woman's strengths balance the man's weaknesses and vice versa. Once the horoscopes match, the two families meet and decide whether they are compatible. It is assumed that they are of the same religion, caste[5] and social stratum.[6]

While this eliminates risk and promotes homogeneity,[7] the rationale is that the 12 personalities of the couple provide enough differences for a marriage to thrive. Whether or not this is true, the high statistical success rate of arranged marriages in different cultures—90 percent in Iran, 95 percent in India, and a similar high percentage among Hasidic Jews in Brooklyn, and among Turkish and Afghan Muslims—gives one pause.

Although our families met through a mutual friend, many Indian families 13 meet through advertisements placed in national newspapers.

My parents made a formal visit to my future husband's house to see whether 14 Ram's family would treat me well. My mother insists that "you can tell a lot about the family just from the way they serve coffee." The house had a lovely flower garden. The family liked gardening. Good.

Ram's mother had worked for the United Nations on women's-rights issues. 15 She also wrote humorous columns for Indian magazines. She would be supportive. She served strong South Indian coffee in the traditional stainless steel tumblers instead of china; she would be a balancing influence on my youthful radicalism.

Ram's father had supported his wife's career even though he belonged to a 16 generation of Indian men who expected their wives to stay home. Ram had a good role model. His sister was a pediatrician in Fort Myers. Perhaps that meant he was used to strong, achieving women.

November 20, 1992. Someone shouted, "They're here!" My cousin Sheela gen- 17 tly nudged me out of the bedroom into the living room.

"Why don't you sit down?" a voice said. 18

I looked up and saw a square face and smiling eyes anxious to put me at ease. 19 He pointed me to a chair. Somehow I liked that. The guy was sensitive and self-confident.

He looked all right. Could stand to lose a few pounds. I liked the way his lips 20 curved to meet his eyes. Curly hair, commanding voice, unrestrained laugh. To my surprise, the conversation flowed easily. We had a great deal in common, but his profession was very different from mine. He had an MBA from the University of Michigan and had worked on Wall Street before joining a financial consulting firm.

Two hours later, Ram said, "I'd like to get to know you better. Unfortunately, I 21 have to be back at my job in Connecticut, but I could call you every other day. No strings attached, and both of us can decide where this goes, if anywhere."

I didn't dislike him. 22

He called ten days later. We talked about our goals, dreams and anxieties. 23

"What do you want out of life?" he asked me one day. "Come up with five 24 words, maybe, of what you want to do with your life." His question intrigued me. "Courage, wisdom, change," I said, flippantly.[8] "What about you?"

"Curiosity, contribution, balance, family and fun," he said. In spite of myself, I 25 was impressed.

One month later, he proposed and I accepted. Our extended honeymoon in 26 Connecticut was wonderful. On weekends, we took trips to Mount Holyoke, where I showed him my old art studio, and to Franconia Notch in New Hampshire, where we hiked and camped.

---

5. caste: one of four social classes in India
6. stratum: level
7. homogeneity: sameness, similarity
8. flippantly: lightly, thoughtlessly

It was in Taos, New Mexico, that we had our first fight. Ram had arranged for 27 a surprise visit to the children's summer camp where I used to work as a counselor. We visited my old colleagues with their Greenpeace T-shirts and New Age commune mentality. Ram, with his clipped accent, neatly pressed clothes and pleasant manners, was so different. What was I doing with this guy? On the car trip to the airport, I was silent. "I think, perhaps, we might have made a mistake," I said slowly. The air changed.

"Your friends may be idealistic, but they are escaping their lives, as are you," he 28 said. "We are married. Accept it. Grow up!"

He had never spoken to me this harshly before, and it hurt. I didn't talk to him 29 during the entire trip back to New York.

That fight set the pattern of our lives for the next several months. In the 30 evening, when Ram came home, I would ignore him or blame him for bringing me to Connecticut.

Two years into our marriage, something happened. I was ashamed to realize that 31 while I had treated Ram with veiled dislike, he had always tried to improve our relationship. I was admitted to the journalism program at Columbia, where, at Ram's insistence, I had applied.

Falling in love, for me, began with small changes. I found myself relishing a 32 South Indian dish that I disliked, mostly because I knew how much he loved it. I realized that the first thing I wanted to do when I heard some good news was to share it with him. Somewhere along the way, the "I love you, too" that I had politely parroted[9] in response to his endearments had become sincere.

My friends are appalled[10] that I let my parents decide my life partner; yet, the 33 older they get the more intrigued they are. I am convinced that our successful relationship has to do with two words: tolerance and trust. In a country that emphasizes individual choice, arranged marriages require a familial web for them to work. For many Americans, that web doesn't exist.

As my friend Karen said, "How can I get my parents to pick out my spouse 34 when they don't even talk to each other?"

Discussion and Writing Questions

1. Why did the author agree to an arranged marriage?

2. What factors did her family consider as they matched her with a husband? Which of these factors do you think are important predictors of success in marriage? Which, if any, seem unimportant?

3. How did Shoba Narayan know, after two years, that she was falling in love? If you have ever fallen in love, how was your experience similar or different?

4. What might be the disadvantages, or even risks, of an arranged marriage?

Writing Assignments

1. Soon after they met, Ram asked Shoba what words she would choose to express what she wanted in life. She said, "Courage, wisdom, change." Ram chose "curiosity, contribution, balance, family and fun." What three to five words would you select in answer to Ram's question? Choose your words carefully; then explain why each one is important to you.

2. Would you consider letting your relatives pick your marriage partner? Take a stand, presenting the two or three most important reasons why you would or would not consider such a move.

---

9. parroted: repeated mindlessly, like a parrot
10. appalled: shocked

3. How important is romantic love in a marriage or other intimate relationship? To help you answer this question, review or read Francine Klagsbrun's article "Forever," on page 444. Klagsbrun states that the "real work of marriage" begins only when romantic illusions wear off. *Is* love just a romantic illusion?

Tortillas

José Antonio Burciaga

As the Mexican national food, the *tortilla* is more than just something delicious to eat. In this selection, José Antonio Burciaga, a prize-winning author, artist, and poet who died in 1996, shares the *tortilla's* larger significance—as well as the unusual history of the *tortilla* in his own life.

My earliest memory of *tortillas* is my *Mamá* telling me not to play with them. I had 1 bitten eyeholes in one and was wearing it as a mask at the dinner table.

As a child, I also used *tortillas* as hand warmers on cold days, and my family 2 claims that I owe my career as an artist to my early experiments with *tortillas*. According to them, my clowning around helped me develop a strong artistic foundation. I'm not so sure, though. Sometimes I wore a *tortilla* on my head, like a *yarmulke*,[1] and yet I never had any great urge to convert from Catholicism to Judaism. But who knows? They may be right.

For Mexicans over the centuries, the *tortilla* has served as the spoon and the 3 fork, the plate and the napkin. *Tortillas* originated before the Mayan civilizations,[2] perhaps predating Europe's wheat bread. According to Mayan mythology, the great god Quetzalcoatl, realizing that the red ants knew the secret of using maize as food, transformed himself into a black ant, infiltrated[3] the colony of red ants, and absconded[4] with a grain of corn. (Is it any wonder that to this day, black ants and red ants do not get along?) Quetzalcoatl then put maize on the lips of the first man and woman, Oxomoco and Cipactonal, so that they would become strong. Maize festivals are still celebrated by many Indian cultures of the Americas.

When I was growing up in El Paso, *tortillas* were part of my daily life. I used to 4 visit a *tortilla* factory in an ancient adobe building near the open *mercado*[5] in Ciudad Juárez. As I approached, I could hear the rhythmic slapping of the *masa*[6] as the skilled vendors outside the factory formed it into balls and patted them into perfectly round corn cakes between the palms of their hands. The wonderful aroma and the speed with which the women counted so many dozens of *tortillas* out of warm wicker baskets still linger in my mind. Watching them at work convinced me that the most handsome and *deliciosas tortillas* are handmade. Although machines are faster, they can never adequately replace generation-to-generation experience. There's no place in the factory assembly line for the tender slaps that give each *tortilla* character. The best thing that can be said about mass-producing *tortillas* is that it makes it possible for many people to enjoy them.

In the *mercado* where my mother shopped, we frequently bought *taquitos de* 5 *nopalitos*, small tacos filled with diced cactus, onions, tomatoes, and *jalapeños*. Our friend Don Toribio showed us how to make delicious, crunchy *taquitos* with dried,

> "While the **tortilla** may be a lowly corn cake, when the necessity arises, it can reach unexpected distinction."

---

1. *yarmulke:* skullcap worn by Jewish men
2. Mayan civilizations: societies that developed from Mexico to Belize between 300 and 900, noted for their advanced culture
3. infiltrated: entered secretly
4. absconded: hid
5. *mercado:* market
6. *masa:* dough

salted pumpkin seeds. When you had no money for the filling, a poor man's *taco* could be made by placing a warm *tortilla* on the left palm, applying a sprinkle of salt, then rolling the *tortilla* up quickly with the fingertips of the right hand. My own kids put peanut butter and jelly on *tortillas,* which I think is truly bicultural. And speaking of fast foods for kids, nothing beats a *quesadilla,* a *tortilla* grilled-cheese sandwich.

Depending on what you intend to use them for, *tortillas* may be made in various ways. Even a run-of-the-mill *tortilla* is more than a flat corn cake. A skillfully cooked homemade *tortilla* has a bottom and a top; the top skin forms a pocket in which you put the filling that folds your *tortilla* into a taco. Paper-thin *tortillas* are used specifically for *flautas,* a type of taco that is filled, rolled, and then fried until crisp. The name *flauta* means *flute,* which probably refers to the Mayan bamboo flute; however, the only sound that comes from an edible *flauta* is a delicious crunch that is music to the palate. In México *flautas* are sometimes made as long as two feet and then cut into manageable segments. The opposite of *flautas* is *gorditas,* meaning *little fat ones.* These are very thick small *tortillas.* 6

The versatility of *tortillas* and corn does not end here. Besides being tasty and nourishing, they have spiritual and artistic qualities as well. The Tarahumara Indians of Chihuahua, for example, concocted a corn-based beer called *tesgüino,* which their descendants still make today. And everyone has read about the woman in New Mexico who was cooking her husband a *tortilla* one morning when the image of Jesus Christ miraculously appeared on it. Before they knew what was happening, the man's breakfast had become a local shrine. 7

Then there is *tortilla* art. Various Chicano artists throughout the Southwest have, when short of materials or just in a whimsical mood, used a dry *tortilla* as a small, round canvas. And a few years back, at the height of the Chicano movement, a priest in Arizona got into trouble with the Church after he was discovered celebrating mass using a *tortilla* as the host. All of which only goes to show that while the *tortilla* may be a lowly corn cake, when the necessity arises, it can reach unexpected distinction. 8

Discussion and Writing Questions

1. What is a *tortilla*? Why doesn't Burciaga define it in the first paragraph or the first few paragraphs of his essay?

2. As a child, what did Burciaga do with *tortillas*? Why did his family claim that he owed his career as an artist to his *tortilla* experiments (paragraph 2)?

3. Have you ever eaten any of the types of *tortillas* that Burciaga describes in paragraphs 5 and 6? If so, discuss your experience.

4. What is Burciaga's tone in this essay? Explain your answer by giving examples.

Writing Assignments

1. Write a personal history of your favorite food. Start with your earliest memory of it, add two or more memories, and conclude with your latest memory. Try to include details that appeal to a reader's sense of sight, smell, touch, and taste.

2. What ethnic foods do you enjoy eating? Put together a menu of three to five tasty favorites, and, in a letter inviting family and friends to dinner, describe what you plan to serve. Follow Burciaga's practice of using italics for foreign dishes. Check a dictionary for spelling if necessary.

3. Burciaga uses the *tortilla* as a symbol of something that has given nations as well as families a shared history. Choose something that has held special importance in your community's history and your personal history. It could be a food, a religious ceremony, an object, a song, or anything that has woven people together. Using Burciaga's essay as a model, write about that symbol.

Perfume

BARBARA GARSON

Some people work year after year at dull, repetitive jobs. Why do they do it? How do they stand it? To find out, journalist Barbara Garson interviewed hundreds of workers for her book *All the Livelong Day.* Here, she visits a factory that makes beauty products.

1 Helena Rubenstein makes over two hundred products (if you count different colors). Here in F&F—filling and finishing—there are usually about two dozen lines working at once. Each line is tended by ten to twenty women in blue smocks who perform a single repeated operation on each powder compact, deodorant bottle or perfume spray as it goes past. . . .

2 There are about 250 blue-smocked women in filling and finishing. They are mostly white, mostly middle-aged, and mostly earning "second" incomes. But there's a peppering of black and Latin women in the room, one or two unmarried girls on each line, and an increasing number of young mothers who are the main support of their families. . . .

3 Herbescence is a relatively simple line. The lead lady takes the filled bottles of spray mist out of cartons and places one on each black dot marked on the moving belt. The next two women put little silver tags around the bottle necks. Each one tags every other bottle. The next nine women each fold a protective corrugated cardboard, unfold a silver box, pick up every ninth spray-mist bottle, slip it into the corrugation, insert a leaflet, put the whole thing into the box and close the top. The next seven ladies wrap the silver Herbescence boxes in colored tissue paper. The women don't actually have to count every seventh box because, as a rule, when you finish the twists and folds of your tissue paper, your next box is just coming along with perhaps a half second to relax before you reach for it. The tissue-papered boxes are put into cartons which in turn are lifted onto skids[1] which, when filled with several thousand spray colognes, will be wheeled out by general factory help or skid boys.

4 Since the line doesn't involve any filling machines, it was a bit quieter at Herbescence. The women didn't have to shout. They could just talk loudly to each other and to me.

5 "You writing a book about cosmetics?" . . . "About Helena's?" . . . And then with greater disbelief: "About these jobs?" . . . "About *us?*"

6 Then I got my instructions.

7 "Write down how hard we work."

8 "How boring."

9 "You ought to come back here on a nice hot summer day. They got air conditioning upstairs in lipsticks but it's not for the women. Don't let 'em hand you a line. It's just 'cause the lipsticks might melt."

10 "Write about how fast the lines are now. It used to be a pleasure to work here. Now you can't keep up. They keep getting faster."

11 "Write about the new supervisors. Why should they treat you like dirt just because you work in a factory?"

12 "Be sure to say how boring."

13 Some twenty years ago, before all the talk about job enrichment, Local 8–149 fought for the right to rotate positions on the assembly line. Now the women change places every two hours. In addition the entire crew of certain particularly unpleasant lines is rotated every three days.

"After four minutes, or about two hundred bottles, the effects of the break seemed to be wearing off."

---

1. skids: platforms for stacking and moving heavy items

"Not that one job is so much different from another," said Dick McManus, 14 local union president, "but at least the women get to move around. They sit next to different women. They get to have different conversations."

Maxine Claybourne, a fortyish, flourishing, light yellow black woman, was 15 the new leading lady of the Herbescence line. Since the break she had been putting the bottles out one on each black line. After four minutes, or about two hundred bottles, the effects of the break seemed to be wearing off. Eyes were hypnotized, hands reached heavily for the boxes, bottles, wrapping paper and tags.

"Here's a gift, girls," Maxine announced. She took a comb out of her pocket 16 and, between every self-confident stroke, set a bottle down on the belt. They came out neatly on every *other* black dot.

Gradually the gift was carried down the line. "This is beautiful," said the boxers 17 as the farther-spaced bottles arrived. "Thanks, Max." Then after a minute it reached the wrappers. "This is how it should always be." And finally: "It used to be this way when I first started here," said the woman filling cartons at the end.

And then, without any noticeable shift, Maxine began putting the bottles on 18 every dot again.

"I can do things like that," she told me, "when the supervisor moves away. 19 When he comes back . . . [and she cast her eyes in the direction of the man I had not seen approaching] well, at least the girls get to enjoy a little break. One way or another, you got to get through the day."

The line settled down to its old pace again. I left Maxine and headed down to 20 the other end.

"I started here," a woman said, answering my question, "to send my kids to 21 college, but they're all grown up now."

"That's what I did," said the woman next to her. "First you put your kids 22 through school, then you start to pay for a car, then it's new rugs, and before you know it—I'm here fifteen years."

The women nodded. That seemed to be the story for the second-income workers. 23

A young black woman who hadn't said a word till then muttered sullenly, 24 "Some of us are here to pay for the rent, not buy rugs."

The older women went on. Perhaps they didn't hear her. 25

"And then you stay because of the other girls." 26

"Yeah, you stay to keep up with the gossip." 27

"And there's self-improvement here. You come to work every day, you get 28 more conscious of your clothes, your hair."

"Real self-improvement," a woman objected. "You should hear the language I 29 pick up. My husband says, 'The language you use, you sound like you work in a factory.' "

The most important benefit from the past struggles in this factory, and from 30 the impartial rotation systems, has no official recognition. There is no clause in the contract that says the workers shall have the right to laugh, talk and be helpful to one another. Nor is there a formal guarantee that the workers can shrug, sneer or otherwise indicate what they think of the supervisors.

But most of the women at Helena Rubenstein are helpful to each other and 31 they present a solid front to the supervisors.

The right to respond like a person, even while your hands are operating like a 32 machine, is something that has been fought for in this factory. And this is defended daily, formally through the grievance process and informally through militant kidding around.

I spent my last hour at Helena Rubenstein back at the Herbescence line, 33 watching hands reach for piece after piece until my own eyes grew glazed and my head throbbed with each bottle that jerked past. And yet, when I looked up it was only four minutes later. I forced myself to stay for a full twenty minutes; then I finally blurted out, "How do you do it seven hours a day?"

"You don't do it seven hours a day," was the answer. "You just do it one piece 34 at a time."

Discussion and Writing Questions

1. Describe the process by which a perfume bottle is packaged on the Herbescence perfume spray assembly line.

2. What reasons do the workers give for working on the line? Why do some of them stay so long if they do not enjoy their work?

3. What "gift" does Maxine Claybourne give her coworkers?

4. Which would you prefer: a boring, high-paying job or an interesting, low-paying job? Why?

Writing Assignments

1. Have you ever worked at a dull, repetitious job? Describe step by step what the job involved and your reaction to it, so that the reader can experience it as you did. Did you do anything to make the job more pleasant or interesting? What?

2. "Most of us, like the assembly line worker, have jobs that are too small for our spirit," says Nora Watson in Studs Terkel's book *Working.* What do you think she means by this? Do you agree? Describe a job that would be "big enough for your spirit."

3. Some people believe that a positive attitude can make even the most boring job interesting. Agree or disagree, using examples from your own or others' experience.

The Hidden Life of Bottled Water

Liza Gross

Consumers buy more bottled water than ever, believing that they are satisfying their thirst with something healthy. In fact, they might be better off just turning on the tap, according to this writer for *Sierra,* a magazine devoted to conservation and the environment.

Americans used to turn on their faucets when they craved a drink of clear, cool 1 water. Today, concerned about the safety of water supplies, they're turning to the bottle. Consumers spent more than $4 billion on bottled water last year, establishing the fount[1] of all life as a certifiably hot commodity. But is bottled really better?

You might think a mountain stream on the label offers some clue to the con- 2 tents. But sometimes, to paraphrase Freud, a bottle is just a bottle. "Mountain water could be anything," warns Connie Crawley, a health and nutrition specialist at the University of Georgia. "Unless the label says it comes from a specific source, when the manufacturer says 'bottled at the source,' the source could be the tap."

Yosemite brand water comes not from a bucolic[2] mountain spring but from deep 3 wells in the undeniably less picturesque Los Angeles suburbs, and Everest sells

---

1. fount: source
2. bucolic: rural

water drawn from a municipal source in Corpus Christi, Texas—a far cry from the pristine[3] glacial peaks suggested by its name. As long as producers meet the FDA's[4] standards for "distilled" or "purified" water, they don't have to disclose the source.

Even if the water does come from a spring, what's in that portable potable[5] may be *less* safe than what comes out of your tap. Bottled water must meet the same safety standards as municipal-system water. But while the EPA[6] mandates daily monitoring of public drinking water for many chemical contaminants, the FDA requires less comprehensive testing only once a year for bottled water. Beyond that, says Crawley, the FDA "usually inspects only if there's a complaint. Yet sources of bottled water are just as vulnerable to surface contamination as sources of tap water. If the spring is near a cattle farm, it's going to be contaminated."

Let's assume your store-bought water meets all the safety standards. What about the bottle? Because containers that sit for weeks or months at room temperature are ideal breeding grounds for bacteria, a bottle that met federal safety standards when it left the plant might have unsafe bacteria levels by the time you buy it. And because manufacturers aren't required to put expiration dates on bottles, there's no telling how long they've spent on a loading dock or on store shelves. (Bacteria also thrive on the wet, warm rim of an unrefrigerated bottle, so avoid letting a bottle sit around for too long.) But even more troubling is what may be leaching[7] from the plastic containers. Scientists at the FDA found traces of bisphenol A—an endocrine[8] disruptor that can alter the reproductive development of animals—after 39 weeks in water held at room temperature in large polycarbonate containers (like that carboy[9] atop your office water cooler).

Wherever you get your water, *caveat emptor*[10] should be the watchword. If you're simply worried about chlorine or can't abide its taste, fill an uncapped container with tap water and leave it in the refrigerator overnight; most of the chlorine will vaporize. If you know your municipal water is contaminated, bottled water can provide a safe alternative. But shop around. The National Sanitation Foundation (NSF) independently tests bottled water and certifies producers that meet FDA regulations and pass unannounced plant, source, and container inspections. And opt for glass bottles—they don't impart the taste and risks of chemical agents and they aren't made from petrochemicals.[11]

* * *

To get information on bottled-water standards—or to find out what's in the water you buy—contact the Food and Drug Administration, Federal Office Building # 9, Room 5807, 200 C St. S.W., Washington, DC 20004, (888) INFO-FDA. To find an NSF-certified manufacturer, call (800) NSF-MARK. For information on your tap water, call the EPA's Safe Drinking Water Hotline, (800) 426-4791.

"Wherever you get your water, caveat emptor *should be the watchword."*

Discussion and Writing Questions

1. Why might tap water be safer than bottled water?

2. Even if bottled water meets all safety standards, what other problems can affect its quality?

3. pristine: pure
4. FDA's: Food and Drug Administration's
5. potable: a beverage that is safe to drink
6. EPA: Environmental Protection Agency
7. leaching: dissolving, draining away
8. endocrine: hormonal
9. carboy: oversized bottle
10. *caveat emptor*: a warning in Latin meaning "buyer beware"
11. petrochemicals: compounds derived from petroleum or natural gas

3. According to the author, how can consumers ensure that the bottled water they buy is, in fact, safe spring water?

4. What is the author suggesting about the American public and bottled water? What is she trying to accomplish by writing this article? Does she succeed?

Writing Assignments

1. Check a campus location that sells bottled water (vending machine, cafeteria, campus store). Which brand of bottled water is sold? Call the Food and Drug Administration, at the number Gross gives in her last paragraph, to find out what information the federal government has collected on that brand. Is it spring water? Tap water from another location? Safe to drink? What ingredients does it have? Have any problems been associated with it? Report your findings in a letter to the campus newspaper.

2. Study the contents label of one of your favorite snacks. What are the ingredients? Consult a dictionary to "translate" those ingredients. Does your appetite diminish as a result? Describe the snack, including what you thought its ingredients were and what the ingredients really are. Conclude with a recommendation for other consumers.

3. Gross suggests that perhaps the public has been fooled by the bottled-water industry. What other products do people buy without really needing them? Find an ad for one such product and describe how it works, how it creates a need where there is none. Attach the ad to your description.

Say Yes to Yourself

JOSEPH T. MARTORANO AND JOHN P. KILDAHL

Do you believe your thoughts can change your life? If you can change the way you think, say therapists Martorano and Kildahl, you will change the way you feel—and act.

It's the classic story with a twist: a traveling salesman gets a flat tire on a dark lonely road and then discovers he has no jack. He sees a light in a farmhouse. As he walks toward it, his mind churns: "Suppose no one comes to the door." "Suppose they don't have a jack." "Suppose the guy won't lend me his jack even if he has one." The harder his mind works, the more agitated he becomes, and when the door opens, he punches the farmer and yells, "*Keep* your lousy jack!"   1

That story brings a smile, because it pokes fun at a common type of self-defeatist thinking. How often have you heard yourself say: "Nothing *ever* goes the way I planned." "I'll *never* make that deadline." "I *always* screw up."   2

Such inner speech shapes your life more than any other single force. Like it or not, you travel through life with your thoughts as navigator. If those thoughts spell gloom and doom, that's where you're headed, because put-down words sabotage confidence instead of offering support and encouragement.   3

Simply put, to *feel* better, you need to *think* better. Here's how: 4

1. Tune in to your thoughts. The first thing Sue said to her new therapist was, "I know you can't help me, Doctor. I'm a total mess. I keep lousing up at work, and I'm sure I'm going to be canned. Just yesterday my boss told me I was being transferred. He called it a promotion. But if I was doing a good job, why transfer me?"   5

Then, gradually, Sue's story moved past the put-downs. She had received her M.B.A. two years before and was making an excellent salary. That didn't sound like failure.   6

At the end of their first meeting, Sue's therapist told her to jot down her ⁷ thoughts, particularly at night if she was having trouble falling asleep. At her next appointment Sue's list included: "I'm not really smart. I got ahead by a bunch of flukes."¹ "Tomorrow will be a disaster. I've never chaired a meeting before." "My boss looked furious this morning. What did I do?"

She admitted, "In one day alone, I listed 26 negative thoughts. No wonder I'm ⁸ always tired and depressed."

Hearing her fears and forebodings² read out loud made Sue realize how much ⁹ energy she was squandering³ on imagined catastrophes. If you've been feeling down, it could be you're sending yourself negative messages too. Listen to the words churning inside your head. Repeat them aloud or write them down, if that will help capture them.

With practice, tuning in will become automatic. As you're walking or driving ¹⁰ down the street, you can hear your silent broadcast. Soon your thoughts will do your bidding, rather than the other way around. And when that happens, your feelings and actions will change too.

2. Isolate destructive words and phrases. Fran's inner voice kept telling her ¹¹ she was "only a secretary." Mark's reminded him he was "just a salesman." With the word *only* or *just,* they were downgrading their jobs and, by extension, themselves. By isolating negative words and phrases, you can pinpoint the damage you're doing to yourself. . . .

3. Stop the thought. Short-circuit negative messages as soon as they start by ¹² using the one-word command *stop!*

"What will I do if . . . ?" *Stop!* ¹³

In theory, stopping is a simple technique. In practice, it's not as easy as it sounds. ¹⁴ To be effective at stopping, you have to be forceful and tenacious.⁴ Raise your voice when you give the command. Picture yourself drowning out the inner voice of fear.

Vincent, a hard-working bachelor in his 20s, was an executive in a large com- ¹⁵ pany. . . . Although attracted to a woman in his department, he never asked her for a date. His worries immobilized⁵ him: "It's not a good idea to date a co-worker," or, "If she says no, it'll be embarrassing."

When Vincent stopped his inner voice and asked the woman out, she said, ¹⁶ "Vincent, what took you so long?"

4. Accentuate the positive. There's a story about a man who went to a psychi- ¹⁷ atrist. "What's the trouble?" asked the doctor.

"Two months ago my grandfather died and left me $75,000. Last month, a ¹⁸ cousin passed away and left me $100,000."

"Then why are you depressed?" ¹⁹

"This month, *nothing!*" ²⁰

When a person is in a depressed mood, everything can seem depressing. So once ²¹ you've exorcised⁶ the demons by calling a stop, replace them with good thoughts. . . . Be ready with a thought you've prepared in advance. Think about the promotion you got or a pleasant hike in the woods. In the words of the Bible: " . . . whatever is honorable . . . whatever is lovely, whatever is gracious . . . think about these things."

5. Reorient yourself. Have you ever been feeling down late in the day, when ²² someone suddenly said, "Let's go out"? Remember how your spirits picked up? You changed the direction of your thinking, and your mood brightened. . . . Practice this technique of going from painful anxiety to an active, problem-solving framework. . . .

By reorienting, you can learn to see yourself and the world around you differ- ²³ ently. If you think you can do something, you increase your chances of doing it.

> *"Listen to the words churning inside your head. . . . Short-circuit negative messages as soon as they start."*

---

1. flukes: accidents, random events
2. forebodings: feelings that something bad is going to happen
3. squandering: wasting
4. tenacious: holding on; stubborn
5. immobilized: kept from moving
6. exorcised: gotten rid of evil spirits

Optimism gets you moving. Depressing thoughts bog you down, because you are thinking, "What's the use?"

Make it a habit to remember your best self, the you that you want to be. In partic- 24 ular, remember things for which you have been complimented. That's the real you. Make this the frame of reference for your life—a picture of you at your best.

You'll find that reorienting works like a magnet. Imagine yourself reaching 25 your goals, and you will feel the tug of the magnet pulling you toward them.

Over the years we've discovered that when people *think* differently, they *feel*— 26 and *act*—differently. It's all in controlling your thoughts. As the poet John Milton wrote: "The mind . . . can make a heaven of hell, a hell of heaven."

The choice is yours. 27

Discussion and Writing Questions

1. What is the point of the story of the traveling salesman and the jack (paragraph 1)?

2. Martorano and Kildahl say that negative inner speech "shapes your life more than any other single force" (paragraph 3). Do you think this statement is true? Why or why not?

3. The authors offer five suggestions for changing negative thinking to positive thinking. Which suggestion do you think would be most useful for you? Why?

4. What is the meaning of John Milton's line "the mind . . . can make a heaven of hell, a hell of heaven" (paragraph 26)? Give examples from experience.

Writing Assignments

1. Describe a person you know who always makes you feel good about yourself. What does he or she say or do that makes you feel that way? Describe a time when you acted in a positive way because of that person's influence.

2. Most of us have negative mental "tapes" that influence the way we feel or act. These might concern our physical appearance, our abilities as a student or worker, or our relationships with other people. In your first sentence, describe a negative thought you have had about yourself. How could you change it and think more positively? How might your feelings and actions change if you did?

3. For a day or two, try using one or more of Martorano and Kildahl's suggestions for changing negative thoughts. Then write about your experience. What negative thoughts did you notice? Were you able to stop those negative thoughts? If so, did you feel better? Did you act in a more positive way? If the experiment didn't work, do you think it might work if you had more time or practice?

Emotional Intelligence

DANIEL GOLEMAN

How important to a person's success is I.Q.—that is, his or her score on an intelligence test? According to a widely read recent book, other personality traits and skills are even more important than I.Q. The author, Daniel Goleman, calls these traits and skills *emotional intelligence*. How would you rate your emotional I.Q.?

It was a steamy afternoon in New York City, the kind of day that makes people 1 sullen[1] with discomfort. I was heading to my hotel, and as I stepped onto a bus, I was greeted by the driver, a middle-aged man with an enthusiastic smile.

1. sullen: gloomy

"Hi! How're you doing?" he said. He greeted each rider in the same way. 2

As the bus crawled uptown through gridlocked traffic, the driver gave a lively 3 commentary: there was a terrific sale at that store . . . a wonderful exhibit at this museum . . . had we heard about the movie that just opened down the block? By the time people got off, they had shaken off their sullen shells. When the driver called out, "So long, have a great day!" each of us gave a smiling response.

That memory has stayed with me for close to twenty years. I consider the bus 4 driver a man who was truly successful at what he did.

Contrast him with Jason, a straight-A student at a Florida high school who was 5 fixated[2] on getting into Harvard Medical School. When a physics teacher gave Jason an 80 on a quiz, the boy believed his dream was in jeopardy.[3] He took a butcher knife to school, and in a struggle the teacher was stabbed in the collarbone.

"How could someone of obvious intelligence do something so irrational?"

How could someone of obvious intelligence do something so irrational? The 6 answer is that high I.Q. does not necessarily predict who will succeed in life. Psychologists agree that I.Q. contributes only about 20 percent of the factors that determine success. A full 80 percent comes from other factors, including what I call *emotional intelligence.*

Following are some of the major qualities that make up emotional intelli- 7 gence, and how they can be developed:

1. Self-awareness. The ability to recognize a feeling as it happens is the key- 8 stone of emotional intelligence. People with greater certainty about their emotions are better pilots of their lives.

Developing self-awareness requires tuning in to . . . gut feelings. Gut feelings 9 can occur without a person being consciously aware of them. For example, when people who fear snakes are shown a picture of a snake, sensors on their skin will detect sweat, a sign of anxiety, even though the people say they do not feel fear. The sweat shows up even when a picture is presented so rapidly that the subject has no conscious awareness of seeing it.

Through deliberate effort we can become more aware of our gut feelings. Take 10 someone who is annoyed by a rude encounter for hours after it occurred. He may be oblivious[4] to his irritability and surprised when someone calls attention to it. But if he evaluates his feelings, he can change them.

Emotional self-awareness is the building block of the next fundamental of 11 emotional intelligence: being able to shake off a bad mood.

2. Mood Management. Bad as well as good moods spice life and build charac- 12 ter. The key is balance.

We often have little control over *when* we are swept by emotion. But we can 13 have some say in *how long* that emotion will last. Psychologist Dianne Tice of Case Western Reserve University asked more than 400 men and women about their strategies for escaping foul moods. Her research, along with that of other psychologists, provides valuable information on how to change a bad mood.

Of all the moods that people want to escape, rage seems to be the hardest to 14 deal with. When someone in another car cuts you off on the highway, your reflex-ive[5] thought may be, *That jerk! He could have hit me! I can't let him get away with that!* The more you stew, the angrier you get. Such is the stuff of hypertension and reckless driving.

What should you do to relieve rage? One myth is that ventilating[6] will make 15 you feel better. In fact, researchers have found that's one of the worst strategies. Outbursts of rage pump up the brain's arousal system, leaving you more angry, not less.

A more effective technique is "reframing," which means consciously reinter- 16 preting a situation in a more positive light. In the case of the driver who cuts you

---

2. fixated: rigidly focused
3. jeopardy: danger
4. oblivious: totally unaware
5. reflexive: automatic
6. ventilating: "letting off steam," raving

off, you might tell yourself: *Maybe he had some emergency.* This is one of the most potent ways, Tice found, to put anger to rest.

Going off alone to cool down is also an effective way to defuse anger, especially 17 if you can't think clearly. Tice found that a large proportion of men cool down by going for a drive—a finding that inspired her to drive more defensively. A safer alternative is exercise, such as taking a long walk. Whatever you do, don't waste the time pursuing your train of angry thoughts. Your aim should be to distract yourself.

The techniques of reframing and distraction can alleviate[7] depression and 18 anxiety as well as anger. Add to them such relaxation techniques as deep breathing and meditation and you have an arsenal of weapons against bad moods. "Praying," Dianne Tice also says, "works for all moods."

3. Self-motivation. Positive motivation—the marshaling[8] of feelings of enthusi- 19 asm, zeal and confidence—is paramount for achievement. Studies of Olympic athletes, world-class musicians and chess grandmasters[9] show that their common trait is the ability to motivate themselves to pursue relentless training routines.

To motivate yourself for any achievement requires clear goals and an optimistic, 20 can-do attitude. Psychologist Martin Seligman of the University of Pennsylvania advised the MetLife insurance company to hire a special group of job applicants who tested high on optimism, although they had failed the normal aptitude test. Compared with salesmen who passed the aptitude test but scored high in pessimism, this group made 21 percent more sales in their first year and 57 percent more in their second.

A pessimist is likely to interpret rejection as meaning *I'm a failure; I'll never* 21 *make a sale.* Optimists tell themselves, *I'm using the wrong approach,* or *That customer was in a bad mood.* By blaming failure on the situation, not themselves, optimists are motivated to make that next call.

Your . . . positive or negative outlook may be inborn, but with effort and 22 practice, pessimists can learn to think more hopefully. Psychologists have documented that if you can catch negative, self-defeating thoughts as they occur, you can reframe the situation in less catastrophic terms.

4. Impulse Control. The essence of emotional self-regulation is the ability to 23 delay impulse in the service of a goal. The importance of this trait to success was shown in an experiment begun in the 1960s by psychologist Walter Mischel at a preschool on the Stanford University campus.

Children were told that they could have a single treat, such as a marshmallow, 24 right now. However, if they would wait while the experimenter ran an errand, they could have two marshmallows. Some preschoolers grabbed the marshmallow immediately, but others were able to wait what, for them, must have seemed an endless twenty minutes. To sustain themselves in their struggle, they covered their eyes so they wouldn't see the temptation, rested their heads on their arms, talked to themselves, sang, even tried to sleep. These plucky kids got the two-marshmallow reward.

The interesting part of this experiment came in the follow-up. The children 25 who as four-year-olds had been able to wait for the two marshmallows were, as adolescents, still able to delay gratification in pursuing their goals. They were more socially competent and self-assertive, and better able to cope with life's frustrations. In contrast, the kids who grabbed the one marshmallow were, as adolescents, more likely to be stubborn, indecisive and stressed.

The ability to resist impulse can be developed through practice. When you're 26 faced with an immediate temptation, remind yourself of your long-term goals—whether they be losing weight or getting a medical degree. You'll find it easier, then, to keep from settling for the single marshmallow.

5. People Skills. The capacity to know how another feels is important on the 27 job, in romance and friendships, and in the family. We transmit and catch moods

---

7. alleviate: reduce, make better
8. marshaling: gathering together, using
9. chess grandmasters: experts at the game of chess

from each other on a subtle, almost imperceptible level. The way someone says thank you, for instance, can leave us feeling dismissed, patronized or genuinely appreciated. The more adroit[10] we are at discerning the feelings behind other people's signals, the better we control the signals we send.

The importance of good interpersonal skills was demonstrated by psychologists Robert Kelley of Carnegie-Mellon University and Janet Caplan in a study at Bell Labs in Naperville, Ill. The labs are staffed by engineers and scientists who are all at the apex[11] of academic I.Q. tests. But some still emerged as stars while others languished.[12]   28

What accounted for the difference? The standout performers had a network with a wide range of people. When a non-star encountered a technical problem, Kelley observed, "he called various technical gurus and then waited, wasting time while his calls went unreturned. Star performers rarely faced such situations because they built reliable networks *before* they needed them. So when the stars called someone, they almost always got a faster answer."   29

No matter what their I.Q., once again it was emotional intelligence that separated the stars from the average performers.   30

Discussion and Writing Questions

1. Goleman names five qualities that contribute to emotional intelligence. What are they?

2. Describe someone you observed recently who showed a high level of emotional intelligence in a particular situation. Then describe someone who showed a low level of emotional intelligence in a particular situation. Which of the five qualities did each person display or lack?

3. Did it surprise you to read that "ventilating" is one of the worst ways to handle rage? Instead, experts suggest several techniques. Suppose you are in the following situation, and your first reaction is anger: *You ask a salesperson for help in choosing a CD player. As she walks right past you, she tells you that the boxes and labels will give you all the information you need.* What might you do to calm yourself down?

4. In paragraphs 24 and 25, Goleman discusses a now-famous study of children and marshmallows. What was the point of this study? Why does Goleman say that the most interesting part of the study came later, when the children reached adolescence?

Writing Assignments

1. Write a detailed portrait of a person you consider an "emotional genius." Develop your paper with specific examples of his or her skills.

2. Daniel Goleman claims that weak emotional qualities can be strengthened with practice. Choose one of the five qualities (self-awareness, people skills, and so forth), and recommend specific ways for a person to improve in that area. Your audience is people who wish to improve their emotional intelligence; your purpose is to help them do so.

3. Review or read "The Gift" on page 427, and evaluate the emotional intelligence of Jermaine Washington. Washington saved a friend's life by giving her one of his kidneys after her two brothers and her boyfriend refused to be donors. Most people in their town still think Washington was "crazy" to make this decision. What do you think? Does he have a high level of emotional intelligence? A low level? Why?

---

10. adroit: skilled
11. apex: top, topmost point
12. languished: stayed in one place

Quotation Bank

This collection of wise and humorous statements has been assembled for you to read, enjoy, and use in a variety of ways as you write. You might choose some quotations that you particularly agree or disagree with and use them as the basis of journal entries and writing assignments. When you write a paragraph or an essay, you may find it useful to include a quotation to support a point you are making. You may simply want to read through these quotations for ideas and for fun. As you come across other intriguing statements by writers, add them to the list—or write some of your own.

Writing

Writing, like life itself, is a voyage of discovery. 1
—*Henry Miller*

Writing is the hardest work in the world not involving heavy lifting. 2
—*Pete Hamill*

I think best with a pencil in my hand. 3
—*Anne Morrow Lindbergh*

I write to discover what I think. 4
—*Daniel J. Boorstin*

A sentence should contain no unnecessary words, a paragraph no unnecessary 5
sentences, for the same reason that a drawing should have no unnecessary lines
and a machine no unnecessary parts.
—*William Strunk*

To me, the greatest pleasure of writing is not what it's about, but the inner music 6
that words make.
—*Truman Capote*

Writing is the only thing that when I do it, I don't feel I should be doing some- 7
thing else.
—*Gloria Steinem*

I never travel without my diary. One should always have something sensational 8
to read on the train.
—*Oscar Wilde*

Write something to suit yourself and many people will like it; write something to 9
suit everybody and scarcely anyone will care for it.
—*Jesse Stuart*

A professional writer is an amateur who didn't quit. 10
—*Richard Bach*

Learning

Teachers open the door, but you must enter by yourself. 11
—*Chinese proverb*

The "silly question" is the first intimation [hint] of some totally new development. 12
—*Alfred North Whitehead*

The mind is a mansion, but most of the time we are content to live in the lobby. 13
—*William Michaels*

Education is . . . hanging around until you've caught on. 14
—*Robert Frost*

Prejudices, it is well known, are most difficult to eradicate [remove] from the 15
heart whose soil has never been loosened or fertilized by education; they grow
there, firm as weeds among stones.
—*Charlotte Brontë*

Many receive advice; few profit from it. 16
—*Publius*

Pay attention to what they tell you to forget. 17
—*Muriel Rukeyser*

Education is what you have left over after you have forgotten everything you 18
have learned.
—*Anonymous*

Only the educated are free. 19
—*Epictetus*

The basic purpose of a liberal arts education is to liberate the human being to 20
exercise his or her potential to the fullest.
—*Barbara M. White*

Love

We can only learn to love by loving. 21
—*Iris Murdoch*

To love and to be loved is to feel the sun from both sides. 22
—*David Viscott*

So often when we say "I love you," we say it with a huge "I" and a small "you." 23
—*Archbishop Antony*

Choose your life's mate carefully. From this one decision will come 90 percent of 24
all your happiness or misery.
—*H. Jackson Browne, Jr.*

Marriage is our last, best chance to grow up. 25
—*Joseph Barth*

A divorce is like an amputation; you survive, but there's less of you. 26
—*Margaret Atwood*

No partner in a love relationship should feel that she [or he] has to give up an 27
essential part of herself [or himself] to make it viable [workable].
—*May Sarton*

I can't mate in captivity. 28
—*Gloria Steinem*

Gold and love affairs are difficult to hide.   29
—*Spanish proverb*

Love doesn't just sit there, like a stone; it has to be made, like bread, remade all   30
the time, made new.
—*Ursula K. Le Guin*

To be loved, be lovable.   31
—*Ovid*

Work and Success

The best career advice to give the young is, find out what you like doing best and   32
get someone to pay you for doing it.
—*Katherine Whilehaen*

Measure a thousand times and cut once.   33
—*Turkish proverb*

There are two things to aim at in life: first, to get what you want and, after that, to   34
enjoy it. Only the wisest . . . achieve the second.
—*Logan Pearsall Smith*

Money is like manure. If you spread it around, it does a lot of good, but if you   35
pile it up in one place, it stinks like hell.
—*Clint W. Murchison*

If you have built castles in the air, your work need not be lost; that is where they   36
should be. Now put foundations under them.
—*Henry David Thoreau*

It is never too late to be what you might have been.   37
—*George Eliot*

A celebrity is a person who works hard all his [or her] life to become well known,   38
then wears dark glasses to avoid being recognized.
—*Fred Allen*

I think most of us are looking for a calling, not a job. Most of us, like the assembly   39
line worker, have had jobs that are too small for our spirit.
—*Nora Watson*

I am a marvelous housekeeper. Every time I leave a man I keep his house.   40
—*Zsa Zsa Gabor*

A good reputation is more valuable than money.   41
—*Publius*

If you aren't fired with enthusiasm, you will be fired with enthusiasm.   42
—*Vince Lombardi*

Very little is needed to make a happy life.   43
—*Marcus Aurelius Antoninus*

When you reach for the stars, you may not quite get one, but you won't come up   44
with a handful of mud.
— *Leo Burnett*

Family and Friendship

Making the decision to have a child—it's momentous. It is to decide forever to have your heart go walking around outside your body.
—*Elizabeth Stone* 45

Any mother could perform the jobs of several air-traffic controllers with ease.
—*Lisa Alther* 46

Familiarity breeds contempt.— *Aesop;* 47

—and children.—*Mark Twain* 48

It takes a village to raise a child.
—*African proverb* 49

Nobody who has not been in the interior of a family can say what the difficulties of any individual of that family may be.
—*Jane Austen* 50

You know the only people who are *always* sure about the proper way to raise children? Those who've never had any.
—*Bill Cosby* 51

Insanity is hereditary—you get it from your children.
—*Sam Levenson* 52

Govern a family as you would fry small fish—gently.
—*Chinese proverb* 53

Everything that irritates us about others can lead us to an understanding of ourselves.
—*Morton Hunt* 54

The meeting of two personalities is like the contact of two chemical substances: if there is any reaction, both are transformed.
—*Carl Jung* 55

The only way to have a friend is to be one.
—*Ralph Waldo Emerson* 56

Wisdom for Living

It is not easy to find happiness in ourselves, and it is not possible to find it elsewhere.
—*Agnes Repplier* 57

Seize the day; put no trust in the morrow.
—*Horace* 58

Don't be afraid your life will end; be afraid that it will never begin.
—*Grace Hansen* 59

My life, my *real* life, was in danger, and not from anything other people might do but from the hatred I carried in my own heart.
—*James Baldwin* 60

No one can make you feel inferior without your consent. 61
—*Eleanor Roosevelt*

Too much of a good thing can be wonderful. 62
—*Mae West*

What we anticipate seldom occurs; what we least expect generally happens. 63
—*Benjamin Disraeli*

Take your life in your own hands and what happens? A terrible thing: no one to 64
blame.
—*Erica Jong*

Regret is an appalling waste of energy: you can't build on it; it is good only for 65
wallowing in.
—*Katherine Mansfield*

It is good to have an end to journey toward; but it is the journey that matters, in 66
the end.
—*Ursula K. Le Guin*

Flowers grow out of dark moments. 67
—*Corita Kent*

Lying is done with words and also with silence. 68
—*Adrienne Rich*

Pick battles big enough to matter, small enough to win. 69
—*Jonathan Kozol*

You can't hold a man [or a woman] down without staying down with him 70
[or her].
—*Booker T. Washington*

A fanatic is one who can't change his [or her] mind and won't change the subject. 71
—*Winston Churchill*

Nobody cares if you can't dance well. Just get up and dance. 72
—*Dave Barry*

Time wounds all heels. 73
—*Jane Ace*

When you come to a fork in the road, take it. 74
—*Yogi Berra*

Acknowledgments

Index

Index of Rhetorical Modes

The following index classifies the paragraphs and essays in this book according to rhetorical mode. Although we do not teach the rhetorical modes in this text, these examples are included for instructors who wish to use them.

No writing containing errors for correction is listed, with the exception of four Writers' Workshops — marked *WW with errors* — where otherwise excellent writing warrants inclusion.

Index to the Readings

Rhetorical Index to the Readings